HERO BOOKS

'59

AN EYEWITNESS ACCOUNT OF HURLING'S GOLDEN AGE

BY BRIAN KELLY

HEROBOOKS

PUBLISHED BY HERO BOOKS
LUCAN
CO. DUBLIN
IRELAND

First Published 2024
Copyright © Brian Kelly 2024

Without limiting the rights under copyright reserved above, no part of this publication may be reproduced, stored in or introduced into a retrieval system, or transmitted in any form or by any means (electronic, mechanical, photocopying, recording or otherwise) without the prior written permission of the publisher of this book.

A CIP record for this book is available from the British Library

Cover design and formatting: jessica@viitaladesign.com

DEDICATION

To Laura, Hannah and Theo.

CONTENTS

FOREWORD

INTRODUCTION

Chapter 1 – Road to '59

Chapter 2 – The Landscape

Chapter 3 – Railway Cup

Chapter 4 – National League

Chapter 5 – Munster Championship

Chapter 6 – All-Ireland Final

Chapter 7 – All-Ireland Final Replay

Chapter 8 – The Celebrations

Chapter 9 – Rest of Ireland

Chapter 10 – Wembley Stadium

Chapter 11 – New York City

EPILOGUE

ACKNOWLEDGEMENTS

APPENDICES

REFERENCES

FOREWORD

JARLATH BURNS
PRESIDENT GAA

A Chairde,

On a July summer Sunday in 1959 the great Michael O'Hehir was relaying half-time scores on radio. According to one of the great anecdotes of the GAA championships, the broadcasting legend refused to read out the half-time score from the Munster senior hurling semi-final.

The score that was handed to him read Waterford 8-2, Tipperary nil. All conquering Tipperary were the reigning champions. It was, surely, a mistake or worse, an attempt at a practical joke.

No half-time score was given. But the full-time score would confirm that this was no mistake. Waterford 9-3, Tipperary 3-4.

The Déise, triumphant, were far from finished. Having accounted for Galway, Tipperary and Cork, they advanced to Croke Park and a meeting with their border neighbours, Kilkenny. After securing a last gasp replay, Waterford would defeat Kilkenny in the second outing to reach The Promised Land.

It is a campaign worthy of commemoration and celebration, and that is why I am delighted that this book has arrived in tribute to the 1959 All-Ireland Hurling Championship winning team from Waterford.

Collecting first-hand oral history of surviving players from the white and blue ranks, as well as some of their famed opponents, does the association some service in securing this eyewitness testimony for future generations.

Without doubt, the style of hurling has changed significantly over the decades since then. But, unquestionably, what has not changed is the power and potency of the championship winning teams who represent our clubs and counties, and make us proud of who we are and where we are from.

Although the yearning for Liam MacCarthy Cup continues, the ability of Waterford to always produce iconic hurlers is a testament to the impact and legacy that the heroes of 1959 had on the GAA in the city and county, and ability to inspire others to keep the flame alive and pass it to future generations.

I would like to thank Brian Kelly for ensuring that the memory and contribution of this great team is preserved.

Thar ceann Chumann Lúthchleas Gael, comhghairdeas agus míle buíochas.

Le meas,
Iarlaith Ó Broin

INTRODUCTION

WATERFORD CITY
JULY, 2024

Another All-Ireland Hurling Championship has been logged in the game's rich history. Clare's brilliant triumph over Cork in the high summer of 2024 has also been catalogued as perhaps one of the greatest finals of all time.

Perhaps. We all live with our own memories of All-Ireland campaigns and finals of times past, and for all of us... our own rank close to the top!

For the Waterford hurling public, we have lived with 1959, and when the curtain was lowered on the 2024 All-Ireland Championship, it was our 65th attempt to win the Liam MacCarthy Cup since the last win in '59.

'59 – it has taken on a mythical status.

Mention that number in Waterford and the first thought will always be the last All-Ireland victory. The players of that year wrote their names into history, and they believed that many more Waterford players would follow them in quick succession. It just hasn't happened.

The '59 team became the '63 team which won the league, Munster and Oireachtas titles, but not the All-Ireland. What followed was a genuine sporting famine. The next Waterford appearance in Croke Park was the All-Ireland quarter final of 1998 against Galway. I attended that game with my mother, a teenager back in 1963, who couldn't have predicted that her next visit would be with her adult son.

The heroes of '59 had long retired and successive generations had brought new heroes to the fore. We have enjoyed exciting days out since 1998 but also continued disappointment, losing 12 All-Ireland semi-finals and three finals. Covid caused everyone to miss the most recent final loss, but it also allowed for some positives. In re-evaluating what is important in our lives, how much more do we now appreciate the opportunity to see Jamie Barron and Dessie Hutchinson play live? How much more do we realise what a privilege it has been to watch Brick Walsh and Kevin Moran, John Mullane and Tony Browne, Ken McGrath and Paul Flynn, Fergal Hartley and Stephen Frampton, John Galvin and Mossy Walsh, Pat McGrath and Jim Greene?

How much more do we appreciate the heroes of '59?

For me, Covid provided a chance to research and write this book. It brought with it the honour of speaking to the team and the players who played with and against them. Throughout the book, I have relied on direct quotations and stories from the Waterford players and their contemporaries. These men are now generally in their eighties or nineties, and they are looking back on a time when they were in the prime of their life and at peak physical fitness. They were single and without children, and for the most part worked in tough manual jobs. It resulted in a group of strong, tough, young men who enjoyed life through their hurling.

They look back with pride in their achievements, and with the honesty and lack of pretention that comes with age. All of the surviving Waterford panel were interviewed, mostly by phone because of Covid concerns. During breaks in Covid, some interviews were carried out in person, and it was a privilege to be welcomed into the players' homes. Nobody refused to be interviewed and all were open, honest (sometimes, brutally so), funny, and insightful in their analysis. Players from other counties were just as supportive. The list of interviewees reads like an All Star team of 1959. In addition to the Waterford players, Eddie Keher and Johnny McGovern of Kilkenny, Jimmy Brohan of Cork, Donie Nealon and Tony Wall of Tipperary, Jimmy O'Brien of Wexford, and Jimmy Gray of Dublin all contributed.

Many of the players mentioned in the book have now passed away. Where possible, their voices have been included by using the direct quotes they gave to authors of other books or journalists writing feature articles. Every effort is made to credit the correct sources. Sadly, during the writing of the book, several more of the players passed away, including Austin Flynn, Mick Flannelly, Tom Cunningham, Jackie Condon, Johnny McGovern, Jimmy Brohan, and Jimmy Gray.

Ar dheis Dé go raibh a n-anamacha.

Many, like Eddie Keher, openly admit that they cannot remember the detail of individual games.

'I don't know about other players. My recollection of matches, strangely enough, is poor. I might remember one or two incidents in a match. I always felt that match is over and done with, now there's the next one to focus on. It's only maybe at this stage where things like your promptings... or you see old matches on television, that things start coming back to you.'

The details of matches and scores may have been prompted by me, but the players will always remember the battles, the fun, and the friendships. While reliving the glories of 1959, my conversations with the players also covered the aftermath of their win. The excitement of foreign travel for the first time to London and New York was a strong memory for many, illustrative of a time before televisions, phones, and foreign holidays. In many ways, this is a social history as much as a sporting one. For some of the players, the aftermath of their win had its downsides.

Local heroes in their time, they were never properly replaced, and the local fame and attention became a drag. Some rarely spoke about hurling with family or friends, and several walked away from the game in the following years.

Whatever their particular story, it was a pleasure to discuss hurling with them. Considering all the research I'd done, it felt like I had lived through 1959. The greatest compliment I received was from Tipperary captain, Tony Wall, a man who wrote his own book on hurling.

'I'm here on my own in the night-time. I'm well able to look after myself. I'm not lonely or anything. Here I am talking about hurling back in the old days. I never met anybody who knew so much about all these things. I'll tell you this, it's great to talk to a fella who knows something about hurling. You can never have a proper conversation with somebody who doesn't know what you are talking about. Fellas ask stupid questions, but a fella who knows his stuff… there is a pleasure in it. It would keep you going all f***in' night.'

I also spent a very pleasurable afternoon with Joe Condon in his garden. As with all the players, I was anxious that they wouldn't be misrepresented and that they would be happy with the final draft. When I asked if Joe would like to review the book before I published it, he confidently said there was no need, wished me well, and said that he'd buy a copy in the Book Centre. His brother, Jackie Condon, probably has the best approach. Having been very open with his recollections and stories, he answered the same question by saying 'No, I'll deny it all anyway!!'.

As much as possible, this book is in the players' words. I hope they enjoy reliving the triumphs of their youth. If it evokes a smile or two, or helps recall a treasured moment for them, it will be worthwhile.

We already look ahead to another championship in 2025; we live in hope of another win, but we will always have '59.

Brian Kelly

WATERFORD
ALL-IRELAND CHAMPIONS 1959

Back - Freddie O'Brien (Mount Sion), John Barron (De La Salle), Ned Power (Dungarvan), Jackie Condon (Erin's Own), Martin Óg Morrissey (Mount Sion), Joe Harney (Ballydurn), Austin Flynn (Abbeyside), Phil Grimes (Mount Sion), Mick Lacey (Cappoquin), Joe Coady (Erin's Own). Front - Paudie Casey (Ballygunner), Tom Cheasty (Ballyduff), Larry Guinan (Mount Sion), Mick Flannelly (Mount Sion), Frankie Walsh (Mount Sion), John Kiely (Dungarvan), Tom Cunningham (Dungarvan), Seamus Power (Mount Sion), Michael O'Connor (Cappoquin), Charlie Ware (Erin's Own), Donal Whelan (Abbeyside).

1

THE ROAD TO 59

'WAVING UP AT FRANKIE'

It is October 4, 1959, and Frankie Walsh raises the Liam MacCarthy Cup aloft. President of the GAA, Dr. JJ Stuart has handed over the cup in the presence of President of the Ireland, Éamon de Valera. In front of the new Hogan Stand is a sea of Waterford supporters, deliriously happy to have beaten the old enemy, Kilkenny. Beyond them, on the pitch, Larry Guinan waves up at his great friend Frankie, while the disappointed Kilkenny team applaud the new champions.

Of the men behind the victory, Pat Fanning is front and centre, casting an avuncular eye over his Mount Sion clubman, while John Keane is nowhere to be seen. The celebrations have just started and the confidence levels of all involved with Waterford hurling is at its height. This was the team's second All-Ireland final appearance in three years. With a young team of skilful hurlers, there was no indication that their success would not be repeated regularly.

However, despite a National League win in 1963, and another All-Ireland final appearance in the same year, this was to be the peak of Waterford's hurling history… never again to be repeated.

In the introduction to their match report of the All-Ireland final replay, the Dungarvan Observer of October 10, 1959, exclaimed:

To the individual who eventually gets around to writing up the history of Waterford hurling is offered this suggestion in the name of every son and daughter of Port Láirge who was in Croke Park for the county's second All-Ireland victory on Sunday: mark down the events of October 4th 1959 as a chapter apart, the day on which eleven years of disillusionment and bitter disappointment were bridged with a victory that even shaded the never-to-be-forgotten victory of '48.

From a distance of 65 years, this is the story of that famous year and the men of 1959. It tracks their development as a team, charts a path through the hurling world of 1959, celebrates

Frankie Walsh's view of the Waterford supporters.

their victory, and revels in the brief but positive glow of being All-Ireland champions; and, yes indeed, there is a specific chapter devoted to the events of October 4.

'WATERFORD EMERGED AS A HURLING COUNTY'

The team was supported by administrators and coaches who were steeped in Waterford hurling tradition. All of the experiences gained in the four decades leading to 1959 were brought together to support the county's most talented-ever group of hurlers. By tracing the highlights of Waterford hurling the cast of characters who played a part in 1959 can be assembled.

While hurling in Waterford has historic roots dating back to Thomas Francis Meagher and beyond, the local county championship only came into its own during the early part of the 20th century. With a variety of teams coalescing and disbanding, it was the early 1920s and the birth of Erin's Own that brought structure to the championship and fed into a strengthening county team. The first breakthrough came in 1925, when Erin's Own's Charlie Ware led Waterford to victory against Clare in the first round of the Munster Championship. Though beaten by Tipperary in the Munster final, the team had shown signs of promise.

It wouldn't be long before a Waterford team won their first All-Ireland at any grade, the 1929 Minor Championship, featuring a young Declan Goode from Dungarvan. Goode was also on the junior team that won an All-Ireland in 1931. A predominantly Erin's Own team, led by Charlie Ware, and including his brother, Jim, represented Waterford into the mid-30s, based on their incredible nine-in-a-row winning team. As the power balance in Waterford City shifted from Erin's Own to the newly formed Mount Sion from 1932, it was also augmented by strengthening teams from around the county.

By 1938, the experience gained was starting to bear fruit. Despite playing in the full-forward line, Declan Goode was already the County Board secretary, and John Keane had emerged as one of the game's greatest players. They were making progress on the field and inspiring the next generation. Goode's goal, along with two each for Pa Sheehan and Locky Byrne, booked Waterford's place in the Munster final when they beat Cork 5-2 to 1-3. It was a very wet day and a seven-year-old Tom Cunningham, later a star of 1959, watched from the shelter of the stand. Thanks to his family friendship with Waterford player, Jimmy Mountain, he managed to get a seat on the team bus for the short trip back to O'Connell Street. It was the young hurler's first experience of being cheered through Grattan Square, but not his last.

Waterford beat Clare by a goal (3-5 to 2-5) at the Athletic Grounds in Cork, giving Waterford their first ever Munster title. Johnny Fanning was the hero of the hour as he made a last ditch save as he 'pounced on' Mick Hennessey who was about to strike for an equalising goal. William Doyle-Walsh accepted the trophy in the absence of Mick Hickey, who had been sent off against Cork and was suspended. The delay in scheduling the Munster final had a knock-on effect and the All-Ireland semi-final against Galway was played only a week later. In the first championship match between the counties, Waterford had a relatively easy 4-8 to 3-1 victory to set up a first All-Ireland senior final against Dublin.

The final was Waterford's first match in Croke Park, and their surroundings included the new Cusack Stand which had opened just two weeks previously. The attendance was quite small by comparison to later years at only 37,129. Cost was a limiting factor for some fans, so many stayed at home and listened to the match on the wireless. The commentator, Michael O'Hehir's predecessor, was a Dungarvan man named David Hanley. As the Waterford team gathered for a photograph before the match, they found that one of their number was missing. Declan Goode had realised that he was missing his lucky holy medal, so he dashed back to Barry's Hotel to collect it. While he made it back in time for the throw-in, he missed the photo. Most people who saw the team group in the newspapers the next day failed to notice Waterford were a man short. The medal may have helped as Goode went on to score a goal in the game.

Both captains were from Carrick-on-Suir, Mick Hickey of Waterford and Mick Daniels of Dublin. In fact, almost all of the Dublin team were from outside the capital, with wing back Jim Byrne being the only Dublin native. Waterford had a good first 10 minutes but were starting to slip behind by half-time when they trailed 2-3 to 1-3. Dublin's back-line gave away fewer frees than their Waterford counterparts. Frequent stoppages for frees and injuries detracted from the flow of the game, and it failed to live up to expectations. Dublin's half-backs were particularly good in the second-half as Waterford made a strong push in the last few minutes.

Generally, Dublin had the best of the midfield play where Daniels and Gray outplayed Moylan and Feeney. In the half-forwards, McDonald did well against John Keane, scoring three points from play. John Keane was uncomfortable in his boots, so he discarded them after 10 minutes and played for 50 minutes in stockinged feet. From the half-back line, he outscored his marker, scoring four points in the game. Without the strong performance of the full-back line of Hickey, Ware and Fanning, Dublin would have won by more than their ultimate two-point victory of 2-5 to 1-6.

While Waterford were disappointed, it was generally felt that good progress had been made in winning the Munster Championship for the first time. The final appearance boosted interest in hurling and the number of clubs registered in the county jumped from 47 in 1938 to 65 in 1939.

Charlie Ware announced his retirement in 1939 and his last match was in the Munster Championship against Cork. John Keane was initially brought back from centre half back to full back until a replacement could be found. Keane was the team's leader and most influential player. When trying to recruit him back to Waterford in 1943, it was John Keane's idea to move to centre forward to allow Vin Baston to play at centre back, creating a strong spine that would later challenge for the All-Ireland in 1948.

'IT BROUGHT US ON A MILE'

The home ground for Waterford hurling was the Gaelic Field, to give its official name, on Slievekeale Road in Waterford City. It hadn't yet been named Walsh Park and most people referred to it by its traditional name, the Sports Field or often just 'the field'. Many of the players who would play in 1959 grew up around 'the roads' during the 1940s and within minutes 10 of the squad could walk to training. Also nearby was the school many of them had attended, Mount Sion on Barrack Street.

These streets were where players like Jackie Condon learned their hurling.

> 'I went to Mount Sion school and I came through the street leagues. I captained a team which won the street league when I was 12 years of age, Griffiths Place. That street league brought on hurling no end in Waterford. There was eight of the players on that All-Ireland team that came from up those streets – Griffith Place, Ard na Greine, Keane's Road – they all came from that area. If you take the county players out of it, that is where the hurling was done in Waterford.'

One of Jackie's neighbours was Freddie O'Brien. In the many interviews with his teammates of the time, all refer to him by his nickname of Taylor O'Brien, but nobody seems to know why, most not even aware of how it was spelled, assuming it was tailor. Freddie explained how this nickname came about.

> 'Robert Taylor was a film star at that time. My mother had a little huckster's shop in Ard na Greine. Her main customers came from the Jute Factory. She used to do a bit of buying of clothes, women's stockings and women's underwear... and things like that. It was a sweet shop and a vegetable shop, but she was a bit of an entrepreneur for the time. She used to go to Dublin to the big sales after Christmas and she used to go to the Monster House in Kilkenny... they used to have great sales. She used to bring home a load of stuff and there would be 60 to 80 employees of the Jute Factory

pass down the street in Ard na Greine. Any kind of a bargain she got on clothes that would suit herself, she would keep. She had me very well dressed, I was the eldest of the family. There was Keatings beside us, and Mattie was there – he was a bitter oul' bastard. He'd be there saying 'Oh, here's Robert Taylor' ... that's where I got the nickname.'

Martin Óg Morrissey also picked up a new name, courtesy of his Mount Sion teammates.

'When I hurled minor with the club, there happened to be three Morrisseys playing on that particular team... and their first names were Martin, Mattie and ... yea, Martin. Martin, from Griffith Place, was two years older than me, so the fellas looking after us started calling me Martin Óg... and all I was ever called after that when we played was Óg. And it has stuck ever since.'

As Jackie points out, there was another cluster of players from the west of the county, including Mick Lacey and Michael O'Connor from Cappoquin, Ned Power, John Kiely and Tom Cunningham from Dungarvan, and Donal Whelan and Austin Flynn from Abbeyside. Tom Cunningham also remembers the impact of street hurling.

'I was always interested in hurling, from the time I was seven, and in playing hurling out on the street. The Christian Brothers, at both primary and secondary, really promoted hurling. And there was the radio... you would hear all the great hurlers' names on the radio, and you would start to dream a little by yourself.'

A common theme linking many of the players was their experience of hurling in school. The majority of the panel attended Mount Sion, De La Salle, or Dungarvan CBS. Playing for their college was their first experience of competition and marked them out as talents to watch. It also gave them exposure to colleges from other counties and players who would later oppose them in inter-county hurling. Jimmy O'Brien remembers the strength of opposition at Mount Sion.

'I went to the Christian Brothers in New Ross. There used to be a competition between the CBSs in Wexford – Enniscorthy, Gorey, Wexford and New Ross – which we won. It was a big thing to go on a bus. There would be a load of lads come from the school for the trip. We came down to Waterford to play Mount Sion in a practice match. Well, they bet us out the gate. There was one fella went to town on us. It was Larry Guinan. We were brought into the school then and we were given tea and buns. We didn't worry then... it didn't matter a damn about the match!'

There was stiff competition between the Waterford colleges in their attempt to win the coveted Harty Cup, as Noel Dalton described in his book *A Deise Boy*.

'I made the (De La Salle) Harty Cup team which was every hurler's dream in the college. We started well and beat Carrick CBS comfortably. The draw pitted us against Dungarvan CBS in the next round. We had a surprise win and John Barron as ever was the main man in defence. We were in the semi-final against our arch-rivals, Mount Sion. Mount Sion had a very good team with brilliant players like Frankie Walsh. The game attracted the national press, which was a bit unusual at the time... and rarer still was the fact that 10 goals were scored. We were a point ahead going into the last minute when a high ball going into our goalmouth fell short and Tom Flynn caught it securely.

'Not being a goalkeeper, instead of striding clear of the goalmouth, he threw the ball up to drive it long down the field. In a flash from nowhere came Frankie Walsh who flicked the ball into the net before Tom's hurl met it. The puck out was still in the air when the final whistle sounded. I remember the Irish Press newspaper proclaimed the next morning in banner headlines 'Sixty Seconds Enough for Mount Sion'. They had won 5-3 to 5-1. Mount Sion beat St. Flannan's of Ennis and became the first Waterford team to bring home the most coveted of all schools' hurling trophies.'

The ultimate individual accolade for a player was to be chosen to play for the Munster Colleges in the inter-provincial colleges championship. Over the years, many of the Waterford team of 1959 received this recognition and gained experience playing with the best hurlers of their age group. Tony Wall recalls Austin Flynn being a teammate.

'I won the Harty Cup twice in 1950 and '51 with Thurles CBS. It was huge for my development. Austin Flynn and myself were on the Munster Colleges team. He was full back... I was centre back.'

The next year's team brought Martin Óg Morrissey into the reckoning, along with Jimmy Brohan of Cork. Tony Wall continues:

'59: AN EYEWITNESS ACCOUNT OF HURLING'S GOLDEN AGE

'Colleges hurling helped an awful lot. I knew a lot of the lads from Munster Colleges games. I played on the Munster Colleges team two years in 1952 and '53. They would have been the equivalent of the Railway Cup. Martin Óg Morrissey would have been on that, and I was always friendly with him from then on.'

In 1953, John Barron of De La Salle was on an All-Ireland winning Munster team. He retained his position for 1954, joined by several of the Harty Cup winning Mount Sion team of 1953, who had beaten Donie Nealon's St. Flannan's.

'I was a sub on the St. Flannan's team in 1953. I came in a sub in the Munster semi-final. Mount Sion beat Flannan's in that final. Then in 1954 we won the Harty Cup with St. Flannan's. The way they picked the Munster colleges team was if you won the final that team got four on it. If you were beaten in the final, that team got two or three, then a number of the other colleges would get representation as well. In that particular year with Munster colleges, I played with John Barron, he was corner-back, when Leinster beat us.

It brought us on a mile. We hurled nearly every single day in Flannan's. We called it at one time the hurling school. It was hurling day in and day out. The most amazing thing that we did was on most of the Sunday mornings we would play a practice match against a Clare club senior team... maybe Clarecastle, maybe Newmarket... maybe Eire Óg. They would go handy enough on us but it was a great preparation for us. We hurled and hurled... and hurled. It sure hardened us up. I thought that was great.'

Unlike today, very few of the players went to university, so the experience of Fitzgibbon Cup hurling wasn't open to many. On the '59 panel, Donal Whelan and Ned Power were teachers. Ned attended St. Pat's Teacher Training College and Donal went to University College Cork. Ned was a little unlucky as hurling wasn't the main sport in St. Pat's, as another graduate Donie Nealon remembers.

'In St. Pat's the hurlers were only the second relation. You see there were so many there from Mayo, Galway, Cork, Kerry... and from the western way, and football was the priority, but we had a nice hurling team there. We played in the Dublin Intermediate Hurling League. Later on, I hurled with UCD and played against St. Pat's. They had a very good hurling team a few years after I left. They had a right good team and they played in the Dublin Senior League.'

However, in UCC, hurling was central to college life. Donal Whelan had a very successful university career and played in several Fitzgibbon Cup competitions. This led him to be selected to captain the Combined Universities team which beat an Ireland XV in 1955. Donie Nealon thinks his friend, Duck benefited enormously from this experience.

> 'I won three Fitzgibbons with UCD. In 1959 I was captain. While there were only four colleges in it in those days... the four universities, Galway, Queens, Dublin and Cork but, my God... the standard was very high. I always said that if you could play well in the Fitzgibbon you were ready for your county team. It was still a very high standard at that time.'

Following Donal Whelan's university education, he became a teacher and was later principal of Kilmacthomas Vocational School. His work brought him to Dublin for a period where he captained the Civil Service Club.

For most of the Waterford players, the next stage of their development as hurlers, after school, was selection for the county minor team. After minor hurling, there generally followed a period of a couple of years for most players, as they developed physically, before they would be considered for the senior inter-county team. Many played junior hurling during this time before being drafted into the senior squad. For example, in 1955, the Waterford junior team included future senior players Tom Cheasty, Frankie Walsh and John Barron. Junior hurling was a more important grade in the 50s. As most players didn't attend third-level education and there was no under-20 or under-21 championships, the junior inter-county team helped to continue the players development.

Some also developed by playing senior club hurling but many of the 1959 squad lacked that opportunity as clubs like Ballydurn (Joe Harney), De La Salle (John Barron) and Ballyduff (Tom Cheasty) were not senior clubs at that time. This led to some unusual fixtures for players. For example, in the weeks after starring in the 1959 All-Ireland, Tom Cheasty was back to Ballyduff to lead them to a Junior County Championship win over Dave Leamy's Gael Óg.

'I WANT ONE OF THOSE'

Waterford started the Munster Championship campaign of 1948 in both senior and minor against Clare. A successful day in Thurles at the end of May qualified them for the Munster final. This was the Phil Grimes' championship debut, and he was highly praised by the Waterford News in the lead up to the final. *'Barely 19 years of age, Philly had already made his mark in the hurling world, and his brilliant debut in senior championship hurling against Clare this year marked him as a boy with a great future in the game. Following that match, he was hailed as the second John Keane, surely a wonderful tribute to one so young'.* The Munster final wasn't played until August 9 and there were concerns that Waterford might be ring-rusty when facing a Cork team featuring Christy Ring and Jack Lynch.

Such was the confidence of the Cork supporters that only two of the four special trains laid on for the trip to Thurles actually made the journey, with the other two diverted to serve day-trippers to Youghal. With veteran Christy Moylan brought back into the team and the spine of the team reinforced by Jim Ware on goal, Vin Baston in defence, and John Keane in attack, Waterford edged Cork by a single point to win by 4-7 to 3-9. Vin Baston, a captain in the army, based in Galway, was recognised as the Man of the Match by the *Cork Examiner*. Their headline read *'Capt. Baston's Magnificent Display in Waterford Defence'*. The sub-headline read *'C. Ring's Great Effort to Get Equaliser'*.

In a typical Ring display, he was the game's top scorer with 1-4 and he refused to give up. His shot in the last minute following a 40-yard solo run grazed the upright. Credit must go to Mick Hayes who tackled Ring just as he struck the ball. Recognising the significance of the victory, Ring commented to the Waterford players at full time that 'Ye have an All-Ireland'. Jack Lynch wasn't quite so sure and his comment to Mick Hayes was 'Don't make a hash of it this time'. With the minor team beating Tipperary on the same day, the double was still on.

In the semi-final against Galway, Waterford had a relatively easy win by 3-7 to 1-6. Tom Keith in his book, *The Colours Blue and White*, quotes Pat Fanning as saying *'They were lordly against Galway, but it must be recalled that if the western county had had the services of Capt. Vin Baston, the army officer who was based in Galway, then it was debatable whether Waterford would have won the All-Ireland semi-final. Such was the contribution he made, so much did he tip the scales in favour of his native county, that without his services, we would surely have been lost'.* His 1-1 along with John Keane's two goals saw the team safely into their second All-Ireland final.

Pat Fanning was unlucky not to be in that final. At 30 years old, he was already an experienced administrator with Mount Sion, while being in contention for a place on the county team. In controversial circumstances surrounding the running of the county selection committee, Pat lost his place on the panel and his opportunity to win a Celtic Cross.

The minor team had also qualified for the All-Ireland final with a facile 8-12 to 3-2 victory over Galway in their semi-final. Seandun, writing in the *Examiner*, picked out future senior stars of 1959 Mick Flannelly and Michael O'Connor in his report.

> 'Waterford's win of eight clear goals was a fair reflex of their superiority over the Western side. The Waterford forwards were a treat to watch, and with McHugh, M.

'59: AN EYEWITNESS ACCOUNT OF HURLING'S GOLDEN AGE

O'Connor, P. O'Connor and Flannelly all at the peak of their form, they wove patterns around the Galway defence time and time again.'

Team training for the minor final was held in Dungarvan and there was a good combination of players from the east and west of the county. The common denominator in most cases was the influence of the Christian Brothers on their development, whether they were from Waterford, Dungarvan or Lismore. One player, Michael O'Connor, who would be part of the 1959 senior panel, had transferred from the Christian Brothers school in Lismore to become a boarder in Mount Mellary. He was one of six Cappoquin men in the team (Michael Kelleher, Vincent Walshe, Joe Flynn, Michael O'Connor, Billy Conway and Michael Browne) who, along with trainer Paddy Cunningham became known as 'The Magnificent Seven'.

Tom Cunningham recalled that he had attended county trials earlier in the year and not been selected for the panel. However, after a strong performance in a game for his club Sarsfields against this powerful Cappoquin side, his display couldn't be ignored, and he was drafted into the team. Michael O'Connor recalled reminiscing with Tom about his promotion to the squad.

> 'Tom told me some time ago, and I didn't know this... that we played Dungarvan in a minor match some Tuesday evening. I remember that I was working with my father in the factory in Cappoquin. After work, I got into the car and went over to play the match. We had six of the Waterford team... but Dungarvan beat us. I couldn't believe it. In hindsight, what we were doing was stupid, thinking we could do a day's work, jump in a car and go and play a match. We were playing guys that were more intellectually trained... students.
>
> 'Cunningham was put on me seemingly and he obviously did very well... he told me this himself! He wasn't on the minor panel at all but "after that game, because I held you, I was on the minor panel" he told me. It was only a year ago he told me that. I was complaining to him, and I said "I remember the match because you cost me a lot of money. You blew out my front teeth. You cost me a lot of shagging money!"'

Tom recalls that his selection for the team was at the expense of a clubmate.

> 'The 1948 minor team beat Clare in the first match, and I wasn't even at it. At that time, there used to be a trial every year. I mustn't have been a very good triallist. When they picked the team for the Munster final, I was picked to replace a fellow

Mick Flannelly being carried from the field after the 1948 Munster Minor final.

clubmate. Michael Shalloe was a half-back against Clare and he was a schoolmate and a very good friend of mine. He got dropped instead of me... not that I had any objections.'

Having stayed in Naas the night before the final, the team was transferred to Croke Park in a fleet of cars. The Cappoquin group were ferried in a large Dodge vehicle and almost missed the throw-in. Their car was in an accident en-route to Croke Park, and they had to wait for the investigating Garda to release them to continue their journey.

Once the match started, nerves subsided, and Waterford led from start to finish. Playing with the breeze, they got off to a dream start with a goal from Browne, two points from Gallagher and one from McHugh, without reply. Connolly scored Kilkenny's only point of the half and at half-time they trailed Waterford by 2-7 to 0-1. The second-half saw the appearance of Donal Whelan as a substitute for McHugh, joining future 1959 teammates Tom Cunningham, Michael O'Connor, and Mick Flannelly. Michael O'Connor remains full of praise for one of his brothers in arms.

> 'The big thing from my point of view was that I scored. I was playing in the forwards. I scored because there was one man on the team, and he presented the ball to me... and I had to score. That was Mick Flannelly. I was looking at a picture of the minor team and there I am beside Mick Flan and right through most of the team photos I was on for the next 10 years... I was beside Mick Flan.
>
> 'We had a bond... we were like brothers. It was extraordinary.
>
> 'As a player, he was a real team man. He played for the team. I thought he read the game intelligently. In my case, he laid on passes for me when I was in the forward line. With present day hurling, he would be perfect for it. His awareness was amazing. He was a small little man... but he was hardy. In that minor final, I scored a couple of goals and a few points but really it was Mick Flannelly who scored. He laid the ball on for me. I was playing wing forward and he was playing centre-forward. He was a brilliant player, completely underestimated.'

Mick Flannelly went on to be the most decorated Waterford hurler of all time. In addition to All-Ireland medals at minor and senior levels, three Munster medals, league and Oireachtas titles, he has the distinction of winning more county titles than any other player, an incredible 15 hurling and four football championships. He played at minor grade for three years, winning a county championship each year but came to national prominence as captain of the Waterford minor team who won the All-Ireland in 1948. He recalled this time in interviews with Michael Moynihan of the *Irish Examiner*.

> *'It's a long time ago now... 65 years. We were only young fellas. I was serving my time as a printer with the* Munster Express *down on the quay... jobbing work, but regular hours. You could make training easily enough. We hadn't interest in much apart from the hurling. I thought we had an exceptional team, for one reason in particular... there were five from Mount Sion, four from Dungarvan and four from Cappoquin. So, most of the team was from three clubs, and the players knew each other very well, we understood each other and that was a big help all that year.'*

In the Munster Final win over Tipperary, Mick had his first chance to play in Thurles.

> 'Vincent O'Donoghue was chairman of the County Board; he became president of the GAA afterwards. He spoke to us before we played in Thurles: "Remember, lads, this field is as big as a prairie... use it". That's all he said, but it was enough. We played fast hurling... ground hurling, but the game was different back then. You could do that. And he was right about Thurles... to us at the time, it was the biggest field you could think of, but the difference was that at the time you had people in sideline seats... almost in on the field. It added to the whole thing.'

In a precursor to the senior final, Mick recalls the excitement of the minor All-Ireland final.

> 'We knew we were good. Kilkenny had a few players on that minor team who would have gone on to play senior, but we were confident enough. We played a good brand of hurling and we trusted in it. We didn't see much of Dublin the night before the game. They kept us outside in Naas on the Saturday night... near Punchestown. For entertainment, we walked the racecourse the night beforehand. We won handy enough. It was only three points, but we were the better team over the hour alright.
>
> 'I didn't get a cup after the game, mind you. There was a pitch invasion because Waterford were in the senior game as well, and there was a big crowd there from the county. There was no presentation... though we were carried off the field afterwards, which was great.'

'59: AN EYEWITNESS ACCOUNT OF HURLING'S GOLDEN AGE

Noel Dalton, later a top-class referee, was at the match and recalls it vividly in his book *A Déise Boy*.

> 'Waterford had been knocking on the door for a couple of years in this grade but had now reached their Holy Grail. They came bounding out onto the pitch in royal blue jerseys with white collars and cuffs. Unknown to myself at the time, I was going to play against many of them in club games in later years, but now they were my heroes. Unlike the senior team who were like gods to me, these lads were still going to school and of course I knew the Mount Sion players who contributed one third of the team, to see in the street. Cappoquin and Dungarvan schools contributed the remaining two thirds in equal measure. The cognoscenti around us were of the opinion that the minor game always produced the best hurling. It seemed so as Waterford played brilliantly to move comfortably ahead but, whether it was because of the heavy showers that poured down or the three huge lads Kilkenny put in as subs, we were back-pedalling as the game ran to its conclusion. The skill of Mick Flannelly and Budge McHugh, the tenacity of Tom Cunningham and John Hayden and the flowing hurling of Pat Boyle ensured we kept our noses in front at the final whistle.'

Kilkenny made a strong comeback, but the Waterford lads held their nerve to win by 3-8 to 4-2. Strangely, there was no cup to present to the minor champions. It wasn't until the following year that the *Irish Press* newspaper provided a cup for the competition. Instead, they celebrated in their dressing-room and having changed, took their place on reserved sideline seats in front of the Hogan Stand. Luckily, the team had the TWA Cup from the Munster final win to bring with them on their celebrations around the county.

Excitement surrounding the senior final was high and stand tickets for the final were sold out two weeks in advance of the game. Every mode of transport was employed to get to the match, including chartered airplanes from the USA which landed at Collinstown Airport on the outskirts of Dublin. The American group, including Philly Grimes, present as a spectator, marched to Croke Park, headed by the Transport and General Workers Band who played *The Star-Spangled Banner* in their honour.

Mick Foley and Jack Ware, brother of Charlie and Jim, were responsible for training the team but there was concern that the squad were older and heavier on average than the young, fit and fast Dublin team. A rain shower before the start made the pitch greasy and the odds seemed to favour Dublin, but it was to be Waterford's day. From Christy Moylan's brilliant opening point, Waterford were in charge. Even playing against the wind in the first-half they took a 2-5 to 0-2 lead. They never looked back and two goals each from John Keane and Willie Galvin, and goals from Christy Moylan and Eddie Daly ensured victory by 6-7 to 4-2.

After a long history of hurling in the county, on September 5, 1948, Jim Ware of Erin's Own, finally became the first Waterford man to accept the Liam MacCarthy Cup. Waterford had its first All-Ireland medals and future 1959 players Philly Grimes and John Kiely both received one, having featured in that year's Munster Championship first round win over Clare.

In Kilkenny, young hurlers were taking note. Johnny McGovern still remembers going to see the new All-Ireland champions.

> 'The first time I saw Waterford play, they were after winning the All-Ireland in 1948. Kilkenny were playing them in a league game after the All-Ireland. There was a train going down from here, so we all went. I was only a young fella... about 16 at the time. The place was packed. I remember John Keane at centre-forward that day, Vin Baston centre-back, Andy Fleming corner back. Jim Ware in goal. John Keane was a great player. As a centre-back, he could handle any forward he ever played on. Even Mick Mackey found it hard to shake him off. He moved up centre-forward in 1948.'

Eddie Keher, who was to feature on the Kilkenny team in 1959, was still only a young boy in 1948 but recalls how he came to meet one of the heroes from his scrapbook in real life.

> 'Kilkenny won the All-Ireland in 1947. I would have been six when Waterford won in 1948. I remember myself and my friend next door, we started in '47, cutting out the pictures of the players out of the paper and pasting them into a book. We used to sit naming out all the teams. Waterford won in '48... which was in the next pages. We knew all the players... Jim Ware, Vin Baston, Eddie Carew... all that team.
>
> 'That would have been my first coming in contact with the Waterford team. A quick story about Jim Ware... We were in Tramore one day. I'd say I was about seven. We were walking along the street... my mother, father, myself and my sister... and my mother said "Oh there's Jim Ware" so we went over to talk to him. The thing I remember about him was that he shook my hand and nearly broke my bloody hand. 'He had a big strong hand on him.'

In Waterford, a 12-year-old Frankie Walsh was brought by Brother McGill on a visit to John Keane, something he never forgot.

Declan Goode

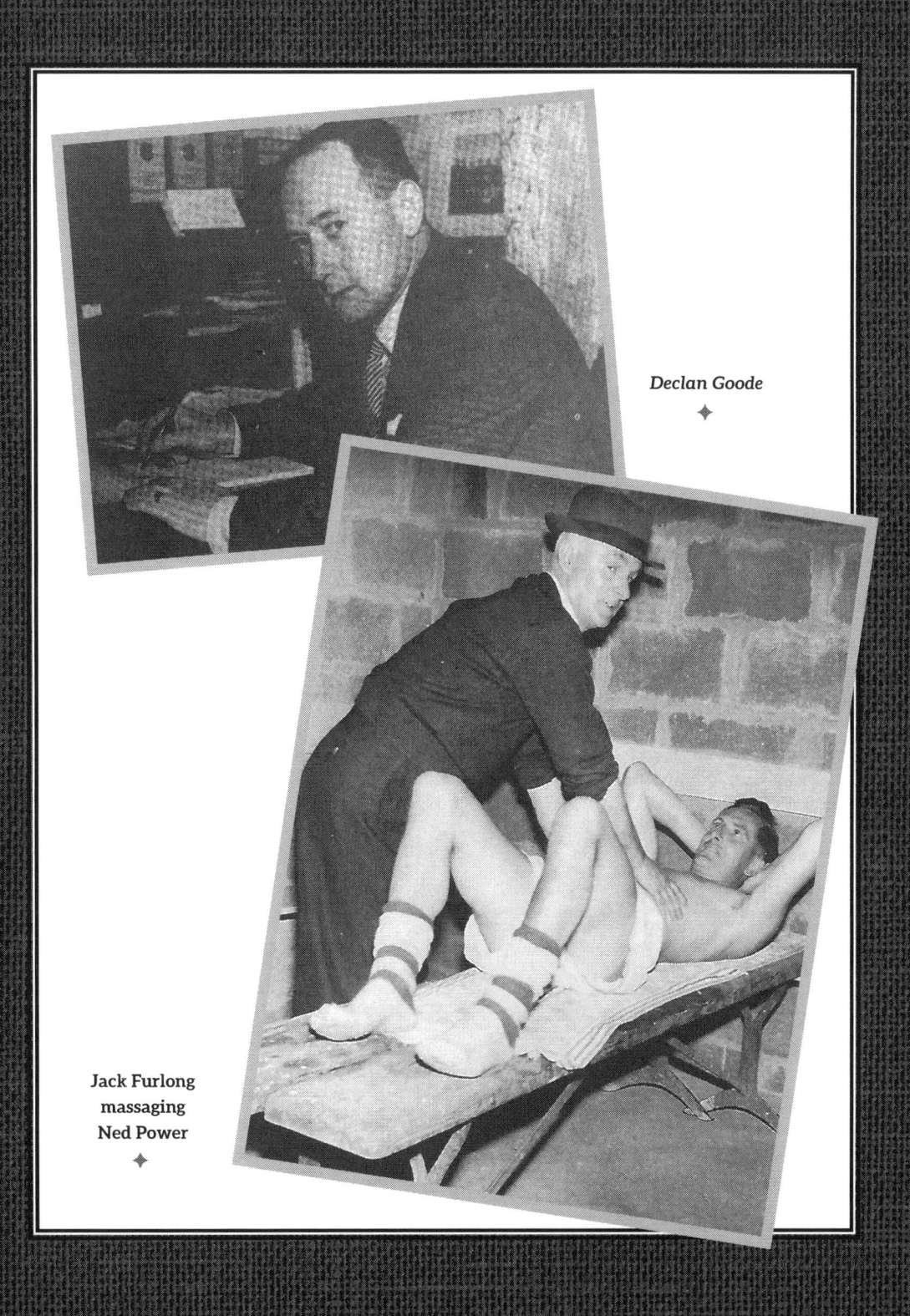

Jack Furlong
massaging
Ned Power

'We were given a cup of tea and biscuits. Then John said to me "Did you ever see an All-Ireland medal?" I said I hadn't. He went upstairs and brought down the medal he won in 1948... when Jim Ware was captain. When I looked at it the first thing I said was "I want one of those".'

In the years following the 1948 final, some of the key players in the 1959 story retired from playing and transitioned into the management and administration roles. With the benefit of these experiences, the cast of supporting characters was now in place for an assault in the summit again in the late 50s.

By 1959, they held all of the key positions in the county set-up.

>Pat Fanning was county chairman.
>Declan Goode was county secretary.
>Charlie Ware represented the county on the central council.
>Vin O'Donoghue was Waterford's representative at congress.
>John Keane was the team trainer.
>Jim Ware was a selector.

Jack Furlong of Erin's Own came to receive more recognition in later years. A hurley carrier and repairer of broken hurleys, first-aid man, water carrier, masseur, and general factotum, he was a one-man support team for the players. An annual trophy named in his honour is now awarded to personalities who work tirelessly behind the scenes. Considering the number of injuries sustained at the time, the medical officer, Dr. Milo Shelley was the necessary final piece of the group. With this management team in place, it was now time to prepare a team capable of winning the All-Ireland again.

'GOING OUT WITH A WEAKER SIDE'

The All-Ireland winning team of 1948 was a relatively old side. With an average age of 28, they were expected to be overrun by a younger, fitter Dublin team, who were, on average, five years their junior. While the experienced heads won the day, none of that team survived until 1959. The next generation of success would be in the hands of the minor champions of 1948 and the rising young star, Philly Grimes. He had a baptism of fire when introduced to the Waterford senior team in 1947.

In a league match at Dungarvan, he faced the legendary Christy Ring. Even then, Ring had five All-Ireland medals and was nine years older than Grimes, but the 18-year-old acquitted himself well. By the following year he was an automatic choice for the championship opener

'59: AN EYEWITNESS ACCOUNT OF HURLING'S GOLDEN AGE

against Clare, as he recalls.

> 'I was 19 at the time and played against Clare in the first round before emigrating to America. Waterford went on to beat Cork in the Munster final… and Dublin in the All-Ireland final, and because they only had 20 players on the panel, I received a medal. It was a great honour, but as I had played in only one match, somehow… it lacked something.'

Having played for New York for two and a half years, his return to Mount Sion was confirmed in December 1950. In addition to the already established Grimes, there was a crop of minor players who had just won the 1948 minor All-Ireland. This team included Mick Flannelly Michael O'Connor, Tom Cunningham and Donal Whelan, who would become senior players by 1959.

Following the victory in 1948, Waterford went on to suffer some lean years. Up to 1956, they only managed two championship wins, both in the first round. Jim Fives who, although born in Waterford, played for three counties (Waterford, Galway and Roscommon), recalls those years leading up to his transfer to Galway in 1955.

> 'The Waterford team that won the All-Ireland in 1948 was a relatively old team and the team broke up straight after that. We had a poor team while I was there. You have to remember that it's a small county and that the number of clubs playing the game is small. Another problem was that we had not the right management structures. We had far too many selectors and this led to a lot of political selection decisions, with selectors sometimes more interested in having players from their club on the team than having the best 15 players. Of course, that was not a problem unique to Waterford… but at the time, we couldn't afford to be going out with a weaker side. The biggest disappointment of my time with Waterford came when we lost to Tipperary by two points in the Munster Championship in 1951. They were the big power then and we were so close. We never put it together after that.'

One by one, the players that were to become the heroes of 1959 were being added to the championship squad. In 1949, Seamus Power, still playing his hurling in Tipperary with Roscrea came on as a sub in the game against Limerick. The following year, Mick Flannelly made his breakthrough when he appeared as a sub against Cork. By 1951, Phil Grimes was back from America and took up his place in the team with Flannelly, Michael O'Connor and John Kiely.

'59: AN EYEWITNESS ACCOUNT OF HURLING'S GOLDEN AGE

Waterford were still without that elusive championship win but it finally came against Clare in 1952 when Tom Cunningham and Austin Flynn made their breakthroughs. Austin Flynn, far from showing delight with his call-up to the team, felt it was too soon for him and that he might be better not being picked. He did play throughout that campaign but then dropped out of the team until 1955. He was surprised that despite the 'amazing achievement' of winning an All-Ireland senior and minor double in 1948, that 'things had slipped so much in a short space of time. We were so disorganised'.

The defeats to Limerick in 1954 and '55 didn't bring any respite but it allowed for the debuts of Donal Whelan, John Barron, Martin Óg Morrissey, Tom Cheasty and Charlie Ware. Frankie Walsh even appeared on the team-sheet as a substitute. By the time of the Munster Championship game in Fermoy against Cork in 1956, there were 10 of the 1959 team in place and, despite defeat by six points, there was a feeling of change in the air.

'THEY WERE LIKE GODS TO US'

While the peak years of Waterford hurling are usually defined as 1957 to 1963, during which time they won an All-Ireland, the National League, the Oireachtas Cup, and three Munster finals, a more specific starting date was defined by County Board stalwart Seamus O'Brien.

> 'Waterford's golden years extended from October 1956, when they drew with the All-Ireland champions, Wexford in a thrilling National Hurling League encounter at Walsh Park… until that era came to an end in 1963, when we lost to Kilkenny in another thrilling final.'

It proved to Tom Cunningham that better times were ahead.

> 'Nick O'Donnell of Wexford was marking me that day. Waterford's first breakthrough was a draw against Wexford… after Wexford winning the 1956 All-Ireland. That was the first signs of light that we weren't as bad as we made ourselves out to be.'

Waterford had been beaten in the championship that year by Cork in Fermoy. Frankie Walsh made his championship debut and received a fractured skull from a blow by Pat Philpot. He was so badly injured that he recalls 'I spent over a month in hospital. I was allowed no visitors, no papers… no nothing. As I lay on my back, I wondered a lot about the future'. Frankie did come back though, much to the relief of all hurling fans. Phil Fanning was at the match with his father and was in the car as Frankie was transported to hospital. His interpretation of the incident was that it was intentional.

'That day marked the debut of Frankie Walsh who came on as a substitute only to be forced to leave the field with a horrendous head injury, the infliction of which was never regarded as an accident. When Waterford played a thrilling draw with All-Ireland champions, Wexford in the league later that year, Walsh was only allowed play with what was then a rubber ribbed cycling headgear, which was covered by a tweed cap... not an unusual sight at the time. It was soon discarded.'

In a conversation for this book, Phil Fanning elaborated on the incident.

'Frankie was a substitute against Cork down in Fermoy. He would have been 19. He went on as a substitute in the second-half and made an immediate impression. That was the day he got creased by Paddy Philpot... the Cork half-back who gave him an awful crack in the head. He had to go off immediately. He was knocked out practically. I remember getting him into the taxi coming home... the hackney car. I was with my father who used to take me to the matches. I would have been 12 at the time.

'I remember rushing back to Waterford to get him into the hospital to get him fixed up. He was really in a bad way. They were wondering how it would go, but he got over it all right. The day the league campaign started later in the year, I remember Frankie going out against Wexford wearing a cyclist's helmet. They used have a rubber ribbed helmets at the time for cyclists. Frankie went out wearing a rubber ribbed helmet and he put a cloth cap over it so fellas wouldn't see the helmet. By the time the game was over, the two of them were thrown away... and thrown on the sideline

'That was an awful injury he got that time. It was really amazing the way he came back from it. It was an injury that would have put quite a few fellas out of the game... saying I have enough of this thing. He didn't... he stuck with it and that was it. It is amazing to say that at the age he was, to captain an All-Ireland team, especially a Waterford team of that time, he would have been only 22 or 23 when he captained the team in '59. I thought that in itself must be something of a record. There were very few lads at that age captained All-Ireland winning teams.'

Frankie's son, Peter takes up the story of that day.

'My mother said, it was the crack in the head that had him mad. She always maintained it was the fractured skull that made him as odd as he was. In the infirmary he spent several days in darkness. Pat Fanning pleaded with him to give up the hurling, actually. He got Brother McGill, who was a great mentor of Frankie's... who had taught him in school and got him started into the hurling. At that time the Christian Brothers weren't their own bosses... they weren't allowed to do anything, it was very controlled and rigid. He ducked out of the monastery in Cork and got a bus, and came to Waterford. He went up to Frankie and got down on his bended knee and begged him not to play hurling again. The cycling helmets were leather. It was at home for years.'

Another player who started that day was Tom Cheasty.

'We were beaten by a couple of points by Cork in Fermoy. That was the first time I made any real impression. Christy Ring was playing... he beat us that day... scored a couple of goals. We should have beaten them. I was playing on a young fella. I was only 22 and he was younger than myself. Mick McCarthy was the fella I was playing on. They brought Willie John Daly out on me. I got on almost as well on him. It was a bit of a breakthrough for me... I scored five points from play. I was picked for the Rest of Ireland team later that year.'

Echoing the frustration of Austin Flynn, Tom Cunningham pulled out of the panel in 1956 but recognised that there as a change in the air.

'I always considered myself a back, but I kept being shunted up into the forwards... I sort of became a moveable feast. I just said I'd had enough of it. I went back for 1957 and everything had changed... for the better. Pat Fanning was the County Board man and Pat was a brilliant organiser. John Keane came in to train the team, and he was excellent. No roaring or shouting... or embarrassing anyone in front of everyone else. John would just have a quiet word here and there, as required.'

Writing in the *Cuchulainn Annual* shortly after the 1959 victory, Pat Fanning, Chairman of the Waterford County Board recalled:

'The story starts in Fermoy on a summer day in 1956, for it was then, in a Munster championship game with Cork, that this present Waterford team had its beginnings. Waterford were beaten that day but out of defeat was born a resolve to stick together and win another All-Ireland for the county."

'59: AN EYEWITNESS ACCOUNT OF HURLING'S GOLDEN AGE

The disorganisation experienced by Austin Flynn and the rest of the team was corrected by the appointment of John Keane as the team trainer to work in tandem with Pat Fanning who, despite being the chairman of the County Board, was the de facto team manager. When it was suggested to him in later years that he was a manager in a time before the rise of the modern Bainisteoir, Pat Fanning agreed.

'I suppose that's fair to say. John Keane was the team trainer. I was the one who did the talking. I would talk to them before the game... during the game and after the game. I would do the motivating factor during that whole period. They were a great bunch of boys.'

Fanning had an eye for a player. Austin Flynn recalled one of his earliest games.

'When I moved to secondary school at Dungarvan CBS (thanks to extra tuition from a dedicated teacher named Michael Foley who had in fact helped train the 1948 successful All-Ireland team) I was immediately involved in school hurling under the guidance of Brother Murray, who did great work for college hurling. Shortly after starting at the CBS, I remember playing in a schools final in Waterford... when I learned a lot from an umpire at the match. The match was in progress for about 10 minutes, and I hadn't struck a ball. We were under great pressure and every time the ball came my way the full-forward, who was much bigger and stronger than I, was pushing and shoving and getting himself tangled up in me. I was really frustrated and did not know what to do.

'At this point the goalkeeper asked me to puck out the ball. I went back to pick it up and as I did so the umpire whispered, "Keep away from your man until the ball arrives... he can't hurl". Well, I was open to suggestions.

'The next ball that came I pretended to go for it, but let the full-forward off. He was now dealing with a dropping ball but with nobody to tangle with, he did not know what to do. I just arrived at the right time (by accident) to gather the ball and clear. It was the first decent puck of the ball I got in the match, and I remember thinking that this was a great idea. Afterwards, whenever I had to mark anybody that was bigger or stronger than me, I knew I had no business standing with him and I tried to implement this idea... not always with the same success, however.

'The umpire was unknown to me then and little did I know of the influence he would have on my hurling career, and that of Waterford hurling during the most glorious years (so far) from about 1956 to 1963. I later got to know him as Pat Fanning of Mount Sion.'

John Keane was an obvious choice for team trainer. He had the respect of all of the players and officials. Pat Fanning, while a clubmate of Keane's was never in doubt about his greatness.

> 'John Keane, the greatest hurler Waterford ever produced, a man who ranks with Ring and Mackey and Keher and Lynch... and the rest of them. When people ask me, who was the best man that ever played for Waterford, I say... take the name of John Keane, put it to one side... and discuss the rest. He was that good. He was a selector, and he was our star player.'

Larry Guinan was a young player and remembers Keane with a mix of respect and awe.

> 'John Keane was a bit strict. As Frankie always said, "Did you get your Munster final haircut?" I always got it cut into the bone when we'd be playing the matches. I put a bit of Vaseline on the bit of hair I had, and John Keane saw me in the toilet one day and I was lighting a match or something to dissolve this Vaseline before I put it on my hair... he f***in ate me! He read me!
>
> 'I remember another time up in the Sports Field and we were training for one of the games. John Keane said to us that nobody... now nobody, was to touch a ball, to catch a ball or to lift up a ball and put it in their hands. He wanted the balls on the ground the whole time and go from one end of the field to the other. Frankie and myself were great for crossing over from one side of the field to the other, and Frankie hit this ball over. Just as it came over to me, didn't it hop and the natural thing was to grab it.
> 'He came out on the field and what he didn't say to me... and I actually cried, I had so much respect for the man. John Keane was a God. He was brilliant. He had everything. Pat Fanning and John Keane, they were like Gods to us.'

His coaching style received the approval of Tom Cheasty who analysed his own playing style.

> 'John Keane took over and he probably saw something. I was a tough aggressive player and had a bit of speed as well. I admired John as a trainer, but I could have done with a lot more coaching. I didn't develop my right hand until just about All-Ireland

John Keane training the team

Pat Fanning, John Keane and Jim Ware

time in 1957. After 1957 I trained and developed it myself. My particular thrill was the solo-run. Beating a tackle maybe or putting the ball over the bar... maybe passing the ball on to a better placed team-mate. You'd either score yourself or make the play.

'I liked the physical contact. You know the way a fella would go for you... try and sink you altogether, that's when you could really make a cod of them. It's the cute fella that shadows you is the hardest man to beat. It's the man with his dander up is the easiest man to beat. I'd like to make a fool of a fella and then score if possible.'

Austin Flynn spoke about the respect that came with Keane's hurling ability.

'Talk about being overawed! Here was this legendary figure treating me as an equal and without any condescension. He was a great man. He had a knack of putting you at your ease. You know... he never raised his voice. He didn't need to. He had done it all and when he spoke about hurling, he did so with authority. We often hear of managers who break down doors and who never stop roaring and shouting at players. That was not John's way. His approach was the quiet word in your ear.

He was a sports psychologist long before that type of person was ever thought of in Ireland. He never criticised a player in front of others. He never even took us aside from the others to speak to us. When he had to impart advice or otherwise you would suddenly realise that you and he had somehow drifted apart from the others without anyone noticing and then... after your talk, you would rejoin the group... again without anyone noticing.'

John Barron emphasised the psychology behind his actions.

'John's training method consisted mainly of hurling skills allied to explosive sprints. The training was enjoyable but intense. We didn't know how much work we were doing because of the way John operated. He had enormous hands, you know, and he had wrists like steel cords. He would stand in the midst of a group of players with the hurley in his right hand and flick the ball one-handed for a player to chase and hit, right or left. What we didn't realise was that he kept hitting the ball just that little bit farther each time, so we were doing these really intense sprints that were getting progressively longer. And all the time he was encouraging us with that soft voice.'

'WE CAN WIN AN ALL-IRELAND'

The players could feel the momentum building and were looking for indications of progress. It didn't lead to any trophies, but the team were moving in the right direction. Tom Cheasty felt that it was a matter having the right personnel, both players and coach.

> 'After 1956, I remember John Keane was thinking that maybe we had the makings of a reasonably good team... the kind of team where fellas would believe they had a chance of winning. That's an important thing with any team... to believe that you have a chance of winning.'

Austin Flynn has been interviewed extensively on this subject and agrees that the team of officials was important to setting the correct tone.

> 'Things were now definitely changing and for the 1957 championship, the panel was brought together in Dungarvan for collective training under John Keane as trainer and selector. Also present that evening were the other selectors, Jackie Goode, Mickey Feeney, Seamus O'Brien, and the Chairman, Pat Fanning.'

The most influential in setting the tone was Pat Fanning, who was now two years into his role as chairman of the County Board and was frustrated with playing second fiddle to the big three of Cork, Kilkenny, and Tipperary.

> 'I became chairman of the County Board in '55. I had been sick and tired of the Cork and Kilkenny and Tipperary tapping you on the shoulder after a match and saying "God, ye were great, lads". We were great... but we had lost. I remember putting it to the team that we formed at that time, 1955 to '63 was one of the finest teams any county ever produced... and putting it to them that we should be sick of being patronised and that we should realise that we had the ability and we had the will to do great things, and the story of '55 to '63 is a demonstration of what the will to win, coupled with ability, can achieve in the county. The rivalry between Waterford and South Kilkenny is tremendous but we were the poor relations and felt it. They were the lords and demonstrated it, but between '55 and '63 there was born a new relationship... a new world as Waterford came out of the blue, and the three All-Irelands were among the finest All-Irelands of the era. It never became a battle of equals and that's why I'm saying Waterford had taken its place as a hurling county par excellence, the equal of the best.'

'59: AN EYEWITNESS ACCOUNT OF HURLING'S GOLDEN AGE

This was a message that was to be repeated regularly, so much so that Tom Cunningham considered it to be a mantra.

'Before that, we were regarded as underdogs against most teams, particularly all the teams in Munster. Pat was impressing upon us how good we were. He was praising us. We had no reason to feel like second-class citizens compared to the other teams in Munster or Leinster. We were as good if not better than most of the other teams and there was no reason why we couldn't win an All-Ireland. We shouldn't have any doubts about our own abilities. That was his mantra.'

Austin Flynn, Tom Cunningham and others pinpoint a training session in Dungarvan in 1957 as the real starting point. Enda McEvoy, following an interview with Austin Flynn, recreated the scene vividly for his article in the *Irish Examiner*.

'Early 1957, an evening in Fraher Field. The Second Coming of Austin Flynn. This time it's serious. This time it's for keeps. Because Waterford, at long last, are serious. Pat Fanning, the new chairman of the County Board and a future GAA president, is addressing the members of the panel. Fanning is a wonderful orator and tonight he isn't sparing the rhetoric. "As God is my judge," he announces, "I believe there's the winning of an All-Ireland for Waterford in this team. It will take a great effort. You will have to give a great commitment. You will have to give until it hurts and then give more. Everything possible will be done by the County Board. But lads, it's a matter of pride in the Waterford jersey. Cork and Tipperary and Kilkenny have their tradition. But we have our tradition too. It's easy to come back when you're winning. Picking yourself up and coming back for more — that's Waterford's tradition." To Flynn the words were nothing less than an epiphany. He'd been happy with life as it was, playing hurling and football for Abbeyside and messing about with boats. He'd just finished building a 16-footer with his brother, based on the model of a stormy petrel in a book of boat plans someone had given him and, in the absence of marine plywood, fashioned out of larch from the priory in Mount Melleray. "I was fulfilled. I had no great ambition to play for Waterford again. That all changed that night in Fraher Field."'

Pat himself later referred to this Waterford tradition, of which he was so proud.

'Ours is a tradition of continuing effort. The county has never ceased in its striving for success. Through good times and bad times Waterford remains staunchly faithful to the association and I'm proud of that.'

While the vision was inspiring and the support from the County Board and management was welcomed, Austin still had doubts, especially when comparing himself to more established players.

> 'Pat Fanning who made a famous address to the players which, for me, was the actual night it all started. I remember the way he spelt out his firm belief in the capacity of this group to win an All-Ireland for Waterford... the efforts the County Board would make towards this goal... and the total commitment, dedication and pride in the county that would be expected from the players. I didn't know most of the other players at that time and I remember thinking... *this is serious stuff*... and I remember looking across at Seamus Power and Philly Grimes and thinking... *my God am I out of my depth here... could I be in the same league as these fellas?*'

In turn, Pat places the credit with the players who grasped the opportunity and started the new era on the pitch against Limerick in the 1957 championship.

> 'Well do I recall the coming together in Dungarvan... the players, the few officials. And well do I recall putting it for all of us that we had grown weary of recurring defeat, sick of being sympathised with, and patronisingly praised by our conquerors for "doing well". That was the day a group of hurlers determined to prove themselves in victory and make their county the equal of the best. The rest is history... a history that had one of its prominent chapters when we faced and beat a great Limerick team in the very first round in the Cork Athletic Grounds.

Having avoided the draw for the first round, Waterford's game against Limerick was a Munster semi-final. Their 4-12-to-5-5-win set Waterford on a path that would eventually lead to glory. Mick Dunne reported for the *Irish Press*.

> *'If Waterford folk do some wild celebrating for a few days, you cannot really blame them. For the first time they have teams in both Munster finals. Their hurlers are back there after a lapse of nine years. They reached the final with a spirited display of forceful hurling that decisively beat Limerick's young team on the sun-drenched*

'59: AN EYEWITNESS ACCOUNT OF HURLING'S GOLDEN AGE

Athletic Grounds in Cork yesterday. And there were none greater than the two veterans, Johnny O'Connor, and John Kiely.'

Agreeing with the assessment of Johnny O'Connor's performance, Seamus Power pointed to the team's resilience in overcoming injuries on the day.

> 'We played Limerick in the first round. Limerick had a young team with players like Liam Moloney, Mick Tynan, Tom McGarry, Dermot Kelly, and Vivian Cobbe. Waterford had a narrow win, but Phil Grimes suffered a shoulder injury... Austin Flynn had to go off, and Frankie Walsh wasn't on for the full hour.'

The Limerick win led to the Munster final against Cork, recalled by Philly Grimes.

> 'In 1957, we beat Cork by five points in the Munster final at Thurles. Christy Ring was missing that day, but they had so many good hurlers... Willie John Daly, Matty Fouhy, Paddy Barry, Terry Kelly and Johnny Clifford... to mention but a few. Seamus Power and I were at midfield together by now and we got on superbly. We had been friends from our earliest days and even sat together at school.'

Waterford beat Cork by 1-11 to 1-6 to win just their third Munster title. There was always a question mark against any victory over a Cork team which didn't include Christy Ring. Cork were also missing Pat Philpot and Gerry Murphy. The Waterford defence was resolute, and it wasn't until the twentieth minute that Cork scored a point. After a very low scoring first-half, Waterford led by just three points to two. From Dickie Roche's important saves to Mick Flannelly's goal, Waterford were stronger throughout the pitch and deserving of the win.

In the All-Ireland semi-final on July 28, Waterford hammered Galway by 4-12 to 0-11. In the *Irish Press*, Padraig Puirseal described it as *'The most disappointing and the stormiest game that any lover of hurling could wish not to see'.* Waterford players were far from blameless, but it was Tommy Kelly and Billy Duffy of Galway who were sent off. This left their 13 teammates with no chance, particularly having conceded two goals... one from Guinan, and one from Kiely.

'WE SHOULD HAVE WON'

Waterford received a strange request in the build up to the 1957 All-Ireland final from film director George Pollock to allow an actor to line up with the team before the game, with the footage to be integrated into his film *Rooney*. Feeling it would be too much of a distraction, the County Board refused. Kilkenny, obviously more relaxed in the environment of Croke Park accepted the offer and allowed British actor John Gregson to march in the parade with them. He was supposed to be a Dublin hurler in the film, so the black and amber jersey must have been confusing to Irish audiences. Eddie Keher remembers:

> 'I was in the minor dressing-room that year which adjoined the senior one, and there was equal consternation there as we emerged to see this strange figure in the black and amber strip surrounded by a weird bunch who turned out to be film directors and crew.'

Tom Cheasty recalled that there was some Waterford involvement. 'We went up then about a week or so after the All-Ireland to do shots to put into the film. I think some of the lads couldn't go back there. They were so disappointed.' Philly Grimes felt the experience of Croke Park made a difference for Kilkenny.

> 'They had been through four successive Leinster finals with a magnificent Wexford team. That experience stood to them whereas it was our first appearance in a final... an indication, perhaps, of how green we were was that Larry Guinan had never been in Dublin before that weekend.'

Showing the strength in depth in Kilkenny hurling, seven of their team played junior club hurling. Dick Rockett described Kilkenny in 1957 as 'an average team overall but then we had a great goalkeeper and that counted for a lot. If Ollie was playing today, nothing would pass him'.

In front of a 70,594 attendance, Waterford were slight favourites in this first ever championship meeting of the two counties, due to their impressive march through Munster and their semi-final win over Galway. After a bright start, Kilkenny went five points up. Waterford then took the initiative and actually led at half time by 1-6 to 1-5. Were it not for some brilliant saves by Ollie Walsh, Waterford's lead might have been enough to put them out of reach. Tom Cheasty thought 'Ollie was unbelievable that day in his first All-Ireland final' and Mick Flannelly recalled the Thomastown man's heroics.

> 'He had a quick eye... great hands, brilliant sidestep... and was able to make great clearances. Of all the great saves which Ollie Walsh made over the years, the shot that he saved in the All-Ireland final of 1957 stands out. Larry Guinan, was no more

than 15 yards out when he shot low and hard for the corner of the net. But Ollie... at full stretch... dived across the goal, got his hurley to the ball... and turned it round the post. Devastating for Waterford but brilliant for the keeper and Kilkenny.'

John D. Hickey's report emphasised these saves as crucial events in the game.

'I was privileged to see the match and my only regret was that the match did not end in a draw. I feel that three miraculous saves by Ollie Walsh in the first-half should be awarded a particular mention. Three times within a few seconds in the 18th minute he brought off saves from point-blank range, twice when off-balance.'

Despite an early Kilkenny goal by Billy Dwyer on the restart, Waterford again took over. Now on top in midfield, Waterford went into a six-point lead with the game entering the final quarter. The Kilkenny comeback started with a clever goal by Billy Dwyer in the 47th minute. With 10 minutes to go, Waterford led by six points. Then, seemingly against the run of play, Kilkenny struck back. Billy Dwyer, the stocky Kilkenny full-forward, scored a goal. But Grimes, with two points, put Waterford five points ahead with full-time nearing. Then the Kilkenny half-forward Mick Kenny scored a point and followed it with a superb goal. While the bewildered Waterford side, who had been anticipating accepting the MacCarthy Cup, seemed mesmerised by how suddenly the game had changed, Sean Clohessy from Tulloroan levelled. Mickey Kelly, the Kilkenny captain, got the winning point three minutes from the end. Phil Grimes just missed a last minute free to draw the game. Waterford were beaten by a point, 4-10 to 3-12.

In a review of the game in 1991, James Grant, County Secretary, pointed out that that Waterford should have had extra time to equalise at the end.

'Waterford mounted a magnificent assault that almost brought a score before the ball was shot wide... and in among the spectators at the Canal End. Some onlooker... maybe he had his fill of excitement, did not return the ball. There was a delay of at least a minute before the new ball was thrown in. But those who had timed this epic accurately can vouch for the fact that Stephen Gleeson of Limerick was remiss in as much as he did not allow *lost* time for the lost ball. He whistled the end of the glorious encounter with a Waterfordman in possession in the Kilkenny half of the field.'

Michael O'Connor names that player as Mick Flannelly.

'59: AN EYEWITNESS ACCOUNT OF HURLING'S GOLDEN AGE

'In the 1957 final, he had the ball in his hand... when the ref blew the whistle. It would obviously have been tipped over the bar because he was very accurate. It was terrible... I can't believe it. We threw it away. We allowed them score two goals with 10 or 15 minutes to go. We had them hurled off the field... we allowed two easy goals from Kenny... from way out the field. I couldn't believe it. That shook us. My own personal view was we hurled ourselves into the ground and had them hurled off the field. For this to happen, it was really like the stab of a knife.'

This was the common view across the team. John Barron couldn't believe that a team with a centrefield pairing of Philly Grimes and Seamus Power would lose the game.

'I always maintain that we should have won the 1957 All Ireland final. That team was hurling with great fluency... particularly Seamus Power and Philly Grimes... and it was a big shock when Kilkenny got there by a point.'

Those two players in particular were devastated. Philly Grimes described it as 'the most shattering disappointment of my life' and Seamus Power's reaction was 'complete and utter amazement that we had lost'. He was... 'numbed, shattered... bewildered'. Philly, as captain, was also disappointed not to lift the trophy.

My saddest moment was, of course, the 1957 All Ireland, in which I had the honour of being captain of the Waterford team.'

Tom Cheasty was worried that he may have lost out on the chance of a lifetime.

'If you are one of the 'Big Three'... Cork, Tipperary and Kilkenny... you're going to be there every three or four years anyhow. It's not that much of a disappointment to the players that are used to winning. But it's a terrible disappointment when you're not used to winning. You're going to say to yourself... *we'll never be there again.*'

Comparison to the big three was taken up by Martin Óg Morrissey.

'I still look back on the 1957 final against Kilkenny and say that we had it in our pocket with about seven minutes to go. I've said this before... that if it had to be Cork or Tipperary playing against Kilkenny that day, they would have put them away in the final quarter of an hour... but it was a case of them putting us away. If they had to be playing any of the two teams I've mentioned, they would have knuckled them whereas we would be playing hurling against them.'

The press reaction echoed the feelings in the Waterford camp, the Irish Press commenting that *'Kilkenny had stolen the All-Ireland medals from Waterford in the closing minutes of one of the most agonising and thrilling finals ever played'*. John Keane was more philosophical and felt the team would learn from the defeat, possibly recalling his team's defeat in 1938 before their win in 1948.

'What won for us in 1959 was the loss of the 1957 crown. The 1957 defeat made our players more steady and they did not make the same mistake twice.'

This was Kilkenny's third All-Ireland win in-a-row by a single point... 'The usual point' as Jack Lynch described it. At a reception for the winning team held in the Hollybrook Hotel in Clontarf, Bob Aylward, the Kilkenny chairman sympathised with Waterford, who unlike his own county 'had to put up with foreign elements and foreign games'. Things were to go from bad to worse for Michael O'Connor.

'Three weeks after playing the '57 final, I was in hospital for five months. I got TB. I had X rays and I probably had done too much. I had played in the football team as well and I shouldn't have. I played against Kerry and against Cork in the football championship. It was ridiculous trying to play the hurling as well. I just overdone it... I was five months in Ardkeen. I came out in February 1958.'

'THE TEAM WAS LEARNING'

After being so close to the summit in 1957, the following year brought Waterford down to earth with a bang. After an easy win over Kerry in the Munster semi-final, Tipperary were the opponents in the Munster final. Raymond Smith reported at the time that Waterford made the mistake of agreeing to play Tipperary in Thurles which gave them home advantage. Pat Fanning confirmed that the Waterford County Board had agreed to the Thurles fixture, but only as part of a reciprocal agreement which should have brought Tipperary to Waterford in the 1959 championship. This was disputed by Tipperary, and after much discussion at the Munster Council, the 'agreement' was broken and the 1959 game was played in Cork.

Waterford were badly beaten by Tipperary, 4-12 to 1-5. While disappointing for Waterford, it led to an unexpected All-Ireland win for Tipperary. Donie Nealon recalled that great year for him and his team.

> 'We weren't given much chance that year either because a number of the older team had retired. They had won the league a year or two before that and went to America… and then Paddy Kenny and others finished up. Waterford, of course, had been beaten in the '57 All-Ireland by a point. They had only played Kerry, so they had very poor preparation for the Munster final, whereas we had played two hard games against Limerick and Cork. Then… it was in Thurles as well, so we won very easily.'

Pat Fanning recalled there was a lot of negativity around the team that year.

> 'Remember '58… and the disappointment of Thurles when the heroes of '57 failed inexplicably to Tipperary? To this day I cannot explain the extent of that defeat. And again, there were men of little heart among us who said, "We told you so, '57 was but a fluke… the flame had died, this team… these men had shot their bolt, they were done". And truth to tell, the signs were ominous. The unexpectedness of the defeat, compounded by the totality of it, was a shattering blow to morale. But, in a way, and in the light of subsequent events, '58 was a necessary factor in establishing the true greatness of these hurlers. Many lost faith in them, but they retained faith in themselves. That was all that mattered.'

Despite the disappointment, Frankie Walsh 'felt that the team was learning'. This was borne out by winning three games at the end of the year in the league, against Dublin, Wexford and Cork.

'KNITTED AS A FAMILY'

It seemed that the difficult experiences of 1957 and '58 had forged a strong team bond entering 1959. Writing in *The Sunday Press*, Seamus Power emphasised the team spirit that was building.

> 'Thirteen of our team last Sunday played in the 1957 All-Ireland series and in the interim, they have gained that extra craft and experience which is now manifesting itself. Moreover, six of the side played together for Mount Sion, the county champions, for the past five years and have developed a style of their own which is being copied

> *by the whole Waterford team. We are fortunate also in having a new captain, Frankie Walsh, who is a born leader, radiating a spirit of determination which seems to spur all players to sustained action.'*

Mount Sion wasn't the only connection. John Barron, Jackie Condon, and Joe Coady, while they played for De La Salle and Erin's Own also lived near the Mount Sion players as Martin Óg Morrissey points out.

> 'You had seven fellas from Mount Sion... 10 from the parish of Ballybricken. They would have been close enough to one another... they would really know one another. That Guinan was a bit of a card. A tough rooster, that Guinan. You couldn't f***in' separate the two of them (Larry and Frankie). They were like the terrible twins. Then you had Mickey O'Connor, Austin Flynn... Tom Cunningham and Duck Whelan. They were after been on the '48 minor team with Flan.'

The city versus county divide, which Joe Byrne once described at a County Board meeting as being like Vietnam, was real. Humphrey Kelleher, from Abbeyside in the west of the county described the split.

> 'I have to explain it to people in Dublin that the west of Waterford is different. We only considered the west only. The mindset of the Waterford City lads was, I believe, that the east/city lads looked down on those from the west.'

Seamus Power's son, Tom, and Frankie Walsh's son, Peter reframed the discussion as being about urban versus rural.

> **Tom Power:** 'One of the things that was key to that team, even though there was seven from Mount Sion and it was predominantly a city team, they needed a few from Dungarvan and Abbeyside to actually get a strong team. They managed to overcome any differences in how they approached hurling and gel together, which I think was the key to them winning. Lads that all lived around Walsh Park and that area had it tough. To go back to the social side of it, they were tough times in Waterford City in the mid-50s. In Seamus' eyes the farmers were far better off and had it easier. He brought that to his game. When he was playing Kilkenny... they were all more rural. That geed him up. All his life he regarded hurlers from city areas as being better. Just

as well he wasn't captain!'

Peter Walsh: 'They did gel as a squad. They always had a great affinity. Joe Harney and Frankie were great friends… and their wives all their life after. It didn't end. They always checked in on each other. John Kiely, when he retired… he got all the Mount Sion fellas together and told them first. They had a great mutual respect between them all. Austin loved the Mount Sion fellas… Philly especially.'

Traditional barriers between east and west were broken down and Austin Flynn felt 'the Mount Sion lads went out of their way to make people like Ned Power and myself feel welcome'. Tom Cunningham also credits training sessions for bringing together players from east and west.

'I started my senior hurling inter-county career in 1952 and it wasn't very organised until Pat Fanning and John Keane took over. They introduced a system of collective training. In other words, we came together twice a week. Whereas before, it was more or less off-the-cuff… fellas nearly trained on their own. I don't remember training before that as a group. We generally trained down in Walsh Park; they gave us tea and sandwiches after in the dressing-rooms.'

One of the Mount Sion players, Larry Guinan, also appreciated the team bonding sessions, even with Erin's Own players!

'We often went for walks out the roads getting to know each other… blackguarding, you know… pushing and shoving. We kind of knitted as a family. It wasn't just Mount Sion… it was Pat Fanning, John Keane, and we were all as a group. The lads came from Dungarvan, Lismore, Cappoquin… they all came as if it was a training night. They made it a kind of get-together for us before we really started training… getting to know each other and getting to be friendly and, as I say… knitting as a family. We'd head off out the six cross roads. There was no east-west divide. There was no animosity about anything. I remember breaking a hurley across Charlie Ware's legs above in the field in a county final and the next week or so we were back playing as if nothing happened.'

It was one of the major achievements of Pat Fanning's stewardship.

'59: AN EYEWITNESS ACCOUNT OF HURLING'S GOLDEN AGE

'It was a team in every sense of the word. Previously, if I may say so, I used to go to matches before I became chairman of the County Board, and you would see the Erin's Own people sitting in one corner of the room at a meal... and you would see the Mount Sion fellas in another... and the Portlaw fellas in another, and they seemed to be disparate groups without anything in common. I saw to it that that was broken up and there was born a great spirit which carried that team through from '57 to '63... and made them one of the most memorable teams in the history of hurling.'

The psychology employed by John Keane gave confidence to the players and his approach was appreciated by Martin Óg Morrissey.

'John Keane was a good trainer. He never roared at anybody. I never saw him losing his cool with us. If he thought you were doing something wrong, he would walk over and just say it to you. I remember coming out of Walsh Park on day. I was walking down Slievekeale and he said... "Another game or two like that... and you'll be up with the greats like myself!"'

While teams have their own psychologists today, Austin Flynn points out that it was completely new to hurling in their era.

'We heard a lot about psychology. I didn't know what psychology was. Pat Fanning and John Keane were using psychology on us... looking back. John Keane would sit down beside you. After the training you'd have your sandwich and John would be saying... "Austin, things are going well now, but I'd say if you did such a thing...". Or you might be out training and John would tap you in the shoulder and say... "Austin, you have enough done now for tonight".

'You'd feel like doing more but he was pulling you back a bit, trying to get you just dead right on the day. We didn't know that was psychology... we didn't know that was going on, because it was done in a very quiet way by very gentle people. They were able to do all that and I never heard Pat Fanning or John Keane using a dirty word in motivating us.'

The closest comparison that Mick Flannelly could find in modern hurling was Brian Cody.

'You could put down John Keane and Brian Cody as the same... very quiet, knew the game inside out, wouldn't be giving anyone bad advice. He was just very cool and calm, after being a great hurler himself. Brian Cody always reminds me of John Keane... two great men. John Keane would be walking up and down the sideline just having a smoke.'

The concern for the players mental welfare was matched by their economic welfare. Larry Guinan recalls how close he came to missing out on his Waterford hurling career.

'At the end of 1956 or the start of '57, I was going to emigrate... I was going to England, I had my ticket to go. My father worked on the Great Western on the winch... that was the ship that used to come in. I was going on that. I went down and got my ticket one day. I had an aunt living in England and I was going to her. Pat Fanning and Mick Miniter, he was a detective above in the barracks, they called out to me down on the Quay outside the *News & Star* offices. I met them there on the corner and we said something about hurling, and I said "I'm going away tonight"... which I was.

'I had to go because I had no job or anything. I was just 18. I'd had a few jobs. I was a messenger boy. I used be getting in on the train to go to Tramore to deliver chickens, believe it or not. I had a bike with a basket in the front of it. That's what I used be doing, working in Flanagans... up John's Hill. It was only the rich people who could buy the chickens at the time. I got another messenger boy's job then in opposition to Flanagan... I think it was Powers or something. They offered me a job and maybe sixpence or ten pence more and I went into that. Then I decided... *There's nothing here for me so I decided to go.*

'When I was 18, I loved hurling... I lived and died for hurling, I just loved it. It broke my heart to be going away. That was an awful time but then, as I said... Pat and Mick Miniter, they just asked me there and then if I got a job would I stay? I said, "Would I!". They said, "Hold on there for a minute"... and within a half an hour they were back to me and they said, "Will you start on Monday?". This was on a Friday or Saturday. The job was in AB Services in Greyfriars... it was to do with Lucas Batteries. I was there for 10 years and then I went with O'Briens.'

The net result was a confident team which Larry Guinan and his teammates felt was ready to take on the championship in 1959.

'The team knew at that time in our heart and soul that we were good enough to win an All-Ireland. It's as simple as that. We just knew. You'd know yourself that you were good enough... that's the attitude we had anyway. We were confident after '57 because, I know I was a bit young at the time, but to go into an All-Ireland in '57... an All-Ireland that we should have won... we should have had a bit of confidence. Tipp did knock the shit out of us then in '58. In '59 we came back strong. We hated losing games. We played, loving the bloody matches and the challenges.'

'WIN... OR DIE IN THE LOSING OF IT'

A new Waterford squad had now been put together to take on the championship in 1959, but back on the club scene there was still huge rivalry between Mount Sion and Erin's Own. With eight Mount Sion players and three Erin's Own in the reckoning for 1959, Phil Fanning points out that the numbers didn't change the intensity of the games.

'Great club games at that time were Mount Sion versus Abbeyside... and Mount Sion versus Erin's Own. Regardless of how many players each club had on the county team, the games were very competitive. These days there is a county panel, and fellas can't go their clubs for about six months. In those days there was no question of it at all.'

Freddie O'Brien emphasises the strength of the rivalry.

'There was wicked rivalry... it was like Fianna Fail and Fine Gael, Erin's Own and Mount Sion... they hated one another at that time. The individuals, we were butties, like Jackie Condon, John Meaney, Harry Hurt... we were all reared up the streets and there was never any animosity amongst us, but that rivalry was there. Erin's Own ruled the roost for the early years in the 30s and 40s, and Mount Sion came on the scene then and they ruled from the 50s, 60s, and into the 70s.

'Charlie Ware was a nice fella... I've nothing against him, but he wasn't worth his place on the team ahead of Mick Flan. Jim Ware was his uncle. Pound for pound, Mick Flannelly was as good a man as you'd get in my opinion. I played football for Mount Sion, in centrefield, and I could go up as high as you like for a ball, and I wouldn't be too concerned about catching it. I'd hit it and Mick Flan would be down underneath. He was as cute as the day is long.

'You'd get a big strong back... if he got a shot at the ball, he'd drive it 90 or 100 yards, but Mick would be in and just tip the ball out of his way. He was very disruptive in that sense. Some of the county players, because of the fact that they were on

'59: AN EYEWITNESS ACCOUNT OF HURLING'S GOLDEN AGE

the Waterford team... they thought they could take days off when club tournaments came around. One thing I'd say about Mick Flannelly, he was the most dedicated player Mount Sion had.'

From the Erin's Own side. Jackie Condon agreed on the rivalry.

'It was a huge rivalry, but it made for great sport. A lot of fellas got injured at one time or another but that's the type of game it was in those days... tough stuff. Whatever used to happen on the field, it was just bad. You could play any other team and it wouldn't make any difference, it didn't matter too much, but against Mount Sion you had to win... or you had to die in the losing of it.'

There was mutual respect between the players though. John Flavin of Mount Sion had great time for Jackie.

'The Condons were very good. Joe and Jackie were lovely hurlers, but they had a brother called Reg who was the dirtiest hurler I ever in my life seen. He'd kill ya. Jackie wasn't dirty but he was tough out.'

Jackie is wholesome in his praise for his friends, neighbours, and Waterford teammates from the Mount Sion team.

'I remember Larry Guinan used to run with his head out in front of him and it was hard to knock him over, but I knocked him over one day. By Jesus, five minutes later I got the same dose off of him. You wouldn't get the end of Larry Guinan too easily. I used to love his attitude to the game and the way he used to knuckle down and do the job. When I'd get the ball in the half-back line and I'd be in trouble with two or three fellas around me, I'd be looking for somebody to shunt the ball off to... I'd fire it up to Larry up the sideline... and he'd always hold on to it and you'd always get a chance to get your wind back.

'Larry could hold on to a ball and he'd go off on a run with the ball. Larry was a great little hurler altogether. I liked Philly, I thought he was a smashing chap. He was an honest man. He was a plasterer. I spent most of my youth going around with Tommy Cheasty from Doyle Street and he was a plasterer as well. He was working with Philly and the two of them were great butties, so in that sense I was tied up in different ways with Philly. I used to meet him a lot. He was a quare fella, Philly, when we used to go off to the matches. He was the one fella wanted to go home all the time. He'd demand a car and he used to go home in a car on his own. The fellas that were in his car... he'd try to pile into other cars. We'd all go down to Clonmel if we were coming back from Thurles or Limerick for a dance... or Youghal if we were coming back from Cork. That used be great craic altogether. Of course, you'd be announced from the stage as soon as you'd get in there. All the women would be after you, no end. You'd have to bate them off, as the fella said. How bad.

'If I had the ball coming out from a melee, I'd never throw it to Philly, because it might come back at you... and you're knackered at that stage. I'd always throw it to Power or up to Larry Guinan because you'd get a break while they held on to the ball. Grimes always played hot and cold. You could never trust him. He looked lovely on the field... lovely striker of the ball, but there were some days he just didn't play. I don't know what used be wrong. Hot and cold is the only way I can describe it. He'd be great for 10 minutes and the next thing... you wouldn't see him for maybe 15 minutes.

'The funny thing is, that when you are on the field playing you can feel where the pressure is coming from. You are throwing the ball to Philly, and you are hoping to get a bit of a rest... and it comes back to you and you have to go through the whole shebang again. Send it out to Powerie... and he'd hold on to it, and he'd run and bust his way through... and the ball would go up the field and you'd get a break. I'm talking honestly about things and how I felt. I have no prejudice or anything against the lads. They were great fellas.

'Seamus Power in my opinion was the best hurler that Waterford ever saw. He had a heart like a lion. A tremendous man. His name was Power... and he was powerful. He tried his heart out. I had some wicked tussles in matches with him.'

'TRADITIONAL REASONS'

A team had now been assembled which balanced the traditional rivalries of east and west, and the city rivalry of Erin's Own and Mount Sion, and this was also reflected in the choice of selectors. Tom Cunningham describes how the selection committee came together for 1959.

'In 1958, Waterford were trimmed by Tipperary in the Munster Championship. Arising from that, the County Board always gave the county champions two places on the selection committee. Because of what happened in '58, the County Board decided that it was no longer a good idea so they decided they wouldn't give Mount Sion two representatives on the selection committee for 1959... they'd give them one. Mount Sion wouldn't accept it and they nominated two in their places... Dec Goode and Terry Dalton of Dungarvan. The others were Michael O'Connor of Cappoquin, Paddy Joe O'Sullivan of Clonea and Jim Ware. Pat Fanning was the chairman of the County Board. John Keane was the trainer of the team. Jim Ware and John Keane wouldn't have been the best of friends, for traditional reasons!'

Michael O'Connor explains how he came to be part of that group.

'I was invited to be a selector in 1959. I didn't influence the thing a whole lot... I wouldn't be that type of man. I had my say in the picking of fellas. Pat Fanning was more the chairman, but he was a man we had a lot of respect for. He was a very good orator before a game. He stood back a bit and didn't try to influence the selection. We had a meeting about two weeks before a match to select the team. Looking back on it, a lot of it was built up on the spirit of the individual and his attitude to the game.'

The greatest former players and the most able administrators of the game joined forces to create an environment which could guide a team towards the heights of 1959. Considering the strength of the rivalry between Erin's Own and Mount Sion, and traditional east-west rivalries within the county, this structure gave Waterford their best ever chance of success.

'

THE FUNNY THING IS, THAT WHEN YOU ARE ON THE FIELD PLAYING YOU CAN FEEL WHERE THE PRESSURE IS COMING FROM. YOU ARE THROWING THE BALL TO PHILLY, AND YOU ARE HOPING TO GET A BIT OF A REST... AND IT COMES BACK TO YOU AND YOU HAVE TO GO THROUGH THE WHOLE SHEBANG AGAIN. SEND IT OUT TO POWERIE... AND HE'D HOLD ON TO IT, AND HE'D RUN AND BUST HIS WAY THROUGH... AND THE BALL WOULD GO UP THE FIELD AND YOU'D GET A BREAK. I'M TALKING HONESTLY ABOUT THINGS AND HOW I FELT. I HAVE NO PREJUDICE OR ANYTHING AGAINST THE LADS. THEY WERE GREAT FELLAS.

JACKIE CONDON

2

THE LANDSCAPE

Ireland in 1959 was a completely different country.

Hurling was a different sport…

In an era when each player was in an individual battle of strength and skill against his opposite number, it was usually felt that 'A good big fella is better than a good small fella'. Eamonn Sweeney in *Munster Hurling Legends* describes how the smaller Waterford players turned their physique to their advantage.

> 'The Waterford men were light, quick and skilful. They kept the ball moving first-time constantly and used the wings intelligently, and what they lacked in strength they compensated for with pace.'

Their small size could have held the team back. Phil Fanning recalls that even by the standards of the time, Waterford weren't a big team.

> 'To make comparisons with teams going out now. You look at any programme and you will see that they are nearly all six foot. Tom Cheasty was described as a 'Giant of a man', but he was no more than 5'8"or 5'9". Mick Flan was only about 5'5". Johnny Kiely was the same way. People would talk about Philly as a giant of a man, but he was just below 6 foot… he was 5' 11.'

In fact, Donal Whelan was the only six-footer on the team although at 5'11" Austin Flynn wasn't far behind. Rather than see this as a disadvantage, Waterford played to their strength and the smaller, faster players used their talents effectively. Seamus Power described how the smaller Waterford players outplayed bigger, heavier opponents.

'59: AN EYEWITNESS ACCOUNT OF HURLING'S GOLDEN AGE

'We were all fairly light, and many were small, so we had to rely on speed and skill in playing fast balls into the forwards. When light forwards are up against big heavyweight backs… as many back lines were in those days, you have to whip the ball in quickly to give advantage to speed. We were basically an attacking side… all players felt they were part of the attack.'

As one of the smallest, Mick Flannelly was aware of necessity of this approach from a young age.

'I wasn't a big man, and I was playing centre-forward on the minor team, but my father used to advise me… he always said to spread the play, that you'd have the winning of the game that way. And that's how we played… there wasn't any barging through fellas, we moved the ball fast through the lines, and we had plenty of speed on the team. It suited us to move the ball… so we did.'

In an interview with Diarmuid O'Flynn, Frankie Walsh brought out similar points.

'Size wasn't that important though, not if you were pretty quick, which I was. I was able to get out of trouble. The tendency now is for big half-forwards under the puck-outs, but in my day the ball would usually only reach to centrefield anyway. I was able to double on the ball… most times, but not all the time, that was a big help also. At my size, you can't really contest the ball in the air, but you can keep it moving on the ground and the breaks will come. Throw it up the wing… the corner-forward might get it… keep going and you might get the return pass. That was our forte in those days. If you were under pressure, if there was someone on your back, you just let the ball in. By all means though if you were in the clear, have a go.'

Nicholas Furlong described Waterford as an 'innovative team of hurlers' which is again supported by Frankie Walsh.

In the All-Ireland of 1959 we had a system where we'd interchange, which was unheard of at the time. John Kiely to full-forward… Duck Whelan moving out… Philly Grimes, Larry Guinan, Seamus Power, myself… if the inside forwards wanted to move out the field a bit, we might move out to midfield, under the puck-out. People were wondering what was happening, but we knew. And always… you covered.

'59: AN EYEWITNESS ACCOUNT OF HURLING'S GOLDEN AGE

'No good having a midfielder in corner-forward and the ball being pucked out... no one on the opposition midfielder. Even if someone was down injured, someone would drop in to fill the gap... wing back to corner-back, midfielder to wing back, wing forward to midfield, corner-forward to wing forward... fill in the gap back along, leave it up in the full-forward line. If the centre-back comes out on a solo run, fill in behind him in case he loses the ball.'

Everyone in the team knew their roles and even set-plays were defined in advance. In his private notebook, Pat Fanning noted the role of each player:

- Puckouts – **Ned Power, Austin Flynn.**
- Frees – each back in own area; each midfielder to 50 yards of goal; Frankie Walsh from 40 to 21 yards; John Kiely off 21 yards.
- 70s – Philly Grimes, Martin Óg Morrissey.
- Sideline – corner-back, wing back, midfield.

The individual responsibilities of each position tell a lot about the style of hurling played in 1959. Starting with the goalkeeper, the best analysis comes from a star goalkeeper of the day, Dublin's Jimmy Gray.

'I think it's a cinch playing in goal these days. You were fair game at that time. It was up to your full-back line to protect you. I was lucky in that respect. I had a good full-back line. It was essential to catch the ball. I always believed you should have the ball in your hand... because when you have it in your hand, you are controlling things. The sliotar was much heavier, totally different to what it is now. You'd be doing well to puck it out 70 or 80 yards. The reverse was true also... a '70' was more likely to land in the square, but generally if a '70' was any way reasonably central, it would wind up over the bar.'

Jimmy O'Brien, who played many times against Austin Flynn, describes the role of the full-back at the time.

'A full-back was rooted to the square... protecting the goalkeeper and not doing anything stupid. A steady player. Austin must have been very good to be there that long time.'

'59: AN EYEWITNESS ACCOUNT OF HURLING'S GOLDEN AGE

Austin's modesty comes across strongly in his interviews with Brendan Fullam for the book, *Hurling Giants*. *'I was a stupid hurler you know – I could only play a full-back. I never missed a match once I established myself – I was afraid they might find someone better.'* Austin also described the role to Enda McEvoy as being to *'protect the goalkeeper from being killed'*. Eddie Keher feels that Austin was doing himself a disservice in describing himself that way.

> 'At that time the full-forward line and the full-back line was nearly a wrestling match. You had big strong fellas playing in the full-back line and their job was to protect the goalie. That all changed in the 1970s with the rule changes... when they brought in the semi-penalty. I always felt that Waterford were way ahead of their time... the team from 1957 to '63. They played the game by moving it fast. The backs attacked... like John Barron and Joe Harney in the corners. To call him a 'stopper' doesn't do Austin Flynn justice, but he was the strong man in front of the goal. The two corners and the half-back line were attacking as they are now.
>
> 'That was new in the game at the time. I often felt that if that Waterford team were playing in the 1970s when the rule changes came in that made a significant change to the game... that they would have been exceptional... they would have been way ahead of the posse.'

The corner-backs, in standing firm against the full-forward line, had their hands full, literally, as Freddie O'Brien describes.

> 'You could hold on to fellas that time. You could have your hurley cross-ways across your body and you could have your two hands behind the fella's jersey to hold him. I was playing another day and the pair of us were heading out for the sideline, neck and neck. Our hands were in motion, and I was able to get my right hand in under his left elbow... and I pulled him back a yard or so. You were able to do those things then. There were several ways. If you were playing left corner-back, you could hold the length of the hurley out and hold your man at bay at an angle that he wouldn't have much of a chance to get away from you.
>
> 'There were tough hurlers then. I played on Timmy Sweeney of Galway, and I played on Jimmy Doyle. I played on Billy Dwyer... Liam Devaney, and John Kiely. They were the kind of players that were built very low to the ground, and it made it hard to get over or get under them. They were physically very strong. John Kiely wasn't a big man, but he had powerful strength in his body. Billy Dwyer was like a tank... you'd want a

tank to hold him! Paddy Barry too. They were the best I came across. They were able to get over the ball. They could cover the ball well and get away from you fairly fast.'

Waterford's corner-backs, while capable of doing a marking job, were also the launch pad for moves up the field. At exactly that time a new skill was being developed for corner-backs which Tony Wall described in his book.

'In batting the ball, the player stands directly facing the ball with the hurley held overhead by both hands. As the ball drops or approaches, the hurley is allowed to come back directly behind the head and then the ball is batted forward. Jimmy Brohan of Cork is the best exponent I have seen. Jimmy can send the ball fifty yards out the field and never misses.'

The innovator himself, Jimmy Brohan, remembers that the move was born out of the necessity to clear his lines.

'I developed a batting style myself. We were always told to get the ball away from your own goal as quickly and as far as possible so the other team can't score. At that time, it was get the ball away from your own goal and a lot of ground hurling. Waterford were good ground hurlers.'

Raymond Smith in his *Book of Hurling*.

'There was something in John Barron's hurling when he was at peak form that impelled attention. I have seen him in Thurles, against Cork in the championship, coming through from his own goal line almost to midfield, controlling the ball beautifully with the stick and to me on such occasions he epitomised quality and class. Like Jimmy Brohan of Cork, he could do wonderful things to delight the eye. In the long run, however, men who play it close can be far more successful and concede fewer scores, but they are not the same adornment to the game. The classic defenders are few.'

John even played in goal for Waterford in 1958, in the first round championship match against Kerry, while the selectors were in the process of searching for a replacement for Dickie Roche. Ned Power, who became the first choice goalkeeper, appreciated John's awareness of the oncoming danger.

'59: AN EYEWITNESS ACCOUNT OF HURLING'S GOLDEN AGE

'John had great peripheral vision, a knack of seeing players in positions where other guys wouldn't dream of looking. A snappy type of hurler and another man who gave me good cover.'

Michael O'Connor, who would have played in front of John at wing back, had a similar view.

'He was a nice fella... that John Barron. Obviously, he was able to read the game well. The fella he'd be on he'd have his man sized up."

Michael's view of John's personality is echoed by Jackie Condon who said 'John Barron was a very quiet man. He was a real gent' and Mick Flannelly who described him as 'a real nature's gentleman, great hurler, great head, and very shy'. Playing alongside the equally genial Austin Flynn, their off-pitch personas didn't match their role on field. Humphrey Kelleher recalls that 'Austin had a different persona on the pitch. Off the pitch, you would hardly hear him. A gentle giant' and Billy Kelly of Erin's Own recalls that 'you wouldn't hear either of them behind a paper bag'.

While Tom Cunningham played in the forwards during 1959, he was a stylish corner-back who wouldn't have attempted many catches.

At that time, there was no such thing as putting your hand up and catching the ball. That wasn't a feature of any team. Wexford were the first team that handled the ball a lot because they were all big men. In general, the ball didn't go as far as it does now. All the balls now are passing over midfield, whereas back in the 50s it was a different type of ball, so it was generally contested between the centrefielders. They contested it by pulling, for or against. Ground hurling was the only hurling that was really well known at the time, or moving the ball along.'

This is confirmed by Eddie Keher who would regularly play Wexford in the Leinster championship.

'The Wexford team of the 50s developed catching. There was no catching of the ball at that time. They developed the skill of catching the ball as those hurls were flying to pull on it, by protecting their hand and catching the ball... and they had possession. That style was coming in and Waterford developed it in a different way. They weren't catchers of the ball to the same extent as Wexford but they were playing the ball intelligently to their colleagues.'

One of that Wexford team, Jimmy O'Brien, credits Billy Rackard with that innovation.

'Wexford... Billy Rackard mainly, started catching the ball. He was a huge, big fella so he was able to protect himself. If a man was in on him, he could lie back and get the ball. We had some good ground hurlers too. It wouldn't have been the style for Wexford though.'

Waterford prided themselves on their ground hurling in a style that Seamus Power describe as 'embracing all that was best in the Munster and Kilkenny traditions'. Tony Wall described that Munster style.

'Ground hurling, as it is played in Tipperary, is very effective hurling. I feel, however, that people are apt to confuse ground hurling with first time pulling. There is a certain amount of first time pulling involved, but ground hurling is not dependant on a first time pull. A Tipperary hurler will pull first time all right, if he sees the opportunity of getting in his stroke. However, this is not always practical, and it is often much better to block the ball first, and divert it out of the opponent's reach to a position where it can be struck. When this happens, it is not always picked up. It is struck immediately from its position on the ground. This is ground hurling. It is not first time pulling. This ground hurling as I have just described it is the essence of good effective hurling. As long as I have been hurling in the back line I have been told "block the ball first and then clear".'

The Kilkenny tradition at that time was being adapted by the coaching of Fr. Tommy Maher, a style personified by Johnny McGovern.

'The style of play for a half-back was to get out first to the ball and move it on. Fr. Maher pushed for ground hurling too. He was all in favour of it... keep it moving. The ball would often come to me from the opposing half-back line. You would be studying the opposing half-back line in matches. Some of them would rise the ball... and more of them would hit it on the ground. You'd get to know them and anticipate what they were going to do. Like, Tony Wall... a fine centre-back from Tipperary, he was a great man for the ground hurling. When Tony got on to the ball he'd play a long ground stroke out to the wings, whereas the Rackards were the opposite. They would always rise the ball and play a big, long, high ball down the middle.'

While the half-back line was the launch pad for attacks, they still had to defend, and Jackie Condon describes his approach.

'In those days you didn't go away from your man. You didn't travel with the ball much. You'd have to go a bit further down the field to score... so we just held back. The measure of your game was if you stopped someone from scoring... everyone was man to man... that was the arrangement then. You mark your man and if he scores... it was down to you, so you had to stop him from scoring. But these half-forwards were the best fellas on most teams. They were all the classy hurlers... Jimmy Doyle and all those fellas were able to score. If you were playing on those fellas, you had to have some kind of a plan to stay with them or be able to get into them. They were all handy players and speed merchants. That's one thing with me. I had no speed. What I developed was an anticipation of where the ball is going so I'd be running to where the ball is going to land shortly after the man hit it, whereas the other fella would be still standing.'

One of his fellow half-backs, Michael O'Connor, feels that push to get the ball as far down the field as possible was naïve. Having played with Mick Flannelly for 10 years, he was more likely to play the ball to the wing forwards, Frankie Walsh and Mick Flannelly, in the same way as their club teammate Martin Óg Morrissey.

'You'd try to get the ball into the full-forward. My memory is that I was able to get the ball and hit it long... and hit it into John Kiely at full-forward. In hindsight, the backs had the advantage with the ball flying in and the forward trying to reach it. It was a different time. The ball was heavier and slower and the hurleys were a bit longer. At my best hurling at wing back... if the ball broke at all, I would get it and lob it into the corner. The amount of scores we got from that was very small. I should have been playing the ball out to Frankie Walsh or Flan, not trying to drive it into the full-back line, but my mental thing at that time was to get the ball and get it way up the field as far as I could. There is no question we weren't coached to play it into the wing forward as it would be played now. I would say it was a natural build-up of teamwork we had from playing with each other. I was playing with Flan for 10 years!'

'59: AN EYEWITNESS ACCOUNT OF HURLING'S GOLDEN AGE

A quiet man, Mick Lacey's contribution to the team could easily be overlooked but his work colleague and teammate John Flavin feels that is unfair.

> 'Mick Lacey was very good. I worked in Cappoquin in 1960 as a van driver in the bacon factory so I knew Mickey O'Connor and Mick Lacey. I played on Mick Lacey in club games. He was a quiet fella... a big man. A good hurler... he wasn't dirty in any way.'

Pat Fanning praised both his technique and attitude.

> 'He places his clearances with cleverness and accuracy. Boundless energy and stamina, Lacey chases the ball when most have given up, and it is this quality which makes him a valuable man to have around. Mick Lacey is strong... resolute and determined. He will not fail for want of trying.'

When it came to midfield, Waterford had an exceptional pairing. In The Hurling Immortals, Raymond Smith singles them out for praise.

> 'The Seamus Power-Philly Grimes midfield partnership was to my mind, as strong a pairing as has ever represented any county. Grimes brought style and class to everything he did on the hurling field. Few could play John Doyle better.'

Midfield play was different then, as Jimmy O'Brien recalls.

> 'You wouldn't drive the ball. You had a little patch to protect. You'd get it up to the next person as best you could... as quick as you could. The ball now is after destroying hurling, it's too light. We had two fellas playing in the middle of the field and they were as good as were around and I never even saw them shooting for a point. They never scored one that I could see. You never expected you could do it. A '70' was often dropped in the square.'

The weight of the ball meant that it landed in midfield a lot, but Jimmy Brohan points out that the number of plays didn't necessarily make midfield play more tactical.

> 'The ball would land in centrefield from a puck out. There was a lot of centrefield

play... there was no tactics really. There was a lot of ground play but there was no real tactics.'

One of the skills that Power and Grimes were renowned for was overhead striking, a skill that Eddie Keher has seen die out.

'The older fellas... older than me even, always lamented the passing of the overhead striking. Fr. Maher didn't really favour overhead striking. The game at that time was about the ball landing in the middle of the field and two fellas stood shoulder to shoulder and pulled... and the best man won, but God knows where the ball is going to go. Fr. Maher brought in to get possession rather than to pull wildly.'

The half-forward play on the Waterford team revolved around Tom Cheasty who would drive forward with the ball, attracting several defenders towards him. He would either handpass the ball to the now unmarked wing or full-forwards or, if he burst through his markers, he would scoop the ball over the bar. In various interviews over the years, Tom described his own role in the team.

'I always saw myself as a supplier of the ball to the inside forwards. It was my job to keep the ball going goalwards. If the centre back was starting to win some ball it was up to me to do something about it. I was never a player who laid down. If things were going against me, it made me try that much harder. I was lucky to play in the same team as men like Philly Grimes, Austin Flynn, John Kiely... these men were like brothers to me.

'I always took the view that as well as scoring and distributing the ball, I should at least neutralise my opponents. No good in a forward playing a good game if his opponent is allowed to get in telling clearances to his forwards'

'(Taking on the man) makes the game more physical. I was the kind of fella who didn't care if I sidestepped an opponent or if he hit off me. I took some punishment, but I punished the fellas tackling me.'

Tom's wife. Kathleen remembers his love of all sports, particularly rugby, which he learned in Waterpark College. Ned Power felt that it helped his hurling – 'Tom had a great sidestep developed from his other love, rugby' – which made for exciting viewing according to Austin Flynn.

'59: AN EYEWITNESS ACCOUNT OF HURLING'S GOLDEN AGE

'He was, in my opinion, the most exciting man on the Waterford team in this time. He could bob and weave through a defence like no other. When Cheasty was on one of his runs, the crowd was on its feet in admiration of his very presence.'

In reflecting on his career, Tom expressed one regret.

'At times I played a very negative type of game. I tried to play negative if I had one of my off days... I tried to snuff out my opponent more than play myself.'

On occasion, that player would be Tony Wall of Tipperary, who described how the centre-forward could gain the advantage over the centre back.

'The cardinal rule is to get between your opponent and the ball. In this position you have the advantage. You can see the ball more easily and indeed your opponent may not be able to see the ball at all.'

Jimmy O'Brien also felt his job as a half forward was to supply the ball to the full forward line.

'To be a half-forward at that time, you got the ball in. You could score sometimes but it would be a lottery. My first thought was get it into the full-forward line and let somebody else worry about it.'

While Cheasty was the fulcrum of the attack, Seamus Power felt that Waterford's competitive edge was in the speed and agility of their wing forwards.

'The cornerstone of this eminently successful brand of hurling was the unrelenting sweeping movement of the ball form wing to wing. To achieve this movement, of course, each player had to be competent at the art of swift striking of the ball in flight... on the ground, or in the air. You will notice I have deliberately described it as an art. Of course, it is, because hurling at its most graceful best is essentially a game of movement of the ball... with the minimum of picking-up and dawdling.'

As a wing back tasked with marking them, Johnny McGovern agreed with the sentiment.

'59: AN EYEWITNESS ACCOUNT OF HURLING'S GOLDEN AGE

'They were all good players. They had a lovely brand of hurling. They spread the ball out along the wings. They were all fairly fast, and they kept the ball moving. They were a grand team to watch. Flannelly was very fast and when he got to the ball, he kept it moving. Unless you were there in time… it was gone. If you were slow at all he'd beat you to it.'

Not only was Frankie Walsh fast, he also never stopped moving, as he described himself.

'I didn't stand… I'd bring him on a little journey. Wherever the ball was I'd be moving… be ready for the break. I wouldn't be lying up against him, anyway… put it that way. I'd do the running… let him do the chasing. But always, you have to be looking for the ball.'

Frankie was also unusually strong off his left side which gave him the opportunity to play the ball into the square from either side. Tony Wall praised both Frankie and Seamus Power for having very strong left-handed strokes… *'So strong in fact that I suspect that they are really 'ciotógs' who hurl with the right had on top. An analysis of their swing is particularly useful to the player attempting to develop his left'.*

Full-forward play was essentially the opposite of the full-backs, but Waterford had forwards who brought a variety of styles to the role. In 1959, Waterford played 18 games. Donal Whelan appeared in all 18, starting 17 of them and scoring 17 goals. According to Billy Kelly it was a simple equation.

'Duck Whelan was always standing there on the edge of the square and if the ball came at all… it was buried.'

This approach was no surprise to Jimmy O'Brien.

'I saw Duck Whelan playing a fair few times. He was a big fella who in my memory always stayed in the square. When a fella stays in… he will always get chances.'

Humphrey Kelleher remembers his clubman's approach to the position.

'The forwards were cute. They knew they weren't going to go by the corner-back so they hit the ball first time or went through the guy. Duck would have been a hatchet man… he was the nemesis for Ollie Walsh. Duck would go for Ollie Walsh. The ball was incidental. Duck was strong, powerful, and deceptively quick. He had a great pair of wrists. He was a big broad man... he wasn't afraid of anything.'

Duck's only appearance from the bench was the All-Ireland final replay, when he came on for Tom Cunningham. Ned Power recalls that decision.

'Donal was unlucky not to get his place on the team itself, but he also came on during the replay to play his part in the victory.'

John Kiely, as the senior member of the panel was more likely to keep his place. Billy Kelly remembered his debut on the Waterford team.

'On his debut, John Kiely was only up to Phil Shanahan's elbow, but he hurled the ears off him. He even beat him for balls in the air.'

His own clubman, Ned Power, particularly praised John Kiely's teamwork.

'He was a very quiet, shy fellow. He was another convert from midfield where he played most of his early hurling. He never realised how much he meant to our team but we other fellows did. John was a great hurler.'

Sean Clohessy of Kilkenny thought that John Kiely was 'one of the most complete hurlers he had seen, though seldom given the praise he deserved'. In Jack Mahon's book, *The Game of My Life*, Tom Cheasty paid particular tribute to John.

'I'd like to pay tribute to the whole team I played with in 1957 and onwards. John Kiely at full-forward, a great bit of stuff altogether. John was from Dungarvan and was very nearly over the top. He was brought back at the veteran stage, and he took terrific punishment in at full-forward. He had a great drive on a ball. A wristy drive and he could double on it. Small too, five foot five inches about. He was hardy. Frankie Walsh and Mick Flannelly each side of me in the half forward line. Both very fast. We played well together.'

The other guaranteed starter in the forward line was Larry Guinan whose precocious talent was recalled by players like Ned Power and Donie Nealon.

'59: AN EYEWITNESS ACCOUNT OF HURLING'S GOLDEN AGE

> 'As Donie Nealon said of Larry, he had a wonderful powerful body. Larry had a low centre of gravity and great balance and when he hit you... you knew all about it. The youngster of the side in 1957 when he was 19... Larry was still only 21 when he got his All-Ireland medal.'

Outside of sport, Larry worked in a garage owned by Jimmy O'Brien, the Wexford hurler.

> 'Larry Guinan worked with me for a long, long time... about 20 odd years. Larry Guinan was a great hurler. He had it every way. Larry was a wonderful hurler... he could play anywhere. He was even a great back. To my mind, he was one of the most natural corner-forwards... and they are rare. Most corner-forwards are fellas getting slow. Larry could play corner-forward as one of his best positions. He was brave, quick and well able to hurl.'

Outside of these strong forwards, there was also a place in some games for more stylish full-forwards. Billy Kelly recalls his Erin's Own teammate as one who didn't rely as much on his strength.

> 'Young Charlie (Ware) was great... there was great spirit in him. He wasn't wicked robust. With the father behind him, he used to put himself in danger.'

Another Erin's Own man, Michael Dowling, described Charlie's first touch.

> 'He was a very good athlete. He might not even stop the ball... he'd just flake it and he was reasonably accurate. He had a right belt on a ball.'

On his return from injury, Tom Cunningham was asked to play in the forward line. A team player, he was willing to do so and was obviously chosen for his unselfish distribution of the ball.

> 'My favourite position was as a back because that was my natural position with the club. I had never played as a forward before. In that time, you tried to bring a bit of cohesion into the forward line. I don't think I ever scored anything... I wouldn't have been a scoring forward anyway!'

'59: AN EYEWITNESS ACCOUNT OF HURLING'S GOLDEN AGE

It was the story of his entire career.

'For my debut in 1952, I played against Clare down in Walsh Park. I was playing centrefield that time. I was kind of a utility player.'

This flexibility probably led to him being considered as 'one of the most underrated players', as his clubmate Humphrey Kelleher described him.

EQUIPMENT

While the style of play was very different in 1959, it was also influenced by the equipment being used. There were very obvious differences in the hurleys and sliotairs of the day, compared to modern equipment. Considering the current discussions about the light weight of the sliotair, the most relevant difference was the heavy weight of the ball. Johnny McGovern of Kilkenny recalled the effect of the weather. 'It was a heavier ball at that time. If you had a wet day the ball was very soggy and heavy.'

While Eddie Keher wasn't impressed with their quality, he also recalls their scarcity.

'The sliotar, certainly if it was wet, was a ton weight. It was like a ball of soap if it got wet. There was big rims on it. There seemed to be only a few balls available. Nowadays, each goalie has a bucket or a bag of balls. As soon as it goes wide, he pulls out another one. The ball was rarely changed, even though there was no high ball nets in those days. They had to be thrown back from the crowd. You were playing effectively with the same ball for the whole match.'

Echoing various controversies in recent years, which have been highlighted by Donal Óg Cusack, it is interesting to understand that differences in sliotair design and manufacture have always had an influence on the game. Diarmuid O'Flynn asked Frankie Walsh about the difference between the balls.

'We used the McAuliffe ball in the Munster Championship… made in Limerick. A week or two before the championship we'd get them. The Munster Council used those… it was a very big ball, a big rim, with a different flight to it. In training we used a Lawlor number one and number two. I'm not sure what the difference was between those two, I think it was the ridge size. Later then, if we got to the All-Ireland series, we were playing with an O'Neills ball, which was different again… almost oval shaped, and a very hard ball. After training with the Lawlor ball, I found it difficult to adapt to the other balls.

'All the balls that time would lose their shape very easily. Another problem we had too was that if the ball was hit into the crowd, very often it didn't come back… the game would be held up for a while. The modern ball is more like a tennis ball with a leather cover… I cut one of them open one day with a hacksaw, it was like a sponge ball.'

Tony Wall, in his book *Hurling* also discussed the impact of the playing surface on the ball.

'The hurling ball is small. If the grass is more than one inch high, it just will not travel freely along the ground and ground hurling is out. It is easier to lift the ball in two-inch-high grass, but it is much more important for good hurling to have it short.'

This comes up again when players compare their experiences of Wembley Stadium with Thurles and Croke Park in a later chapter. In an interview which took place in the Mount Sion club, Frankie Walsh, Martin Óg Morrissey and Dickie Roche discussed their favourite grounds.

FW: 'I thought Thurles was the ideal spot for a match. It is the atmosphere coming into the place. And also, the type of hurling that Waterford played at the time… Thurles was about that yard extra on either side. You had plenty of time… you'd think you were near the sideline, but you still had that extra yard. The atmosphere in Thurles… you walk into the square and the whole place is uplifting. It is so convenient. You have a short walk to the pitch. We used to tog off in the FCA Hall. We'd be nice and relaxed.

For the Athletic Grounds, you'd tog off in the Metropole Hotel. You drove out and then you had to walk back in the whole way because you couldn't get back in for about two hours after it.'

DR: 'The least one anyone would like was Limerick… nobody liked playing in Limerick.'

MOM: 'I never minded playing in Limerick. I fancied the Athletic grounds more so than any of the rest of them. Out of all the championship matches we won, we must have won half of them in Dungarvan.'

FW: 'We had no objection going to Dungarvan. We often opted to go to Dungarvan… we weren't frightened to play anywhere. We didn't mind where we played… tt didn't matter. It was only another pitch. That's the way we looked at it.'

'59: AN EYEWITNESS ACCOUNT OF HURLING'S GOLDEN AGE

MOM: 'If you are going to play well, if you are playing in a bog... you are going to play well. If you are not going to play well, if you are in Croke Park... you won't play well.'

The other significant difference was the hurleys of the time which Eddie Keher compares to a hockey stick.

'I was looking in a shed here recently and I found one of my old hurls. I think it was 36/37 inch and the bas was not too far from a hockey stick... a thin narrow bas. Now they are playing with 33/34 inch hurls... lighter, and a big bas, and the sliotar is lighter.'

The hurleys were also more likely to be home-made rather than mass manufactured. Even inter-county hurlers like Theo English of Tipperary made his own.

'Back in those times I made all my own hurleys. I made them for other hurlers or whoever wanted them. Ten bob each... or six pounds for a dozen. I made them at home and then cut the butts as well. I would have an eye on a tree for a while... until it was time. We knew when the ash would be ready, be it months or years. Everyone knew where the timber for their hurley came from back then. Often a few fellas would go together to cut a butt, get it planked out and make the hurleys together. Ash grows best by the riverbanks they say, and if the soil and climate is right you get better hurleys. We knew the location of all the ash trees for miles around. It was common, even in club matches, that there would be five or six hurleys broken in a game. It took longer to make them than to break them!'

Tony Wall referred to the age-old practice of kids taking a broken adult hurley and fashioning something useable for their smaller frame.

'The hurleys used by many are worth examining. Sometimes they are the genuine article, purchased by a harassed parent. More often than not, they are the patched-up relics of sterner battles, snatched by eager hands from the scramble when a broken stick is thrown out to the sideline.'

Larry Guinan remembers this as his introduction to hurling and described his first real hurley.

'59: AN EYEWITNESS ACCOUNT OF HURLING'S GOLDEN AGE

'Hurleys were hard to get. Talking about the streets, you see I went to Saint Patrick's school. That's where I started the hurling... below in the yard there. There was tough lads going to that school. You had to be as tough as them. Every minute that I could have, I had a hurley in me hand... wherever I'd get a hurley. This is a fact now. I'd only be a young lad. I'd go out the country on my own and I'd be looking at ash plants and I actually tried to cut one one day.

'I remember getting my first hurley. I cycled out to a fella by the name of Johnny Cahill. It was on the way out to Portlaw... he was working in Mount Congreve. He said come back another day, so I said I'll wait for it. God, didn't he cut an oul' thing and he made a hurley for me. He broke a bottle and cut it down... and pared it and everything. That was the first new hurley I ever had. I remember coming in the road on the bike and I never rode a bike without my hands on the handlebars, but I remember swinging this hurley coming in the road, no hands on the handlebars.'

His Mount Sion teammate, Martin Óg Morrissey had the same source.

'My first few hurleys were sourced from a fella called Cahill out in Mount Congreve Estate and Gardens, a few miles outside Waterford City. He lived in a gate lodge next to the main entrance. He used to gather the ash from around the estate to make his hurleys... all by hand, and I bought mine for half a crown. Some of the hurleys he made you could nearly use as a belt on your trousers... they were fantastic.'

As a farmer, Joe Harney was more inclined to make a hurley than buy it.

'Money was tight in those days and I can remember one day when I broke my hurley, and I could not replace it. I got a hatchet and climbed up a tree... cut down a big branch and made my own hurl. It was probably the best hurley I ever had.'

Having a 'proper' hurley really helped each player's development. By the time they were playing senior hurling, the hurley was the tool of the trade and each player modified his own to suit his size, strength, or style of play. Tony Wall captured the idiosyncrasies of some of the stars of the day.

'Very few hurlers prefer similar sticks. Jimmy Doyle prefers a small light one. Ollie Walsh prefers a heavy one. I like a stick with a heavy bas. Some hurlers like large

'59: AN EYEWITNESS ACCOUNT OF HURLING'S GOLDEN AGE

round handles, others like small oval ones. Tony Reddan used a hurley as thick at the top as at the pole. The hurley for the senior player should be 37 inches or so. Some years ago, I got great results by shortening hurleys by about one inch. Jimmy Doyle and Donie Nealon shorten theirs. I believe Tom Walsh of Kilkenny also uses a short stick. I use a hurley which weighs 23 ½ to 24 ounces, Jimmy Doyle's hurley weighs 21 ounces. I hear Ollie Walsh's hurley weighs 28 ounces.'

Martin Óg Morrissey's choice depended on his position and his team's style of play.

'Compared to the rest of the lads, I used a heavier hurley. A light hurley was no good to me as I'd be first-time pulling, so I needed something substantial. Usually, we all had two hurleys, with Wattie Morrissey holding one in reserve for each of us during a match... and he was always on hand to replace the broken hurley.'

It was a bone of contention for Jackie Condon that the Waterford players were not supplied with hurleys and the comparison to Kilkenny let them down.

'The Kilkenny hurlers were just treated so well. I remember coming off the field one day, talking to John Sutton. We were chatting and I had the hurley in my hand and it was getting pulled. Wattie Morrissey... he was the fella in charge of the hurleys. I broke my hurley and he fired this one out to me. He wanted it back and he annoyed me, so I got the hurley, put it across my knee and broke it. "Now", I said "You can have it". John Sutton said to me "Jaysus, that's awful. We were all supplied with seven hurleys each and we all get them banded the way we want them. We use them at all different games, and we bring three hurleys with us everywhere we go. So, if you want a hurley, they fire out your hurley to you". That's the difference. It's small things. We had to bring along our own hurley and pay for it.'

Another piece of equipment which was related to style of play were shin-guards. Their use has almost completely died out now, but Phil Fanning recalls their use in 1959.

'There was a lot of ground hurling, so you were likely to get a belt in the shin. These days everyone wants the ball in their hand so there is less ground hurling. That leads to fewer sore shins... and less need to wear shin-guards. The modern ones are not as big and awkward as the old shin-guards used to be.'

'59: AN EYEWITNESS ACCOUNT OF HURLING'S GOLDEN AGE

Universally accepted as one of the toughest hurlers ever, even Tom Cheasty wore shinguards at the time. They were folded pieces of cardboard stuffed down his socks. He tried to convince Austin Flynn to do the same. Austin said 'They wouldn't be much use Tom, I'd need them up around my ears!' Tom's regular opponent, Tony Wall, was not so keen on shinguards, but did predict the introduction of helmets as far back as the 1960s.

> *'Shin guards are a matter of personal preference. Some players insist on wearing them while others (myself included) never use them. I can only remember getting one really hard blow on the shin and I so not see the need for them. I keep my socks up for the parade, but I like the freedom of having them down in warm weather. Others seem to like this too and you will often see shin guards being discarded during the game. I would much prefer to see every hurler wearing some sort of light weight helmet which would protect the head and face from the cuts which are the most common injuries in hurling. Every hurler should wear an athletic support.'*

Tony's mention of his socks brings up a topic that modern players would never need to consider. Larry Guinan draws our attention to this element of the player's kit.

> 'If you look back at 1957 and even '59, we all had different socks. They had the home colours. Cheasty had Ballyduff... John Barron had De La Salle. It was terrible. It's an amateur game and that was it.'

According to his son, Peter, Frankie Walsh laughed when he saw the All-Ireland team of 2008 being measured for suits. He joked that in 1959 they got measured for a pair of socks. If only that had been the case! In his book about his father, Ned, Conor Power described the lead up to the '59 final.

> *'In advance of the All-Ireland final, the players received the standard letter notifying them of the date of the game, and the details of pick-up and accommodation arrangements. It also requested that "All players to have complete set of clean playing togs and hurley".'*

In the same book, Tom Cunningham reveals the full story of the 'sock protest' which went unnoticed at the time.

John Barron's socks

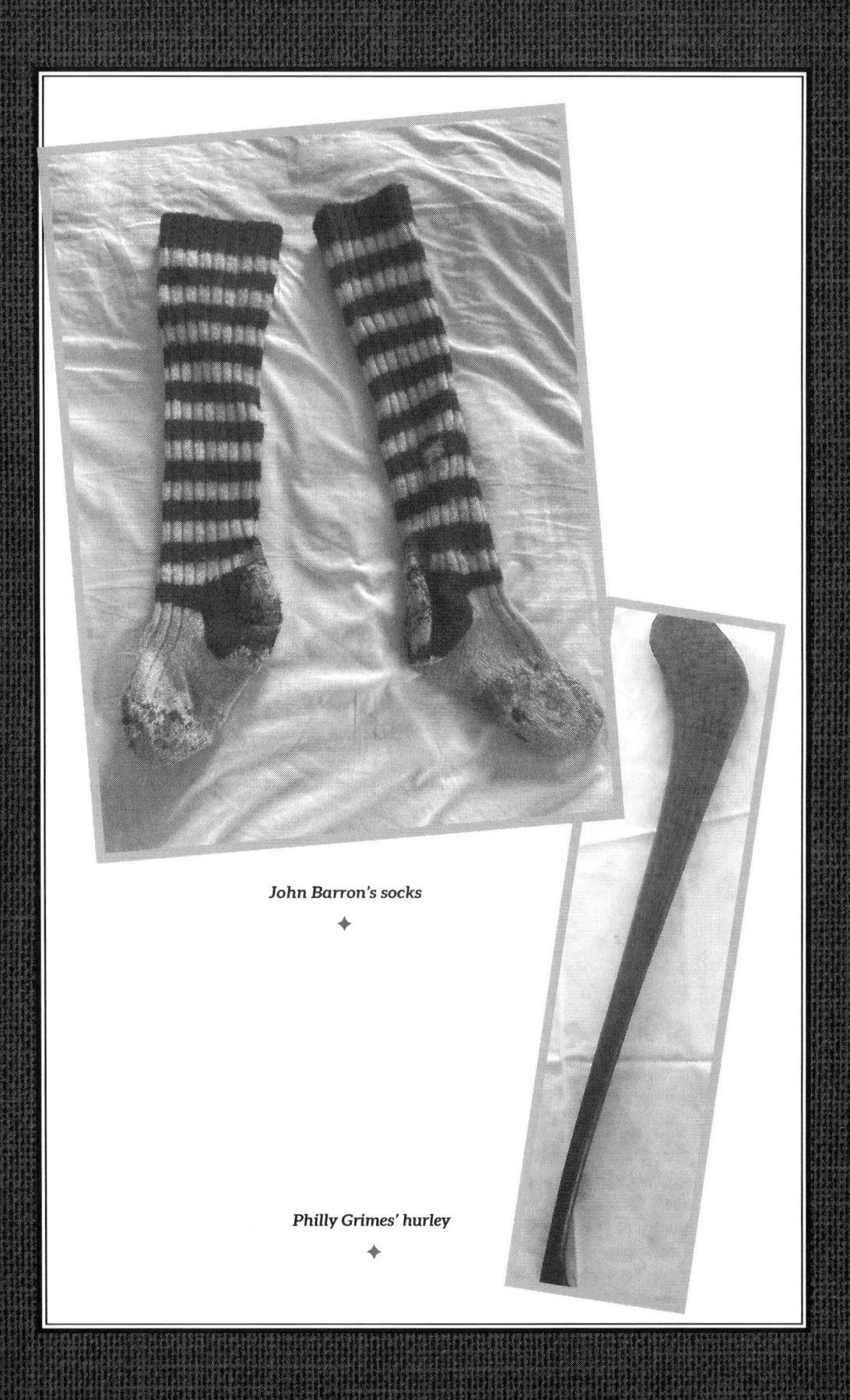

◆

Philly Grimes' hurley

◆

'59: AN EYEWITNESS ACCOUNT OF HURLING'S GOLDEN AGE

'Ned Power had distinctive socks… they were red and black. It didn't occur to me at the time, but I remember being asked about it years later when I noticed it in a colour photo. This had gone past me altogether. In those days, the jersey was supplied, but you had to supply everything else yourself… boots, shorts, hurley. According to Ned Power, prior to the 1959 All-Ireland there was some suggestion that the County Board were going to supply stockings to the players. This was being mooted as a kind of gesture by the board, but apparently this idea was not carried through and so everyone had to bring their own socks. So, Ned Power, as a protest against what he called a meanness on the part of the County Board, decided that he's go out and buy a pair of distinctive socks.'

The protest didn't gain any traction and the players wore their own choice of socks or whatever came to hand. As Kathleen Cheasty points out 'Tom was careless… he could have two different socks on him'. As a unique element of strip, and a nod to his love of his college and club, the Barron family still have the maroon and gold De La Salle College socks John wore in the final. They have obviously been darned multiple times, not something a modern hurler will ever experience. John's family also have the jersey he wore in the All-Ireland final. The v-neck is laced up, but the players discarded the lace while playing and it was only relaced for photo opportunities. There are also bloodstains on the shirt but, as his son, John, points out, it was unlikely to be his own blood!

TOUGH PLAY

It is a truism to say that 'the past is a foreign country' and in hurling they certainly did things differently there. In his book, *Over the Bar*, Breandán Ó hEithir, from the relatively recent vantage point of 1984, looked back on the toughness of a previous generation of hurling.

'Rough and sometimes brutal hurling was common enough in those years. It was usually confined to the lower grades of club hurling, or to meetings of parish teams with a long history of spites and spleens behind them. I saw it too in some of the Munster finals I now see described as "great", very often by people who did not see them. The GAA's attitude to it was that of the three little monkeys who neither see, speak nor hear evil. This did a lot to bring the game into disrepute, particularly with parents who worried about injuries to their children.'

No discussion of this toughness in the late 50s and early 60s would be complete without

'59: AN EYEWITNESS ACCOUNT OF HURLING'S GOLDEN AGE

mention of 'Hell's Kitchen', the nickname applied to the Tipperary full-back line which at various times included Mickey 'The Rattler' Byrne, John Doyle, Kieran Carey, and Michael Maher. When pressed as to the style of play of the full-back line, Tony Wall admitted to a curious blind spot that required prompting from other players.

'When the Rattler retired, John Doyle went back into the full-back line with Maher and Carey. We got a few good half backs, young fellas like the two Murphys, Len Gaynor, and Matt O'Gara. That settled in that fearsome backline. They were formidable people. They were tough out. There was nobody got through them. They were big fellas and strong. Doyle was a fine hurler. Sure Mickey Maher couldn't hurl at all. He was a great wrestler. The ball was being dropped in on top of them. Carey was tough out too. I saw very little dirty play. I never really saw a dirty stroke but when the ball was dropping in you wouldn't know what the fuck they were up to. I was talking to Paddy Cobbe one time, or was it Vivian, the fella in the Army anyway, and I said I never saw Carey hitting anybody. He looked at me and he said, 'are you fuckin serious?''

Even Eddie Keher, the fairest and most balanced of commentators, agrees with the reputation built up around the Tipperary defenders.

'They were tough. In the era that we are talking about, that was the style of play. Kieran Carey, he would have been regarded as dirty, that would be the word to use in their case. The others like Mick Maher would have been a stopper, I wouldn't see him pulling on anyone. John Doyle would have been the same, a good hurler, but they were physical and strong. That's the type of game they played, and they had that reputation. If you tried to match them physically you were certainly up against it.'

At a time when Cork v Tipperary was the biggest match in Munster, Jimmy Brohan of Cork recalls the mixture of styles his team were up against.

'They didn't get that name Hell's Kitchen for nothing... they were something else. They were fair enough at times, but they wouldn't take any prisoners. Tough or dirty? There was a mixture. I wouldn't be putting myself on the line now about individuals, but Kieran Carey was an awful man... oh, he was cynical. He'd be laughing at you when he'd be hitting you. Having said that there were some Tipperary players who

'59: AN EYEWITNESS ACCOUNT OF HURLING'S GOLDEN AGE

were outstanding hurlers... Tony Wall and Pat Stakelum in particular. They were thorough gentlemen. Theo English was non-stop. He covered a fierce amount of ground. Jimmy Doyle was a gentleman too. Jimmy was a very nice lad, very shy. John was John! He was a tough man.'

The rivalry that developed between Waterford and Tipperary at the time took on a bitter edge and Larry Guinan, who played corner-forward, still recalls the treatment he received from the full back line.

'I always found the Tipperary defenders dirty. John Doyle... he was a dirty article that fella. He was dirty out. In fact, there was two of the back men and one of them... the full back, Mick Maher, he was Munster Council Chairman later on. Maher and that Doyle fella and there was another fella, Kieran Carey. I can remember playing in a League final above in Croke Park against Tipp and we beat them the same day. I remember the ball was way down the field I remember getting two knees into my back and knocking me onto the ground. That was that Carey fella... he stuck his two knees in my back.'

Depending on your position, you were less likely to encounter Hell's Kitchen but even from the half-back line, Martin Óg Morrissey had some experience of these opponents.

'Tipperary always had a couple of tough fellas on the team. I won't say dirty, but they dished it out. John Doyle said when Kieran Carey, Michael Maher and himself gave up hurling, they closed the hospital in Nenagh! None of those three fellas would stand on any ceremony. I played on Carey once for Mount Sion and I found him okay. He didn't do anything to me.'

One incident, where John Doyle split open Charlie Ware, is remembered by all involved, with Phil Fanning even finding the irony in the situation.

'It was an accepted thing that you were going to get a crack in the head at some stage. Some guys made a speciality of it alright. There was the time that John Doyle creased Charlie Ware and apologised about it afterwards... because he thought he was hitting Larry Guinan, as if that made it alright.'

'59: AN EYEWITNESS ACCOUNT OF HURLING'S GOLDEN AGE

It outraged the other Waterford players, and Jackie Condon remembers a Mount Sion man standing up for his Erin's Own colleague.

> 'When Charlie got split open by John Doyle, Philly Grimes went up to have it out with Doyle... and Doyle jibbed it. He pulled the hurley out of Doyle's hand. Philly was a boxer you see. I suppose Doyle might have had some inkling. Doyle was a dirty hurler... he used to use the hurley on people. That's not playing the game at all. My forte in the game was the fair shoulder. I used to go into guys and just bowl them over... hit them hard and knock them over... and most of them will get up again. Not with the hurley. I never hit a guy with the hurley... not deliberately.'

It is probably apocryphal, but, in a similar vein, one inter-county hurler was supposedly asked if he had gone to John Doyle's funeral. His joking response was that he had... 'to make sure he was dead'. As the earlier discussion showed, hurling was a tough sport back in 1959. Mick Flannelly in discussion with Michael Moynihan of the Irish Examiner questioned whether the Tipperary full-back line was really much worse than any other.

> 'They were as hard as other defenders... no more, no less. Mind you, the odd time against Tipp you were going in from half-forward for a '70', and the entire full-forward line would be on the ground before the ball dropped in.'

Waterford had a couple of their own hard men who would be mentioned in the same breath as Hell's Kitchen by Tipperary opponents. For example, Donie Nealon, while admitting that Kieran Carey was 'an awful tough man' had to point out that Joe Harney 'was a hardy boy' too. Martin Óg Morrissey also grouped Austin Flynn, Joe Harney and Johnnie Kiely as 'tough men'. However, the one player that was constantly in the wars with Tipperary seemed to be Tom Cheasty. His style of play continually led to clashes with the opposition half- and full-back lines. Tony Wall had one unusual battle with Cheasty in the 1959 league final.

> 'Waterford played the same way as we did, man for man, you win your ball, and you passed it along. There was nothing greatly scientific about it. There was nobody picking the ball and running. Well, Cheasty did it alright, but he was the only one. He was a bit of a rooter, but he'd pick it up and start running for goal. If I say so myself... one of the things I said to our lads was I'll stop him from scoring, you mind your own men... and I don't think he ever scored much against me. He looked terrible dangerous

'59: AN EYEWITNESS ACCOUNT OF HURLING'S GOLDEN AGE

running towards goal hopping the ball.'

(Note - Tom only scored 1 point in the league final and nothing in the Munster semi-final).

'That day in the League Final, I was centre-back, and he was centre-forward. He was the only fella that ever hit me when the ball was gone... and he did it that day. I looked at him and I did nothing. I got free after free... and as far as I know the Waterford fellas were saying "Will you stop that"... because of the frees. I didn't retaliate, I took the frees. What happened then though was people thought I was afraid of him. It was unheard of not to retaliate. I was looking at the referee, who would have put the two of us off... and I was getting the frees from the referee.

'Cheasty was the worst of them. When the ball was gone wide and wasn't even pucked out, he started this thing. I played him before that, but I think he was frustrated... or if it was a policy that day for them. He came out with the policy to do it and I don't think it worked. As far as I'm concerned, I took the frees and we won the match.

'Cheasty was the only one. The rest were all decent hurlers... they were fine fellas and I had good time for them all, except for my friend.'

John Flavin who also played that day does recall that particular encounter.

'Cheasty was renowned for it. He was some hurler that Tony Wall... a brilliant hurler. No way could you ever say he was dirty, he wasn't.'

In a nice turn of phrase, one player said 'Tom Cheasty wasn't what you'd call a tourist!' As farmers, Tom Cheasty and John Doyle had a lot in common and they encountered each other many times on and off the field, as Tom's wife, Katheen remembers.

'Just before he died, Tom was nominated for the Farmer 15 on the Farmer's Journal. John Doyle's son was at the banquet in Kilkenny and Tom said to him that "Doyle and myself had a pact, we'd only stay down as long as it would take us to get up again".'

Tom had filmed an ad for Leo Laboratories with John Doyle at a farm in Co. Wicklow in the 1980s but Kathleen recalls that he wasn't prepared for the shoot.

'John had a Tipperary jersey. We couldn't get a Waterford hurling jersey anywhere... so I bought him a soccer jersey in the same colours. The children loved watching the

'59: AN EYEWITNESS ACCOUNT OF HURLING'S GOLDEN AGE

ads when Tom was on the television.'

Interestingly, Kathleen's memories of Doyle and her husband are at odds with their public personas.

> 'He was so funny... John Doyle. I never laughed more than that weekend. You can never judge a book by the cover.'

The same reaction could be made of her comments on Tom.

> 'Tom nearly regretted being a farmer because he just drifted into farming. Tom was a fantastic reader. Oh my God, he was. Tom went to Waterpark for two years and he was handy at the rugby as well. John Goff often said he was one of the brightest in the class. He read morning, noon, and night... everything and anything. Even when he was busy working, he'd still have time to read every night. Donie Ormond's wife Greta said "You know Tom, when I retire, the two of us will go to UCC and do a history degree". He was interested in poetry too. If there was something sad on the *Late Late Show* and they needed funds... he'd always donate. And then he'd be so different on the field.'

John Doyle, the comedian, and Tom Cheasty, the shy, soft-hearted intellectual. Not exactly the image they held amongst the hurling community!

The idea that you must retaliate was commonplace in the game. Depending on your circumstances, that might necessitate the help of your teammates. John Flavin recalls one encounter with the Rattler Byrne where his county teammates joined the fray. John was a flying forward but was relatively light and relied on the extra strength of others.

> 'There was a fella called Micky Byrne. We were playing against him for Mount Sion... I think against Thurles Sarsfields. Who was refereeing the match... only Theo English. I was going through on a solo in the first-half, and he came out and never went near the ball... just absolutely took me out, cleaved me out. The blood was everywhere. I was pulled onto the line... a big bandage around me head, a slap on the back "Go on, you're grand... out you go", and I finished the match. During the match Grimes and Power, every chance they got... they hit the Rattler. They'd really back you up. If they thought that some fella was after doing you, they would nail yer man. When

'59: AN EYEWITNESS ACCOUNT OF HURLING'S GOLDEN AGE

the match was over, I was brought up to hospital and I got eight stitches... and I after getting the belt early on in the match.'

Billy Kelly recalls that as well as supporting their teammates, they were well able to look after themselves.

'If you didn't hit a fella back when he hit you, they'd go to town on you. You had to be brave... whether you could hurl or not. Grimes and Power looked after Flannelly. If you hit Flannelly... you'd have to hit one of them. They'd murder you. I couldn't hurl Philly Grimes. He was like lightning... so I hit him across the side of the knee to slow him up. He hit me up under the chin with the handle of the hurley. I couldn't eat for a fortnight... but you'd be the best of pals afterwards and have a drink together.'

Jackie Condon, with his no-nonsense style, was sometimes used as an enforcer but he didn't start out that way.

'I remember the first hurling game I played for Waterford. It was against Cork down in Cork. The lad who was on me was a Guard called Riordan. He was running rings around me. When you go into the county hurling after leaving the club hurling, the pace is twice as quick. I was just standing looking around... I didn't know what was going on. Philly Grimes came down to me and said "Jaysus Jackie, will you give that fella belt of the hurley... he thinks you are gone home". That got me going. I hit yer man a whack of the hurley and he said "What the f***in hell are you doing that for?". "That's for luck" I said. He was really after me after that. Really, you have got to let a fella know that you are around. Let him know you are there.'

Remembering a conversation with Kilkenny's Sean Clohessy, from that time, Clohessy, according to Jackie himself, said 'Remember that match we played in the Sports Field in Waterford? You broke my nose... I couldn't go to work for weeks. I had two black eyes, and you didn't even know you did it. You were just rough out'. Jackie recalls one occasion when he combined with Joe Harney to avenge John Barron.

'You met all types when you were hurling, and you had to have something in your armour to tackle it. You had to work out what a fella was like after a few minutes and deal with it. I played a match one time against Cork and John Barron was playing...

'59: AN EYEWITNESS ACCOUNT OF HURLING'S GOLDEN AGE

Christy Ring was on John Barron. John was a nice quiet chap. Ring hit John with the handle of the hurley up under the nose. John came out to me and said, "I can't take that, this fella is just a scamp" and I said "John, he knows he's getting to you".

'John had to go off and they brought Joe Harney in instead. I said to Joe "You hit him, and I'll meet him coming out". Harney and myself… we murdered Ring that day. We gave him an awful doing altogether. When he was coming off the field he called me a choice name! "Good luck to you now", I said.'

With that approach to the game, Jackie had plenty of experience with Hell's Kitchen. He described Mickey Byrne as 'a small man but, by God, he was dangerous'. Naturally, he had a John Doyle war story but, as always, he could find the humour in it.

'John Doyle… he was a ferocious man. Erin's Own played Holycross in Carrick for suit lengths. We won the suit lengths but there was about 15 fellas went to hospital after it! That John Doyle… he was a terror. When I went down to get that suit, they handed them out in Erin's Own… I got a brown oul' suit length. It was like something the fellas up in the mental hospital used to wear.'

Jimmy Brohan equally finds the humorous side of Christy Ring's encounter with Micky Byrne.

'I suppose you have the story about himself and The Rattler. We were coming off the field after a game between Cork and Tipperary. Ring was outstanding as usual. He came off the field and the Rattler says "Jaysus, we'll have to shoot ya". "Ye may as well," said Ring, "Ye tried everything else!"'

The rest of the Tipperary team were generally regarded to be stylish hurlers but one of them surprised Jackie Condon and tamed him.

'The one fella that fooled me from Tipperary was Liam Devaney. The first ball that came down, he dropped the ball between my knees, and he nearly broke my two legs, and he came back to me and said "Jaysus Jackie, I'm awful sorry… I didn't mean to hit you". A nice fella. I couldn't hurl him at all after that. I couldn't tackle him because my style of hurling was to bowl the fellas over all the time. I learned psychology from him!'

'59: AN EYEWITNESS ACCOUNT OF HURLING'S GOLDEN AGE

The combination of pride, toughness, respect, and bravery still comes through from all of these hurlers, even when talking about games from 60 years ago. Phil Fanning summarises the approach well.

> 'You never wanted to lie down. If you got a belt in the head and you were bleeding, you got up... and you'd run around like mad after it. Now a fella gets a tap on the leg, and he's gone down rolling around on the ground... and he has about six fellas out to have a look at him. In those days, if you got a belt in the head and you were bleeding, you gave it a wipe... unless somebody told you it was a bad one and they'd pull you aside. The last thing you wanted to do was lie down because if you lie down, you show the other fecker that you couldn't take it. You'd be ashamed to lie down after getting a belt... particularly in the head.'

Players just took it in their stride. Larry Guinan shrugs it off with the comment that 'I got a fair few belts and a fair few stitches but I didn't mind that. Believe it or not, I never got a broken bone'. These attributes were never better captured than by Freddie O'Brien recalling an incident in the Sports Field. He was well aware of the toughness of the game, having seen his friend and teammate Frankie Walsh have his skull fractured twice. He accepted that and admitted 'I hit fellas and they hit me, but I never had an enemy afterward'. There was one occasion when he needed Frankie's help though.

> 'I got split open playing against Wexford. I needed 11 stitches. Frankie was the first over to me. I could feel his two hands holding my brains together. He was saying "Stay down... stay down". I said "I can't! My mother is watching from the sideline"!'

Two other Mount Sion men, Seamus Power and John Flavin had an unusual relationship.

> 'The other fella... the Hammer as we used to call him, Seamus, he'd feckin' kill you. I remember playing with the fecker, I was only about 18 and we were playing down in Poleberry where Erin's Own pitch is... on a Sunday morning, seven-a-side... the Shops versus the Public Authorities. I was playing on the Hammer. I was fast and I was running around the Hammer and shouting "Go way with your big belly on you, Power... out drinking last night".
>
> '"I'll cut the effing head off you Flah." he said, "If you don't stop". And sure as Christ, he cleaved me... and he meant to. He was standing over me. He broke my nose in

three places and I got nine stitches. He was my teammate at Mount Sion. I was up in the Infirmary on the Sunday morning and the Mount Sion Social was on the Sunday night. Of course, I was in the bed... I heard him coming up the corridor. I knew by the walk on him... the big flops. He had a half pound of jelly sweets.

'I can still see him. He comes in and he fired the half pound of jelly sweets up on the bed. "That'll f***in' teach you," he said... and he walked out. Jaysus he was a wicked man... he was a hardy bit of stuff.

'I went off on holidays with him on the back of his scooter later on that year!'

Frankie Walsh, looking back on his career took all of this in his stride.

'I wouldn't change a thing. The friendships you gain... even though things happen on the field. I have a saying that my son laughs at... "You'll never see a hurler being canonised".'

TRAINING, FITNESS & HEALTH

In 1965, at the peak of his career, Tony Wall, the Tipperary captain wrote his fascinating book on hurling. One section examined the ideal of a healthy lifestyle.

'Smoking has a definite adverse effect on athletic performances, and it is best to abstain completely. If the habit has been formed, it may be better to smoke in moderation than to stop completely prior to a game.'

This might seem obvious to a modern reader, but smoking was ubiquitous at the time. Even on the day of the 1959 All Ireland final, newspaper adverts for Players Cigarettes showed cigarette stick figures playing hurling with the scoreboard in the background reading Port Lairge and Cill Chainnigh. Wall had a similar approach to alcohol.

'Much the same comments apply to alcohol. Taken in moderation there are not many serious ill effects. Indeed, there seems to be a lot of goodness in the traditional pint. However, the consumption of large quantities is very harmful and should be avoided.'

This parroting of the Guinness advertising tagline that 'Guinness is good for you' emphasises how embedded a pint of stout was in the collective consciousness. After the All-Ireland finals of the era, the teams would visit the Guinness Brewery on the morning after the match in the same way as their modern counterparts visit the Crumlin Children's Hospital. While the championship wasn't sponsored by Guinness as it would be in later years, tie-ins with alcohol advertising were common, with Smithwick's claiming to be 'The All-Ireland Drink'. There was an acceptance of both drinking or smoking, and it certainly wasn't seen to be detrimental to a player's hurling. Phil Fanning remembers it in the context of their overall lifestyles.

> 'Lads would play matches week in and week out. All you wanted to do was play hurling. It wasn't a question of minding yourself. I remember lads on Saturday nights going into Norriss's and playing cards and having a little bottle. There would be a big match the following day. They were all fit and well... it wasn't that they were abusing themselves, that's the way things were at the time.
>
> 'I remember Philly having a slug of brandy out of a Baby Power bottle at half-time in a match. Seamus would be the same way. Jack Furlong might have it... and Billy Jones certainly had it when he used to go around with the team. A quick slug of brandy even at half time... it was a thing. When they were training for the All-Ireland, the idea was that the lads would have a small stout after training each night. If a fella wanted a small stout, he got Maureen Quane and Johnny to bring up the stout from the pub. Martin Óg gave out. He said "I don't drink stout... you'll have to bring up a bottle of Harp for me". Imagine that now!
>
> 'The idea was that fellas wouldn't be going to the pub. It was a relaxing kind of thing... and a small bottle of stout wasn't going to kill you. These fellas were physically fit. They were all working men... a lot of them doing heavy work during the day on building sites or doing factory work or farming. All they wanted to do was play hurling and enjoy it.'

Not all players smoked or drank and some, like Michael O'Connor, specifically credit the GAA with supporting their healthier lifestyle.

> 'I never drank or smoked in my life. That's one of things I thank the GAA for. They got me involved in sport and I was always half training myself. I was a pioneer all my life, but I was one of those fellas that didn't want to display it with a Pioneer pin.'

Several of the hurlers from the west, including Ned Power, Austin Flynn, Tom Cunningham and Michael O'Connor, were Pioneers. Friends of the players remember others who followed an equally strict regime and dedicated themselves to their sport. John Barron was a non-smoking Pioneer. He featured in an article in the Pioneer magazine leading up to the All-Ireland final and it helped him bond with Tom Cheasty, as Tom's wife, Kathleen remembers.

> 'Tom always felt that because he didn't drink, he'd have an edge. Tom was quite friendly with John Barron, through the Pioneers. We'd be at Pioneers socials together.'

Eddie Keher interviewed Tom and recounted his approach.

> 'Tom's training partner was Mick Power, who worked on the family farm. Mick was two years younger and played centrefield on the Ballyduff team. When the day's work was done, they hurled every evening until nightfall. Tom credits Mick with the development of many of the skills that were to stand to him later in his career. He remembers that he was weak and had little confidence in shooting for scores on his right side. They spent hours working on that deficiency and it paid off in the 1959 All-Ireland replay when he soloed in to finish two first-half points on his right side.'

Tom did extra training with former Olympic hammer thrower, Pat O'Callaghan and was among the first GAA players to use a weights programme during a career which stretched into the 1980s. Kathleen recalled Tom meeting O'Callaghan in Bonmahon and sharing training tips.

> 'Tom was before his time with weightlifting. He had all kinds of weights at home, a rowing machine... we could start up a gym!'

Mick Flannelly wrote an excellent article in the Dunhill GAA Centenary Book on the topic of dedication and fitness.

> *'To reach a high standard in any sport, or better still to get a lot of pleasure out of playing games, requires a lot of serious training and dedication. Serious training should consist of at least three nights hard work, be he a senior or a junior player. Players should do extra training on their own, practicing the skills of a game, skipping or exercises. When you train hard and get fit, that is the time you will enjoy the hard competitive games. Sixty minutes will not be long enough for you.*
> *'A lot of money is spent on drink and cigarettes by young people today. Moderation*

Player's Cigarettes advert

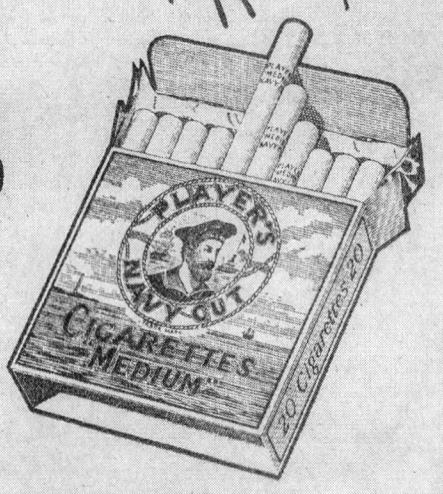

'59: AN EYEWITNESS ACCOUNT OF HURLING'S GOLDEN AGE

in these would be of great benefit to themselves and to the games they play. Why not spend some of this money on good playing gear for themselves, also on extra nourishment for their bodies to make them strong and fit for hard competitive games. Honey and glucose are great for all sportsmen.'

Flan lived these lessons himself. His next-door neighbour in Griffith Place, Michael Walsh remembers his match preparation.

'Mick Flan would skip for at least 20 minutes. It was poetry in motion to watch Flan skipping. I have never witnessed anything like it... like a machine, never miss a beat. To warm up. Then... the hurley and the ball against the back wall. Nothing else... just lacing the ball against the back wall. Doubling on it and hitting it any and every way it came... brilliant.'

Michael also had another privileged insight to the training regime, as he was one of several teenagers who helped out at training sessions.

'Liam Power and myself used to get jobs above in the field. You'd be sent off with Seamus Power... or off with Grimesey. Nobody wanted to go with Seamus Power. I'm serious. One would be throwing the ball to him to double on it... and one would be going to collect the ball after he belting it. You'd get a bucket of sliotars. My God... did they train. Most of it was running, but there was a lot of hurling in it as well. From what I can remember of it, there was very little contact hurling. You know like they say about Kilkenny that Cody blows the whistle and he'd blow the whistle again after an hour. There was none of that. John Keane coached them on the skills, but Fanning played a major part. Pat Fanning was the brains behind the whole thing.

'They'd all have to go in then, one by one, for the rub down with Jack Furlong. John Fraher used to give a hand out. The stuff that they used to rub down with... they used to use on horses. I'm serious. It was a formula made up by John Fraher. John was a chemist in Bells. For f**k sake... what dynamite, boy! When he left Bells, he went to work for the veterinary man on Ballybricken. John would bring all his mixes with him. A smell between eucalyptus and wintergreen... dynamite!

'There was no such thing as going for showers or going for a meal. They'd have sandwiches there... and a bottle of milk. The conditions that they trained under and stripped off under above in Walsh Park were absolutely atrocious. There was mud on the floors that wouldn't be swept from one week to the other. The dressing-rooms were out opposite the convent... just there at Keane's Road. They were big black tin sheds. There were four of them... and a small place where they used to keep the flags and the machine for lining the pitch.'

Martin Óg Morrisssey recalls the structure of the week's training.

'We did our training in Walsh Park under John Keane. He was a good trainer. He'd never roar at you. If he thought you were doing something wrong he'd nice and quietly tell you what he thought. We usually played a mixed match. If we had 20 fellas there, you had 10 fellas on each side and you played a match the full length of the pitch. The 10-a-side matches meant you were doing a lot more running than normal. We were fit alright. We used get a cup of tea and a sandwich after training. If you wanted a bottle of stout, it was there... or a bottle of lager and lime, it was there for you. You'd start at half seven and it could be half nine and you finishing.'

When it came to training for the championship. Freddie O'Brien recalls the priorities in training.

'John Keane would concentrate on your hurling skills and your level of fitness, to stay the distance... to stay the hour. We were all fairly physically fit at the time. It was only a matter of keeping peak fitness in us... not to be overburdened.'

Waterford's training plans were captured by Pat Fanning in his private notebooks. Pat's son, Phil joined a discussion of training methods with Frankie Walsh's son, Peter, Philly Grimes' daughter, Kay and Seamus Power's son, Tom.

Peter Walsh – 'I think the nature of the training was simple. Philly used always say to me that when they would say "Let's throw in the hurleys and have a match"... that's when Philly would leave the training pitch. He just wanted to hit ball after ball... after ball. They would have straight lines up and down the pitch hitting the ball and doubling on it... on the ground and in the air. At the time, striking the ball in the air was very prevalent and ground hurling was very prevalent. Philly had no time for these practice matches... they didn't achieve anything. What he wanted to do was hone his skills and be sharp.'

'59: AN EYEWITNESS ACCOUNT OF HURLING'S GOLDEN AGE

Phil Fanning – 'Training was much simpler. Most guys were natural hurlers. They honed their skills on the roads... they learned their hurling that way and they were all ball players. The main thing about the Waterford team of that era was their speed. In '57 when they were playing in Limerick, Limerick were referred to as 'Mackey's Greyhounds'... they were a very young team and a very fast team, but Waterford matched them for speed. At training, you did your short sprints, laps of the field to build up your stamina. The most elaborate exercise they were doing was leap-frogs around the field, that's all. It was all about moving the ball fast. That's why, when you look at the old films you see there is an awful lot of ground hurling. The whole idea is getting the ball in fast into the full-forward lines.

'When Frankie played for Munster first, he was wing forward and Ring was inside, and they won the Railway Cup. Somebody said to Ring, you have so many Railway Cup medals and seven All Irelands and Ring said "I'd have seven more if I had that little fella outside me hitting balls in fast to me like I had today". Frankie was a great man to whip a ball along the wing... or whip a ball across the field. There was no dilly-dallying at all... get the ball in fast to the full-forwards. That was the name of the game.'

Peter Walsh – 'A couple of them might make the Railway Cup squad. They wouldn't have hurled that much over the winter... so if some of them made the Railway Cup squad, some of the others would go training with them. They would wear hob-nailed boots running around the field. That was their element of strength and conditioning.'

Phil Fanning – 'Very few fellas had cars then and that's why very few had hamstring injuries. These days, fellas are sitting down all day. In those days, they walked to work, walked home from work every evening... they walked or cycled to the field. They were moving all the time.'

Tom Power – 'I wouldn't say Seamus was the fittest man in the team. I'd say he struggled with his fitness quite a bit.'
Kay Grimes – 'When Phil was coming close to the end of his career, and he had been left out of the team a couple of times, he'd get really annoyed and he'd layer up with jumpers and he would put on his rubber boots... and he'd go running round the town at night to muster up on the fitness. In his own head he'd be daring them to leave him on the sideline and when he'd go on, he'd have to hurl twice as hard as he ever did to

try and stay with the pace. Not only was he doing that, he was on the tools all day. They were probably doing strength and conditioning all day long in the work they were doing. Philly was with a mortar board and trowel... up and down ladders or on scaffolding... Tom Cheasty was out on the farm doing manual work and he was a bull of a man... Larry was physically very strong... you'd see him wearing short sleeves and you'd see the size of his arms... they were huge. Obviously, they were doing very physical work all day on top of the training.'

THE BAN

The long history of the ban and its place in the GAA is covered elsewhere, notably *The Steadfast Rule* by Breandan MacLua. In 1959, it was wrapped up in social issues related to Ireland emerging from its situation as a rural isolated island nation and beginning to interact economically with the world. This brought with it foreign music, foreign movies and most notably, foreign games. In the *News & Star* in 1959 there was an item about an under-16 hurling league established in Lismore, to which the reaction was 'This is great news from a town suffering from infiltration by the devotees of Empire games'. Pat Fanning wrote an impassioned defence of the Ban in the *News & Star* in the week after the GAA's Annual Congress on Easter Sunday 1959. This was consistent with the views of his predecessor, Vincent O'Donoghue, who 'explained that the ban was a defence against forces – sporting and cultural – which sought through their promotion of "imperial" pastimes, to "blunt the national conscience, weaken the national fibre and sabotage the national revival effort".'

While these senior officials maintained these lifelong positions on the matter, many of the players held different views. This had traditionally been the case. In his book *Over The Bar*, Breandán Ó hEithir referenced GAA President Dan McCarthy who, at Congress in 1924 said that 'If a plebiscite was held among players of hurling and football the ban on foreign games would go'. Declan Goode was playing at the time and was also secretary of the County Board. He later described how the ban had an impact on his younger brother, Jackie, who had won an All-Ireland medal in 1948 and five Railway Cup medals.

> 'He had been selected for his sixth final. The day before, he attended a rugby match in Dublin. He was in the Croke Park dressing-room changing for the match when the stub of the Landsdowne Road ticket fell out of his pocket. A selector who was standing by picked it up and reported him to the chairman of the Munster Council. He lost his place on the team as a result.'

'59: AN EYEWITNESS ACCOUNT OF HURLING'S GOLDEN AGE

Players from the 1959 team were also impacted by the ban over the years. John Barron's view was quoted by Brendan Fullam in *Giants of the Ash*.

> 'John was glad to see the ban go. He considers that it was retained for far too long and that it led to unnecessary dissension within the GAA and within counties. He also feels that some counties adapted a tougher vigilance policy than others. John was a victim of the ban. He was suspended for six months at the age of 16 and recalls that Seamus Power also incurred suspension under the ban.'

John wasn't just a victim of the ban, he was actively opposed to it, as Jackie Condon recalls.

> 'I was in the car one day with Pat Fanning and John Barron... and John was going on about the ban. I was working in Hearne's cabinet factory at that time, and they had a soccer factory league team. I went out and played. The lads brought out all the gear first and I went out on the quiet. They had the vigilante committee and they twigged that I was there... so I got suspended for six months. This was the part that went up my nose altogether.
>
> 'You had to write an apology when you wanted to come back to the GAA in Irish, on Irish watermarked paper, and a fine of ten shillings. I'm telling you... you can go take a running jump. This is what John Barron was arguing with Pat Fanning over. It was an awful thing altogether... that bloody ban. John was against it as well, big time. He was having a right go at Pat Fanning.
>
> 'Fanning was out of breath going on about it. All the Mount Sion fellas were all for the ban... but they were being indoctrinated by Pat Fanning. His opinion was their opinion. Outside of that, nobody else wanted the ban. I mean, Tom Cheasty got suspended as well for going to a dance... a foreign dance. It was ridiculous, absolutely ridiculous. It was out of its time anyway and well out of its time. It went anyway and I was an advocate for it going. I just thought it was nonsense.'

Even winning an All-Ireland was no protection, as Jackie Goode had found out. Mick Lacey was banned in 1960 for attending foreign games and missed the trips to Wembley and New York. While these games were not significant, the 1963 National League final certainly was. Tom Cheasty played in the league 'home' final against Tipperary, but he missed the actual final against New York after being suspended for attending a dance run by a local soccer club.

'59: AN EYEWITNESS ACCOUNT OF HURLING'S GOLDEN AGE

'I wasn't on the team for the drawn game and the victorious replay against New York. There is a story behind that. I went to a soccer dance in the Olympia and got suspended. I got no league medal. If they offered it to me now, I don't think I'd take it.'

There is a lesser-known story about Tom Cheasty being banned, that was told by Freddie O'Brien.

'Tom Cheasty was suspended for life… did you ever know that? Back when he was playing minor for Ballyduff in about 1952. I was at the match the same day. De La Salle were allowed play their boarders that time on their minor team and a fella by the name of Daverin… he was from Tipperary, played. Tom gave him a bit of a plastering on the field, and he was put off. It was fairly rough, there were hurleys swinging. This Guard Cullen came up to Tom and he said "What's your name?" and Tom did nothing only hit him a clatter.

'He was suspended for life that time. I believe that when he went home his father took the hurley off him and burned it, and said you'll never play hurling again. I think he was out of it for about three years… and then he came back. He was a funny fella. We'd have a mixed match in Walsh Park. He was in front of me, and I was chasing him, following him and trying to go to the right side… and didn't I tap his heel unintentionally and he tumbled over. He came up with his chest out and he was facing me. "I think that was serious," he said. I said "Jaysus, go away Tom… it wasn't. It was totally accidental". He'd blow a gasket fairly lively.'

John Flavin corroborates the story.

'Tom Cheasty… he was a lovely fella, but he was banned for life. He was playing for Ballyduff, and they were playing against De La Salle. At that time, a boarder in De La Salle College could play for their minor team. I can't remember yer man's name, but he was playing centrefield on Cheasty. I'm not telling you a lie… four men from the sideline had to come out and pull Cheasty off yer man. He had him down on the ground and he had one knee on the left hand shoulder and one knee on the other side… and he was hitting him with the hurley. He was suspended for life and within two or three years he was back again. I was there…. I was at the match. I couldn't believe it.'

'59: AN EYEWITNESS ACCOUNT OF HURLING'S GOLDEN AGE

Tom's wife, Kathleen, was aware of the early ban but Tom never mentioned it. She brought the story of the 1963 ban up to date, revealing that Tom did eventually receive his league medal.

> 'He was banned for going to a dance. Paddy Buggy of Kilkenny was at that dance as well that night. There were other Waterford hurlers at the dance too, but Tom was singled out. The way Tom looked at it was, he played Tipperary in the 'Home' final… and he played one of the best games he ever played. He got Sports Star of the Week in the *Irish Independent*. By the time they were playing New York he was suspended, and Tom didn't get a medal. In a book about Feile na Gael Tom mentioned that he didn't get the medal. In 1996, they put it in the book, and they commissioned a medal for him. Seamus Grant and a lot of the hurlers from Portlaw presented it to him at the Waterford Crystal Sports Centre… 33 years later. Pat Fanning was probably the cause of Tom being suspended but Tom got on grand with him. He wouldn't hold a thing in for you, but he'd just rise above it. Tom just took it in his stride.'

Even those with a strong interest in all sports had to respect the rules, particularly if they held a prominent position in a traditional club, like Michael Dowling at Erin's Own.

> 'Erin's Own and Mount Sion would have stuck rigidly to the non-attendance. I was never at a soccer match in Kilcohan, even though I knew a lot of fellas that played soccer… like Dixie Hale and Jack Fitzgerald. It was said that any amount of fellas from south Kilkenny went out to Kilcohan in the heyday of Waterford but there wasn't a word in Carrick about it. But if I was seen going in… it would be "Yer man from Erin's Own is up". I was interested in the Ireland rugby matches but I could never go and see them.'

One of those Waterford players was Jimmy Brohan's brother.

> 'I had two brothers who played League of Ireland soccer… I never saw them playing. I just accepted it. I had to accept it. I didn't want to be causing any problems for the club because you'd be suspended straight away if you were caught. They came to see me alright. Bobby was a goalkeeper… he got a few international caps at amateur level. Bobby was transferred to Waterford for a couple of years.'

While some were banned for watching soccer or attending soccer club dances, Ned Power was banned for actually playing soccer, albeit at a very casual level, as his son, Conor described.

'In the early 50s he was suspended for six months while playing with Dungarvan for being spotted playing soccer in Quann's field with three friends by a Waterford County Board official. He felt it was an excessive punishment and that his club hadn't been very helpful in trying to overturn the decision. As a result, he signed up with rival club Affane.'

The most ironic turn of events led to Phil Grimes' pub soccer team becoming Pub League Champions in 1970, months before the ban was to be discussed at Congress.

'Phil does not subscribe to the ban but despite this he has never seen a soccer or rugby match and while the ban is there he doesn't intend to. It's a matter of principle with him. Yet the customers of the pub he owns won the Public Houses' soccer competition in Waterford this year, and Phil is proud of this. Most of his customers are soccer followers who respect him for his feelings on the ban. Phil says 'The Ban is there and though you mightn't agree with it... it doesn't automatically mean that you should break it, but I think the GAA would be better off if they got rid of it. It has only helped to tarnish the association's name. It has given its enemies a weapon to use against the association.'

While the nature of the ban caused people to take entrenched positions on either side, Eddie Keher provides an even-handed viewpoint.

'It was always out there. I could understand the reasons when it was set up. It is like people talking now about things that happened 50 years ago... times were different. When the ban was introduced, it was introduced with a good purpose. The difficulty over the years was that the association was so democratic that it came up at Congress nearly every year and it was defeated, because the Six Counties would be voting to retain it. You would have a lot of people in the south supporting their view as well, including Pat. It was ironic he was president when it was removed. I would like to think I was a very good friend of Pat Fanning's and I had huge admiration for him. I saw a reason for it when it was introduced and when it was eventually removed, I suppose I wasn't sorry. I suppose I had an even view on it.'

'59: AN EYEWITNESS ACCOUNT OF HURLING'S GOLDEN AGE

Eddie refers to Pat being president when the ban was lifted. Despite his strong opposition to the motion, Rule 42 was struck from the rule book during Congress in 1972, to universal acclaim of the manner in which he handled such a delicate situation. Looking on from Erin's Own, Michael Dowling admired the approach he took.

> 'Pat Fanning was left in the position, and he had no option but to do what was done. The motion was put up... it was voted on, it was carried, and then he did the right thing. He accepted it as it was and let's get on with it.'

Pat Fanning was a man of strong beliefs, sincerely held, and he always acted in what he felt was the best interests of the association. However, in his later days, even Pat admitted that while he was a self-confessed 'walking rule book', the application of the rule wasn't always easy.

> 'The ban was a symbol. Terrible things were done in the name of the ban. I did them myself when I was chairman of the County Board. I suspended people for going to soccer matches. People used to say to me that this was disgraceful... that they were as true to the association and loyal to the association as I was. My only comeback and it was rather trite was "This is the rule... we live by the rule, and we apply the rule" and that is the way it was.'

Jimmy Gray recalls that Pat's legacy was far greater than this single issue, but the ban loomed large over his presidency.

> 'I knew Pat Fanning well. He was a good friend of mine. He was one of the best presidents. He was the first president that recognised the importance of Dublin... his general support for Dublin was strong. Dublin City and County was growing at a pretty big rate. It needed a County Board to be able to cater for that. He showed great maturity in Congress of 1971. He recognised the changing times. Dublin was generally in favour of removing the ban... largely through the offices of Tom Woulfe of the Civil Service club. It was passed at convention with a huge majority.'

Another star player, turned senior administrator, Donie Nealon, also discussed Pat.

> 'I knew Pat very, very well. He was some man to give a speech... to talk to a team, or at a function. He was one of the best speakers that I ever came across... fantastic, from

the heart! I don't know did he even have a note. It (congress 1971) was a great credit to Pat, and it was a magnanimous gesture for him to be so democratic and to let that go through. He would have been against it, but he didn't come out against it.'

Pat earned the right to define his own legacy and it is a fair assessment of his life's work.

'I'd like to be remembered as one who served the association to the best of his ability and who would like to be recognised for that, as a man who all the time put the association before himself… and I did that.'

3

RAILWAY CUP

While the National League programme was still being played through the winter, the newspapers at the start of January were always full of speculation about the selection of the Railway Cup teams. The competition, which pitted the best players of each province against each other in a four-way tournament, gave players the opportunity to be recognised individually in an era before the All Star awards. A prestigious tournament, it usually involved a semi-final played in February and the final played as a double header with the football final on St. Patrick's Day.

The Munster hurling team for 1959 was announced on Saturday January 10 in Limerick. The six selectors, one from each county (including Tom Penkert of Ferrybank) selected five Waterford players in the panel of 20 – John Barron, Seamus Power, Martin Óg Morrissey, Larry Guinan, Phil Grimes (four in the starting line-up and Grimes in the subs). At the same meeting, Tom Cunningham was chosen as centre half-back on the Munster football team for the second year running. Martin Óg Morrissey would start his season at that point.

> 'It was a great honour to play for Munster. In January I'd be out on the roads doing a bit of road work in anticipation of getting my place on the Munster team. Jimmy Smyth was a great player. At that stage you could say he was the Clare team. He was a fantastic hurler... a lovely hurler. Battles in county games were all forgotten when you went out for Munster. At that stage, you could play the game on a Sunday, and you had a go at a fella, or he had a go at you... and the following Sunday you could be out against him again, maybe in a club match... and it wouldn't make a bit of difference. My favourite position was left half-back. I played two years at centre half-back and two years at left half-back for Munster. Tony Wall and myself used to swap positions.'

Hogan Stand ten-year ticket

Railway Cup final programme and ticket

'59: AN EYEWITNESS ACCOUNT OF HURLING'S GOLDEN AGE

Central Council also announced in January their decision that Ulster, which was effectively an Antrim team, would not be accepted into the Railway Cup hurling competition. The *Irish Weekly Independent* of January 22 reported that *'The standard of hurling in Ulster is so far below that of the other provinces that the only result there could be from such an uneven contest is a discouragement for players who find themselves so completely out of their depth. Encouragement through equality in competition and an occasional victory is the tonic required by Ulster hurling. This they could not get from meeting the pick of Munster one year and the pick of Leinster the next'*. Despite Ulster's objection, the decision stood, and Munster received a bye into the final. Central Council also announced their decision that the Railway Cup hurling final would be the match to feature at the opening of the new Hogan Stand on June 7. The Leinster v Connacht semi-final was played on St. Patrick's Day as a double header with the football final.

In the semi-final, Connacht had a surprise 2-14 to 3-7 win over Leinster. As all 15 Connacht players were from Galway and wore the Galway colours, the *Irish Independent* headline the next morning announced, *'Galway Storm to Hurling Final'*. Only Gerry O'Malley of Roscommon merited a place in the substitutes. Leinster, featuring eight Kilkenny players and O'Donnell, Wheeler and Kehoe from Wexford, were *'strongly fancied'* but the midfield pairing of Joe Salmon and P.J. Lally gave Connacht the edge. Goals from corner-forwards Egan and Conway ensured they qualified for the final against Munster.

The celebrations on final day began with the blessing of the stand by Monsignor T. O'Reilly, the parish priest of St. Agatha's on North William Street, the parish in which Croke Park is located. This was followed by the official opening by President Seán T. O'Kelly. Reported to be a good hurler in his youth, he recalled that his own association with the GAA went back over half a century, and he referred to the completion of the work *'as a magnificent and most creditable achievement'*. He also praised the GAA leadership, saying 'Your President, Dr. J.J. Stuart, is to be congratulated on his spirited and impressive address on declaring the stand officially open'. In this 75th year of the association, Stuart noted that the GAA 'was built on the dreams of a handful of men". Many of these were recognised with invitations to the ceremonies. Twenty Waterford All-Ireland medal winners from 1948 were invited to attend and clubmates remember Jim Ware, captain in 1948, attending with his wife, Alice.

The 'Pageant of the Flag' began at 2.30pm. The pageant, written by Listowel playwright Bryan MacMahon, honoured four generations of militant patriots who died so that the flag might fly freely. Scenes were enacted by members of the FCA who played the parts of 1798 Rebels, the Fenians, the Soldiers of the 1916 Rising, and the Volunteers of 1920. Camogie players from Dublin represented the members of Cumann na mBan. Tipperary's Donie

'59: AN EYEWITNESS ACCOUNT OF HURLING'S GOLDEN AGE

Nealon recalls that the players 'were getting ready to play the match so we weren't out on the field for the official opening' and Cork's Jimmy Brohan, equally focused on the game, ignored the ceremonies, commenting 'We didn't know anything about that'.

The new Hogan Stand, with a seating capacity of 16,000 was one of the largest in Europe at the time. With the seating capacity of the Cusack Stand adding another 7,000 seats, it brought the total capacity of the stadium to 85,000. The stand was designed with modern convenience in mind and had the major advantage of only using three narrow roof supports, the only viewing obstructions in the entire stand. There were five levels to the stand including office space and catering. It was constructed by McInerny & Sons Ltd who started work early in 1957 and built in stages to allow the pitch to be available for inter-provincial and final matches. Over 700 tons of steel bars from Haulbowline, stretching almost 500 kilometres if laid end to end, were used for reinforcement. The roof was fabricated from more than 350 tons of structural steel and 6,000 cubic yards of concrete was used for the beams, supports and terracing.

In order to defray some of the construction costs, the GAA put in place a 10-year ticket scheme, which allowed supporters to secure tickets for the All-Ireland hurling and football finals from 1959 to 1968. The cost of the tickets was £16 for the Lower Deck and £11 for the Upper Deck, and initial sales were brisk. The back page of the programme for the Railway Cup football final was a full-page application form for the scheme and by March 24 there were almost 1,000 sold. However, approaching the deadline of August 15, sales were not as expected and a final push from each county was encouraged.

The ticket holders received a certificate with their name and address, marked with a two-penny stamp and the signature of General Secretary, Pádraig Ó'Caoimh. The ticket was valid for replays at no extra charge so there was an immediate extra value offered in 1959 as the hurling final was replayed. The scheme brought in revenue of £70,000. To put this into context, the GAA's total income in 1959 was £98,000, so the ticket scheme made a huge financial contribution to the association. The assets of the GAA at year end amounted to over half a million pounds, of which £470,000 represented money invested in Croke Park.

With all the preliminaries out of the way, the important matter of the Railway Cup final was still to be decided. With their bye into the final, the Munster team had yet to play a game. At a Munster Council meeting at the end of May there was a discussion as to whether the team needed to be re-selected 'as some of the players had lost form' but it was decided not to make any change. The Munster team included four Waterford starters and lined out as follows.

'59: AN EYEWITNESS ACCOUNT OF HURLING'S GOLDEN AGE

- Mick Cashman (Cork)

- Jimmy Brohan (Cork) • Michael Maher (Tipperary) • John Barron (Waterford)
- Tom McGarry (Limerick) • Tony Wall (Tipperary) • Martin Óg Morrissey (Waterford)

- Theo English (Tipperary) • Tom Casey (Limerick)

- Donie Nealon (Tipperary) • Seamus Power (Waterford) • Jimmy Doyle (Tipperary)
- Jimmy Smyth (Clare) • Christy Ring (Cork) • Larry Guinan (Waterford)

Martin Óg Morrissey remembers the morning of the match.

'We were up in Dublin the night before and we stayed in Barry's Hotel. In the morning, Larry Guinan and myself were coming down for our breakfast. We walked into the dining-room and Guinan said "Where will we sit?". I looked around… and here was Christy Ring on his own. I said let's go over and sit down with Ring and have a chat. We sat down with him, and he spoke about nothing else only hurling. He looked at me and said, "I'd say ye will win the All-Ireland this year". It's a bit too early to be talking like that I said. "No," he said, "Who will beat ye?"

'I said what about Limerick?. "No," he repeated. Tipperary? "No". Kilkenny? "No." Wexford? "No." Dublin? "No."

'What about yourselves?' I said. He said to me "Who have we?" I said ye have Cashman on goal. "He's a good goalie," he said. Ye have Jimmy Brohan… corner-back. "I'll tell you something about Cork," he said, "Cork have two… John Lyons and myself, and Lyons is nearly bet". Lyons was playing full-back.

'He said, "No one will beat ye this year. Ye will win the All-Ireland".'

In front of an attendance of 23,248, Christy Ring, appearing in his 18th successive Railway Cup final, scored 4-5, a performance praised in the *Cork Examiner 'as much for the quality of the scores as the quantity'*. Donie Nealon has good reason to remember the occasion.

'1959 was my first Railway Cup appearance. We had won the All-Ireland in 1958. Ulster didn't field at all… so we got a bye into the final. Strangely enough, Connacht had beaten Leinster. The final was postponed. Normally it would be Patrick's Day, but it was postponed to coincide with the official opening of the Hogan Stand. It wasn't played until June. We beat the guts out of Connacht. Christy Ring was full forward… what age was he that time? He was born in 1920… so he was 39 and he scored four goals and five points.

'59: AN EYEWITNESS ACCOUNT OF HURLING'S GOLDEN AGE

'The Galway lads were always tough on him. A high ball came in and he got a belt on the head and down he goes. Somebody cleared out the ball, but I could see him. He wasn't concussed because I could see him peeping out of the corner of his eye. I hit the ball straight back into him on the ground. Up he hopped... doubled on it, and into the back of the net. He was something else.

'The first ball I got that day, I was wing forward, it was down near the corner flag. Ring, if he was full-forward, would always run out to the '21' so I hit it out to him and he scored a goal or a point off it... but, by God, if I hit it wide, I can tell you one thing... you'd hear about it from him. He was well able to take the punishment. He was very strong.'

Connacht had a strong breeze in the first-half but were unable to take advantage. In the opening 10 minutes goals from Smith and Guinan, and two points from Ring, put Munster eight points up. John Barron, still affected by a nagging leg injury, opened cautiously but settled into the game. He combined well with Maher and Brohan to keep Galway out. Martin Óg Morrissey was reported by the *Waterford News & Star* to be *'the most competent defender Munster had'* and was praised for his anticipation, interception and striking, both overhead and on the ground. Seamus Power, like Barron, was also suffering from an injury. His duel with Jim Fives was a tough battle and he retired injured just before the end. The game was effectively over at half-time. An early second-half goal for Donie Nealon was followed by Ring's goals in the 36th, 40th, 46th and 50th minutes. Larry Guinan supported Ring well and scored two goals of his own, but this was Ring's day as he won his fifteenth Railway Cup medal as Munster triumphed by 20 points on a score line of 7-11 to 2-6. Ring ultimately won 18 in total from 23 consecutive final appearances between 1941 and '63.

The late 50s were the heyday of the Railway Cup. Slowly and steadily, it declined in popularity. Eddie Keher played through those years and his regret at the demise of the Railway Cup is clear.

'We had a great run in the Railway Cup with Leinster in the 70s particularly. Munster were dominating the Railway Cup for years and years... and we took over in the 70s. I remember witnessing the demise of the Railway Cup from 40,000 to 50,000... to about 18,000, that sort of a drop.'

Donie Nealon also expressed his sadness that 'it is an awful pity that the Railway Cup is gone'. During its lifespan, many Waterford players were honoured by Munster. Interprovincial

1959 Munster Railway Cup team: Back – Larry Guinan (Waterford), John Barron (Waterford), Tom McGarry (Limerick), Michael Maher (Tipperary), Jimmy Smyth (Clare), J. Quaid (Limerick), Jimmy Brohan (Cork), Jim Barry (Cork). Front – Seamus Power (Waterford), Theo English (Tipperary), Jimmy Doyle (Tipperary), Mick Cashman (Cork), Tony Wall (Tipperary), Christy Ring (Cork), Martin Óg Morrissey (Waterford), Donie Nealon (Tipperary).

✦

1960 Munster Railway Cup team: Back – Vince Murphy (Cork), Austin Flynn (Waterford), John Doyle (Tipperary), Tom McGarry (Limerick), Jimmy Smyth (Clare), Seamus Power (Waterford), Jimmy Brohan (Cork), Phil Grimes (Waterford), Jim Barry (Cork). Front Row – John Barron (Waterford), Paddy Barry (Cork), Tom Cheasty (Waterford), Mick Cashman (Cork), Martin Óg Morrissey (Waterford), Christy Ring (Cork), Frankie Walsh (Waterford), Jimmy Doyle (Tipperary).

✦

Seamus Power and Philly Grimes in Munster gear

'59: AN EYEWITNESS ACCOUNT OF HURLING'S GOLDEN AGE

hurling competitions began in 1927 and the first Waterford player to play for Munster was Charlie Ware in 1930. Charlie won Waterford's first Railway Cup medal that day, the first time the final was played on St. Patrick's Day. Another Waterford man featured that day as the game was refereed by Willie Walsh, after whom Walsh Park is named. Charlie was selected five times, and his brother Jim was chosen three times.

Of the players who won an All-Ireland in 1959, here is how often each player was selected for Munster:

- 7   Seamus Power
- 6   Frankie Walsh, Larry Guinan, Austin Flynn
- 5   Martin Óg Morrissey
- 4   John Barron, Tom Cheasty
- 3   Philly Grimes, John Kiely
- 1   Mick Flannelly, Tom Cunningham (plus 6 for football), Donal Whelan, Ned Power, Michael O'Connor

That is a total of 49 appearances by 14 players, winning 35 Railway Cup medals. In addition to this impressive haul, Tom Cunningham was also selected for the Munster football team on six occasions. If trainer John Keane's nine appearances and selector Declan Goode's one hurling and four football selections are included, it truly was a golden era for Waterford.

The highest representation ever achieved by Waterford was following the 1959 All-Ireland. In January 1960, the selection committee of Pat Fanning (Waterford), Conn Murphy (Cork), P. Purcell (Tipp), Vincent Murphy, and M. MacAodha (Limerick) announced a panel with seven Waterford players in the starting line-up, plus Larry Guinan in the subs.

The Railway cup semi-final victory by 5-12 to 1-9 over Connacht on February 21 was a facile win in which 'the Munstermen were not at their best, for the simple reason that they played just as well as they had to'. Connacht, playing a full Galway team, were reported to be unfit and were no match for Munster. While Christy Ring had a quiet hour, he still scored 1-2, which along with 2-1 from Paddy Barry and two goals from Jimmy Doyle, scored within 90 seconds, was easily enough for victory.

'59: AN EYEWITNESS ACCOUNT OF HURLING'S GOLDEN AGE

On St. Patrick's Day, this team lined out again in the final at Croke Park.

• Mick Cashman (Cork)

• Jimmy Brohan (Cork)   • Austin Flynn (Waterford)   • John Barron (Waterford)

• Tom McGarry (Limerick)   • Martin Óg Morrissey (W'ford)   • John Doyle (Tipperary)

• Seamus Power (Waterford)   • Philly Grimes (Waterford)

• Jimmy Doyle (Tipperary)   • Tom Cheasty (Waterford)   • Frankie Walsh (Waterford)

• Jimmy Smyth (Clare)   • Christy Ring (Cork)   • Paddy Barry (Cork)

An attendance of 36,295 appreciated the display of Mick Cashman in the Munster goal and at the other end, the four goals scored by Jimmy Smyth of Clare. His first came from a speculative shot from Phil Grimes which deflected off Smith's hurley on its way to the net. Smith managed another two goals in the first-half giving Munster a 3-3 to 1-4 half-time lead. A Paddy Barry goal in the second-half killed the tie as a contest and even though Leinster had a period of dominance, Munster regained control and finished the game with a goal from Frankie Walsh and Smith's fourth of the day. Munster won 6-6 to 2-7. Jimmy Brohan recalls his Munster teammates' performance well.

> 'Jimmy Smyth from Clare... he was a regular. Jimmy must have played 10 or 12 times for Munster. He scored four goals that day. Jimmy was deadly but, you see, when he was playing with Clare, he was on his own most of the time, but with a bit of help from other players he was able to get the goals. He was a great player, but he had an unusual strike. He wouldn't have had a full swing at all, most of the time. You couldn't hook him or anything. He was a strong man too.'

The domination of the competition by Munster that year emphasises the strength of the Waterford All-Ireland winners. The crucial central positions of full-back, centre half-back, both midfielders, and centre-forward were all Waterford players, and they brought the largest haul of Railway Cup medals ever won back to Waterford.

"

'1959 WAS MY FIRST RAILWAY CUP APPEARANCE. WE HAD WON THE ALL-IRELAND IN 1958. ULSTER DIDN'T FIELD AT ALL... SO WE GOT A BYE INTO THE FINAL. STRANGELY ENOUGH, CONNACHT HAD BEATEN LEINSTER. THE FINAL WAS POSTPONED. NORMALLY IT WOULD BE PATRICK'S DAY, BUT IT WAS POSTPONED TO COINCIDE WITH THE OFFICIAL OPENING OF THE HOGAN STAND. IT WASN'T PLAYED UNTIL JUNE. WE BEAT THE GUTS OUT OF CONNACHT. CHRISTY RING WAS FULL FORWARD... WHAT AGE WAS HE THAT TIME? HE WAS BORN IN 1920... SO HE WAS 39 AND HE SCORED FOUR GOALS AND FIVE POINTS.

DONIE NEALON

4

NATIONAL LEAGUE

The National League was the ideal opportunity to trial players for the championship. Leading up to 1959 much of the team was in place since the 1957 All-Ireland final. There was some rotation of players in the forward line but, most critically, there was a corner-back slot up for grabs with contenders including Joe Harney, Freddie O'Brien, Billy Kelly, Tom Cunningham and Joe Coady. The two Erin's Own players, Kelly and Coady, were played in the league in 1958 although Billy Kelly is still modest in describing his inter-county appearances.

> 'They had no one else. Myself and Joe Coady were always drafted in when the good fellas wouldn't want to play.'

The league ran through the winter months so the Kinane Cup in early summer was also a useful testing ground. In the 1958 Kinane Cup final Waterford beat Wexford 10-6 to 2-12. Without the full Mount Sion contingent, the Dunhill pairing Mick White and Billy Dunphy were given a chance in midfield with Mick Kelly of Dungarvan given a run at wing forward.

- Ned Power
- Billy Kelly (Erin's Own) • Austin Flynn • John Barron
- Jackie Condon • Martin Óg Morrissey • Joe Coady
- Mick White (Dunhill) • Billy Dunphy (Dunhill)
- Mick Flannelly • Tom Cheasty • Mick Kelly (Dungarvan)
- Tom Cunningham • Seamus Power • Larry Guinan

Two Erin's Own players also played, and Michael Dowling of Erin's Own recalls Joe Coady's performance.

Train from Waterford Dept 10 a.m.
Meal on train 11/45 a.m.
Train Dept Dublin 6/30 P.M.

CUMANN LÚITHCHLEAS GAEDHEAL

Coisde Co. Phortláirge

17 Sraid an Teampuill,
Dungarbhan.
(Date as Postmark)

PORTLAIRGE V. _Ath Cliath_
AT _Páirc an Chrócaigh_ ON SUNDAY _8/11/59_

A Chara,

Kindly note that you have been selected on the Waterford _S.H._ team to play _Dublin_ at _Croke Park_ on Sunday _8/11_. You are requested to make yourself as fit as possible in preparation for this very important engagement. If, for any reason, you are not available to travel, you are requested to notify me in writing at the very earliest, so that a substitute may be selected to travel in your place.

Players failing to notify me of inability to travel or field out will be reported to the County Board.

Players will travel by ~~car~~ _train_ on Sunday _8/11/59_ and you are requested to meet ~~car~~ _train at Waterford 10 a.m._

All players to have complete set of clean playing togs and hurley.

Teams will stay at the _Castle Hotel_ where you are asked to report on arrival, not later than _1/30 P.M._

Call up letter to player for league match

Mise,
Deaglán Fuitt
Runaidhe

'59: AN EYEWITNESS ACCOUNT OF HURLING'S GOLDEN AGE

'He was an outstanding clubman. He was small and had a low centre of gravity, but he used to play very well for Waterford in challenge matches. I clearly remember him in the Kinane Cup playing on Hopper McGrath from Wexford. The two of them would be at it hammer and tongs.'

While Tom Cunningham could easily have taken the corner-back position, he was being tried in the forwards and he scored 2-1 against Wexford in a forward line alongside Seamus Power and Larry Guinan, who scored 3-3 and 3-1 respectively. The management continued to try players and in the league in 1958. Billy Kelly played again as an *Experimental Waterford team beats Antrim* according to the headlines of the day. With limited slots available, decisions at club level had to be made by Erin's Own, as Billy describes.

'Joe Coady was slow but wicked strong. He was a good hurler, more suited to the corner than wing back. Jim Ware approached me in 1959 about going on the panel. I said let Joe Coady go forward. We wanted to build a team in Erin's Own and Joe was more of a soccer man. Young Charlie said we have to get Coady, so I said to Jim, "Put Joe on". Joe knew that himself and he got an All-Ireland medal. Joe was a modest fella anyway. We were great friends... we used all go out together. I'd be drinking large bottles and he'd be drinking pints of Cidona... I don't know how he didn't explode!'

Waterford had an unbeaten start to the league campaign of 1958/59 with three wins before the turn of the year. A four-point win away to Dublin set the tone. At O'Toole Park on October 26, Waterford won by 1-12 to 1-8. Describing a close game, Mitchel Cogley writing in the Independent felt that *'If Waterford and Dublin can maintain the form shown in their opening National Hurling League game at O'Toole Park yesterday, they will make matters hot indeed for any opposition'*. Both teams were evenly matched as reflected by the 1-6 to 1-6 score at half-time. With solid defending, Waterford pulled away in the final quarter. Jackie Condon was recognised as Man of the Match – *'The best player afield, however, was the Waterford right-half back John Condon, whose general all-round excellence was highlighted by two second-half incidents (in the happy sense of the word) when he emerged triumphant from sorties against three and four rivals'*.

Two weeks later, Waterford beat Wexford by 2-8 to 1-8 in the Gaelic Field, Waterford. This was a deserved victory as Waterford were never behind during the contest. The *Irish Press* reported that *'unless there is a series of fantastic upsets in the remaining rounds, a new name will be inscribed on the National Hurling League trophy for 1959. Holders Wexford virtually kissed*

'59: AN EYEWITNESS ACCOUNT OF HURLING'S GOLDEN AGE

goodbye to their chances of retaining it at Waterford yesterday'.

On November 23, Waterford wrapped up the year with a third win against Cork, by 4-5 to 2-3. Mick Dunne, writing in the *Irish Press*, predicted *'watch Waterford surging into the National League final. After collecting further points with this impressive victory over Cork, at Dungarvan, they are now the only side with full points in Division 1A. And I say they won't be stopped'*. Larry Guinan led the scoring with three of the four goals. The feeling was that Waterford had recaptured the form of 1957. According to Mick Dunne *'now they are a side of vim and vigour. They approached their work with a zest that overcomes the best of opposition, and their combination is so well knit together that they are a formidable force'*. Having come on as a sub in the previous two games, John Flavin started his first game. The *Press* described him as *'19-year-old newcomer, Sean Flavin, fleet as a greyhound, did well'*. He recalls the crowd's excitement at the end of game. 'We apparently played very well that day. We were nearly carried into the square in Dungarvan… and it was only a league match'.

Entering 1959 full of confidence, Waterford's first league game was against Kilkenny on February 8. A win for Waterford would virtually assure them of a place in the league final so a huge crowd was expected. The match was all-ticket with no cash being accepted at the turnstiles. Instead, ticket sellers were operating on the approaches to the ground selling 1-shilling tickets for entrance to the field and 2 shillings and sixpence tickets for access to the sideline. The sense of excitement spread to the travelling supporters. The match started late but not due to the large crowd. The Waterford team responded to the referee's call at five to three, but the Kilkenny team did not appear for a further 20 minutes. On a cold day in February, that must have affected the Waterford players. The Kilkenny players and officials apologised for the delay. Without stars like Ollie Walsh and Sean Clohessy, they were forced into four changes with Cleere, Heaslip, Kelly and Carroll coming into the side, the line-up not being finalised until the last minute. For Waterford, Tom Cunningham was ruled out due to a hand injury suffered the previous weekend against Tipperary in the National Football League. His hand was in plaster, so Donal Whelan was brought in to replace him.

The St. Patrick's Brass Band played while the crowd were waiting. Kilkenny won the toss and elected to play against the breeze. Centre half-back Hogan broke down the first attack and Liam Cleere, replacing Ollie Walsh in goal, saved from Frankie Walsh soon after. It was all Waterford, but each attack was foiled in succession by a different Kilkenny defender. Finally, when Seamus Power was fouled in midfield, Phil Grimes scored the free from 80 yards. Heaslip managed a break for Kilkenny but was stopped by the combined strength of the full-back line. Waterford had two wides from Grimes and Cheasty but, despite their dominance, it was not reflected in the scoreline. Brophy, who was playing well for Kilkenny, shot wide. As Waterford came back up the field, Grimes crossed to Guinan, who lost his hurley but hand-passed across to Whelan, who struck the ball to the net from the ground.

The defences were on top, but Kilkenny's forwards were now looking more dangerous and Kelly scored their opening point. After wides from both sides, Walsh lobbed the ball into the square where, in a skilful move, Whelan doubled the ball over the bar, only for it to be ruled out by the umpires. Walsh won a free from a pass from Guinan and pointed it himself. Just before half-time, Kilkenny forwards were rewarded for their hard work when Dwyer, the strong full-forward, gathered the ball from a Brophy centre, burst through and shot to the corner of the net. The half time score was Waterford 1-2, Kilkenny 1-1

At half-time White was replaced at corner-forward by Mick Flannelly and he scored Waterford's first point of the second-half. After two close efforts by Frankie Walsh, Kilkenny broke down the field with a combination of passes from Carroll to Dwyer to Kelly, who scored a hand-passed goal. Flannelly kept a ball from going wide on the end-line and sent the ball across to Guinan who scored a point, followed quickly by one from Walsh to make it level at 1-5 to 2-2. A Kelly free restored their lead, while Heaslip and Power traded frees. In the turning point of the second-half, Ned Power made a good save, but a fumble in the Waterford defence let Kilkenny in for a goal from which Waterford never recovered. While Grimes scored from a '70', Kilkenny ensured victory with two further points. Lacey's point in the last minute was no consolation as Waterford lost by four points. Waterford's play was criticised for trying to pick the ball too often, allowing their fast opponents to converge on them before they had full control. This was counter to the ground hurling which had won them their earlier league games. This criticism was particularly levelled at the back lines and midfield, although it was noted that two of Kilkenny's scores came while John Barron was lying injured. Kilkenny were deserving winners by 3-6 to 1-8.

Padraig Puirseal, reporting for the *Irish Press* enjoyed the game. *'After as hard and enjoyable an hour's hurling as I have watched for many a day – hurling, fast, fierce and yet admirably fair – Kilkenny sprang a major surprise before nearly ten thousand spectators at the Waterford Gaelic Field yesterday. They halted the hitherto unbeaten league match of the Deisemen in a thrill-packed game that for dash, daring and fearlessness was almost of All-Ireland standard.'* Martin Óg Morrissey remembers the difficulty of playing against Johnny McGovern, Kilkenny's wing back.

> 'Philly wasn't feeling up to scratch one day and he said to the selectors "Don't put me centrefield... put me in the forward line" so they put him at right half-forward which would have put him playing on Johnny McGovern. I was talking to him before the match, and he asked if I knew anything about McGovern. I told him he wouldn't

hit a ball in the air, even though Philly was pretty good at that. I said when you are getting ready to pull on the ball, he'll give you a little tip on the back with his elbow... and he'll be picking up the ball 10 yards behind you. The first two balls that went in, that was exactly what happened. The third one went in and Philly only missed McGovern's head by about two inches... and he hit every ball after that.'

The unfortunate wing forward in this game was John Flavin who, having made the starting lineup, faced his toughest test yet.

'I played on a fella called Johnny McGovern, left half-back. Mother of Divine God... a small man, he was an absolutely brilliant hurler. As a fellow hurler, there was no dirt or anything in him... he was great.'

Dublin drawing with Cork on the same day, meant that Waterford only needed to beat Antrim to qualify for the league final. The Antrim league game was set for Loughiel in the Antrim Glens on April 5. Waterford had requested that it be played in Casement Park in Belfast, but it was undergoing improvements and was unavailable. Loughiel is 40 miles further north and extended an already long journey. The cost of travel to this game for the County Board was £200. The team travelled to Dublin by car on the Saturday, took the train to Belfast on Saturday morning, and got by bus to the venue. To return home, they needed to catch the 6.40pm from Belfast to arrive home late that night. John Flavin recalls the impact of the travel arrangements.

'They were tough boys up there. We went up by car to Dublin and got a train to Belfast. We had to get back very fast for a train afterwards. We didn't even have time for a wash or anything... we just got on your clothes and off you went. Most of them used to hold the hurley left over right. They'd be hitting you with the hurley the whole time... keeping you occupied, as the fella said.'

Waterford were fielding a full-strength team and not taking the challenge of Antrim lightly. Paddy Downey, writing in the *Sunday Review* on the morning of the match suggested that *'the price in toil and tension should not be too high, for their opponents, Antrim, are not expected to put up more than a token resistance. Waterford are fortunate that the last hurdle on the way to their first ever league decider is little more than a practice run among the Glens'*. Antrim were trying a new goalkeeper, Eugene Collins, who was expected to have a busy day. For their part,

'59: AN EYEWITNESS ACCOUNT OF HURLING'S GOLDEN AGE

Frankie Walsh had to pull out due to illness and Dominic Enright, who was named as a sub, withdrew due to injury. An option which had yet to be deployed was the return of John Kiely. It was announced before the Antrim game that if Waterford qualified for the league final, the County Board would consider his recall from London.

The game in Antrim was the expected easy victory, with Waterford cruising to a 2-13 to 0-5 win. They also had two goals disallowed so it could have been an even wider margin. Waterford started out in control at defence and midfield but were sluggish in the forwards. As the scores were not flowing in the first 10 minutes, some switches were made. Tom Cheasty was brought out from full-forward to his customary position in the half-forwards. Troy went to the corner, Lacey to the wing, and Guinan into full-forward. The reorganisation paid dividends and by half-time Donal Whelan had scored two goals and Waterford held a comfortable lead of 2-4 to 0-3. In the second-half Guinan, Troy, Dunphy, Grimes and Lacey all picked off points before Donal Whelan bundled goalkeeper and ball to the net. The referee judged it to be a free out. Minutes later Seamus Power broke through and with defenders hanging from his arms, he opted to hand pass to the goal. He scored, but the play was brought back to award him a free instead. Neither of these incidents mattered much as Antrim only managed two points in the second-half and Waterford ran out easy winners by 14 points.

The scene was set for a Waterford versus Tipperary league final to be played on May 3. There had been some discussion as to where the final would be played. As Croke Park was still closed due to work on the new Hogan Stand, Limerick and Cork were possibilities. Even Thurles was mooted, but a neutral venue was more suitable. Nowlan Park in Kilkenny, 30 miles from Waterford and the same distance from Thurles, was the ideal compromise.

Leading up to the final, Tom Cunningham's arm was still in plaster and would remain so until after the match. There was a central council rule that only 20 players could be named in the squad. In the year leading up to 1959 John Kiely was working in London where he played for the recently formed Sean McDermotts club. Having missed the league campaign, he was brought back from London for the final and the successful championship run. This news meant that somebody in the panel was going to miss out. It was decided to wait until after the challenge match with Galway on April 19 to name the final squad. This game was played at the Athletic Grounds in Cork as part of the Cork City Juvenile Board Tournament.

Without Cunningham and Kiely, Waterford needed a full-forward. Larry Guinan had performed well in the position against Antrim, but that was only seen as a temporary fix. In a surprise move, Charlie Ware of Erin's Own was called up. He had not appeared in any of the league games, and he generally played in the half-forwards for his club, but his speed fit well with the team's style of play. Seamus Power was suffering from a cold but took up his place in midfield. Galway were seen as a sterner test than Antrim. They had represented Connacht in the Railway Cup semi-final on St. Patrick's Day and beaten the combined strength of Leinster. Twelve of that Connacht team were on show against Waterford, one of the missing three being Waterford native Jim Fives. While it was not a brilliant performance, it was satisfying to beat Galway, as both teams had an eye on their Munster Championship fixture in June and tried to stamp their authority on the other. They took the fixture seriously and both teams travelled to Cork on the Saturday to avoid fatigue.

Walsh and Troy opened the game strongly for Waterford, but Galway's Sweeney scored the opening point. Applying pressure to the Waterford defence, Galway were held off by cool play from Austin Flynn. The sustained pressure led to scores and a further goal and two points were added. Now Waterford took a turn to dominate play. Another good combination between Troy and Walsh led to a narrow wide. Immediately after though, Cheasty latched onto a pass and charged through to score a great goal. A team move started with a cross from Frankie Walsh and added to by a pass from Charlie Ware allowed Paddy Troy to score from a handpass. Within minutes Mick Lacey dropped a ball into the square and Cheasty again drove home a goal. Waterford, from a bad start, were now leading 3-0 to 1-5.

Galway pushed on again and took the lead after another two points. Waterford swept up the field in a terrific team move. John Barron made a relieving clearance to Jackie Condon who charged up field. He passed to Donal Whelan, who drew several defenders, but got the ball to Paddy Troy, and the Ballygunner man struck home a goal. The midfield battle was intense, but Waterford were on top, with Mick Lacey getting the better of Joe Salmon. In the minutes before half-time, Ned Power caught a ball in the square and made a long clearance to Mick Lacey who scored Waterford's first point of the day from long distance. Waterford were happier going into the break but a severe head injury to Charlie Ware, who was replaced by Michael White, was a setback. At half-time Waterford led 4-1 to 1-8.

Galway came out strongly in the second-half and an early goal pushed them in front. Condon was playing brilliantly and keeping Galway out, but Galway scored another point, while Walsh and Troy hit wides. Flavin came in to replace White and it coincided with an upturn in Waterford's fortunes. Frankie Walsh scored a point to equalise at 4-3 to 2-9. Walsh dropped a ball into the square and while Power restrained Duffy, Whelan scored a well taken goal. Waterford drove towards goal again, but stout defence led to a sending off for Galway's Burke. Waterford were now in command and Flavin and Troy scored points, and Whelan scored again from another Walsh centre. As the half-backs and forward pushed forward, points were claimed by Guinan, Morrissey and two from Walsh. Galway scored two consolation points at the end but Waterford had won convincingly by 6-9 to 2-11. Jackie

'59: AN EYEWITNESS ACCOUNT OF HURLING'S GOLDEN AGE

Condon was Man of the Match with a powerful performance in the half-backs, while John Barron's stylish hurling seemed to appeal to the Cork crowd.

The squad for the league final was named after the Galway game but the selectors were waiting to see how training went before naming the team. John Keane's aim was not just to sharpen their fitness but also to get them focused on their performance in those two weeks. In the end, Paddy Troy's 2-1 against Galway secured his place for the final, and Charlie Ware lost out to John Kiely, possibly suffering the after-effects of his injury in Cork.

Arrangements for the game were taking shape. Waterford and Tipperary were responsible for the ticket selling, gate supervision and stewarding at the final. Each supplied 35 volunteers and a special bus was run to bring the Waterford group to Kilkenny. In Kilkenny, the County Board played their part in making the game a spectacle. The goal areas of Nowlan Park were resodded and the grass was cut as short as possible to encourage fast hurling. Having qualified from different groups of the league qualifying competition, Waterford and Tipperary had not met in competitive action since the 1958 Munster final. A crowd of 21,870 made their way to the neutral venue of Nowlan Park in anticipation of a hard-fought game, but with the Munster and All-Ireland champions the clear favourites. There was great praise for the pitch, the general arrangements and choice of Kilkenny for the game. The pitch was deemed to be *'every bit as fast as Thurles'* and with sideline seating and the stand providing seating space for 10,000, the overall capacity of almost 50,000 made it the ideal choice of venue for the meeting of the south-east rivals. The rain which persisted from early morning to early afternoon may have put off some spectators from travelling but it did not impact the playing conditions.

From the throw-in Tipperary immediately sprang into attack but their first two forward waves were repelled by Jackie Condon. In clearing, he sent the ball to Frankie Walsh who passed to Donal Whelan. Whelan's shot brought a fine save from Terry Moloney in the Tipperary goal, and he parried the ball for a '70' as Paddy Troy rushed in. Phil Grimes sent the ball into the square, but it fell wide, as did Mick Lacey's effort after winning a tough clash with Theo English. Waterford had started well, despite not scoring, but, consistent with what was to come over the rest of the hour, the scoring opened with a free.

In the fifth minute Jimmy Doyle shot at goal but Joe Harney deflected the ball out for a '70'. Tony Wall lobbed the ball into the goalmouth and when Ned Power handled it on the ground, Doyle took his chance to score from the resultant free. Another Waterford attack saw Larry Guinan break past John Doyle. He passed inside to Tom Cheasty, who played in Kiely. His shot was again saved by Moloney at the expense of a '70' which was also put wide. In the eighth minute another free for Jimmy Doyle doubled Tipperary's lead. Donie Nealon followed this with two points from play, one an exceptional score from a very acute angle, and

craob iomána.

SRAIT COMÓRTAISÍ NA hÉIREANN

AR 3.30 p.m.   3 bealtaine, 1959.

port Láirge
v.
Tiobraid árann

Réiteoir: Stiopán Ó gliasáin (Luimneac).

clár oifigiúil.

Luac—3d.

Rúnaí.

"The Tipperary Star," Thurles.

1959 League final programme

'59: AN EYEWITNESS ACCOUNT OF HURLING'S GOLDEN AGE

Waterford were down by four points.

Frankie Walsh started to bring Waterford back into the game. When Byrne pulled down Whelan, he opened Waterford's scoring with a point from the free, only for Devaney to reply with his own pointed free. Walsh created the next opportunity for Kiely and when he was brought down, Frankie scored another free. His third point in-a-row came when Tom Cheasty was impeded as he ran for goal. At 0-5 to 0-3, Tipperary now unleashed an attacking onslaught that led to points from Devaney, Doyle, McDonnell, and Connolly within just two minutes. Six points behind, Waterford needed a goal, but despite having the ball in the net in the 24th minute, it was disallowed. Jackie Condon had cleared down the line to Larry Guinan. He first broke past John Doyle and then Tony Wall and had managed to take the ball from the right wing to the edge of the square. Guinan was tackled, but as he fell, he managed to pass the ball across the square for Paddy Troy to fist the ball to the net. The goal was disallowed as Troy was adjudged to have been in the square before the ball.

At this stage, Tipperary employed the tactic of pushing Donie Nealon into the forward line from midfield and this overload helped the Tipperary forwards to dominate the second quarter. In the last four minutes of the half, Tipperary piled on the pressure with a pointed free from Jimmy Doyle and one each from play from English and Connolly, bringing their haul at half-time to 0-12. Donal Whelan scored his only point of the game from a Walsh centre just before half-time to bring Waterford to 0-4.

As mentioned in almost every match report throughout the year, the Waterford full-back line invariably receive praise as a threesome for their ability to protect Ned Power in goal, mark the opposing forwards closely, and play stylish ground hurling, overhead strikes and effective clearances. Joe Harney, Austin Flynn, and John Barron were again praised for their performance in this game and managed to keep Tipperary goalless. This was the only game of the 18 played by Waterford in 1959 that had no goals on either side. From the half-back line forward, individual outstanding performances are recognised regularly but there is no doubt that the consistency of the full-back line added strength and confidence to the entire team. On this occasion, John Barron was noted as Waterford's *'star performer'* and Phil Grimes marking of Jimmy Doyle also earned individual praise. For Tipperary, Terry Moloney was deemed to have *'attained an entirely new rating in this game with a succession of spectacular saves in the first-half under exceptionally heavy pressure'*. Under the headline of *'Terry Moloney Was Brilliant'*, Mick Dunne, wrote in the *Irish Press 'in the distribution of bouquets let not the champions' goalkeeper, Terry Moloney, be forgotten. This former St. Flannan's College star outshone even the sparkling displays of his minor days with the daring saves he made when the Waterford forwards did succeed in breaking through'*.

'59: AN EYEWITNESS ACCOUNT OF HURLING'S GOLDEN AGE

The second-half was extremely low scoring with only three points added by each team. The Tipperary forward line which had been quite accurate in the first-half had three wides in the first two minutes of the second-half. John Kiely moved to centre half-forward and it helped Waterford towards a 20-minute period of attacking dominance. Even corner back John Barron, joined the attack with a spectacular 60-yard run. However, the outstanding Tipperary defence lived up to its reputation on the day and Waterford only managed a return of two points one from a free by Frankie Walsh - although he missed two others - and a point from play from Tom Cheasty, who finished a pass from Kiely. John Flavin replaced Paddy Troy and Bill Dunphy came on for the injured Seamus Power, but the game was slipping away.

It was 23 minutes into the second-half before Tipperary finally added to their score when Donie Nealon scored an effortless long-range point. This contrasted with the Waterford attack who only managed two points from play in the entire 60 minutes. Jimmy Doyle added another pointed free and in the last minutes Mick Lacey had Waterford's final score of the game with a long range free. Tipperary finished with a point from Nealon and the final score of 0-15 to 0-7 gave Tipperary an eighth league title.

John D. Hickey in the *Irish Independent* noted that *'the forwards were out of their depth against Michael Maher and his colleagues'*. Maher was variously described as *'majestic'*, *'outstanding'* and *'one of the best full backs playing'*. *'A real rancour crept'* into the game during the second-half. Waterford were seen to be the aggressor and two players in particular were lucky to avoid being sent off, being *'most fortunate to find referee Stephen Gleeson in most indulgent mood'*. Demonstrating a reticence that would not be seen in the modern age of instant replays, video analysis and studio pundits, the *Irish Independent* refused to name the two Waterford players and also allowed them to *'plead provocation'*. The number of frees bears this out as Waterford were awarded 20 frees in the 60 minutes, to Tipperary's 11. John Kiely and Tom Cheasty were accused of using questionable methods and Seamus Power was deemed lucky to escape the vigilance of the referee. Michael Maher was also described as *'performing with customary legitimate ruthlessness'* so there can be no doubt that it was a tough game, even by the standard of the time. One newspaper had Tipperary centre half-back, Tony Wall, as the Man of the Match and noted that *'Tom Cheasty was no worry to him, and Cheasty's approach to marking the top hurling star of 1958 left much to be desired. It only showed all the more the coolness and efficiency of Wall'*.

The reporting of the game from the Dublin media drew an immediate response in Waterford which is best captured in Pat Fanning's column, 'The Gaelic Arena', in the *Waterford News & Star* the Tuesday after the game.

'59: AN EYEWITNESS ACCOUNT OF HURLING'S GOLDEN AGE

'Tis amusing, indeed, to read one man in particular on the 'toughness' of the game, He thought the exchanges so nasty that at least two of our team deserved to be sent off, and escaped only because the referee was in a lenient mood, Well, well, for years we have been told that we lacked that very toughness, that it was the reason why we failed so often in the past. We lacked 'legitimate' devil; we were not ruthless enough – 'legitimately' ruthless, of course, Anyway, last Sunday, our lads showed a little devil and a meed of ruthlessness and 'our man' who had bemoaned the lack of these 'qualities' in our makeup, threw up his hands in holy horror, raised his eyes to heaven and pronounced that our 'devil' and our alleged ruthlessness were not of the 'legitimate' kind – born out of wed-lock, I suppose! Anyway 'tis true that we played a tough game on Sunday. This time we gave as good as we got, perhaps a little more. But the toughness was not all on one side; it could not be so, unless the nature and character of Tipperary hurling has changed overnight. Our lads – some of them, at any rate – were too open in their methods. We all saw what they were up to. But if you think that we were not on the receiving end of a little toughness – all of the legitimate brand, of course, then have a chat with any of our forwards.'

While this might seem to be a straightforward defence of the Waterford team's play, it equally acknowledges their aggressiveness. The column goes on to say that this tough play is a part of the game and hurling is the better for it. It is consistent with the prevailing view of hurling as a manly game which was a battle on the pitch, but which was forgotten afterwards. The Waterford and Tipperary players actually shared a meal at a hotel after the match where *'there was no bad blood between the players. They joked together and dined together and parted on Sunday night the best of friends'*. The News & Star article finished, after a description of the play, with the sentiment that *'Tipperary won well and thoroughly deserved their victory'*.

In planning ahead for the championship, Waterford may have been concerned about the lack of goals scored in the league final, but local opinion was that *'Waterford did in fact break through not once, but several times, but they did not score'*. This was attributed to the *'superb – and completely unexpected – performance of Terry Moloney in the Tipp goal'* who *'came to the rescue of worried backs and on at least three occasions, he saved 'impossible' shots which, had they gone home, would have changed the outcome of the game'*. He even saved three points which most goalkeepers would have let go. It seems clear that, for all the admiration of the legendary Tipperary defence, the Waterford team felt that they could use their speed and guile to break through and expected a better goal return against Moloney in their next fixture. At the other end of the field, Ned Power had only two saves to make and another consistent performance by the Waterford full-back line was generating a quiet confidence in the camp. While disappointed to lose a major final, they may have been happy to fly below the radar and allow the narrative

'59: AN EYEWITNESS ACCOUNT OF HURLING'S GOLDEN AGE

to be written by *'a biased commentator'* and use the defeat as *'the springboard to future triumphs'*.

The players recollections of the game bring up some interesting viewpoints. Larry Guinan recalls the intensity of the play.

> 'You had to try to be as tough as them. I remember that league final below in Nowlan Park. Jeez... there was a fifty-fifty ball going between Theo English and myself and there was no give from either of us. We just f***in' went for this ball and crossed together. It was often afterwards when we'd be playing for Munster maybe together and Theo and myself would have a chat and say "Do you remember the day in Nowlan Park?" Our bones rattled that day... honest to God. Both of us went down. We hit one another like two bulls hitting together and down we went... but we got up again and played on. That was a thing always stood in my mind and it was the same with Theo.'

Tony Wall remembers another tough match-up on the same day.

> 'I'll tell you one great story. The Rattler against Waterford in the league final was playing right corner-back against the Duck Whelan. The Duck was about five inches taller than Mickey and he was a big strong fella. There was a lot of speculation before the match as to how they would get on. Would Mickey be able to hold the Duck? So, when the match was over... Duck, I think he only scored one point... I said to Mickey "Jaysus, that was great stuff, how did you do that?". "Well, the first ball that came down." says he "I shoved the hurley up under his throat and his eyes popped out the same as a rabbit in a snare". There was a photograph on the feckin' paper showing it happening. He had the hurley across the Duck's throat with his head pushed back, so the poor old Duck wasn't going to get much with him.'

The overall effect of these individual battles was to stifle any free-flowing hurling. Donie Nealon made a realistic analysis of the game.

> 'In 1959 we had won the league against Waterford in Kilkenny. It was a poor dull kind of oul' match... there was nothing very great about it. Fifteen points to seven which would tell you a lot. Waterford were poor the same day. It was very tough. Poor oul' Cheasty, God rest him... he was playing very tough the same day. It was more tough against our backs, I think... it was a very dogged oul' game. There was nothing very free flowing in it.'

'59: AN EYEWITNESS ACCOUNT OF HURLING'S GOLDEN AGE

Typical of all these battles and adversaries, the heat of the situation has long disappeared, and the players love to reminisce on old times. After an article in *The Irish Times* in the build up to the Waterford v Limerick All-Ireland final in 2020, Larry Guinan received a surprise phone call.

> 'Who rang me recently… was Tony Wall. He was an army man, played for Tipp at was centre-back. He was good. He rang me there lately when this thing came on the paper there… on *The Irish Times*. He was very nice and wished us well in the All-Ireland. It was nice out of Wall to ring me.'

To complete the story of the league campaign, we return to John Flavin who, in addition to the disappointment of losing the final, lost his place in the team for the championship. Looking back on it, he raises some of the issues involved in picking a county team, but he is philosophical about the decision and its timing.

> 'I didn't start the league final. I came on for Paddy Troy… Lefter. He was a gas man. He was a corner-forward and was older than I was. At that time, there was six on the team from Mount Sion and Taylor O'Brien was a sub. They were all saying "Ah, there's too many Mount Sion on the team"… but we were winning everything. In club matches we beat Glen Rovers, Thurles Sarsfields and Bennettsbridge. We were the top club team in the country.
>
> 'That was the only change in the panel… I was dropped off the whole lot and Charlie Ware was brought in. They didn't let you know… they'd tell you nothing. At that time, if there was three city fellas on it, they wanted three fellas from the county… even though they mightn't have been the better hurlers. They wanted representation. There was always a Mount Sion and Erin's Own rivalry. The likes of the Condons… they were Mount Sion originally and they went to Erin's Own.
>
> 'You wouldn't feel like going back out playing again. But, sure, it's like everything else, c'mon get a grip of yourself… you'll be grand, you have plenty of time… you are only a young fella. You have plenty of time to get on the county team. The thing about it is, 1959 is the last time we won an All-Ireland. We are still waiting to win one.'

Once the league was completed, there was a hiatus before the start of the Munster Championship. This was usually filled by tournaments and challenge matches. For Waterford

Invitation to Dr. Kinane's funeral

clubs, the biggest tournament was held in Dunhill through the month of May. For the inter-county team, the Kinane Cup, a tournament featuring Waterford, Wexford, Kilkenny, and Tipperary, allowed for some testing games before the championship.

CHAMPIONSHIP PREPARATION

In preparation for the championship, Waterford had two games in June, a challenge against Kilkenny on the 11th and the Kinane Cup semi-final against Wexford on the 18th. In the challenge match Paudie Casey was tried at wing back against Kilkenny along with some other prospects for the upcoming championship. His performance in the three-goal win was good enough to secure him a place in the championship squad against Galway. He maintained that place throughout the year but was an unused sub in each of the championship games. In his report for *Waterford News & Star*, Pat Fanning, writing as 'Deiseach', descried the newcomers on the Waterford team, Joe Coady, Freddie O'Brien and Paudie Casey.

> 'The newcomers to the team last Thursday played well – better than that – and they helped prove the old theory that a new team, seemingly shot to pieces by late directions, can, by dint of spirit and whole-hearted effort, do splendid things. But, I hasten to add, there is a world of a difference between a mid-week challenge and a critical Munster Championship tie, and with the Galway game little more than a week away, the time for experiments has gone. The tried and true are our best bet for this test. After that, if things go wrong, as many new men as possible may be brought in and vetted for another year, and if things go right and we beat Galway, a little new blood here and there will suffice to give us that Munster crown.'

Freddie O'Brien was ever present in the Waterford squad through 1959 and was unlucky not to make it as the seventh Mount Sion player on the All-Ireland team. Freddie was a sporting prodigy at the Mount Sion club. Superbly fit, he has the distinction of playing on 10 teams in a single year, a feat he recounts himself.

> 'I won minor and senior county championship medals in the same year. I played on 10 different teams. I played the six club championships but once I had played senior I was gone out of junior. I played minor hurling, minor football and junior hurling for Waterford and I played on the factory league team at the time.'

The Kinane Cup was named after the donor of the cup, his Grace, the Most Reverend

'59: AN EYEWITNESS ACCOUNT OF HURLING'S GOLDEN AGE

Dr. Kinane, Archbishop of Cashel and Patron of the GAA. The trophy was sponsored by the Waterford Gaelic Field Committee. Games were usually played around Ascension Thursday and were often a good indicator of form approaching the championship. Erin's Own's Michael Dowling recalls that 'at that time there was no back-door system or under 21s so thousands would attend tournament matches. On the Thursday of the holy day, there could be six or eight thousand people in the sports field'. Dr. Kinane was a familiar figure at Munster and All-Ireland finals and regularly attended club matches in Co. Tipperary. Having played in his youth, he appreciated hard hitting hurling at any level. He had died in March of 1959. Due to his strong association with the GAA, several officials from each county were invited to his funeral, including Charlie Ware, Waterford's representative on Central Council.

These were attractive games. Kilkenny, All-Ireland winners of 1957, Tipperary, the team which succeeded them in 1958, the Waterford team who were destined to win the All-Ireland in 1959, and Wexford, who would take the title in 1960. Any one of them could beat each other and the crowds flocked to see attractive games on summer evenings. On the evening of June 18, Waterford played Wexford in the semi-final of the tournament. There was a strong breeze blowing which made the pitch play fast and a crowd of 8,000 attended in anticipation of a close game.

On the same day, Clover Meats played in the Leinster Factory League Final. They were a very strong team and had been Munster champions for two years. When the Munster competition lapsed, they received special permission to compete in Leinster. The Waterford County Board recognised the importance of that game so, surprisingly for the time of year, they released John Barron and Martin Óg Morrissey. Missing those two regulars, in addition to Tom Cheasty who was injured and Seamus Power who was on the bench, Waterford were weakened down the centre of their team. Wexford also had their trouble and started without Ned Wheeler, Bob O'Leary and John Kennedy as their car was late arriving at the ground. Once they arrived, Wheeler and Kennedy were introduced as substitutes during the game. Wexford player, Jimmy O'Brien recalls 'We never went anywhere only in a car. We used to have a great laugh', although the situation would have been less funny if it had been a Leinster Championship match.

From the start, Wexford hurled with confidence and the Waterford defence was immediately under pressure. The full-back line, with Joe Coady replacing John Barron, was reported to be *'hesitant and slow against fast-moving opponents'*. With the wind at their backs, Wexford ran riot and scored an incredible two goals and eight points before Flannelly set up Paudie Casey for Waterford's opening point. Nick O'Donnell, Sean Power and Tim Flood, who scored 1-3, were singled out for praise by all the newspaper reporters. With Wexford stretching their lead by a further point, Frankie Walsh made the half-time score a little more respectable, latching on to a pass from Charlie Ware and racing through for a well taken goal. Despite the wind advantage in the second-half, Waterford struggled to recover from 11 points down. They had most of the play and had several near misses. Frankie Walsh and Paudie Casey managed two further points each but they were matched by four from Wexford. The final score was Waterford 1-5, Wexford 2-13.

Waterford were still experimenting with their line-up just 10 days before their opening championship game against Galway. The team against Wexford included nine changes in personnel or position since the Kilkenny game one week earlier. There would be another seven changes for the championship match and this was a cause for concern. In the *Waterford News & Star*, 'Deiseach' wrote:

> 'Here we are within a week of the most important game of the year and the team lacks confidence, fitness and, above all, that spirit which is so essential to victory. The cause may be found in the uncertainty which surrounds the team. No man is sure of his place or where he may be played. We should decide on a team now and stick to it. This is not the time for rash experiments. To say the least of it, such tactics are dangerous.'

The Kinane Cup loss to Wexford led to some nervousness about the championship. In their eight games of the year-to-date Waterford had won four and lost four. They had scored as many as 7-9 against Kilkenny and conceded 10-11 against Cork, but they had beaten their upcoming opponents Galway in a challenge match in April by 10 points.

"

THEY WERE TOUGH BOYS UP THERE. WE WENT UP BY CAR TO DUBLIN AND GOT A TRAIN TO BELFAST. WE HAD TO GET BACK VERY FAST FOR A TRAIN AFTERWARDS. WE DIDN'T EVEN HAVE TIME FOR A WASH OR ANYTHING... WE JUST GOT ON YOUR CLOTHES AND OFF YOU WENT. MOST OF THEM USED TO HOLD THE HURLEY LEFT OVER RIGHT. THEY'D BE HITTING YOU WITH THE HURLEY THE WHOLE TIME... KEEPING YOU OCCUPIED, AS THE FELLA SAID.

JOHN FLAVIN

5

MUNSTER CHAMPIONSHIP

WATERFORD V GALWAY

Galway were playing in the Munster Championship for the first time in 1959 and were keen to prove their capabilities. They were holders of the Oireachtas Cup, a major trophy in its day, and playing as Connacht had beaten the best of Leinster in the Railway Cup semi-final. One effect of the decision was to remove the semi-finals from the competition for the All-Ireland, so the Munster champions would qualify directly for the All-Ireland final. Playing for Galway at the time was Jim Fives, a Tourin man who had lined out for Waterford in the early 50s. In books by John Scally, Jim recalled playing his native county.

> 'Really, for practical reasons, the only option was for me to switch to Galway, although I was very sorry not to be playing for Waterford anymore. The hardest part was the two times I had to play against Waterford, in the All-Ireland semi-final in 1957 and in 1959 when we played them in the Munster championship because Galway were 'in Munster' then. It's a very, very difficult thing to do to play against your native county.'

Michael O'Connor recalls Jim Fives and the Galway team of the time.

> 'Jim Fives was a year older than me. I played for Waterford with him. I knew him very well. He was very tall… a big man, and a great hurler. I think the fact that he was based in Galway, the transport was the problem. It wouldn't have been on. He used to drive his own old car up and down. My mother was a Meany… farmers from over in Tourin. The Fives, Shane and them, their mother was also a Meany. They are all related to me.

'59: AN EYEWITNESS ACCOUNT OF HURLING'S GOLDEN AGE

'My memory of Galway at that time is that they were slow and awkward... in my memory anyway. At that time, they were fairly rough.'

Just because Fives was a fellow Waterford man didn't mean that he wasn't involved in the rough play, as Larry Guinan describes.

'It was often Frankie would get into trouble because he was so small. When we played Galway in the semi-final in '57 in Croke Park, Jim Fives hit Frankie. He was an Army man and I remember hitting him... I always backed Frankie up because Frankie was a lovely hurler and he'd never look for trouble. I was a bit of a divil, I suppose. I always said that if someone hit Frankie, I'm going to hit them and that was about the size of it. I remember hitting yer man Fives that day. I hit him a belt of the hurley... a shoulder wouldn't do any harm at all.'

Bearing in mind that Larry is 5'8" and Fives was six feet tall, that was probably a pretty accurate assessment. In 1959, Fives was called upon to captain the Rest of Ireland against All-Ireland champions, Tipperary, whom he had played against in the All-Ireland final in 1958. Unfortunately, a serious back injury caused him to step down from senior inter-county hurling by the end of the year.

An attendance of 15,000 travelled to the Gaelic Grounds in Limerick, which was fewer than expected but the 'stay at home followers' must have been disappointed to miss out. The pitch was playing fast and there was a stiff breeze from goal to goal, but it did not seem to affect the Waterford team. With Power, Cheasty, Barron and Morrissey back, Waterford were described as 'confident, rampant, unbeatable' in the *Waterford News and Star*. Galway won the toss and decided to play against the breeze, a decision which backfired on them. Galway attacked right from the throw-in but shot a couple of early wides. Fives and Sweeney were repelling moves by Phil Grimes and Seamus Power. Lally, Egan and Sweeney combined well only for their attack to be foiled by a cool-headed John Barron. The deadlock was broken in an unlikely fashion. Seamus Power sent a high lobbing ball into the square from long distance. It deceived Ignatius Gavin in the Galway goal and went straight to the net. Gavin had a connection to Waterford hurling as his work for the Bank of Ireland brought him to Waterford where he lined out with Erin's Own.

Waterford struck again in quick succession. Frankie Walsh passed to Phil Grimes who offloaded to Seamus Power. He was in again and lashed the ball to the net. Morrissey, Guinan and Cheasty were dominating and soon Whelan was sent through and slipped

'59: AN EYEWITNESS ACCOUNT OF HURLING'S GOLDEN AGE

the ball nicely past the advancing Gavin for a third goal. Frankie Wash scored a free when Ware was fouled, but the pick of the points was from John Kiely who latched on to a huge clearance from Joe Harney. Within 10 minutes Waterford were 11 points up. Surely there was no way back for Galway?

Galway opened their account with a point and were putting the Waterford full-back line under pressure. Walsh and Sweeney exchanged pointed frees. Frankie scored two more frees, this time from play thanks to passes from Ware and Power. Condon playing brilliantly in the corner stopped another attack, but the next wave led to a point from Sweeney. Points for Cheasty and Guinan and a goal for Walsh, as the culmination of a brilliant movement involving Kiely and Whelan, followed. Frankie was everywhere and played in Larry Guinan for a goal before half-time. The half time score read Waterford 5-7 to Galway's 0-4, an unassailable lead that must have seemed unbelievable on the day.

Galway opened the second-half with a point, but the pattern resumed with points from Ware and three in-a-row from Walsh. Galway managed another point but when Whelan burst through for another goal, it was effectively all over. Mick Flannelly came on to replace Seamus Power but that certainly didn't weaken the team. He set Tom Cheasty off on a run and when he off-loaded to Whelan, the inevitable goal followed. Both teams kept trying to the end, but it was a 7-11 to 8 points win, a twenty-four-point victory which announced Waterford as a team to be watched for the championship.

Ned Power had a seemingly easy match but did have two fine high catches, after which he burst out through the defensive line and cleared. The full-back line was highly praised for keeping a clean sheet again, having done so in the league final. Jackie Condon played amazingly well when you consider that he broke a finger and a bone in his hand after 15 minutes, but played on for the rest of the hour. Jackie recalls his own injury but was more concerned about Charlie Ware.

> 'I broke a finger and a bone in my hand after quarter of an hour, but I played on. That was par for the course. We didn't go down if we didn't have to. When we were playing, if you put a fella down, you made sure he stayed down. Galway were a really tough team. Yer man Burke playing full-back for Galway that day creased Charlie Ware... hit him down behind the two ears, nearly killed the chap. Charlie was always very vulnerable.
>
> 'The thing about hurling when you were playing was, you went into the man... you didn't stand out. If you were any way off and you stood out, you had the hurley come up and you got a belt. Charlie was like that... he always stood out. He was all the

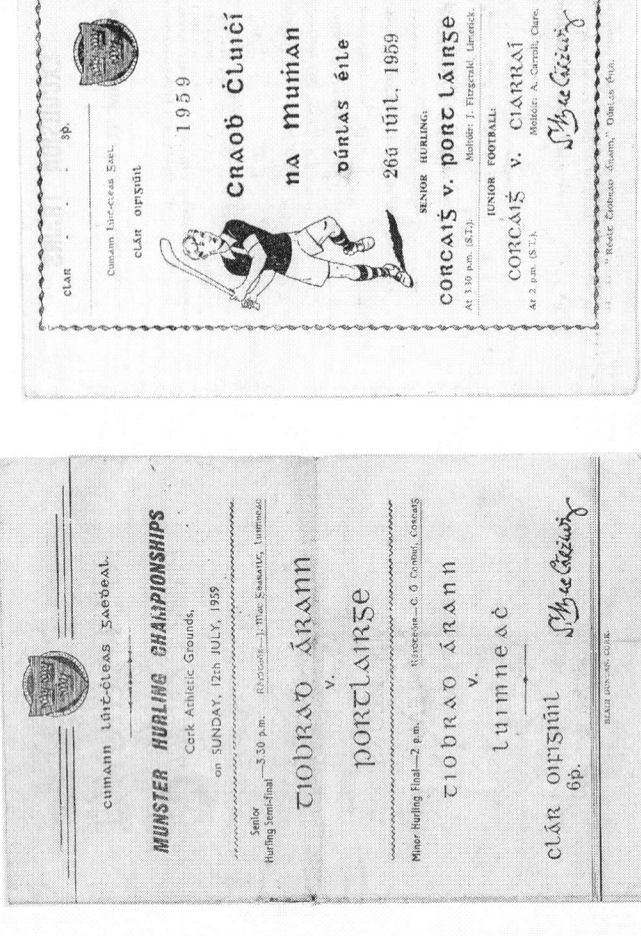

Programmes for Munster Championship matches versus Galway, Tipperary and Cork.

time getting hit but yer man creased him that day down behind the two ears. It was a terrible thing. He nearly killed him.'

PJ Lally of Galway had been in great form in the Railway Cup but was subdued by Phil Grimes. In the forwards, Cheasty outplayed Jim Fives and Walsh was too sharp for Jimmy Duggan. Frankie's 1-7 and Donal Whelan's haul of three goals were the strongest contributors of the seven Waterford scorers. The players were pleased if a little surprised with the size of the win. Larry Guinan recalls it as 'an awful trouncing', Martin Óg Morrissey that 'we hammered them' and Frankie Walsh remembered that 'while we were confident, we didn't expect to beat the Oireachtas title holders by 7-11 to 0-8'. Always confident against Galway, Martin Óg Morrissey described how the team approached the game.

'I was never afraid of playing against Galway. I always thought we were a better team. They had no answers to the type of hurling we played… fast open hurling. They couldn't play that type of hurling at all. I never really worried about Galway. We met them a couple of times and beat them a couple of times, including the All-Ireland semi-final in 1957. The plan wasn't just to go for goal. You took your score when it came. If you got a chance of a point you took it… if you got a chance of a goal you took it.'

It was an experiment to include Galway in Munster and one which lasted for 10 years. In that time, they only won a single game. Following a hammering by Cork in 1968, they returned to the Connacht Championship.

WATERFORD V TIPPERARY

The build-up to the Munster semi-final was coloured by the outcome of the league final and the previous year's Munster final. Reporting of that league final in the national press indicated that 'the Waterford attack was represented as a collection of useless tools who never looked like getting through an impregnable defence'. Waterford fans would have considered that a harsh assessment and would have been more inclined to the *Tipperary Star* view which heaped praise on the Tipperary goalkeeper Terry Moloney, who saved the day on the rare occasions the Waterford forwards broke through the exceptional Tipperary defence.

More controversial though, was the allegations that Waterford had used 'unsporting tactics' and that they needed to 'learn the difference between hard, legitimate tackling and rough play'. This was countered in the Waterford press by reports of 'Larry Guinan, who had the handle of a hurley driven into his throat in the Tipp goalmouth'. No doubt there was tough and even illegal play on both sides and these points were used as motivation for the upcoming Munster semi-final. Frankie Walsh felt that it had been a learning opportunity, and they could beat Tipperary.

> 'We had played them in the league final, lost by 15 points to seven, but we learned from it. We knew we had the beating of them after that... if we could keep the ball moving. And that's what we did. We kept the ball flying, and they had no answer to us.'

Donie Nealon, while acknowledging Waterford's poor performance in the league final, felt that championship form might be more telling.

> 'In the first round of the Munster Championship Waterford beat the living guts out of Galway. They scored 7-11 and against us only a month before they could only score seven points. I don't know why. In the first round in '59 we only beat Limerick by five points... 2-9 to 1-7. Waterford had much better form than we had in the first round.'

Another perennial topic was the choice of venue for the match. The previous year, Waterford had travelled to Thurles to play Tipperary in the Munster final, and it was announced that the next time the teams met in the Munster Championship, other than a Munster final, that Tipperary would travel to Waterford. Now that a Munster semi-final was in prospect, Tipperary claimed that the agreement or arrangement covered only first round games. As it had not been recorded and the Munster Council minutes made no reference to it, this led to the council fixing the game for the Athletic Grounds in Cork. Once again, this added fuel to the fire of an already important fixture. Larry Guinan was happy with the choice of Cork as a venue.

> 'I loved the Athletic Grounds in Cork because the Cork people somehow had an oul grá for Waterford and any Cork people who'd be there would be shouting for Waterford. They hated Tipp of course. They hated them with a vengeance... everyone hated Tipp somehow and you can't blame them because they were an arrogant crowd.'

The small attendance, 27,236, shows that Tipperary supporters did not travel in strength, guided by the recent league win and Tipperary's comprehensive victory in the 1958 championship. It was still fresh in Larry Guinan's mind, but so was another incident in the same week.

'59: AN EYEWITNESS ACCOUNT OF HURLING'S GOLDEN AGE

'When I was talking to Tony Wall, I said to him I'll never forget the game in '58 when we played ye and ye gave us an awful hammering. I crashed the van the following week... an awful accident. I was travelling for AB Services. I came out of Cahir to go through Clonmel and back to Waterford. A truck came across the road, and I hit the truck... I went under the truck actually. I was stuck in the van, and I couldn't get out. There was batteries came in on top of me so I was stuck under the truck. Yer man in the truck came over and he said, "What happened?". I said, "Will you get me out please?" Jaysus, the big f***in' dope he didn't get me out. There was a fella came upon the accident and pulled me out of it. Yer man was to blame... he came right across me!'

Austin Flynn recalls that he couldn't avoid questions about the match and the best he could do was supply a quick answer.

'I remember the day before our championship match with Tipp in 1959... reigning All-Ireland champions. I had been out boating and as I came ashore two hurling fans approached me and enquired how we would fare against Tipp? So as to keep the discussion short I said we would beat the sugar out of them... end of conversation.'

In some quarters it was taken for granted that the All-Ireland champions would make short work of Waterford. Tom Cheasty recalled that 'many Tipperary fans didn't travel expecting another landslide for their team'. Once at the ground, attention was focused on the game, with Larry Guinan crediting Pat Fanning's team talk with firing up the team.

'We were really heated up for it. Pat Fanning had a few words with us... he had the hair standing on our head before the game.'

Seamus Power was initially concerned about the weather as it wasn't a day that suited the fast ground hurling that Waterford preferred.

'We had a bit to prove, and it was payback time. They gave us a trouncing (in 1958) and we were determined we would try to do the same to them. It was a very wet day, conditions which normally don't suit Waterford hurlers and a strong wind.'

'59: AN EYEWITNESS ACCOUNT OF HURLING'S GOLDEN AGE

Donie Nealon even questioned whether it was a day for hurling.

'That was the stormiest day I ever played a hurling match in. Really, it was so bad that the match should not have been played.'

To get a flavour of the weather conditions and the efforts made to get to the match, this extract from Phil Fanning's memories of 1959 is as instructive as it is entertaining:

'It was a day I will never forget, It had been decided that I would travel to the game as a pillion passenger on my father's fine NSU scooter piloted by uncle Larry, himself an experienced purveyor of motorised two-wheel transport of many years on a BSA Bantam. We splashed our way towards Cork through the gale force wind and driving rain, stopping for some respite in the gateway to a big house on the outskirts of Midleton, that I can identify to this day, before resuming the journey. It had been well flagged that one Corporal "Skinny" Fanning of Morrisson's Road, garrisoned in Cork, had secured the rights of the bar for the day in the boat club adjacent to the pitch and that a big stock of Large Bottles had been secured for the thirsty Waterford supporters. That was the first stop on arrival with the cousin duly keeping his promise in the significantly less than luxurious surroundings. With my driver suitably nourished we made our way to the ground for a further soaking.'

While the weather was obviously a factor on the day, John D. Hickey, writing in the *Irish Independent* described it as 'fine but blustery conditions', but almost immediately contradicted himself by blaming Tipperary for contributing to their own defeat 'by electing to play against the wind of near gale force which blew from the City end'. Team mentors advised that if Tony Wall won the toss, they should take advantage of the wind, but the decision was left to the players and they chose to play into the wind, presumably believing that even if they fell behind by half-time, they could catch up in the second-half. They would also have had the memory of their league final defeat to Wexford in 1956 when they ran up a 15-point lead by half-time only to turn into the wind and lose by 5-9 to 2-14. Unfortunately for Tipperary, Waterford 'were a hurling tornado whose great power in defence, grandeur at mid-field and scheming in attack' meant that there was no way back in the second-half. Jimmy O'Brien of Wexford weighs in on this strategy.

'We were at a match in Croke Park that day. I can't remember who, but I wasn't playing

'59: AN EYEWITNESS ACCOUNT OF HURLING'S GOLDEN AGE

(note – it was the Leinster final between Kilkenny and Dublin). I remember somebody giving the score and nobody could believe it. They got a run on them. It had happened with Wexford a few years before. I was at the match. Wexford were way behind at half-time and then they started getting early scores in the second-half and they got going. Tipp didn't die… they kept pegging away points, but Wexford were getting goals easy enough. I always felt it was better to play against the wind in the first-half. You are expecting to get away to a great lead if you have the wind and often it doesn't happen. Whereas if you can improve a bit, you have a better chance in the second-half. It should be a big advantage, but fellas don't settle quickly in matches.'

Despite the weather advantage, Waterford's 'display of supercharged hurling' merited the big lead they took in the first quarter, an impressive 5-1 to no score 'in that spell of sheer brilliance'. The opening goal came in the first minute when Terry Moloney stopped a Seamus Power centre but was slow in his attempted clearance. He was overpowered by the Waterford forwards and the ball was forced into the net by Larry Guinan. Frankie Walsh then scored the first of his two points of the day. Mick Burns, Tipperary's right half-back had received a gash on his shin in a challenge match against Kilkenny the previous Monday evening. He had four stitches removed from the injury and this was enough to slow him down and allow Frankie to dominate him. Walsh won a lot of possession, and each time sent the ball towards the square in search of goals. In response to Frankie's point, Tipperary launched an attack, but McCarthy shot wide. Waterford immediately reapplied the pressure and gained a 21-yard free. Frankie Walsh's shot for goal was parried, but Charlie Ware, positioned on the post got his hurley to the ball and flicked in into the net. Billy Kelly recalls the detail.

> 'Johnny Kiely stopped the ball from going wide and passed it across the square and Charlie buried it for his first goal.'

When Larry Guinan sent one of the many Frankie Walsh centres to the net for the third goal, the floodgates opened. Seamus Power even scored the next goal from close to centrefield, with Moloney surprisingly beaten. Further goals came from Kiely, when Moloney was again slow to clear; Whelan, after a mistake by full-back Michael Maher; and another when Moloney pulled on a centre when he should have caught it. Austin Flynn was effectively a spectator at the other end of the pitch.

> 'As far as I remember, Tipperary won the toss. There was a gale of a wind there that

'59: AN EYEWITNESS ACCOUNT OF HURLING'S GOLDEN AGE

day and Tipperary decided to play against it. Liam Devaney, a great centre-forward, was on me. The match wasn't long in, to my recollection, and we'd a goal went in. That was okay. Then, there was another goal went in. And another… and another. Devaney started scratching his head and looking at me. He was obviously thinking *Jesus, this is a nightmare. Is this really happening?* So, I was conscious of that, and I was trying to keep a straight face, as if it was par for the course, like. But I was as surprised as he was. What happened really was that Waterford had a great open style of hurling and it just happened that everything that day clicked. We were about eight goals up at half-time and walked the match. The fans I met at the Harbour thought I was a prophet.'

When asked about it in recent years, Theo English said that when the ball passed him from the puck out, he closed his eyes because it was going into the net below. Despite the Waterford goals, the Tipperary defending was its usual intensity and injuries were inevitable, the first being to Martin Óg Morrissey.

'I got a belt on the head in the first half hour, and I had to go off. Dr. Shelly put a bandage on me. I was sitting on the sideline for a while coming near the end of the first-half hour saying to myself *If only they could score another goal… if only they could score another goal… if only they could score another goal.* I came back on in the second half hour.'

This explains the unusual pattern of substitutions. Mick Flannelly was brought on for Morrissey when he was injured in the first-half, but Martin Óg was reintroduced for Seamus Power in the second-half. In turn, Seamus Power was brought back on when Charlie Ware was badly injured. Charlie's sister, Mary, remembers 'we went to Cork to see them play Tipp and it was thronged. Charlie was very lucky he didn't get his eye out from John Doyle. He was tough… John Doyle. Head injuries and cuts. That's all they got… plenty of it. Bruising and cuts and you name it'. In this game, John Doyle was supposed to be marking Larry Guinan and Larry recalls the ongoing battle between the pair.

'Those three goals were on John Doyle. I was delighted. He made no bones about it… he hated playing on me. When we were All-Ireland champions, we played the Rest of Ireland… Christy Ring, Wexford men, Tipp men, Galway men, and everyone were on it. We drew with them. I upended Doyle on his arse. I know I was small, but I remember the two of us were charging together and I got under him and up over my shoulders... and down on the ground I threw him. In fact, in '59, he hit Charlie Ware an awful belt and he always said after "I thought it was f***in' Guinan I was going for".'

I scored three goals that day so that was a very special one for me, understandably. Three goals against the All-Ireland holders... days like that don't come around too often. We just ate them without salt... we were bursting with confidence. Everything we were capable of producing as a team came out if us that day."

One of Larry's goals was straight from the training ground.

'We trained hard for that game, and I remember Frankie Walsh... he was brilliant for a small little man... we'd be above in the field and the two of us would be there. Frankie and myself trained crossing the ball from one side to another. In '59, I remember he crossed this ball to perfection right in front of me and all I had to do was stretch out full length and tap the ball into the net. We trained to be as perfect as we could. We had gone through this in training, and it worked to perfection on the day. Charlie Ware was in on it too. I remember looking over at Frankie and putting up the hurl... it was a really fantastic score.'

These rehearsed patterns were essential according to Austin Flynn as Waterford were no match for Tipperary in physical size.

'The Waterford team was in full flight with the ball flying. Frankie Walsh is a small man... Mick Flannelly is a small man... Larry Guinan too. They are small on the outside but inside they are about seven foot tall. They are condensed, I think. They had the ball flying that day and everything clicked.'

One of those small men, Mick Flannelly, emphasised that movement was the key to scoring goals.

'The team played as a team. You had no individuals. Everything was teamwork. There was no sense at that time in giving high balls into the full-forward line. They were only a disadvantage. The balls went in on the ground. Moving about... that's the way the game should be played.'

'59: AN EYEWITNESS ACCOUNT OF HURLING'S GOLDEN AGE

Tipperary were not without chances in the first-half. A great shot by Jimmy Doyle just before half-time was brilliantly saved by Ned Power, and Donie Nealon also missed a goal chance when he tried to rise the ball in front of the goal rather than pulling first time. A final point from Power brought Waterford to an incredible 26-point half-time lead of 8-2 to 0-0. Frankie Walsh regularly recalled the most famous story from half-time.

> 'When the score was sent to Michael O'Hehir to announce it during his broadcast at another venue, he looked at it in disbelief and asked to have it checked. When he announced it, half the country didn't believe it. He told the story that they rang the guards' barracks down in Cork. They got somebody, by bush telegraph or something, to give them the score. I met Michael a few weeks after and I said to him "If it was the other way around, would you have announced it?" and he started smiling.'

Tipperary made some changes at half-time. Pat Stakelum, who had come out of inter-county retirement for the game was introduced. He replaced McDonnell and took up the centre half-back slot, while Tony Wall moved to centre-forward. Wall had received an accidental blow to the head at the end of the first-half and was now bandaged to cover the two stitches in the cut. The goalkeeper, Terry Moloney, was replaced by Roger Mounsey, but that was seen as 'tantamount to shutting the stable door after the horse had bolted'. That was an unusual move, but even national news commentators felt that Moloney had been 'grievously culpable' for three of the goals. Local Tipperary commentators went further, complaining that up to five of the goals could have been saved. Most reports point to the lack of cover afforded to him by his normally dominant full-back line, but it seemed clear by half time that 'his confidence was completely gone'. Donie Nealon remembers half-time.

> 'I often think of going out of the Athletic Grounds at half-time. I don't know what kind of dressing-rooms were there... we didn't go into a dressing-room anyway. There was an old showgrounds behind it. We went out into an open shed, but we didn't know whether to go back out or not!'

Jimmy Doyle recalls the shock in that Tipperary dressing-room.

> 'I'm not sure of the exact score at half-time but it was all over. Even the people who were at the match couldn't believe what they were seeing. We went into the dressing-room and Kieran Carey, John Doyle, Michael Maher... they didn't want to come back

'59: AN EYEWITNESS ACCOUNT OF HURLING'S GOLDEN AGE

out for the second-half... said it was a waste of time, to put in a few subs.'

John Harrington's biography of John Doyle takes these facts and dramatizes the story.

> 'The only sound in the Cork Showgrounds horse-shed that the Tipperary team were using as a dressing-room was the gusting wind that whistled and huffed through every crack and crevice. The damp air was heavy with the earthy smell of mouldering straw and horse manure, but that was a small discomfort compared to the deep shame every man in a blue and gold jersey was feeling. Doyle sat on a bale of hay and stared glaze-eyed at the ground with his head in his hands. All around, his teammates too looked like men who had come home from work to find their house burned to the ground.
>
> 'Terry Moloney was just as upset, and his voice cracked as he broke the silence in the room. "I'm not going out for the second-half. I've had enough". Leahy looked hard at his goalkeeper but could see there was little point in arguing with him. The young lad was broken and there would be no fixing him just like there would be no saving the match.'

In the Waterford dressing-room, Pat Fanning urged the team on, as recalled by Philly Grimes.

> 'They had a fine side... Tony Wall, Jimmy Doyle, Mick Burns and so on, but we ran them off their feet and with the big wind at our backs led by 8-2 to no score at half time. The wind counted, of course, but Waterford were so good and so hungry that day that nothing could have stopped them. Pat Fanning, the chairman of selectors, told us at half-time that if we lost that lead, we could never hold our heads up again. So, we never got complacent... got another goal just after half-time and romped home. It was a day Tipperary don't like to be reminded of.'

Into the second-half, Tipperary, taking advantage of the wind for the first time, hit two wides in the first minute. They must have wondered if they would ever score but finally after 10 minutes Donie Nealon and then Jimmy Doyle pointed to start their comeback. A nice move involving Donie Nealon, Jimmy Doyle and Tony Wall resulted in a goal from the Tipperary captain which brough the score to 8-2 to 1-2 halfway through the second-half. Such was the mammoth task ahead of them that Tipperary needed to score a goal every two minutes to catch up. However, Waterford had not stopped playing and immediately after Tony Wall's goal a breakaway move by Waterford led to their ninth from Larry Guinan. It was a 30-yard shot which Roger Mounsey appeared slow to move towards. When Jimmy Doyle scored a goal, it was counteracted by a point from Cheasty and soon Tipperary were almost out of time. Early in the second-half, Seamus Power also had to be replaced due to injury and Morrissey was reintroduced to replace Power. In Power's absence, the Tipperary midfield of Theo English and Jimmy Doyle, who had switched with Donie Nealon, came strongly into the game. This led to Power also being recalled with Charlie Ware making way for him, having scored a creditable two goals. Tipperary tried different combinations in the second-half. Larry Guinan remembers that 'they made a few changes and Martin Óg was on Tony Wall in the second-half… Óg hurled him out of it'. Jackie Condon was also having a great game and he relished the challenge. 'I was marking Jimmy Doyle that day and they took him off me and they sent up Liam Devaney on me. Then they sent up Donie Nealon. That's one of the best games I ever played… I had a marvellous game. They put three different fellas on me that day and I couldn't go wrong.' For his part, Donie Nealon appreciated his opponents' play.

> 'I loved playing on Jackie Condon. He was a very fair player. You could have a good tussle with him. I was centrefield, and we weren't up to it at all against Power and Grimes. They were some centrefield… the pair of them. It was bad enough to be playing against them but to be playing against the bloody wind. They just overwhelmed us. Very soon in the second-half, Waterford got another goal.'

Frankie Walsh proudly recalled his contribution. 'I was the only forward to score in the second half.' In the final minutes, another goal from Nealon and three more points were tagged on by Tipperary but, on the day, it was 'Waterford ever the masters and Tipperary plodding pupils'. The game ended on a final score line of Waterford 9-3 to Tipperary's 3-4 and it rang out across the country as a sign that Waterford's easy dismissal of Galway was *no flash in the pan and the MacCarthy Cup is theirs for the taking for the second time ever*'. Obviously, that was not a sentiment shared in Cork or by Kilkenny, who had managed their own victory in the Leinster final overcoming Dublin by just a single point in a 2-9 to 1-11 win.

This victory put Kilkenny straight into the All-Ireland final and the summer was now mapped out ahead of Waterford. Eddie Keher who was still only a minor player at this stage of the season said, 'We were playing a club match on that day, and we could not believe our ears when we heard the final score as we came off the pitch'. In later years Eddie interviewed Tom Cheasty and quoted him as saying that 'he really had very little to do, that most of the scores came from their full-forward line who were able to get a step ahead of the Tipperary backs to whip the ball to the net'.

Press reaction was intense. In the opening of their report on the match, the *Tipperary Star* pointed out that *'It must be admitted straightaway that on the day Waterford were a far better team and that wind or no wind they would have won anyway'*. This was a sentiment shared in the *Irish Independent* which commented that *'Yesterday's result may seem like an extraordinary one; but it was as merited a triumph as I have seen and if the game were to be replayed, I have no doubt that the winners would again prevail'*. The *Tipperary Star* analysis went into forensic detail and noted that *'speed was the vital factor'* and *'Waterford were yards faster'* making *'Tipperary look slow and even ponderous in comparison'*.

There seems to be a consensus that the few Tipperary players who could not be blamed for their defeat were John Doyle, Jimmy Doyle, and 36-year-old Mickey Byrne throughout; and Tony Wall and Pat Stakelum in the second-half. Jimmy Doyle seemed to have the beating of Jackie Condon who was carrying an injury, but the strong support play of Condon's teammates limited Doyle's effectiveness. Michael Maher's loyalty to the cause was praised as he had returned from a business trip to Holland which the *Tipperary Star* described as *'almost a fortnight away in a foreign country, in which the heat was very great and he was moving around from one place to another all the time, he could not be expected to be at his best on Sunday'*. The *Waterford News and Star* felt this was *'clutching at straws'* and *'please do not attempt to tell me that a comfortable plane journey from Holland rendered Michael Maher less effective as a hurler'*. On the Waterford side, Phil Grimes joined Frankie Walsh in receiving most accolades for their performances in which they *'touched great heights'*. Grimes was particularly praised for *'his over-head and ground play'* and Walsh for *'another faultless display'*. Writing in *The Sunday Press* the following week, Seamus Power analysed the tactics of the contest.

> *'It has been suggested that we had a secret tactical plan, but I can honestly say that such a suggestion is without foundation as could be seen clearly from our displays in the provincial series this season. True we realised that the present hard condition of playing pitches called for fast ground pulling in order that we could exploit to the full the speed and dash of our wing forwards, but we were not unmindful of the fact that Tipp themselves have a wonderful tradition of ground hurling. As a matter of fact, despite what some may say about the wind advantage in the first half, I believe it was our clear-cut superiority in this aspect of the game which was really the decisive factor.'*

Considering the score, it was difficult to fault any Waterford player, particularly the members of *'as crafty an attack as has been seen in a long time'*. Larry Guinan's three goals while being marked by John Doyle achieved the highest score of the day but rarely has there been a game of such importance in which a team featured six different goal scorers (Guinan, Ware, Walsh, Power, Kiely and Whelan). It led to the unusual honour of the entire Waterford team being jointly conferred with the *Irish Independent* Sport Stars of the Week award.

Little was made at the time of the heavy schedule that the Tipperary players had endured in the lead up to the game. While a cursory review of the fixture list shows a seven-week gap between Tipperary's Munster Championship opener and the semi-final, the players schedules were much more hectic than it might appear. Take Tony Wall for example. On the Sunday before the Waterford match, he led Thurles Sarsfields in the Mid-Tipperary Championship against Boherlan. As Boherlan also fielded Mickey Byrne and Musha Maher, it was definitely a tough game with *'hard-pulling exchanges during the closing stages'* reported. The following night he played for Tipperary in a challenge match against Kilkenny, and on Tuesday he reported for training. Two weeks before the match he had played in the Buttevant Tournament final, where Wall and a number of his fellow county players played two games in one day for club and county. Some of the Tipperary players had played up to five games in 10 days, including the Waterford match. Player welfare was on the agenda and the Tipperary county secretary had repeatedly suggested that tournament games be cut to the minimum and that the county only take part in the established ones.

The same would have applied to the large Mount Sion contingent in the Waterford squad. Mount Sion had played in the Cork Churches Hurling Tournament on Easter Sunday and reached the final of the Dunhill Hurling Tournament on June 4 having beaten Faythe Harriers of Wexford along the way. Add in a Dr Kinane Cup match in June and their challenge match against Kilkenny 10 days before the Munster semi-final, and it can be seen that the Waterford players carried a similarly heavy load. The intensity of fixtures did not let up once Waterford had qualified for the Munster final. On the Friday after the Tipperary match, Mount Sion played a challenge match in O'Kennedy Park, New Ross against Geraldine O'Hallorans. On the same evening, the Carrick On Suir Tournament began with a game featuring the hosts against Austin Flynn and Donal Whelan's Abbeyside; and the following Tuesday Erin's Own, featuring Jackie Condon and Charlie Ware, played Holycross in the same tournament.

Typical of his robust approach to the game, Tom Cheasty would not have thought twice about such a schedule.

> 'I used to train hard anyway. I'd get up in the morning and I might run about three miles. That is even when I'd be training normally in the Sportsfield for big matches.

'59: AN EYEWITNESS ACCOUNT OF HURLING'S GOLDEN AGE

That three miles would be before I would milk the cows. It's more organised now and has been reduced to say Tuesdays and Thursdays only for training. They don't go down every evening to the field like we used to do... that is every evening that we could go. Every evening of the week... Monday to Friday, I did it. That was when I was in my prime.'

In an indirect reference to this game, Cheasty, in that same interview, chose his greatest opponents as Wexford's Willie Rackard and Tipperary's Tony Wall stating that he *'wouldn't like to distinguish between the two'*. Apart from a few instances, particularly the League final, Wall had similar respect for Waterford. 'They were a very fine team. I have good time for Waterford, except that Cheasty acted the b*****ks a few times.'

Jimmy Doyle knew many of the Waterford players as Munster teammates and was aware of the danger they posed.

'We were well beaten. It was a bad loss, especially as All-Ireland champions, but people should remember... that was a fantastic Waterford team, the kind that if they got a run on you at all they'd take you apart... so many great hurlers. Philly Grimes, Seamus Power, Larry Guinan, Tom Cheasty, Austin Flynn, Martin Óg Morrissey, Frankie Walsh... oh gosh, they all played for Munster! Take Philly Grimes... in my book he was the greatest utility hurler of all time. He could play corner-back, wing-back, midfield, centre-forward, wing forward, full-forward... he could play anywhere, he was gifted.'

In the recent series of books titled *Game of My Life*, both Larry Guinan and Tony Wall recall this match as the most memorable of their career. That is no surprise for Larry as he *'always liked beating Tipp, more so than anyone else'* and even chatted to Tony Wall about it when they spoke in December 2020.

'The game against Tipperary below in Cork, that was my favourite game playing for Waterford. I was very pleased. That was a great win, it was great to beat Tipperary. I got three goals against John Doyle... a big, brute of a fella. When I was talking to Tony Wall that was one of the things, he said to me "There's a game I'll never forget, the hammering ye gave us in '59. I'll never forget it".'

Tony is serious about this claim and has recalled it in his own book, *Hurling*, the *Tipperary*

'59: AN EYEWITNESS ACCOUNT OF HURLING'S GOLDEN AGE

Game of My Life book, and again in an interview for this book.

'I gave the game of my life in that book as the 1959 Munster Championship match. It was eight goals and two points to nothing at half-time. That was the most traumatic game of my life. In a lot of ways, it was the most memorable. The game that hops into my mind all the time is that feckin' game in Cork. There was no other match in my whole life that was anything like that. It has me traumatised since.

'When I'm telling the stories, the five All-Ireland wins fade into the background and the f***in' thing that I could dream about is that game below in Cork. I won the toss. I had been playing with Tipperary in 1956 when we played Wexford in the league final. We were in Croke Park, and it was a similar wind down the field... and we bombarded Wexford in the first-half and we were leading by 15 points at half-time. We turned over for the second-half... Nicky Rackard broke through a few times and there was a couple of goals gone... and we got hammered. So, I decided we will hold these fellas for half an hour (laughs)... Jaysus, 8 eight goals and two points!

'Our goalie never made a mistake. Waterford played a brand of hurling that day that I have never come across. They were flying and the ball was hopping their way every time. I remember the ball flashing across the square and Larry Guinan coming in and Larry flicked it... and the ball ended up in the net. We were (laughs)... ah Jaysus, we were hammered!'

The *Waterford News and Star*, while celebrating a famous Waterford victory, also went to some lengths in describing the sportsmanship of the defeated Tipperary team.

'The in-born sportsmanship of the Tipperary lads, who in the bitterness of defeat congratulated their conquerors and wished them well. In the hotel later, they went further. Micky Byrne, as amiable and affable a character as you could wish to meet – off the field, of course – was loud in his praise of this Waterford team and he recalled that he had told Seamus Power after the League final, that Waterford would be a major force in the championship. Micky warned of the dangers still ahead and warned against "spoiling the whole thing by not going all the way". Tony Wall, John Doyle, Liam Devaney all echoed this sentiment. Jimmy Doyle went on record by saying that Phil Grimes was as fair and as good a man as ever he stood against on a hurling field.'

While it may seem that the teams shared a meal, Donie Nealon explains that it was mere coincidence. 'Sometimes the same hotel would be booked after the match for the two teams. You'd be in different rooms. The hotel in Cork that we used go to at that time was the Victoria.' Larry Guinan confirms that 'The only time I remember sitting down with those fellas was when we'd be playing for Munster'.

The game was very tough in this era but, even allowing for the press-speak and the importance of keeping up a public façade, there did appear to be genuine mutual respect between all of the top players of the day. As the game itself had been played in a sporting manner, it also put to bed the questions from the league final of Waterford's inadequacy in the forward line and their rough play further out the field. With a first win over Tipperary since 1943, Waterford had qualified for a third successive Munster final and could now focus on the upcoming challenge of Cork. Without a game that day, several of the Cork team were present. Jimmy Brohan, their corner-back recalls 'I was at that match. They looked a very good team that day. They were actually'. It gave them food for thought for a Cork team who would usually be very confident of beating Waterford. Larry Guinan summed up the belief that was growing in the camp. 'It was a great team… we were all great friends, great comrades.'

Some souvenirs of the game still survive, and Frankie Walsh's son, Peter has the prize possession.

> 'I actually have the sliotar from that game. Frankie pocketed the sliotar at the final whistle and he wrote the score on it. He gave it to a great friend of his, Fr. Brendan Crowley a good number of years ago, but when Frankie died, he gave it back to the family. He had mounted it on a little wooden plinth. It is actually very light… it is like a juvenile ball. It's after drying out a lot over the years.'

WATERFORD V CORK

All Munster finals are eagerly awaited but with Cork having beaten Clare by 21 points, and Waterford having seen off Galway by 24 points and Tipperary by seventeen points, this game had the makings of a classic. The *Irish Independent* opened their match report by reflecting that the *'good name of Munster hurling, much damaged in a series of one-sided contests this year, was well and truly redeemed in a rip-roaring senior provincial decider'*. A record attendance for a Munster final of 55,174 was present in Thurles. This presented record gate receipts of £6,728. Even with the price of a seat at 4-/6, demand was huge from all locations. This was more than twice that of Waterford's semi-final, and more than 5,000 higher than the previous record of 50,071 at the Tipperary-Cork final of 1954.

They came from all directions, and by any means. Brendan Fullam, in *Captains of the Ash*,

'59: AN EYEWITNESS ACCOUNT OF HURLING'S GOLDEN AGE

while interviewing Frankie Walsh, recalled that he travelled from Wexford to Thurles on the back of a motorbike, a 160-mile round trip. CIE planned extra trains to Thurles not just from Waterford and Cork, but from Dublin, Kilkenny, Wexford and other neutral counties. The internal CIE document listing the timetable of special trains running from Waterford to Thurles shows departures at 8.25am, 8.45am, 9.05am, 9.25am, 9.45am and 11am. The 90-minute train journey from Waterford Station cost 9 shillings for a second class return fare. From Cork, there were also six special trains (8.30am, 8.50am, 9.10am, 9.30am, 9.45am and 10am) costing 15 shillings and thruppence for a second class return fare, considerably more expensive for a journey that only took five minutes longer than the one from Waterford.

Confidence was high in the Cork camp. That feeling was reflected in Martin Óg Morrissey's memories.

> 'I wouldn't say we would have been favourites to beat Cork. Cork were Cork and they were superior to everybody else, no matter what other county you were playing against. They had that air of arrogance. When you have that it stands to you. "We are better than the rest"... that was their motto. I suppose we thought we would beat them alright, but we wouldn't be saying we were going to hammer them... because you wouldn't ever hammer Cork at that time. You'd beat them by a couple of points and that would be it... or they'd beat you by three or four goals maybe.'

A lot of the discussion in the build up to the match focused on the result two years earlier, but Ned Power remained confident.

> 'We had no fear of Cork. We had beaten them in the 1957 Munster final, and we knew they had Ring, but we weren't a bit afraid of meeting them.'

In fact, the emphasis on Ring, while understandable, Martin Óg Morrisey feels it was something of an insult to the Cork team.

> 'Cork without Ring at that stage were formidable. It wasn't just left to Ring alone to win matches for Cork, although he did do that. They had some great players. Willie John Daly in '57 was reckoned to be the best centre-forward at that time. I think I made my name that day. They had fair oul' players at that time. I think Paddy Barry reckoned he was better than Christy. I found him tough to play on anyway.'

John Barron and Ned Power in action in the Munster final

♦

Munster final team: Back - Larry Guinan, Jackie Condon, Ned Power, John Kiely, John Barron, Mick Lacey, Seamus Power, Phil Grimes. Front - Tom Cheasty, Donal Whelan, Charlie Ware, Frankie Walsh, Austin Flynn, Martin Óg Morrissey, Joe Harney.

♦

'59: AN EYEWITNESS ACCOUNT OF HURLING'S GOLDEN AGE

Tom Cunningham also brings attention to Paddy Barry, one of the stars of the day and a Munster regular.

'I was corner-back in '57. I'd say my most dangerous opponent was Paddy Barry from Cork. He was a very skilful hurler… he wasn't interested in any physical stuff. He was the opposite to Christy Ring, who was skilful but more competitive.'

One of the other stars of the Cork team, Jimmy Brohan, lacked ideal preparation for the final.

'I worked in Dunlops. They were hopeless… no good. As a matter of fact, I remember that particular Munster final. I was on night shift the week of the final and you know you wouldn't be in form at the weekend after a week of night shift. I looked to get a facility to come off night shift for the week… they wouldn't give it to me. When I started working first in 1953, there was over 2,000 people worked there, so you can imagine they didn't want to be giving benefit to anybody.'

As in the semi-final, Cork won the toss and gave Waterford the advantage of playing with the slight breeze and with the sun at their backs. Waterford started well and after two minutes, in a mass of bodies around the goal, the ball was kicked to the net by John Kiely. Two minutes later Christy Ring opened Cork's score with a point from a free and before another two minutes had passed, they took the lead with a Paddy Barry goal after good work by Eamon Goulding. The game was hard fought and extremely close. Tom Cheasty levelled for Waterford only for Cork to immediately take back the lead with a Paddy Barry point. With a pointed free from Ring and another point by Barry, the Cork lead had been further extended to 1-4 to 1-1 after 15 minutes. A *'hurried discussion between the Waterford mentors'* was noticed by the press box. At this point, it was acknowledged that Paddy Barry, with 1-2, was winning his battle with Martin Óg Morrissey. Phil Grimes was brought back to centre half-back, with Morrissey moved to right half-back and Mick Lacey replacing Grimes in midfield. The move worked perfectly and the commentary was universally positive. John D. Hickey wrote in the *Irish Independent*:

'The transfer of Grimes was as successful a switch as I have ever seen. The Mount Sion man, who had been little more than adequate at midfield, stepped right up into the hall of fame of great centre half-backs as he proceeded to play a previously rampant

'59: AN EYEWITNESS ACCOUNT OF HURLING'S GOLDEN AGE

Paddy Barry out of the game. He dealt just as capably with Ring when the latter went out to the mark him in a desperate effort to save the game. I have seen more great men in the centre half-back position than in any other berth, but Grimes yesterday was as good as the very greatest who ever enchanted me in that onerous post. He was here there and everywhere – in short, unbeatable, and was without question the dominant figure of the game as he hurled back wave after wave of Cork onslaughts, with mighty clearances and an obvious relish that seemed to suggest that he wished more work would fall on him.'

Mick Flannelly described the reason the switch was so successful.

'Paddy Barry was running riot at centre-forward, so they brought back Philly Grimes on him. The big advantage Philly Grimes had on him was that he was quicker than him. Paddy Barry was very quick and would get to the ball first, but Philly Grimes was quicker than him. That's the basis of the game... get to the ball first.'

Behind him at full-back, Austin Flynn had the best view in Thurles of Grimes' play, but he revealed it was a braver performance than most people realised.

'Phil Grimes was my hurling hero, and he was so modest about his performances. I will never forget his display when he moved to centre-back in the Munster final against Cork in Thurles in 1959. We had been under fierce pressure in the full-back line and were almost in a panic trying to contain the Cork attack. There are some performances that stand out... that was one of mine. I always remember playing behind Philly Grimes that day. I remember in the hotel afterwards. I had my leg inside in the bath and Philly had his thumb under the tap. Philly actually had a broken finger that day in the second-half, but he didn't know it until it was over. My ankle was all swollen. I was looking at him and saying God, a fella who gave an exhibition of hurling and he was so meek and mild about it afterwards. "Jaysus, Philly, you had a marvellous match today". "The bloody hand was giving me trouble," he said. He had a broken finger, but he kept going.'

Grimes' contribution was summarised in glowing terms by his Mount Sion teammate, Larry Guinan.

'59: AN EYEWITNESS ACCOUNT OF HURLING'S GOLDEN AGE

> 'My outstanding memory of the Munster final was the game that Philly Grimes had. He was magnificent, that's all I could say. It was the best game I have ever seen any hurler play in all my life. He was absolutely outstanding... he won the game for us.'

The man himself was typically modest in his recollections of the game.

> 'It was some game. Ring was back... and I started on Terry Kelly at midfield. But with Paddy Barry playing havoc at centre-forward, I was moved back to centre-back. After a while, Ring and Barry were having a few words and they duly swapped places so that now I had Ring to contend with. I am reminded so often of my display that afternoon that I begin to wonder if I ever played well in any other match.'

It was no surprise when he was awarded *Irish Independent* Sports Star of the Week for the performance. The changes led to a Waterford resurgence in the second quarter, and they swung the game around. A shot from Seamus Power beat goalkeeper Seanie O'Brien from 30 yards. Kiely and Ring traded points. Waterford's pressure was telling. In the 22nd minute from a free by Morrissey, John Kiely scored his second goal of the game. This contribution from a senior member of the panel inspired some of the younger players like Larry Guinan.

> 'Cheasty was outstanding at centre-forward and when he got a ball, two or three men went to him. He could distribute it to Frankie or Flan or Tom Cunningham or big Duck. They were all a threat. John Kiely, to me, was the best hurler we have ever had. John was an outstanding full-forward.'

In the closing seconds of the half, Phil Grimes took a '70' which led to Frankie Walsh scoring a point. Having outscored Cork by 2-2 to a single point in this period, Waterford went into half-time with a 3-3 to 1-5 lead.

After such an intense period of play, the second-half opened slowly and was without a score until a Frankie Walsh point after seven minutes. Again, points were traded with an immediate Ring response and Kiely scoring from an acute angle in the corner. Another period of Waterford dominance ensued with three points by Frankie Walsh and one from Tom Cheasty achieved with only a Mick Quane point in return. With nine minutes remaining, Waterford led comfortably by 3-9 to 1-7, when Christy Ring pointed from a 21-yard free. Three minutes later Paddy Barry scored another 21-yard free and when Christy Ring scored a brilliant goal the difference was reduced to the puck of a ball. Cork were exerting huge pressure, but a resilient Waterford defence was holding on by its fingertips. John D. Hickey described that *'there followed a period of breath-taking escapes and near misses, particularly in the Waterford goal area, that simply beggared description. I was so enraptured, captivated by the splendour of the fare, that I quite forgot to make a solitary note during the wondrous finish'*. In these closing minutes Paddy Barry, in an attempt to equalise, *'broke through on his own and unleashed a pile-driver, but the eagle eye of Waterford goalie, Ned Power, followed its flight and in a twinkle the ball was on its way outfield and out of danger'*. This wasn't until after he gave nervous Waterford supporters an anxious moment as he brought the ball right across the goalmouth before clearing it to safety. Seán Óg O' Ceallacháin, writing in the Evening Press, claimed *'the closing stage produced as pulsating a finale as one could hope – 10 minutes of pathos, drama and excitement'*. Ned Power thrived on the action.

> 'I'll always remember that glorious last 10 minutes. The shots were flying in, but I was stopping every one of them. I wasn't saying it out loud, but I was just thinking *Hit them again. Keep them coming. I'll stop them!* That period stays in my mind more vividly than even the All-Ireland final."

His ability under a dropping ball was remembered by Michael O'Connor.

> 'Ned Power was outstanding in 1959. He was brilliant on a high ball. His weakness would have been a low ball along the ground. He controlled it and knew when to run forward and was seldom caught out with that. He was an exceptional goalkeeper… he was absolutely outstanding against Cork in the Munster final. He gave an example to the defence that day and he was a very confident guy coming out for a high ball.'

Larry Guinan was called into action to support the defence.

> 'They were under fierce pressure. I was up in the forward line, but I remember being back in the back-line at the end of it. The ball was at our end of the field at it was fierce pressure. I don't know did I catch a '70' or two at the time and there was some pressure under the dropping ball. I remember a '70' coming in and I was after coming back down around the back-line. I remember Ring shouting "C'mon, this is it now… c'mon,"… egging on his men while the '70' was being taken.'

When I asked Jimmy Brohan about the intensity with which Christy Ring closed out

'59: AN EYEWITNESS ACCOUNT OF HURLING'S GOLDEN AGE

the game, he replied with a smile that *'he never did anything else'*. Meanwhile, on the sideline, the selectors were discussing another change, with the possible reintroduction of Michael O'Connor after a two-year absence due to illness. O'Connor hadn't even returned to playing with his club at this point in the year; his first appearance for Cappoquin would be against Aglish Geraldines on August 9; so he was understandably nervous.

> 'My memory of that match is that it was very close, but Waterford did very well. The selectors wanted me to go on and play during the match. They could see I was in good fettle, trained, strong... and I had put on a bit of weight. I had something back here in the back of my head saying Don't play. I suppose I was a bit nervous. I was fit alright but mentally I was afraid. The doctors had warned me don't overdo things. I was mad to play but I couldn't that particular day. They were pushing me to go on... I should have gone on, but I didn't... I was afraid. Thank God, I was lucky I was strong. I was after putting back on weight and I was back to health.
>
> 'It was then I realised that thinking back to end of the match in '57 I was burnt out completely. I just felt so exhausted at the end of that game... and then to lose it. Vincent Morrissey, the builders in Dungarvan... he was a big GAA fan. He told me that I was sitting on his knee in the dressing-room after the match and that I was crying like a child, but I don't remember that. I was a bit afraid... I didn't say it to anyone. My brother-in-law was a doctor, and he was warning me about playing again. And yet I started to play, and I started hurling again... and I loved it! They wanted me to go on in the Munster final. They were pushing me. In hindsight, I should have gone on.'

After his Man of the Match performance, Philly Grimes was delighted but exhausted.

> 'After the match I remember falling face downwards on the pitch. Ring turned me over, pulled me up and brandishing his hurley in my face, said "Go the whole way now"... and he meant it. I think they didn't trust us to go all the way. Quite simply, Ring was the greatest.'

Terry Dalton celebrated with his fellow selectors.

> 'That was a wonderful achievement. Any time you beat Cork, you know what it means to another county... it was the thrill of a lifetime. It was wonderful to be a selector and to win but it was tough being a selector and losing.'

'59: AN EYEWITNESS ACCOUNT OF HURLING'S GOLDEN AGE

In his *Evening Press* column, 'In the Soup', Joe Sherwood found Waterford:

'A beautifully balanced team and quite the best in first time ground pulling and striking I have seen this season. Waterford's well merited victory can be traced to the superiority they held round about the centre of the pitch. In no match I have seen for a long time has there been such well-planned positional play as I saw yesterday by the Waterford halves and centre field pair.'

After the excitement of the game, the stadium emptied, and Phil Fanning describes how the players joined the supporters in the walk back to the Square.

'An amazing sight in those days was that of the players walking, togged out… through the throngs on the way to the field. The dressing-rooms in Thurles at that time, as in most grounds throughout the land, were menial to say the least, and teams togged out in the upstairs of a café cum restaurant called The Glamorgan House on the ground end of the square… from where they walked to the pitch, as transport would be unable to make its way through the crowds.'

This led to an encounter for Jackie Condon that was as memorable as the game itself.

'In those days you had to walk down into Thurles after the match because the crowd blocks up the road so you couldn't get up and down in a car. I was walking down just as I was on the field in my hurling gear… even my boots. I was walking along anyway and down comes Ring shouting "Oi, oi… come here you b*****d". He said "You done me". Paddy Barry used to go down the left side of the field and Ring would move away off to the side. He'd draw you… and Barry would lob the ball across. I twigged it and managed to get in the middle of them and caught the ball going across. Ring reckoned I destroyed their plan. Anyway, he said to me "Come into the pub with me… we might never meet again".'

'We went into the pub on the way down from Thurles and yer man put two pints of Cidona up in front of the two of us. I never remember drinking anything as nice after a match. He was giving out all the time. He was a lunatic… an absolute fanatic but I suppose that's what made him so good. If you were marking him, he was whinging and going on… he was really caught up in the game. What you had to do with him was give him a whack of the f***in hurley and leave him think about something else.

'59: AN EYEWITNESS ACCOUNT OF HURLING'S GOLDEN AGE

He was a fabulous hurler, I must say.

'The crowd was delighted. They wanted us to drink Guinness and they were putting up pints... we left a counter full of drinks. We couldn't drink all that, but I must say the two pints of Cidona went down a treat. The barman was delighted because the crowd was pouring in. They saw us coming in and came after us. That's a very vivid memory I have. He was still giving out in the pub... 'If this didn't happen... or if that didn't happen, if you didn't do that...". "Jaysus, will you go away and drink up the pint" I said, "and relax for a bit". He was over the top. He was hurling when he was 39 and I was only 21. He was very skilful. He used to practice all the time. I was a good hand at pulling in the air. You don't see it anymore in hurling, everyone must pick up the ball. I could hit the ball off the ground and drive it nearly the full length of the pitch. You'd see a clearance and you'd drive the ball up through it. Ring would never pick the ball up if he didn't have to. He'd hit it on the ground, and he'd flick the ball up off the ground into his hand. He had all sorts of little tricks and ways of doing things. He was stocky and strong... hard to shift him. He was very determined. I used to pull in the air with him and when the two hurleys clashed... Jesus, you would know you were after clashing. The power in his wrists! You would know you were in a tussle.'

This game was a repeat of the 1957 Munster final in which Waterford beat Cork by 1-11 to 1-6. On that occasion, Christy Ring was absent which, in the mind of many Cork supporters, left an asterisk against the result. Tom Cheasty took satisfaction in proving Waterford's strength.

'Back in '57 Christy Ring was injured and the Cork fellas were saying "You beat us but we hadn't Christy Ring". Christy was back for '59 but Joe Harney played him very well that day. Christy didn't have a great input to that game at all, for some reason. At least we beat them with Christy and all. We put paid to the idea that we wouldn't have beaten them if they had Christy Ring.'

Larry Guinan is consistent with his teammates and agrees that the significance of Ring's presence on the team.

'To beat them with Ring playing... that was the thing. Ring was some man. He was the best of all time as far as I'm concerned. There'd be no one go near him... he was something else.'

'59: AN EYEWITNESS ACCOUNT OF HURLING'S GOLDEN AGE

Having been beaten by Tipperary in the 1958 final, the performance of the Waterford backs against Ring was bound to be scrutinised. Joe Harney was singled out for particular praise for his *'careful policing'* of Ring. Jimmy O'Brien of Wexford was more direct in his assessment.

> 'I was at the match. Ring was fouled every time the ball came up the field, I thought. Joe Harney was on him… he was wrapped around him every time the ball came up.'

Always dangerous, *'the Cork fans still seemed to think that Christy would emerge from his state of hibernation, forced upon him by when he moved out to the '40' late in the game, he only provided Grimes with a further chance to copper fasten his position as man of the match'*. Although Ring was 38 years old, it seems almost unbelievable that Jim Sherwood in the *Evening Press* would suggest, mirroring similar comments from others before the Railway Cup final, that Ring *'should now hang up his togs'*. Yet, despite all of this solid Waterford defending, Ring followed up his 4-5 in the Railway Cup final with 1-5 against Waterford, more than half of his team's 2-9 total.

This was Joe Harney's finest hour. He gained his opportunity with injury to Tom Cunningham but his performances through the year cemented his spot at corner-back. While Tom was redeployed in the forwards, he acknowledges Joe's contribution.

> 'I was at all the matches in 1959… I wasn't a sub. I didn't actually play any full match in '59. I was on the panel. Before that I was playing regularly at corner-back. When I got injured, Joe Harney took over. Joe was corner-back for the full campaign and deservedly so. I went in as a sub in the Munster final.'

While Tom was injured early in the year, Joe also picked up injuries as he went through the season. He was lucky to be able to play the Munster final, as he recalled variously to Matt Keane and Kevin Casey of *WLR FM*.

> 'I had a really sore ankle after an accident on the farm. I was trying to rescue a cow I think, and really, I was not fit to play in the match, but I decided not to tell anyone for two reasons. People would have said that I was afraid to tackle the likes of Christy Ring again, and secondly… I did not want to lose my place on the team. I could hardly walk, and I had to take my shoe off as we travelled to the game. I didn't say it to anyone in the car. It was a very hot day and when we met the Cork traffic we were only barely crawling into Thurles. I was inside having the cup of tea and I was tossing

'59: AN EYEWITNESS ACCOUNT OF HURLING'S GOLDEN AGE

in my head *Will I play or won't I play?*... because the leg was fairly sore. I decided I'd play it. I said it to nobody.

'I put the pain behind me for the hour and we won the game 3-9 to 2-9. I was in agony, but at least I had my Munster medal, which meant a lot to me and my club. I paid for it the following week. I was at home for about three days in terrible pain... you wouldn't go to a doctor in them times. William Lenihan, he was our secretary, came up to see me and he seen I was only on one leg. About two hours after, he arrived back. 'You have an appointment,' he said, 'with Doctor O'Driscoll, for tomorrow at two o'clock, so I'll bring you in.' He wanted to keep me in hospital, but I wouldn't stay. He put a plaster on me, gave me two crutches and said to come back in six weeks. Six weeks was almost the All-Ireland. I had badly torn ligaments, he told me. I cut it off myself on the 15th of August.'

The intensity of three tough Munster Championship games was beginning to take its toll. The Mount Sion trio of Phil Grimes, Martin Óg Morrissey and Seamus Power all missed their club game at New Ross in the week following the Cork game. Joe Harney spent three of the five weeks leading up to the All-Ireland final on crutches. Tom Cheasty had also gone into the game having received treatment for an injured heel, an injury which was exacerbated in the match. He was required to wear a special boot for a few weeks but was confident of making the All-Ireland final.

Seamus Power was pleased with the progress towards their end goal.

'The All-Ireland was the ultimate goal. The Munster final was a stepping-stone towards that end. A great achievement certainly. We had beaten Galway, Tipperary and Cork to get to the All-Ireland final so our credentials were well marked but nevertheless the All-Ireland eluded us in '57 by one point and we were determined that '59 would be our year.'

Waterford already knew their opponents for the final. As the Leinster Championship had been completed two weeks previously, and there were no semi-finals, the final was to be a repeat of the 1957 final against Kilkenny. In the Leinster final at Croke Park on July 12, Dublin were leading by two points in the last few minutes. Johnny McGovern recalls those crucial few minutes.

'We were lucky to beat Dublin in that match. It was nearly over, and they were leading. We got a cut-in, a sideline ball up in the half-forward line. They were leading by two points. Usually, half backs would go up and take a cut-in to leave the forwards push up. I remember taking it and I hit a low ball across the square. Two players clashed together and let it through them. Sean Clohessy was standing behind them and he doubled on it for a goal. Dublin should have won that match, in fairness... we got the goal in the last minute.'

Dublin's Jimmy Gray recalls it from his point of view.

'We were unlucky not to be in the All-Ireland final in 1959. There was a goal in the five minutes of extra time that were played. We were leading by two points but there was five minutes of injury time. Kilkenny got a line-ball... Johnny McGovern cut it across, and Sean Clohessy pulled on it to the back of the net. I pucked out the ball and the full-time whistle was blown. We played well in the second-half in particular. Typical Kilkenny... you can expect something like that.'

As Kilkenny had already qualified for the final, there was a large delegation present at the Munster final to evaluate their competition. Among those spotted were county chairman Nick Purcell, former chairman Bob Aylward, selector Paddy Grant, Jim Langton, centre-back Mick Walsh, Bob Hicks, 'Builder' Walsh and others. No doubt they were impressed with Waterford's performance but were confident of repeating their win of 1957.

> AFTER THE MATCH I REMEMBER FALLING FACE DOWNWARDS ON THE PITCH. RING TURNED ME OVER, PULLED ME UP AND BRANDISHING HIS HURLEY IN MY FACE, SAID "GO THE WHOLE WAY NOW"... AND HE MEANT IT. I THINK THEY DIDN'T TRUST US TO GO ALL THE WAY. QUITE SIMPLY, RING WAS THE GREATEST.

PHILLY GRIMES

6

ALL-IRELAND FINAL

In the build-up to recent All-Ireland appearances, particularly in 2008, the Waterford County Board received criticism for allowing too much access to the squad, particularly at open training sessions. In 1959, training sessions were generally open all year round, but Larry Guinan recalls the hype surrounding the build-up to the '59 final.

> 'Oh God... it was a huge thing for the people of Waterford. There would be people up to training. I thought that people should have been let in more, but the training sessions weren't open. I thought, to be honest with you, they shouldn't lock the field and hold children out. I love to see children running out on a field. It's great... looking for the ould hurleys when they break and everything.'

This was a real attraction for those in Waterford, but Martin Óg Morrissey points out the difficulty for those supporters in Dungarvan.

> 'There wouldn't be a vast amount of people (in Walsh Park for training leading up to the All-Ireland) but the same people would be up there every night. From time to time, you'd get an influx of fellas that would come in from out around Butlerstown... Dunhill and places like that to have a look at you. As regards coming from Dungarvan to Waterford... no way. They would now, but that wasn't in it in our time. There were no cars in '59, only bicycles.'

There was also less media intrusion at the time and Frankie Walsh was relieved to have some calm in the build-up.

Tickets for the All-Ireland final

TELEPHONE NO. WATERFORD 4463.

BISHOP'S HOUSE,
JOHN'S HILL,
WATERFORD.

1st SEPTEMBER, 1959

My dear Mr. Fanning,

    I write to ask you to be good enough to convey to each member of the Waterford Senior Hurling Team and to all associated with them, my sincere good wishes. It is a source of great joy to me that the young men of Waterford County and City have qualified to play in the All-Ireland Hurling Final at Croke Park on Sunday next 6th September.

    I appreciate the enormous amount of effort and energy that has gone into the preparations for this great occasion, not only on the part of the members of the Team but on the part of many others who have given their time and services so generously. And I am especially proud of the fine Christian and manly spirit that inspires the players.

    To each and all I send warmest good wishes for a most successful All-Ireland Final at Croke Park on Sunday 6th September, 1959.

    I remain, My dear Mr. Fanning,

    Yours very devotedly in Christ,

+ Daniel Cohalan
BISHOP OF WATERFORD AND LISMORE

Mr. Patrick Fanning,
Chairman,
Waterford County Board, G.A.A.,

Bishop's letter of support

'59: AN EYEWITNESS ACCOUNT OF HURLING'S GOLDEN AGE

> 'It was more radio because there was no television. RTE was started in 1961 or '62 or something. They would come down from RTE Radio but there wouldn't be as much build up as such. We used to go to the Grand Hotel in Malahide... it was far away on the other side of Dublin, so we had no visitors... and it was quiet. There wouldn't be the same build-up as there is now.'

Warm-up matches were sought with several counties in the lead up to the All-Ireland final. A game planned against Limerick for Thursday August 13 had to be cancelled. The sponsors of the tournament in Limerick requested a change of date to Sunday 16 which would have attracted a larger crowd but, due to the programme of county championship games already scheduled for that date, the switch could not be accommodated by the Waterford County Board.

Another possibility was a challenge against Dublin to be played in Waterford on August 23. Dublin had been narrowly beaten in the Leinster final and were considered to be ideal opponents. However, on August 13, news came through that the Dublin squad were unable to travel for the game. It seems the Walsh Cup match between Dublin and Kilkenny had been switched at short notice from Sunday 16 to Sunday 23. The commentary in the *Waterford News & Star* exclaims *'I wonder why!'...* as Kilkenny had now secured the ideal warm up for the final.

The next port of call was Wexford, with whom the Waterford County Board had a very good relationship. Unfortunately, Wexford already had a full schedule of county championship games arranged for the 23rd. Tipperary were briefly considered as opponents, but it was acknowledged in the News & Star that there were no 'friendly' games against Tipperary.

> 'Officials feared that this might be too strenuous a venture two weeks before the big day. Tipp, naturally enough, are very anxious to have another go at Waterford before their American tour. We will, I am sure, be only too happy to oblige them – after the final. All our men need just now, apart from training, is an outing together to get used to each other and to test our teamwork. They do not need games of the competition or "needle" variety. And a game with Tipp just now would of its very nature be a "needle" affair in which there would be no punches pulled by either. A battle with the Premier County early in September, and at Waterford, would be a tremendous attraction on the eve of Tipperary's departure for New York.'

It would seem that yet another bruising encounter with the toughest team in the country was too much of an injury risk at that late stage of preparations. Last on the prospect list were

'59: AN EYEWITNESS ACCOUNT OF HURLING'S GOLDEN AGE

Cork. They were contacted and invited to visit Waterford for a game on August 23rd. It seems that Cork would like to have participated but their own county championship prevented them from sending a representative side. County Secretary Declan Goode worked with his counterpart in Cork, Con Murphy, but to no avail. This meant that Waterford went into the All-Ireland final on September 6 without having played a match of any kind since the Munster final on July 26, a wait of six weeks.

As the game got closer, the clamour for tickets increased. With three weeks to go before the final, club members throughout the county received a circular from Declan Goode informing them of the number of tickets to which their club was entitled and inviting applications for those tickets before August 21. Applications received after that date or those not accompanied by money were to be disregarded. Each club was entitled to seven tickets per affiliation, divided as follows: 4 at 15/-; 2 at 7/6; and 1 at 10/-. The 15-shilling tickets would have been for the Hogan or Cusack Stands and the cheaper tickets for other parts of the ground. Larry Guinan recalls that 'People were always asking for tickets. There would be pressure there for tickets alright. I don't know what you'd get. I think we got six at the time but I needn't tell you where they'd go straight away… they were gone. You would have people asking you and it was annoying.' Larry's solution to the pressure was simple. 'I always liked walking out the country… I always loved the country, I'd always stay away from the town.' Members of the 1938, 1948 and 1957 teams also received an allocation of two tickets each. Albeit a long shot, the *News & Star* also ran a competition for 16 readers to win tickets for the final. Entrants were asked to write about their hurling *'moment to remember'* in a letter to the editor.

In the build up to the final, the newspapers had standard items that they rolled out each year. The most common was the 'pen pictures' of each player showing a head and shoulders photograph and a short biography. Another reliable feature was to look at the players in their working life. The Waterford team were involved in a wide variety of jobs. Mick Flannelly and Charlie Ware were printers; Donal Whelan and Ned Power were teachers; Tom Cunningham and Austin Flynn were Co. Council Officials; Frankie Walsh, Martin Óg Morrissey and Mick Lacey were factory workers; Philly Grimes, Jackie Condon and John Kiely were in the building trade; John Barron was a clerk; Tom Cheasty and Joe Harney were farmers; Larry Guinan worked in a garage; Seamus Power was a post office official; and Michael O'Connor worked in and later managed his family business. He remembers, 'I left school at 17 so I was doing physical work in a factory. Most of the lads were working young'. The *Irish Independent* described O'Connor's occupation before the 1957 All-Ireland as an exporter, surely the most exotic job title for a hurler in the 50s.

'59: AN EYEWITNESS ACCOUNT OF HURLING'S GOLDEN AGE

Some jobs were more intense than others and farming was notoriously time consuming, although Tom Cheasty refused to let it interfere with his training, as his wife, Kathleen remembers.

> 'We worked long hours. Tom would be up at six every morning but he couldn't understand why any farmer would be out working at 8 o'clock at night. He'd have it all done by then... be in to have his tea and see the 6 o'clock news. Then he'd be off to training.'

Humphrey Kelleher felt this kept Tom very grounded.

> 'I was privileged to play against Tom Cheasty when he played with Portlaw. When I was a child, I remember going into the dressing-rooms in Fraher Field... an old shed really, to meet him. I went in with a little bit of paper and asked him would he sign. He signed it for me and he said "I'm going off now to milk the cows".'

John Barron and Martin Óg Morrissey both worked in Clover Meats; John in the office and Martin in the factory and the commute kept Óg fit.

> 'Clover Meats was almost four miles from my front door. I cycled to and from work every day... six days a week, which meant that I was fairly fit the whole time. I used to be in Clover Meats for 7am every morning.'

They were also joined there by Kilkenny players John Sutton and the Walshes from Slieverue. Martin Óg remembers it well.

> 'Leave me alone. Anywhere I was working... I couldn't turn my head. I remember they had a song out at that time. Part of the song was *'Martin Óg is too fat to match the wiles of the Kilkenny Cats'*. It was a fantastic atmosphere. The factory league was a big competition at the time... there used be murder at those matches. Fellas from the one club would be playing for different teams and they'd be having a go at one another.'

Clover Meats won the Munster factory league title and latterly ended up in the Leinster Championship. These games were so important that Morrissey and Barron were excused from an inter-county match for Waterford in 1959 to play for Clover Meats. Another group which

'59: AN EYEWITNESS ACCOUNT OF HURLING'S GOLDEN AGE

did well in factory league competitions, particularly a seven-a-side hurling competition which they won, was the printers featuring Mick Flannelly and Charlie Ware.

Everyone became a hurling fan in the weeks leading to the final. Telegrams and letters flooded in from all parts of the world. One letter which Pat Fanning kept in his archives was from the Bishop of Waterford and Lismore who was *'especially proud of the fine Christian and manly spirit that inspires the players'*.

As the day of the match arrived, the crowds descended on Dublin. As the fans walked up O'Connell Street, the usual cry of 'hats, scarves and rosettes' would have rung out. Waterford supporter Liam Gleeson's memories capture the scene well.

> 'I was in the Cusack Stand... I didn't need a ticket. I was 12 or 13 and I sat on somebody's lap. The crowd was bigger than quoted if you take children into account. I got a half crown the morning of the final from my mother... and I got two bob to bring to the replay. The paper hats... if you got a shower of rain, it would be all down in your face. The fellas selling apples, oranges, and lemonade. I remember a big fat fella... he'd be coming across 50,000 people in line after line. He'd be up and down... and he'd be crossing you while you'd be trying to see the match and he'd be trying to get change off a fella while the match was going on.'

Showers in the morning had cleared by the start of the minor final. This helped to soften up the pitch which was probably a little hard because of the prolonged dry weather. Tipperary took on Kilkenny and captured their twelfth All-Ireland minor hurling title with a 2-8 to 2-7 victory. Both teams had players who had tasted success in colleges hurling. Tipperary had a unique midfield pairing of two Tom Ryans, one from Toomevara and the other from Killenaule, and Kilkenny featured St. Kieran's College and Inistioge's Eddie Keher. A draw with only a minute remaining, Tipperary pointed from a free, giving them a dramatic victory. Captain Larry Kiely was presented with the Irish Press Cup.

Eddie Keher recalls the game.

> 'It was a tough one. I can clearly remember the linesman. There was a clear sideline ball for Kilkenny and the linesman gave it to Tipp. It was hit in to the '21', but it was a mis-hit that went in and rolled over the goal-line. It wasn't a hard shot... it came from a wrong decision from the linesman. That was a killer blow for me because I had four Leinster minor medals but no All-Ireland. In 1957, we played well against Tipp, but Tipp were very strong... Jimmy Doyle was in his glory at that time. We weren't that

'59: AN EYEWITNESS ACCOUNT OF HURLING'S GOLDEN AGE

far behind them. In '59, we were definitely the better team, but we just got caught. It was that goal and a final point that won it for them.'

In the senior game, Kilkenny were going for their 15th title and Waterford just their second. Most of the press analysis was focused on the previous clash in the 1957 All-Ireland final. Frankie Walsh was hoping to make up for that defeat.

'This is a day of decision for Waterford hurling and every man in the team is filled with a determination to beat Kilkenny and thus make amends for the failure in the 1957 All-Ireland. That day we had the game won and then we relaxed – always a fatal lapse against the wearers of the black and amber. This time we propose to play at full stretch over the full sixty minutes. This time we aim to win and if we don't there will be no alibis. More than any other county in Ireland, we know the quality of Kilkenny hurling and we are not in the least affected by the fact that they performed indifferently enough when taking the Leinster title. That fact serves only to put us on our guard for Kilkenny, mediocre in Leinster, have a happy knack for becoming men transformed when they scent an All-Ireland.'

In return, Ollie Walsh reflected on Waterford's strong performances in the Munster Championship.

'Waterford's victory over Tipperary, or more to the point, the margin of that win, makes us realise that we have a big task before us today. Because of that we have not spared ourselves in our training and with the advice we got from our very capable trainer, Fr. Maher, we hope to at least justify his confidence in us. Waterford are supposed to be better team than they were in 1957 and, while I have not seen them play in the current championship, I can only hope that's not the case. The men with the biggest task on the Kilkenny team will be the six backs. Their job will be to hold the so-far free scoring Waterford forward line. But having played behind that six so often I have every confidence in their ability to do so.'

Current form made Waterford favourites with some commentators, but the tradition of Kilkenny hurling meant they could never be ruled out. Corkman Eamonn Young referred to Waterford's record as *'nothing to write home about'* but he did proclaim that *'I hope Munster champions Waterford win tomorrow and I think they have the men to do it'*. While not universally considered to be favourites, Waterford did have their champions amongst journalists. Andy

'59: AN EYEWITNESS ACCOUNT OF HURLING'S GOLDEN AGE

Croke writing in the Sunday Independent was confident in them.

'I think Waterford can do it. Physically, they have nothing to fear from the Kilkennymen. In height, weight and even in experience, the sides are exceptionally well-matched. True, the Noresiders may have an edge in craft but can craft alone halt the hurling tornado which crushed the might of Cork, Tipperary and Galway in its merciless grip? It has been said in Kilkenny that they could give Waterford four points anytime and beat them. For want of a better word they call it tradition, for the record books credit Kilkenny with 14 All-Ireland successes while Waterford's only victory was in 1948.'

In *The Sunday Press*, Art McGann, writing as 'Fear Ciuin', described his visit to the Waterford training camps.

'Nothing helps a commentator in assessing values than to move amongst the respective contestants in their days of preparation. To make myself conversant with comparative form I went to Waterford City to study the situation at close quarters. I made early contact with one of the old guard, Jim Ware. Under his direction I attended, with six hundred others, at the training procedure of the Waterford men. Ball play began the proceedings with players extended in single file. First time ground pulling on the hurling leather was a marked feature. There was an absence of lifting or handling, with the odd exception of an air snatch. Alternate sprinting and fast walking, and one endurance spell, proceeded the final leap-frogging exercise. It was a business-like performance all around. The players seemed a happy bunch indeed.'

The skills built on the training ground were central to Seán Óg Ó' Ceallacháin's analysis in the *Evening Press*.

'I have great regard for this Waterford team, which seems to have reached its peak at the right moment. The defence has withstood the best efforts of both Cork and Tipperary attacks, strong qualifications, indeed, for tomorrow. The attack spear-headed by Tom Cheasty, and served by industrious Johnny Kiely, Donal Whelan and Frank Walsh, is the fastest striking unit in present day hurling. Speed, stamina and teamwork are the chief weapons, which they hope will bring them the coveted honours for the second time. Two years ago, when previewing their last meeting in the All-Ireland, I plumped

'59: AN EYEWITNESS ACCOUNT OF HURLING'S GOLDEN AGE

for a Kilkenny win. Tomorrow, I feel that Waterford will avenge that defeat and so carry the Liam MacCarthy trophy back home for the second time.'

In the dressing-room, Joe Harney was still suffering from the ankle injury he incurred on the farm before the Munster final. In an interview with Matt Keane in 2012 he described how he wasn't at his best leading into the All-Ireland final:

'Michael Lenihan was the secretary and he sent me to see Dr O'Driscoll in Waterford and he discovered that I had badly torn ligaments, and he put me in plaster for six weeks. Dr O'Driscoll was a good doctor, but I found him to be a little rough around the edges, and maybe that was the reason why I tore the plaster off my ankle on the 15th of August in 1959 because I did not want to miss out on playing an All-Ireland final against Kilkenny. I was not fully fit for the first game which finished in a draw. That game was played on the 6th of September and the replay was fixed for the 4th of October, so I had four weeks to recover, and I was much fitter for that game.'

It wasn't just a big day for the players. The officials, led by referee Gerry Sweeney of Limerick got ready to take the field. A fact that goes unmentioned in the match reports is the identity of the umpires for the senior final. Unlike today, where a referee might work regularly with a team of umpires, possibly from his own club, a different system was in place in 1959. It may have escaped the notice of many supporters that the M. MacAodha and N. MacRiocaird listed in the programme were actually Mick Mackey and Nicky Rackard, two of the greatest players of all time.

This was not particularly unusual, as Waterford's own John Keane had umpired at the 1954 and 1956 All-Ireland finals. While there are obvious benefits to using experts in the role, Donie Nealon pointed out that there could be a downside, as 'They get too involved in the match'. Strangely, it wasn't just famous ex-players who tried their hand at officiating. Tom Cunningham refereed the Munster Senior Football final in Killarney while he was an active player. On August 2, 1959, Kerry beat Cork by 2-15 to 2-8. Tom's linesmen were Larry Guinan and Frankie Walsh, who had played in the Munster Senior Hurling final just one week before. Looking back, we think of these players as hurlers, but Tom Cunningham was a brilliant footballer and was selected to play for Munster in the Railway Cup on six occasions. Even without their hurling haul, Frankie and Larry would still have seven county championships between them for football (four for Frankie and three for Larry). With a different focus, perhaps Waterford could have been competitive as a football county. The

'59: AN EYEWITNESS ACCOUNT OF HURLING'S GOLDEN AGE

Munster Championship semi-final victory over Mick O'Connell's Kerry in 1957 indicates how good they could have been. Michael O'Connor joked to me that 'Kerry were lucky we didn't take football seriously!' although he did say this in the presence of his Kerry-born wife.

President Éamon de Valera arrived at Croke Park shortly before 3pm and he was met by Dr J. J. Stuart, President of the GAA and Padraig O'Caoimh, General Secretary. The teams paraded behind the Artane Boys Band with Frankie Walsh and Sean Clohessy leading their men around the stadium. The minutes of Central Council meetings reveals that the Artane Boys Band were paid £15-15-0 to cover their fees and bus costs. This compares favourably to the £2 fee received by local bands for their appearances at the Gaelic Field in Waterford. Some of the expenses would have been defrayed by advertising revenue. Lucozade, which was manufactured by Beecham's at the time, were one such company. In 1958 they initiated a scheme to distribute 5,000 free hurleys to boys around Ireland. A similar agreement was put in place with Central Council for 1959.

Croke Park was packed with the third highest All-Ireland hurling final attendance of 73,707. The scene was captured by a record number of photographers from Irish and foreign press. This was the first final to be recorded by TV cameras. BBC television had sent cameras and a reporter (Kenneth Wolstenholme of World Cup 1966 fame – 'Some people are on the pitch; they think it's all over... it is now!') who was housed on the upper deck of the new Hogan Stand. They broadcast highlights on their sports magazine programme, Sports Scene, on the Wednesday after the match. More than two years before the opening broadcast of RTE Television, Gael Linn were also present with TV cameras. This new era was not without its adjustments, as one newspaper reported.

> 'When one TV cameraman decided to stay put as he shot the 'head-on', thousands watched to see what the leader of the band would do; whether he would divert the band or get them to mark time. With a masterly wave of his staff, he took the entire band through a figure march that defies description. The crowd enjoyed the spectacle of a somewhat bewildered cameraman, knee deep in tiny musicians, stopping his work to admire the precision of the performance.'

In addition to TV cameras, the Film Institute recorded a 10-minute colour film in 16mm which cost the association £300. As this was a heavy cost to the Central Council, they decided to restrict other commercial groups from filming the final.

Frankie won the toss and informed referee Gerry Fitzgerald that Waterford would take advantage of the breeze and play into the Railway End. And so, 12 anxious minutes late,

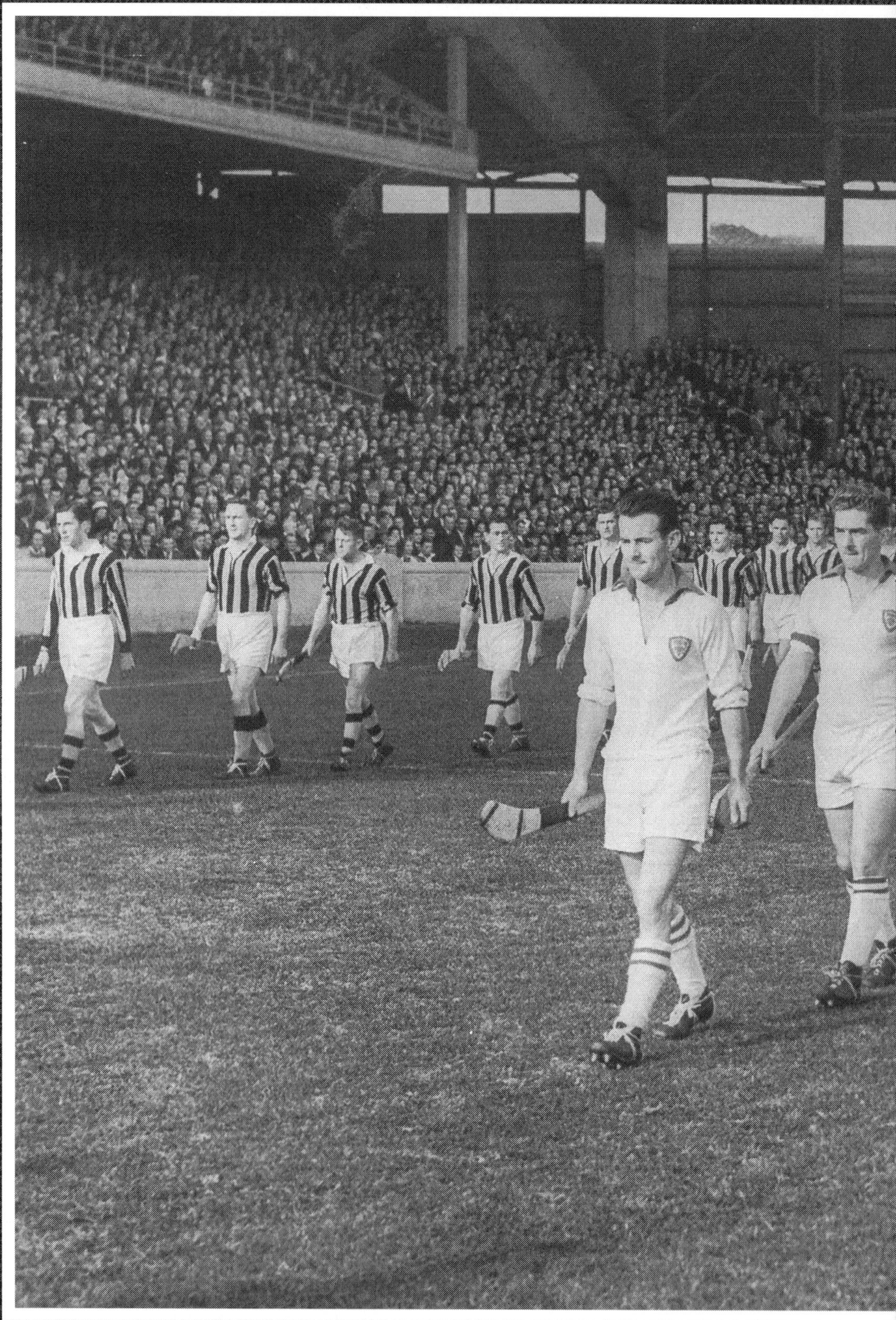

Programmes for the All-Ireland final – official, unofficial, and souvenir versions.

'59: AN EYEWITNESS ACCOUNT OF HURLING'S GOLDEN AGE

the ball was thrown in. After just 25 seconds Waterford had grabbed the lead. Mick Brophy won possession from the throw-in and was penalised for charging. A free from Phil Grimes landed in the goalmouth and Larry Guinan seized on it to tap it over the bar for the opening point, the first of many for the usually goal-hungry Waterford team. The strategy had changed slightly for this game, according to Seamus Power.

> 'We went for points as we were told to do by John Keane. We knew how good Ollie Walsh was and that we had to take our points when we got the chance. As well as that, in an All-Ireland, if you are scoring points, you feel that you are in there... that you are doing what you are supposed to do. It gives the team great confidence.'

That was obvious to Kilkenny too, as Eddie Keher recalls in his book *Hurling Heroes*.

> 'Waterford had been warned by John Keane to take their points and he considered that it would be impossible to get goals against Ollie Walsh who seemed unbeatable. Nevertheless, from my perch behind the goal, I can remember many fantastic saves that Ollie had to pull off to keep his goal intact.'

Within a few minutes Ned Power showed that Walsh wasn't the only shot-stopper on display. His *'tremendous save'* from Denis Heaslip caused Mick Dunne to comment in the *Irish Press* that it was *'the opening act in a drama of spectacular and awe-inspiring goalkeeping by Power and Kilkenny's Ollie Walsh'*. Heaslip again missed out when sending a shot wide from a good position. Jackie Condon recalls how difficult it was in the opening stages for the Waterford team.

> 'We didn't turn up on the first day against Kilkenny... I don't know what was wrong. They were running rings around us, and we didn't seem to be able to do anything with them. I realised after that we had stage fright... we were stuck to the ground. Kilkenny lads are used to Croke Park. It's a whole big occasion going out into the All-Ireland. I remember coming out of the tunnel and the crowd let a roar... and you'd kind of shrink down. You are out there for the first half hour or so and you are so aware of the crowd. If you hit the ball... there is a roar. We weren't getting the ball. Everything was wrong. It was hard to understand.'

Waterford started to get into the game and when Ollie Walsh conceded a '70' under

'59: AN EYEWITNESS ACCOUNT OF HURLING'S GOLDEN AGE

pressure from Cheasty, it was sent back for a point by Phil Grimes. Soon after, Seamus Power pulled down a high ball from O'Connell and from his long clearance John Kiely added a point. Ollie Walsh brought off another fine save, this time from Whelan, before Kilkenny managed to register their first score in the 11th minute, a point from Billy Dwyer. Dwyer's strength was making an impact on the Waterford full-back line. Austin Flynn was drawn out of the square to meet an oncoming Dick Carroll, which left Dwyer free inside. Carroll passed to the edge of the square and Dwyer smashed the ball to the net to give Kilkenny their first lead. It could have been much worse for Waterford as a shot from Heaslip came back off the post to Dwyer whose low drive was deflected wide by Carroll.

Just into the second quarter, Frankie Walsh put Waterford back on level terms with his first free of the day when John Kiely was brought down. Waterford now had a wave of attacks and each one resulted in points by Walsh twice, Cheasty and Kiely, but just as Seamus Power had pointed out, it seemed obvious to Mick Dunne in the press box that each attack failed to bring goals *'because of what seemed to be their forwards complete lack of faith in their ability to beat Ollie Walsh'*. However, John Keane's strategy was working. They dominated midfield and were picking off points. Each team made a change just before half-time with Tim Kelly replacing the injured John McGovern and Charlie Ware being substituted for Tom Cunningham. Johnny McGovern remembers the moment.

> 'I was marking Larry Guinan in the draw. I played left half-back. I went off with a shoulder injury after quarter of an hour or 20 minutes of the first match. I went to clear a ball and I hit it on the ground and one of the lads came in late... at full speed. I didn't see them coming and I got a bad shoulder injury... I could see the whole place, and the stand, spinning around me. It was mostly a muscle injury, so I went off.'

After Walsh pointed another free, there was some wild swinging and heated exchanges in the Kilkenny goal area, but this was the only such incident reported in the press. With that point, Waterford moved into a lead of 0-9 to 1-1 at half time. There was no room for complacency, particularly with Kilkenny's 1957 comeback still fresh in the memory, but Waterford must have been very pleased to go to the dressing-room with a five-point lead while limiting Kilkenny's scoring to just Dwyer's contribution.

The second-half opened with another point from Tom Cheasty. He shot for goal but again Ollie Walsh made a save which deflected off the post and went over the bar. The duel between Cheasty and Walsh was watched eagerly by Eddie Keher and the Kilkenny minor team, who were accommodated in seats to one side of the Railway goal.

'59: AN EYEWITNESS ACCOUNT OF HURLING'S GOLDEN AGE

'It was very hard to see what was going on at the Canal End of the field but being almost on the pitch, we certainly got a worm's eye view of the action in front of the Railway goal. Ollie Walsh performed heroics in the Kilkenny goal, making unbelievable saves right in front of our eyes from a relentless Waterford attack who seemed to take delight in bringing out the best in him. The cavalier centre-forward who was leading most of those attacks was Tom Cheasty. He had just one thing in mind when he ran on to that ball... make for goal, and it didn't matter who came to meet them. Martin Óg Morrissey had obviously been instructed to send every ball down to Cheasty who, with the familiar "genuflect" to pick up the ball on the run... was on his way. If he did find himself in a cul-de-sac, he knew there must be forwards loose, and he had perfected the accurate hand pass to Mick Flannelly, Frankie Walsh or Larry Guinan who capitalised on the space created.'

As expected, Kilkenny came back into the game with a very strong eight-minute spell. They recovered all six points of the deficit by outscoring Waterford by 2-2 to two points (Kelly and Walsh, from a '70', scored points for Kilkenny and Power and Cheasty scored points for Waterford). Central to this effort was Tommy O'Connell, the youngest player on the pitch at 19 years old. He was being marked by Joe Harney who was having an outstanding championship. None of his markers had scored a goal in the three Munster Championship games, including Christy Ring. O'Connell struck in the 36th minute. A long shot rebounded from the upright and he was first to react as he nipped into the square and flicked the ball past Ned Power. Joe Cody in his book, *The Stripy Men*, describes the goal.

> *'The famed Mick Mackey, who was manning the white flag, shouted "Square Ball!". The goal flag was in the control of another legend, Nicky Rackard, who ignored Mackey and waved the green flag. Pressed as to whether or not he was in the square. Tommy laughed and said "I'd say the five years Nicky spent in St. Kieran's College didn't do me any harm."*

Just three minutes later, O'Connell was again right in front of goal when a Paddy Kelly centre from the right touchline allowed O'Connell to run onto the ball and double it to the net. A lesser team than Waterford might have collapsed at this stage, but they rallied well and managed the next four scores, all points. Tom Cheasty produced an incredible piece of individual magic to score his third point of the second-half. His second-half display was described as *'a flood of*

Waterford jersey for the All-Ireland final
◆

Detail of the jersey
◆

Seamus Power's equalising goal

'59: AN EYEWITNESS ACCOUNT OF HURLING'S GOLDEN AGE

thrills' in the *Irish Press*. The BBC commentator, Kenneth Wolstenholme described the scene.

> 'I shall never forget some of the incredible forwards I and 74,000 others saw on Sunday and one man stands in my memory – Tom Cheasty. That time in the second-half when he caught the ball, swerved around an opponent, tipped the ball onto his hurley, started to run, dropped the ball, but regained it, then burst between two men and shot a point which will forever remain as one of my finest sporting memories.'

Eamonn Sweeney in Munster Hurling Legends describes the same point.

> 'With his sights set firmly on the opposition's goal, he took on no less than five strapping Kilkenny defenders, sidestepping a couple of them and shouldering the others out of his way, before striking a perfect shot over the bar. He was completely unstoppable. It was a point no one else could have scored.'

It was not all plain sailing for Waterford though. Ned Power kept Kilkenny forwards at bay with four saves in quick succession. Dominating the midfield, three more points were added by Walsh from play and then two frees from Power and Walsh. Having the game of his life, Tommy O'Connell struck again. The *'teenager displaying all the guile and opportunism of a player much older, again got in behind the defence under a centre from Paddy Kelly. This was his third goal in his first All-Ireland senior appearance in Croke Park'*. Jimmy O'Brien, from his viewpoint at the far end of the Hogan Stand recalls *'every time the ball went up, O'Connell got a goal. I was at the other end of the field so I couldn't really see the play'*. Michael O'Connor appreciated the tactics being employed as it reminded him of his interplay with Mick Flannelly, although he was quite modest about his scoring abilities compared to O'Connell.

> 'That was a lot of scoring… one guy, Tommy O'Connell scored three goals. That cross-field ball was a very clever and effective tactic. It is the perfect way for a forward to latch on to a ball, go up to the corner and get the ball across. That is the way that Flannelly would play in my minor days. He would run over, and the ball would come right across… you had to score.'

While this was heartening for Kilkenny supporters, a point from Larry Guinan kept Waterford two ahead. So far, they had held out against everything Kilkenny could throw at them, but a crucial change was now made. Dick Carroll was brought out from corner-forward

'59: AN EYEWITNESS ACCOUNT OF HURLING'S GOLDEN AGE

to the half-forward line. Minutes earlier, he had sent a relatively straightforward free wide and had another saved, but he now surged into the game. With 10 minutes to play, he scored Kilkenny's fifth goal from a '70' by Mickey Walsh. He then added two further points to put Kilkenny three ahead with less than two minutes to play. Seamus Power, who was playing in midfield drifted up-field. Jimmy O'Brien, who played with Seamus' brother, Sean in Wexford, was tracking his movement.

> 'Seamus Power got a ball... he was playing centrefield and he left centrefield and charged up in a drive up the field... and he lost the ball. He was kinda bet. I saw two Kilkenny forwards get a ball and they started running towards the Waterford goal. They could easily have hit it over the bar, but they carried it too long.'

Grimes, his midfield partner, described the next move.

> 'Seamus and I moved upwards in search of a goal only for the ball to be cleared downfield. Seamus thought that was that... and stayed where he was. Suddenly, the ball was back up again and there he was perfectly positioned to get the most important score of a great career. At the time, I thought it couldn't be Seamus who scored... and it must have been Duck Whelan.'

The pressure was on Waterford and the pace of the game was starting to show. Larry Guinan reflects that rather than a tactical switch, positional changes were more out of necessity.

> 'Seamus ran in, and I was corner-forward... and there was a schmozzle around the goalmouth and ball went wide... and Seamus says to me "I'm f***ed... go out there for a while". This is true. And he leaned with his two hands on his hurley, and he had his head down... "Go out there!" he said to me... so I ran out the field.'

Frankie Walsh describes the finish.

> 'It would take a goal to save the day. We won a sideline cut. Seamus Power moved forward from midfield and raised his hand. I took the sideline cut... I shouldn't have. It only went a few yards. "You little so and so," Seamus shouted. He stayed forward. My memory is that Larry Guinan chased the ball and won possession.'

'59: AN EYEWITNESS ACCOUNT OF HURLING'S GOLDEN AGE

Larry Guinan takes up the story.

'I remember Seamus' equalising goal well. Luckily enough this ball came up the field and I pulled on it. It was out at the corner, and I pulled on the ball and over it went... and into Seamus... and Seamus stuck it in the net.'

Seamus Power completes the tale.

'The ball came up beautifully. I went practically unchallenged for almost 20 yards with the ball on my stick. I was on the 21-yard line and was aiming to strike the ball off my stronger left-hand side, but the Kilkenny backs were beginning to wake up and were converging on my left. I pretended to be going to hit it left-handed... but at the last second, I swung back and let fly from my right for all I was worth. The Link Walsh and Ollie Walsh were in the goalmouth. The goalkeeper seemed to have it covered but the ball was deflected off the stick of the full-back and shot into the net.'

Jackie Condon was confident the ball had got to the right man.

'Powerie could give the ball a good whack when he hit it. He got plenty of time to steady himself and have a go at the goal.'

The man with the best view in the ground described Power's bearing to Pat Fanning.

'Jackie O'Connell... a great Limerick man, he was umpire that day. He told me afterwards that if he ever wants to describe determination in a man's face, he will recall Power bearing down on that goal with that ball.'

Seamus' son, Tom, describes how significant it was to score against Ollie Walsh. 'My father had great time for Ollie Walsh. He believed he was the best keeper there ever was.' While he was delighted with the goal and admitted that it didn't go straight to the net, 'it used to irk him, particularly if Kilkenny people said it to him, that it took a deflection'. The Waterford team were unanimous in their praise of the Thomastown goalkeeper. Larry Guinan recently said:

'I still believe to this day, that Ollie Walsh was the best goalie I have ever seen. He was fantastic. .. he had everything. At that time, you could go in and stick him in the back of the net. Ollie could stand there with you and go shoulder to shoulder if you were

'59: AN EYEWITNESS ACCOUNT OF HURLING'S GOLDEN AGE

going in attacking him. The ball would be in the square, and you could pull on it, but he was there always... he was fantastic.'

He wasn't a one-man defence though and Larry remembers that 'You had the big Link Walsh at full-back and his brother in the corner. I knew John Sutton and I'd know Paddy Buggy from Slieverue'. Of course, Buggy was well known to many in the Waterford team as he had been to school in Mount Sion. Martin Og Morrissey concurs.

'Ollie Walsh was a fantastic goalie. He was the best I ever saw... you could have 10 fellas taking shots at him and he'd stop them. His puckout would be landing on the '21' nearly. If he was playing today... he'd be putting them over the bar from puckouts.'

Unknown to him at the time, Eddie Keher would have a role to play in the 1959 final before it was played out, but he remembers his thoughts about Ollie Walsh and Seamus Power from his role as spectator.

'Ollie was a phenomenon. I was playing the minor that day, of course. There were seats behind the Railway goal... a circle of benches and the minors used to go there for the senior match. We were at Ollie Walsh's goal in the first-half, and he was magnificent... his saves were phenomenal. When you mention Seamus Power's goal... we were at the other side of the field and you can imagine from our viewpoint... low down and through all the players... it was hard to get an accurate view of what happened. I can remember Seamus Power went on a solo run in and hit the ball... and I thought it went off the Link Walsh's shoulder. I think some reports said his hurl, but I thought he lifted his shoulder to block it. It was going for him, and it deflected into the net. Ollie was unbeatable practically at that time.'

Jimmy O'Brien was right behind the flight of the ball, and he agreed with Keher.

'Seamus Power, fair play, he turned and headed for goal but when he hit it... he didn't hit it well at all. It hit the Link Walsh's shoulder and spun back. Ollie nearly had it, but it just barely got in the corner. I thought it hit his shoulder... I was in the Hogan Stand. I remember him heading in about 20 yards. It was a great effort.'

Another Kilkenny player with a sideline view was the injured Johnny McGovern.

'59: AN EYEWITNESS ACCOUNT OF HURLING'S GOLDEN AGE

'In the drawn game, I was in the dressing-room, and I came out to watch the end of it. I was very weak... and I wasn't feeling well after it. I saw the goal coming that Seamus Power scored. I was out for that part of it. Seamus soloed in and Ollie had it covered... he was ready to catch it and Link Walsh put up the hurl trying to stop it and it deflected away from Ollie.'

It is not just the combatants who have strong memories of the match. Donie Nealon of Tipperary was there as a spectator.

'My girlfriend, she later became my wife, and I were on the Canal End. You couldn't see anything. We were sitting up on the wall at the back and if you looked behind you, there must have been a fall of 40 yards down. Waterford were by far the better team that day. That was the day that Kilkenny would come up the field and get a goal. They got five goals... it was ridiculous and here were Waterford a goal behind. Seamus Power poked away from centrefield in between the half-forward line and he picked up this loose ball and he came through right down in front of us... and let fly, and Ollie, God rest him, was ready for it... and the Link Walsh stuck out his hurley... he stuck it out with one hand and put the ball into the far corner of the net, away from Ollie. I'd say Ollie would have stopped it. It was at the right height for him, but the Link turned it into the net.'

The Waterford supporters almost lifted the roof off the new Hogan Stand with their roar of delight, but not everyone joined in. Phil Fanning, when interviewed, admitted that he missed the crucial moment.

'I never saw the goal until afterwards on television and old films. With a minute to go, I'm ashamed to say, I got up and turned around and walked down the steps crying. As I was walking down the steps of the Hogan Stand... it was the new Hogan Stand of course, I heard this roar, and I knew straight away it couldn't be the game was over. It couldn't be the Kilkenny crowd. I ran back up... and looked in and saw that Waterford had got the goal and I swore to myself that I'd never leave a match early again. I was so down in the mouth. I was thinking back to 1957... Here we go again I said. I was 15 years of age and I had tears in my eyes walking down the steps when I heard the roar, and I ran back up.'

'59: AN EYEWITNESS ACCOUNT OF HURLING'S GOLDEN AGE

With the game now tied, Ollie Walsh quickly restarted the action, to push his side towards a winner. With his characteristic swing he launched the ball into centrefield towards Seamus Power.

> 'I was about 75 yards out and I was left all on my own. Like us in 1957 when we thought we had it won, Kilkenny had dropped their defences completely. The ball came straight into my hand. I made ground... five or six yards, with no one to challenge me, over towards the Cusack Stand side. I thought we were a point ahead. The referee had nodded to indicate that time was just up. I hit it an almighty flake... not too concerned about accuracy. It went a yard or so wide.'

Larry Guinan recalls Power's reaction to scoring his goal.

> 'Well Seamus Power charged out the field then... bejaysus as if he was only starting the match. Ollie Walsh pucked out the ball and Seamus caught it around the centre of the field and pucked it up in the air... and he hit it wide. He said, "I could have f***in scored". He always said, "I should have scored that one". We could have won the game... we had a chance of winning the game with the last puck of the ball.'

The referee blew the whistle and the match ended in a draw. The crowd, who had been brought along on this rollercoaster, went wild with both excitement and relief. The Waterford supporters were delighted to see their team survive with a last-minute equaliser and the Kilkenny fans were equally relieved to have survived the last shot at goal and see their team live to fight another day. One journalist commented *'I doubt if I have ever lived through a more exciting second half. If in one way I would have been proud to have had relationship with either of the combatant counties, in that tense finish I was glad I was a neutral; any affinity must surely have been too bad for my blood pressure'*. A huge surge of fans invaded the pitch to congratulate both teams. As they were ushered towards the dressing-room on a wave of goodwill, there was confusion amongst the Waterford players. Seamus Power again:

> 'I thought we had won... there were so many scores on the board that day. With all the cheering and backslapping and everything... I was inside in the dressing-room before I realised that it was only a draw. If I had known we were level, I had all the time in the world... all the time in the world, to steady myself and score a point.'

'59: AN EYEWITNESS ACCOUNT OF HURLING'S GOLDEN AGE

Frankie Walsh was equally confused.

'When the final whistle blew, Seamus thought we had won by a point. I thought we had lost by a point.'

Larry Guinan remembers.

'I didn't know what happened. I remember looking over at Frankie and Jesus he was quare down. We went inside in the dressing-room... and he broke a bottle or something against the wall. He thought we had lost by a point. I didn't know what happened when I saw him like that. I didn't know... did we win or lose.'

Martin Óg sums up the end of the game nicely.

'It was a bit of a fluke for us... Seamus Power's goal. The Link stuck out his hurley and it was deflected into the back of the net. Thanks be to God that he did. I realised it was a draw. I was the only one who could read the scoreboard! I felt lousy... I thought we should have won it.'

Seamus Power acknowledged that Waterford had been fortunate to make their way back into the game, considering Kilkenny's strength of character.

'With the tremendous tradition that Kilkenny had, you don't expect them to throw in the towel... particularly against Waterford. They were going to come back into the game. We had them beaten with 10 or 12 minutes to go but, look what happened in '57. This time... it was we snatched it.'

Mick Flannelly interpreted it as being a matter of experience. In the modern parlance, they would have improved their 'game management' and not put themselves under pressure.

'A bit of an inexperience. I think we were rushing to do everything. When we were in the lead, we should have been slowing it down a bit. Where a fella would be rushing up to take a sideline cut, if he thought and just took 10 or 15 seconds more... 10 or 15 seconds more on a puckout... that little bit of inexperience I'd say. We could have slowed down the game on frees and on puckouts and on sideline cuts... and you might

'59: AN EYEWITNESS ACCOUNT OF HURLING'S GOLDEN AGE

just hold out and sneak a win.'

Typical of his self-confidence and sense of humour, Martin Óg Morrissey saw the funny side and looked forward with confidence to the replay.

> 'Five balls passed me that day… and they scored five goals. I'm only blackguarding!! That's what I said to the boys in the full-back line after. After a bit of a talking to, they didn't score five goals the second day… I'll tell you that much. In the drawn game, we had 18 scores to 10. No matter what way you look at it, we were a better team than Kilkenny on the first day… even though we had to come from behind at the end.'

The match had ended on a scoreline of Waterford 1-17, Kilkenny 5-5, the first draw since 1934's draw between Limerick and Dublin and *'by general agreement any other verdict would have ill-befitted the occasion'*. John D. Hickey, writing in the Irish Independent the next day opened his report by placing the final in context of those that had gone before and estimated its historical significance.

> *'Thank heavens it was a draw. That was my predominant thought at the end of an epic combat at Croke Park yesterday, when, in an All-Ireland senior hurling final that simply beggars description, a game that seems to make all words inadequate, Waterford and Kilkenny ended on level terms in a contest that must rank as a landmark in the history of the GAA. This struggle of breath-taking splendour, astonishing pace and nerve-shattering intensity was the greatest hurling final I have seen – a test of men's skill and courage that will ever be cherished by all who were privileged to see it. In many, if not most, drawn games supporters of either side are wont to make a case that their favourites should have won; but yesterday there seemed to be complete unanimity of opinion that it would have been a hurling tragedy if either side had lost.'*

He went on to point out that 'over the hour Waterford were the better team' and in summing up had to admit *'now, as I look back, it seems incredible that a side which established such a midfield superiority as Waterford's did not win'*. Reflecting in 1984, Pat Fanning agreed with John D. Hickey that a draw was the right result.

> 'The boys had hurled heroically, had amassed a match winning score against legendary Ollie Walsh and, yet, time running out… there we were, three points behind, and

headed for the defeat that must surely present Waterford as the finest team never to win an All-Ireland. I still shudder when I think of it! Then the supreme movement as Seamus Power moves… heads for goal, and delivers the ball that levels the scoring. There is yet another moment as Seamus gets the puck out… and sends wide. It might have been the winner and yet I am forever thankful that it was not. The match-saver was all we wanted… the second chance would be grasped and turned to advantage.'

In a game where one team scored five goals, a critical match-up was the Kilkenny full-forward line against Ned Power and his full-back line. Reading between the lines of the match reports, it does seem that Kilkenny had planned to drop *'high balls from far out'* into the Waterford goalmouth. Where these originated on the right-hand side from Paddy Kelly, it allowed Tommy O'Connell at left corner-forward to drift into the square on the blind side of Joe Harney and Austin Flynn. While this was happening, it was reported that *'Ned Power was impeded by his own backs'*. However, one astute commentator noted that *'while many may incline to the view that the Waterford defenders crowded their goalkeeper, one cannot but assume that they were lured too close by the astute Kilkenny men.'* It certainly seems this was a deliberate tactic by Kilkenny to give their fast young corner-forward some space in which to operate. The full-back line bore the brunt of the criticism in Waterford for their *'poor covering'* but Ned Power, despite conceding five goals *'still left the field with an enhanced record'* thanks to his shot-stopping and clearances. The players when interviewed immediately after the match had some further insights into their thoughts of the game. Frankie Walsh refers to an incident that wasn't covered in the national press reports.

> 'It was a memorable game, and I don't think I'll ever play another like it. I think we were unlucky as I am fully convinced that Phil Grimes scored a point in the first-half that was not signalled… and that score would have made all the difference. Kilkenny can thank Ollie Walsh for earning another chance. I think we will win the replay… if we get the breaks.'

Others were just glad to live to fight another day and were more balanced in their comments. Martin Óg Morrissey said he thought both sides were lucky in their turn.

> 'Kilkenny were lucky in some of the scores they got, and in the end… we were lucky to draw. I am looking forward to meeting them again and I think we should win.'

'59: AN EYEWITNESS ACCOUNT OF HURLING'S GOLDEN AGE

Seamus Power, secretary of the Mount Sion club and well used to dealing with press queries contented himself with neutral comments.

'I am looking forward to the replay and am happy to have another chance of meeting Kilkenny.'

Naturally, Kilkenny were also taking confidence from their own periods of strength and Sean Clohessy said

'They are a grand team. However, I think this game will improve us considerably and we should win the replay. We had the initiative with 10 minutes to go and might have held on. Johnny McGovern's retirement was a terrible blow to us.'

Others, including Mick Walsh, agreed.

'I thought we should have won it on the run of the play. I was afraid that Waterford had us beaten after the first 10 minutes of the second-half but going into the last quarter Kilkenny made a burst and should have won. I think we will win the replay.'

Tom Walsh was more focused on how the game finished.

'I enjoyed the game immensely. We will win the replay by the three points we missed today... the goal we handed to Waterford near the end today.'

The final word was left to Paddy Buggy, a future president of the GAA, who signalled his political astuteness with his comments.

'It was a wonderful game, and I was glad to have the honour to play in it. A draw was a fair result as Waterford missed chances early on and when Kilkenny got the lead near the end, we lost chances of clinching it.'

In the week after the final, Tom Cheasty and Ollie Walsh were awarded joint Sports Stars of the Week by the *Irish Independent*, the closest prize of the era to a Man of the Match award. Walsh's fearsome reputation had withstood the Waterford test with only a single goal conceded. The newspapers heaped praise on him with comments such as *'it must be admitted*

'59: AN EYEWITNESS ACCOUNT OF HURLING'S GOLDEN AGE

that but for goalkeeper genius Ollie Walsh, Waterford must surely have won with something in hand'. In the Independent's match report, John D. Hickey compared him to other great goalkeepers, such as Tommy Daly of Clare, Tony Reddan of Tipperary, and Mick Cashman of Cork, but placed Walsh clearly at the top of the pile. His was *'the greatest display ever by a goalkeeper of outstanding worth and fearless spirit'*. Tom Cheasty received similar praise for his *'hurling bravery'*.

Kenneth Wolstenholme, the BBC commentator was interviewed for a *Sunday Press* article headlined *'Why keep this great game such a big secret?'* He was full of praise for what he had experienced. Admitting that *'he had a wrong impression of hurling – I thought it was just another excuse for a fight'*, he commented 'I've seen sporting events in many parts of Europe and America (both North and South) but I have yet to see a game which keeps the excitement at such a constant fever pitch as hurling. Every other game has its dull moments yet on Sunday there was none at all and I came away wondering how thirty amateurs to whom the rule book says, "full time training is inconsistent with amateurism" could keep it up so long. Happily enough hurling seems to sacrifice nothing of its skill on the altar of speed.'

In the *Evening Herald* of September 7, he was quoted as saying:

> 'If you took those teams on a world tour to play a game like that you would have hurling played everywhere. The amazing speed of the game simply thrilled me. I could not understand how they could control the ball with those pieces of wood. And the wholehearted bodily contact had to be seen to be believed. I had expected to be interested in the match, but it was not long in progress before I was a real fan. Most games have their dull moments, but this hurling is "go" all the time.'

John Keane presented him with a hurley as a souvenir after the match in the dressing-room.

The replay was immediately fixed for October 4 and after such a thrilling draw, it was anticipated that *'while replays seldom touch the standard of drawn games, or attract a better attendance, the second meeting will be a must for those who can make it'*.

The team returned to stay at the Grand Hotel after the match. Martin Óg Morrissey remembers an incident on his arrival in Malahide.

> 'We stayed in Dublin that night in the Grand Hotel in Malahide. We were going into the hotel after the match and there was a woman coming out who asked me if we had won? "We didn't," I said, "it was a draw". "Hold on," she said, and she opened her

'59: AN EYEWITNESS ACCOUNT OF HURLING'S GOLDEN AGE

purse and took out a cross from her purse and handed it to me and she said, "That will bring you luck the next day". I still have the cross... a small little cross. I thought that was very nice of her.'

A dinner was hosted in their honour by the Dublin-based Waterfordmen's Association, also known as Cumann na nDéise. In 1957, there had been a great turnout for a similar event. Tickets were sold at 21 shillings per head and were in strong demand. To boost early purchase of the tickets, the Dublin committee, headed by P.J. Rheinish, included a free draw for six All-Ireland stand tickets to those who purchased their reception tickets by August 27. To entertain the guests at the reception, the committee hired accordionist Albert Healy and tenor Richard Cooper, one of the Radio Eireann Singers who was a former Mount Sion hurler. His son, Risteárd Cooper became famous for playing Bill O'Herlihy in Apres Match.

There was a meal in the Ballroom in the Grand Hotel. Chairman of the association, Sean Feeney welcomed all the guests and had to apologise to those who were absent due to the scarcity of tickets, despite over 300 being present. He paid tribute to the team, all of whom were present, and believed that the MacCarthy Cup would be at the top table of the banquet to be held on the night of the replay and ultimately it would cross the River Suir again. President of the GAA, Dr. J.J. Stuart was 'very proud of the wonderful display by the Waterford and Kilkenny hurlers'. He had 'never seen a finer or more thrilling display of the national game. Pressmen would use many adjectives in the paper descrbing the game, but none could do it full justice'. He also left the audience on a note of encouragement as 'efforts were being made to increase the allocation of tickets for the replay so that more Waterford men and women could see the replay of this memorable final'.

This was a hot topic as many of the 15 shilling tickets which had been allocated to the Ulster counties had been offered for resale in the local newspapers. It was expected that these tickets would be re-allocated to the south east for the replay. Pat Fanning spoke at length in Irish and then in English. He said that 'Every time the hurlers went on the field they gave of their best, and deserved the loyalty and support they were getting. They were all very proud of them who were the stuff of champions'. The Mayor of Waterford, Alderman Dick Jones looked forward to according the team a civic reception, hopefully with the cup in their possession on the night after the replay.

Meanwhile, down the road at the Hollybrook Hotel in Clontarf, The Link Walsh was disconsolate and blamed himself for costing Kilkenny the game. According to Enda McEvoy's *Godfather of Modern Hurling*, he predicted that they wouldn't win the replay. 'The only ray of sunshine for him and his colleagues was the three pounds the County Board gave each of them the next day in lieu of the wages they'd lose through missing a second Monday at work.'

Strangely, there was a reception in Waterford for the team on the Monday night, despite the fact that the final had not been decided. A photograph published in the Munster Express on Friday September 11 shows the team on the back of a lorry driving down the Quay through a throng of spectators. Most of the players were sitting down and, with no trophy to display.

The accompanying reports describe the excitement amongst the huge crowd.

> 'Like the contest itself, the scenes which marked the homecoming almost defy description, so tumultuous were they in character, so compelling in their sincerity. They were of a never-to-be-forgotten kind. And they were enacted in a befittingly gala setting, rendered possible by the profuse display of bunting and other forms of public decoration, into which, on the Mall especially, there was interwoven an artistic arrangement of streamer fairy lights – with star centrepiece – which had already been set in place to proclaim the opening and progress of the first-ever International Festival of Light Opera to be held in this country or across-Channel.'

The arrival of the team at the Sallypark Borough Boundary was announced to the waiting crowd over a network of loudspeakers around City Hall and passed back through the crowds waiting along the quays. It was estimated that 15,000 supporters had gathered, so the truck carrying the players made slow progress towards City Hall behind three local marching bands. Once there, the players were mobbed as the made their way from the truck to the relative calm of the vestibule. They were welcomed to the civic reception by the Mayor, Alderman Dick Jones and members of the Corporation. The players were each introduced to the crowd from an upstairs window by the Mayor. There was a particularly large ovation for Seamus Power who had saved the day in the final by scoring a late equaliser. In the speeches, there was frequent reference to the phrase 'Beidh lá eile ag an bPaorach!' (Power will have another day!), the last words from the gallows of Edmund Power of Dungarvan, executed for his part in the Wexford Rebellion of 1798. Alderman T.A. Kyne TD, commented that 'If they had won, the hurlers could not have got a better reception'. Replying on behalf of the team and the County Board to speeches by the mayor and various TDs and councillors, Pat Fanning urged caution.

> 'Because of the tributes lavished on the team and the enthusiasm aroused by those tributes, it is my duty to stress that the job is not yet completed. The Waterford team hurled heroically on Sunday, but they had failed in their objective in a glorious fight-back. By his goal, Seamus Power had earned for the team the right to fight another

day. They welcomed that opportunity, but it should not be imagined that victory would be won because they had played well on Sunday last.'

That 'lá eile' was scheduled for October 4 and all involved hoped to be celebrating an All-Ireland win at another civic reception on October 5.

In Kilkenny, thousands of supporters also gathered to welcome their team home and lorries draped in black and amber carried the senior team and minor champions to a civic reception at the courthouse. Amongst the speeches was a tribute to the Waterford team.

'We salute and congratulate with our Kilkenny hurlers the great and gallant Waterford team whose skill, courage and determination made possible the most thrilling All-Ireland senior hurling final in the long history of the GAA. In friendly rivalry we wave our hands and hurleys to our neighbours across the Suir and Nore with good wishes now and always.'

7

ALL-IRELAND FINAL REPLAY

The build-up to the All-Ireland final replay was full of excitement for the Waterford supporters but, with the experience of two finals in three years, the players and management had a relatively relaxed approach to the replay. The discussion in newspapers and in every workplace was to be avoided. As Larry Guinan described it, media attention didn't impinge much on his preparation.

> 'I wouldn't be interested in the newspapers in the lead up to the game. I was never a fella for reading anyway. If there was a photo at times... somebody might say "Your photo is in the paper"... you'd look at it, that's all.'

Instead, the squad and trainers plotted the best way to counteract Kilkenny's formidable attack to whom they had conceded five goals. Frankie Walsh focused on defensive frailties as the key factor.

> 'We had to change our tactics. The backs needed a bit of toughening up, so we did "backs and forwards" training.'

They were able to perfect this game plan in the relative quiet of Dunhill, as renovation work at the Gaelic Field forced them to relocate to a quieter environment. This allowed John Keane to play to his strengths and manage each player's individual needs with a quiet word in their ear. It surprised Austin Flynn but he was thankful of the approach Keane took with him.

> '"Austin, you've done enough tonight", said Keane. "Go in and get a rub". We were

'59: AN EYEWITNESS ACCOUNT OF HURLING'S GOLDEN AGE

much fitter... that was the telling factor. John had pulled us back a bit in training because he could see we were just right... and he didn't want us to overdo it.'

Confidence was quietly building in the camp and Larry Guinan thought they were building towards a peak.

'I felt we were good enough to win. We had a really good team and we'd been knocking on the door for a while... I felt we should win something.'

Having failed to secure a challenge match leading up to the drawn final, the team management were keen to have a fixture before the replay. Once again Wexford were considered ideal opponents and as they weren't involved in either the Brendan Cup final or the Oireachtas semi-finals, which were played on the same day. A game was fixed for September 20 at the Gaelic Field in Waterford. Waterford fielded a strong team and also gave four substitutes a run with the selectors making a final choice for the final.

Michael O'Connor started his first game since 1957 in that game and proved that he was ready for action in the replay, if called upon. He took Joe Harney's place at corner-back as Joe was still recovering from his ankle injury. To test his progress, Harney was brought in as a sub at half-time. Jimmy O'Brien was corner-forward and O'Connor's direct opponent that day.

'When Waterford drew the first All-Ireland, we played them in a practice match up in the field and it made a big difference to Waterford. Mick Flan wasn't going well but he had a right good game against us, and he played very well in the replay... he was a great little hurler. Tom Cheasty could have been a disaster because he got a bad belt in the head that day, but he was alright... and he played very well in the replay. It was a late arrangement for Wexford to come in. I played on Micky O'Connor a few times, including that day. He was a fine hurler... a real nice fella and a gentleman. I went through Cappoquin recently and I was thinking of him. He was towards the end of his time, and I was at the start of mine when I played on him. John Kiely... Jaysus, he was a great hurler. He was small and square... but he was great. He was a real handful, but he was at the end of his career, too.'

The match reports support Jimmy's memories. Wexford were short five of their regulars and Waterford had a strong wind advantage in the first-half. However, their play was listless, and only led by a single point at half-time (1-8 to 2-4). Tom Cheasty, having scored two

Tickets for the All-Ireland final replay

◆

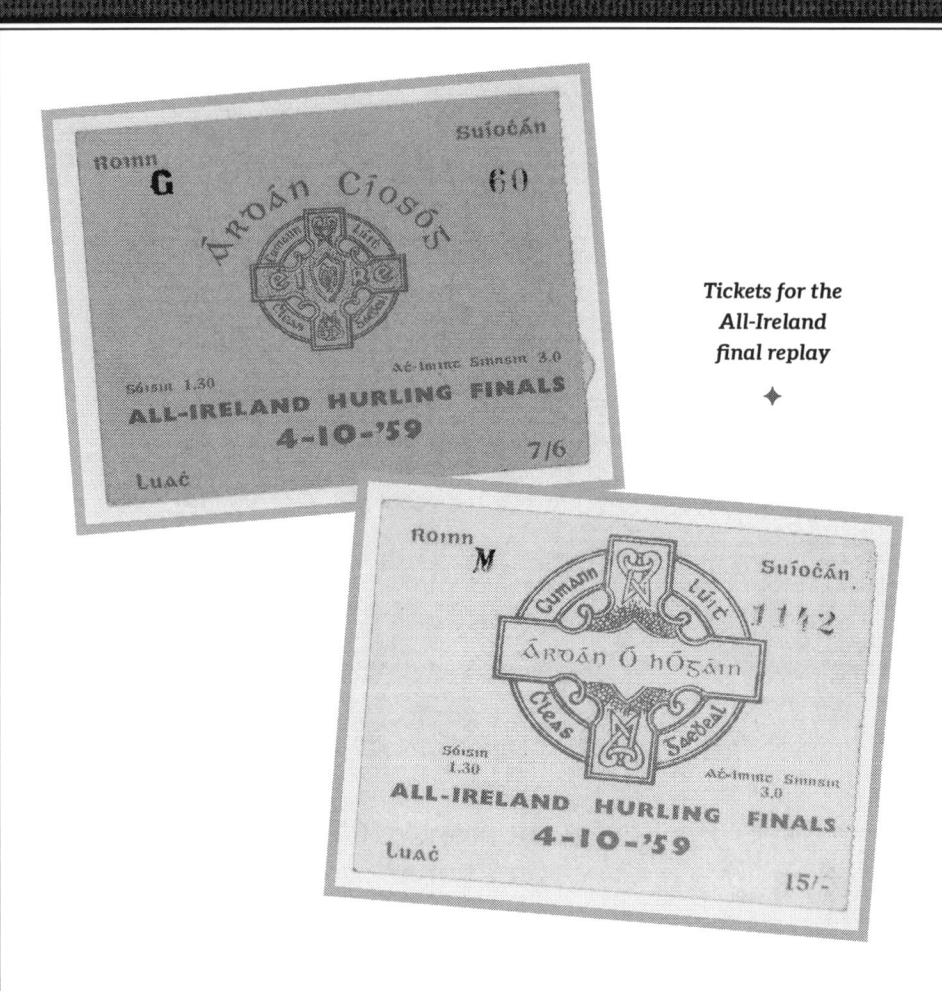

Programmes for the All-Ireland final replay – official, unofficial, and souvenir versions.

◆

'59: AN EYEWITNESS ACCOUNT OF HURLING'S GOLDEN AGE

points, had to be replaced due to injury. Mick Flannelly came in and scored two goals and according to the *Irish Independent* he '*crowned a brilliant outing with two spectacular goals and proved himself the most dangerous forward on view*'. Having only come on as a sub in the All-Ireland Final, the Cork Examiner felt that this display '*strengthened his claim to a forward position in the All-Ireland replay against Kilkenny*'. With John Kiely scoring 1-1, Waterford ran out 3-12 to 2-10 victors.

Obviously, Waterford couldn't play Kilkenny in a challenge, but Johnny McGovern remembers that 'Waterford and Kilkenny had great respect for each other. We played each other a lot'. This is borne out by the statistics from 1959. Of Waterford's 18 games, six of them were against Kilkenny. As they had only played each other once before in the championship, there wasn't the intensity to their rivalry that would have existed with regular Munster Championship rivals, Cork and Tipperary. Kilkenny were generally very respectful of their opponents, and this is borne out by Johnny's comments on the Wexford team of the day.

> 'We had big games with Wexford. Jimmy O'Brien was a hard man to hurl on. You wouldn't be able to get a stroke on the ball. He was good... a real worker. Wexford had marvellous teams, fine sporting teams... Keogh, Ned Wheeler, Tim Flood, Nick O'Donnell and all of those.'

The accounts from the County Board from this challenge match are interesting. They show the receipts for the game and all of the outlay required to run the event. The biggest cost was the rent on the field but even with all expenses considered, more than 90% profit was made, to be split equally between the Waterford and Wexford County Boards.

The players travelled by car to Dublin on Saturday October 3 for check-in at the Grand Hotel in Malahide by 6.30pm. This was their usual mode of transport and avoiding the train kept the team away from the supporters who were flocking to the capital. This isolation all went towards building team spirit and staying calm. Meanwhile, Waterford supporters were availing of any opportunity to get to the match. One Waterford fan, Rue Colbert, recalls the effort his family made.

> 'I was 13 when I saw them win an All-Ireland... that's my claim to fame. I went up on the back of a Lambretta scooter. Myself and my father went up and down on the one day. The weather was grand... it was a good fine day. We started early in the morning. We stopped around Carlow for sandwiches and then we went on to the match. I remember we got to the game and the father knew somebody... and he parked the

scooter in his driveway, and we made our way up to Croke Park. We were up the very back of the terrace to the left of Hill 16. Straight after the game we came home. That is fair going for a Lambretta scooter. The father just kept on going. I remember going across the bridge that night and there were crowds celebrating.'

Another Waterford fan, Michael Cullen found himself in Dublin but with ticket trouble. His grandson, Davy Cullen, tells this brilliant story.

'In October 1959, my grandfather, Michael Cullen formerly of Aird Mhór & Trá Mhór had arranged with a friend to collect a ticket for the All-Ireland final replay between Kilkenny and Waterford from the Clarence Hotel, Dublin. When my grandfather arrived there with my father, Con and other family members, he asked for the ticket but the lady on reception who was expecting my grandfather had changed shift. The next lady did not know anything about the ticket and could not find it. Being the gentleman that my grandfather was, he said to the lady that he would be able to get another one... which he did. A number of days later, a gentleman from the Clarence Hotel posted the ticket to my grandfather accompanied by a nice letter. The additional ticket was never used... was never broken and it's still not broken. The actual stub has remained attached and the print on the letter is clearly visible to this day.'

Paddy Downey writing in *The Sunday Review* two weeks before the replay reported that the Kilkenny selectors' motto was *'don't change horses in mid-stream'* when they picked the team for the replay on the previous Monday night. There had been fears that John McGovern, injured in the drawn match, would not make the replay, but he was fully expected to be in the starting line-up. Fr. Tommy Maher of St. Kieran's College had been training the team and county secretary, Paddy Grace was quoted as saying:

'I think we'll do it this time. All the lads are in tip-top form and we're very confident that our midfielders, Mick Brophy and Paddy Kelly, will at least hold their own with Seamus Power and Phil Grimes. A marked difference from our approach to the last game is that our supporters seem over-confident this time. But we are not allowing that attitude to spread to the players. Of course, the game could go either way, by a few points margin. But, we are determined that we'll pile up a higher points score than we did in the drawn game, and that Waterford will get a lot less than 1-17.'

'59: AN EYEWITNESS ACCOUNT OF HURLING'S GOLDEN AGE

If Ollie Walsh could repeat his performance, with strong coverage from his full-backs, and if Paddy Buggy and Mick Walsh could subdue Frankie Walsh and Tom Cheasty, Downey was sticking with Kilkenny to win their 15th title. He doubted *'Waterford's wisdom in dropping Donal Whelan to make way for Tom Cunningham at full forward'* and felt that Waterford had *'hit their peak'* on September 6. Art McGann, writing as 'Fear Ciuin' in *The Sunday Press*, felt that the introduction of Tom Cunningham made *'their new full-forward line more workmanlike than it was a month ago. Tom Cunningham is a great spearhead who can flip that ball around and make openings to beat the solid Kilkenny full-backs'*. He also didn't think that Kilkenny's right half-back Paddy Buggy, will make as good a job of marking the Waterford captain, Frankie Walsh, as he did on September 6.'

Kilkenny were also making positional switches and it was felt that Sean Clohessy would be more effective at left half-forward than in the right corner where he had featured in the drawn final. Dick Carroll was moved to that position to be marked by John Barron. Having allowed them five goals in the first game, he doubted that the Kilkenny full-forward line would *'get away with much from the Waterford fulls, Joe Harney, Austin Flynn, and John Barron. The southern trio learned a bitter lesson in the drawn game and the Kilkenny full line can now expect close making and no mistakes'*. Indeed, Waterford trainer, John Keane, was confident.

> 'As things turned out on September 6, we were lucky to get a second chance, but the boys are fitter than ever now, and I think we can win this time.'

McGann agreed that with a liberal supply of ball from Power and Grimes to the forwards that Waterford would win. Gerry Ahane in the Irish Weekly Independent, without committing to a forecast, pointed out that Kilkenny had benefitted from two excellent tests in the lead up to the game, first against Wexford in the Walsh Cup final and then in the Oireachtas semi-final. By comparison, Waterford had only had one outing, a challenge against Wexford in Waterford. Ahane commented that:

> 'Waterford on the other hand have been attempting to retain peak form for too long a period, an impossible task, and I anticipate a lack of bite in their play against the wiles of the more seasoned campaigners from Kilkenny.'

The description of the changes in the Waterford team summarised the situation. *'The defence and midfield are the same as that which played against Kilkenny in the drawn game. Changes in attack see Mick Flannelly, who came on as a sub in the drawn game, take over at right-*

'59: AN EYEWITNESS ACCOUNT OF HURLING'S GOLDEN AGE

half forward from Larry Guinan who has moved to top of the right. Tom Cunningham, another sub in the drawn game takes over the leadership of the attack, while Charlie Ware and Donal Whelan, originally right corner and full forward respectively, are now included among the substitutes.'

There was some public debate around whether Mick Flannelly should be brought back onto the team. For a while, Charlie Ware was preferred by the selectors, but Michael O'Connor had his own preference.

> 'Flan would be in my book ahead of Charlie Ware. Flan was always an addition on the team. He might not star but he made the team better. He was a team player.'

With a new line-up in the forwards for the replay, Tom Cunningham recalls the tactical approach.

> 'Larry Guinan John Kiely and myself were the full-forward line. I remember asking John Keane before the match if there would be any objection to John Kiely and I switching places from time to time during the match. He said, "Go ahead". That's what happened... we were trying to confuse the Kilkenny fellas, Tom Walsh at corner-back and John Maher.'

The Kilkenny side was as expected but there were three talking points. Johnny McGovern was confirmed at left half-back. This was only surprising because he had dislocated his shoulder in the drawn game and even in training on the week of the replay *'still found that he was a little sore'*. Mick Brophy had been named at centrefield and this surprised some supporters as he had been suffering from tonsilitis which had kept him out of action since the drawn game. On the day, his place was ultimately taken by Tim Kelly. Finally, there was talk of the emergence of one of the stars of the minor team. Eddie Keher had been brought into the senior panel and had done well against Dublin in the Oireachtas semi-final, meriting his place on the subs bench. Eddie Keher recalls how his call-up came about.

> 'I just got a card in the post to report for training. That's the way it happened at that time... the secretary sent it out. Paddy Grace phoned me to say that Ollie Walsh would collect me. What a start... what a thrill. Ollie would be calling for me in Inistioge! Obviously, I was very surprised and in awe of the whole thing. As you can imagine, the Kilkenny senior team were all my heroes. I had to walk into the dressing-room where they were... it certainly took a bit of getting used to. I remember playing in

Team line-up from Pat Fanning's private notebook.

'59: AN EYEWITNESS ACCOUNT OF HURLING'S GOLDEN AGE

the Walsh Cup final against Wexford and the Oireachtas semi-final against Dublin. What I remember about the Dublin match, which was in Nowlan Park, was Des Foley who played hurling and football for Dublin. We had come up against him when he had played with St. Joseph's, Fairview at colleges level... a great hurler. He made the Dublin senior hurling team also at a young age, only off minor. He might have been a year or two older than me. I was called in to play against Dublin and we went out on the pitch. We were pucking around at each side of the field before the match and Des Foley came up the field and up to me to wish me luck on my first day with the senior team... which I thought was a wonderful gesture. For me, the draw was a mixed blessing. I had to get over the disappointment of losing another minor final, and seeing the seniors hauled back to a draw, but I was surprised to get a call-up to the senior panel for the replay.'

In the *Sunday Independent*, Eamon Young stuck with his prediction of Waterford as he *'cannot see them making the same mistake twice'*. He was referring to the *'juvenile efforts to keep Ned Power's goal clear, which we saw a month ago. We can expect that trainer John Keane and his friends have drilled into their charges that the first principle of defence is to cover the goalie by facing out to oncoming forwards'*.

Television was becoming relevant to the GAA for the first time. On the day of the replay, the *Sunday Independent* launched a brand-new feature in the newspaper, a TV Guide showing a complete list of BBC and ITV programmes for the week. This was in response to the demand for the new technology as *'every day more and more people in Ireland are buying television sets. Soon the demand will grow larger when Ireland's own service begins'*. Looking ahead for the week shows the BBC's *Sportsview* programme scheduled for 8.45pm on Wednesday October 7. This weekly summary programme was due to feature highlights from the All-Ireland final replay. Reporting on the game was Kenneth Wolstenholme again. In *The Sunday Press* he had a column on the day of the match in which he explains that *'so enthusiastic was the reception in England when we showed the first Kilkenny/Waterford set-to that we just had to see it out to the end. So, the BBC Television film cameras are at Croke Park again and I am with them'*.

He had also been at the football final, so he was making his third visit to Croke Park in five weeks. Whether this made him an expert or not, he still voiced his opinion that *'in that first match Kilkenny got the goals, and even a non-hurling expert like this Englishman realises that you've got to score three points to make up one goal'*. This led him to assert that *'my money is on Kilkenny. The great goalkeeping of Ollie Walsh and those tantalising drop shots of Tom O'Connell will tip the scales in Kilkenny's favour. I hope so anyway, because ever since September 6, I've been*

'59: AN EYEWITNESS ACCOUNT OF HURLING'S GOLDEN AGE

having bets with my new-found Irish friends and Kilkenny are carrying my money'. This seems a bit disloyal to Waterford. After all, following the drawn game, the GAA presented him with the hurley that Seamus Power had used to score the equalising goal, a priceless Waterford sporting artefact. The mood in the Waterford camp was buoyant. One of the selectors, Terry Dalton, recalls the drive from the team hotel in Malahide to Croke Park.

> 'Coming in from Malahide, the crowd I was with all started to sing. It was the fourth of October… and it was the most beautiful day. The sun was splitting the stones. Cheasty and John Kiely were in the car, and they were all singing away like Fairhill. They were in the mood, and they had the confidence.'

Joe Harney knew that he needed to improve on his performance in the drawn match but with an extra month of recovery from his injury, he felt more confident.

> 'The first day I didn't play well… I wasn't fit enough to play well. I could have been a doubt for the replay because the defence was poor that day. Father Maher was their trainer at the time, and they'd know how to handle fellas. If you are not fit, you can't follow the man. I remember that day… the man used to go out along and he'd come back… and out and back. I don't know whether he knew that I was in plaster for so long or not… I don't know.'

An unusual feature of the Waterford dressing-room was the visit of some famous Cork hurlers who provided both moral and practical support. They were warmly welcomed by the Waterford management and Pat Fanning described the scene for the *Waterford News and Star*.

> 'Into the Waterford dressing-room before the game came a trio of Cork Gaels to do what they could in these last tense moments. There was Christy Ring chatting with this player and that and looking just as worried as if Cork were about to take the field. There too was Eamonn Young, a man who tipped Waterford from the start, except for one wavering moment before we blasted Cork, and stuck by his choice. Eamonn had the quiet effective word for everybody. Finally, there was that man from Carrigtwohill who worked just as hard on the lads as did our own Jack Furlong. All these were back again at half time, giving a hand with the boys and getting them ready for the second period. Waterford players and official appreciated the presence of these Cork allies.'

'59: AN EYEWITNESS ACCOUNT OF HURLING'S GOLDEN AGE

Larry Guinan still remembers this support.

'Another good thing about Ring. He came into our dressing-room in '59 before the All-Ireland final. That's the sort Ring was. I remember him putting tape around Seamus Power's hurley and saying, "There you go... is that alright now?" Fair play. Other people... other counties, they were behind Waterford.'

Meanwhile in the Kilkenny dressing-room, the players displayed the calm that came with frequent visits to Croke Park. Even young Eddie Keher had played there regularly but, with Johnny McGovern still not operating at 100%, the team's coach had a word with Keher.

'Fr. Maher came up to me before the match just to say "It is very likely you will be going in"... to be ready. I was as prepared as I could be to feel that I was going to get in on the field.'

All was relatively calm, but outside the crowds were starting to arrive. They had plenty to entertain them before the big match. The curtain-raiser for the day was the Junior All-Ireland final between the unique pairing of London and Antrim, the only time that two teams from outside the 26 counties have contested an All-Ireland hurling final. While London won for the junior title twice, in 1938 and '49, Antrim were seeking their first All-Ireland title at any grade. Antrim had beaten Cork in the 'home final' by 3-4 to 2-3 and were favourites to beat the largely unknown London team. London's centre-forward Billy Duffy had previously played with Galway, Des Dillon with Clare and Liam Dargan with Laois. Duffy was one of five Galway natives in the panel which included players from 10 different counties. They surprised Antrim with their superior fitness and, despite playing into a stiff breeze, London were only a point behind at half-time, 2-5 to 1-9. Liam Dargan, who had previously graced Croke Park in the All-Ireland senior final of 1949 for Laois against Tipperary, was the key player for London, along with his midfield partner Eamonn Murray. Antrim made several switches to quell their influence, but London's blend of youth and experience proved too strong, and the game finished London 5-10, Antrim 2-10.

With the preliminaries completed, the crowd of 77,285 were now in place - an increase of 3,000 on the drawn game. Waterford took the field first to a huge cheer and warmed up at the Railway End. Pat Fanning was slightly unnerved by the confident appearance of their opponents. 'Kilkenny came on almost nonchalantly in the manner of many great Noreside teams I have watched in Croke Park. They were at home there'. Conditions were good and the hard ground, as described by Carbery, would have suited the Waterford style of play. 'I walked

'59: AN EYEWITNESS ACCOUNT OF HURLING'S GOLDEN AGE

the Croke Park pitch shortly after noon and found it bone hard. There was a slight covering of grass after the long drought.'

After the parade behind the Artane Boys Band, the teams took their positions on the pitch and faced the flag flying from the roof of the Cusack Stand for the national anthem. The wind had not died down since the junior final and Carbery described the conditions.

> 'Sean Clohessy, the Tulloran and Kilkenny captain won the toss for Kilkenny, but as usual the black and amber men decided to play against the sun and wind... into the city goal. "It helps our lads to steady their early shots," I was told by a wise Kilkenny veteran once. It has worked well for the Noresmen and seemed lucky for the first quarter. Kilkenny opened so brilliantly that the prophets who told us to expect a Waterford debacle were clapping their hands for joy.'

Sean Clohessy's decision to play against the strong breeze was a significant choice as John D. Hickey in the *Irish Independent* considered that *'even the most conservative hurling man would regard as worth four points over half an hour'*.

Mick Flannelly won the ball from the throw-in and had the first shot of the game, but it drifted to the right and wide. Power, Kiely, and Grimes got involved quickly and Larry Guinan flashed the ball wide. Two wides in just the first minute. Clohessy had a wide for Kilkenny and it wasn't until a Kilkenny free conceded by Jackie Condon, that Mick Walsh scored the opening point of the game. Frankie Walsh had the opportunity to level from a free gained by Tom Cunningham but, very unusually, he missed. 'We got off to a bad start… a bit nervous. I failed to lift a close-in free but whipped it off the ground over the bar.' Waterford were taking time to settle into the game. The crucial difference in the replay was the performance of the backs. Having conceded five goals in the drawn game, Frankie Walsh was pleased that 'our backs were tighter the second day". Martin Óg Morrissey agreed that 'the reality of the situation was that we conceded too many goals. Thankfully they didn't get them in the second game'. In reviewing the year, the *Carbery Annual* concluded that the full-back line were the winning difference.

> 'A feature of the Waterford hurlers was their fearless tackling. They were not in the least awed by Kilkenny's great name. The blue and white clad backs showed surprising improvement on the drawn game. Austin Flynn, Barron, and Harney kept well clear of Ned Power, who kept an impeccable goal from end to end. He saved quite as many shots and had as sound a record for the run of the hour as the better-known Ollie Walsh.'

'59: AN EYEWITNESS ACCOUNT OF HURLING'S GOLDEN AGE

Tommy O'Connell, the danger man from the first game was closely held by Joe Harney who *'outplayed'* him according to Carbery. When O'Connell moved out to the half-forwards to create space for himself, he was met by a hard shoulder from Jackie Condon which quelled the immediate danger. Waterford attacked again and when Flannelly sent in a low ball, Tom Cunningham doubled on it but again it went wide. This was compounded by a Kilkenny point from Billy Dwyer and a goal from Dennis Heaslip. Heaslip's flashing movement was compared memorably by Carbery to *'a kingfisher over a stream'*. Despite setting a lot of the early pace, Waterford were already four points down. Seamus Power sent in a ball which Frankie won. As he moved towards goal, he was brought down but he took the free himself and opened Waterford's account.

Waterford continued to press forward and a seemingly unstoppable shot from Larry Guinan was pushed wide by Ollie Walsh. When nothing came of the resulting '70', nerves were setting in. Kilkenny were coming by their scores easier, and two more points put them 1-4 to one point up. Frankie Walsh recalls his surprise at this scoreline. 'I think we were six points down after 10 minutes... and we were playing with a strong wind.'

At about this point, 10 minutes into the game, Philly Grimes broke the index finger of his left hand. He informed John Keane, but he was told to forget it and play on. He moved to right half-back. In a sweeping move from the back, via Seamus Power in midfield, the ball got to Mick Flannelly on the left wing. He took a left-handed shot to the top right corner. Ollie Walsh moving to his right, twisted in the air but couldn't keep it out. The goal was a huge morale boost for the Waterford team and supporters. Frankie remembers the confidence boost that brought.

> 'Then it all began to happen for us. Mick Flannelly, the lightest man on the team after myself... goaled.'

Mick Flannelly had turned the game, but he credited to teamwork in the build-up play.

> 'I got a beauty. I hit it left-handed and got a good goal. It was a good goal but the work up to it put me in the position to have the shot. I didn't beat six or seven players to get a goal... the ball came up the whole field and it was being moved around. There was no fella trying to beat two or three men... the ball was kept moving. That's the only way you will beat backs, to keep the ball moving.'

Despite stout defending by Martin Óg Morrissey, Clohessy managed to score a point,

'59: AN EYEWITNESS ACCOUNT OF HURLING'S GOLDEN AGE

but Tom Cheasty started to come into the game and scored his first point of the day. Johnny McGovern, who'd gone off with a shoulder injury in the drawn game, had to be replaced after 15 minutes. His influence was emphasised by Frankie Walsh *'when Johnny McGovern played well, Kilkenny played well'*. With McGovern replaced. Clohessy was moved to midfield and Walsh was brought back to mark Flannelly. It also allowed Eddie Keher to make his championship debut, a moment he will never forget.

'It's funny, I would have played in the minor match before the drawn match and in All-Irelands before that for the minors. I tend to be fairly good at focusing on the important things and blocking out the crowd noise. In the first days that I played for Kilkenny, in the other two matches and the All-Ireland, I was in awe of the players around me. I was more tuned in to when I'd get the ball... pass it to one of them. At that stage Kilkenny were being fairly well beaten and everyone was fairly well tied up. It took me a little while to get into the game... to get the run of it. I was a bit in awe of the situation for the '59 final. I was up against Mick Lacey. He was a solid wing back... good under the ball. He was a strong fella... unspectacular, I suppose, which is why he didn't get mentioned a lot, but he was doing a solid job at wing back.'

Johnny McGovern recalls the build up to this moment.

'Fr. Maher was telling me to do plenty of walking before the replay. I used to go down by the river every day for a walk to keep fit. I had my arm in a sling. It was a month after that the replay was played... it was marvellous weather for October. He said you'll be okay when you get warmed up. I was marking Mick Flannelly, but I only lasted about 20 minutes... and then Eddie Keher came on. Eddie had played minor in the first game. In the replay, for the first quarter of an hour, I wasn't playing well, and I knew myself that I shouldn't have played at all. Of course, when you get out first, you forget about it. They brought in Eddie Keher at half forward and brought some of the other lads back to the half back line. He was there from 1959 up to 1977, an amazing career.'

Frankie Walsh pointed from a free and Dwyer responded with a point keeping the gap between the teams at three points. Mick Lacey, now in midfield instead of Grimes, lobbed a '70' to the edge of the square and Tom Cheasty, really taking charge now, doubled on it and scored a goal to bring the teams level. Straight after, Frankie Walsh sent in a low ball which was collected by John Kiely and passed to Tom Cunningham, who passed it onwards to Cheasty. He twisted and turned before sending the ball over the bar for Waterford's first lead. Billy Dwyer was doing just as well at the other end and brought Kilkenny back to level scores. Tom Cheasty was hitting peak form though. He won the ball again and drove towards goal. His powerful shot was saved well by Ollie Walsh, but Cheasty was first to the rebound and put Waterford a goal ahead. Tom Cheasty recalls his two goals in the final in the book *Hurling Heroes*.

> 'The first goal was from a 70 by Mick Lacey. As the ball dropped in the square, I got my hurl to it and deflected it past Ollie. If he stayed back, he might have been able to stop it. For the second goal. I slipped my marker, Timmy Kelly, and went on a solo run and sent in a shot which Ollie saved. However, I met the rebound just before Ollie reached me and the ball hit the net.'

This was the turning point of the game and Waterford were never behind after that. At half-time Waterford lead 3-5 to 1-8. Right from the start of the second-half, Waterford were on the offensive. Tom Cunningham's shot was saved by Ollie Walsh. In the next attack he fed John Kiely instead. Kiely caused panic in the Kilkenny defence and was brought down. Frankie Walsh pointed the free. Tom Cheasty had been injured but played on and kept several defenders occupied, a trait admired by Johnny McGovern.

> 'Every team should have a Tom Cheasty... Cheasty was a great player for Waterford at centre-forward. We had to join in to try and put him off or he'd end up in the square with the ball. He was the ideal centre-forward... especially as they had the fast players on either side of him. John Kiely had been a centre-forward, but he went in corner-forward. He was a good hurler... a good striker of the ball.'

His own teammates were just as effusive in their praise with Larry Guinan agreeing with McGovern's analysis.

> 'Cheasty got two goals that day... he was a tower of strength. The way he took stick was unreal. Often after a game the bruises on that man's body were unreal. Cheasty never complained. He could draw two or three players and distribute the ball then to the wingers... he was great at that. His swerve... he'd remind you of Muhammad Ali.'

Ollie Walsh clearing from Larry Guinan and John Kiely.

Ollie Walsh under pressure from Larry Guinan and Tom Cunningham

'59: AN EYEWITNESS ACCOUNT OF HURLING'S GOLDEN AGE

The saviour of the drawn game, Seamus Power, gave credit where it was due for the replay.

> 'Tom Cheasty was our lynch pin that day. He was the centre of every attack we made. He was a courageous man... strong as an ox, God be merciful to him. He certainly gave the Kilkenny backs considerable worry and torment.'

Jimmy O'Brien of Wexford emphasised Tom's strength.

> 'They wouldn't have won it only for Cheasty. He was a hard man to manage. If you talk specifically about the All-Ireland, he was going well in the second-half. He got a ball out near centrefield, and he turned around and headed for goal. Johnny McGovern met him, ran straight into him and he spun him. Cheasty slightly changed his direction but kept going. Paddy Buggy met him on the other side and hit him but straightened him up! Cheasty went in and scooped it over the bar. It was some point! The strength to do it! His real benefit was that they had very good players like Frankie Walsh... great hurlers but a bit light. Cheasty was the ideal ram. He was a great centre-forward. He was a gas man. I liked Cheasty. At that time a man running at a defence was rare because you'd get clobbered... there would be no doubt about it. If you took him out... you'd be a hero. Cheasty had that ability and the courage and speed to do it.'

Larry Guinan now showed his strength to battle through the Kilkenny defence to score a great point to make it 3-7 to 1-8. Eddie Keher came into the game and scored two points, sandwiching one from Frankie Walsh. As the only two Kilkenny scores in the half, it was a great performance for a minor player and signalled what was to come from one of the game's greatest ever players.

> 'One of them, I just took it and hit it without catching it. The other I think I caught it, broke away and hit a left-handed shot over the bar. I was aware that it was very tight in the defence. With Waterford on top and defending to avoid any goals being scored, they were playing very tight, and it was very hard to get space. The first ball I think... it just broke out and I put my hurl to it and hit it over the bar and the second... I think I got my hand to it and turned left-handed over the bar.'

At this point Waterford were gaining in confidence and 10 minutes into second-half, Austin Flynn felt the game was going Waterford's way.

'59: AN EYEWITNESS ACCOUNT OF HURLING'S GOLDEN AGE

'We had training for about a month in between. I'd say Waterford was tuned better. After about 10 minutes of the second-half, I felt that we were going to win it... but you never know until it really happens.'

The game was at its most intense and in a bout of hard hurling Mick Lacey went down injured. He was replaced by Michael O'Connor who came on at wing back while Grimes resumed his usual position in midfield. O'Connor recalls that this was the end of long road back to championship hurling.

'I was back on the Waterford panel in 1959, but I didn't play during the campaign. I only came on as a sub in the All-Ireland final. As an act of appreciation, I was picked as a selector so that kept me involved. I really looked up to the chairman, Pat Fanning and the trainer, John Keane. I had a good relationship with Pat. I was reluctant to go on in the final, but I was delighted to get the opportunity. I felt great but I had put on a bit of weight. My confidence wasn't as good.

'I came on for Mick Lacey. I think it was just tactics... they wanted fresh legs. I was on Eddie Keher... he was only 18 or 19... a fast young fella at that time. I remember going for the first ball on the wing. I rose the ball and gave a little swerve. I thought that I would drive it into the opposition square, but he was able to hook me. I was surprised at it. It was unbelievable.

'Eddie Keher was a very good player, and he was strong even at that young age. He was a good player and quite fast. I was fast but he was fast too. I remember blocking him and that was the big thing I was trying to do... to block him... block him. I don't think he scored while I was on him.'

With quarter of an hour to go, Ned Power was shadowing a ball which was going wide when he was hit. A melee developed and was quickly quelled but erupted again between John Barron and Dick Carroll, both of whom were sent off. To this day, the sending off of John Barron is still a surprise amongst Waterford GAA people. Michael Dowling of Erin's Own captures the general feeling when he described John. 'He never smoked or drank. He wasn't a glad handler. John Barron was an outstanding man, but saying that, he got thrown off in the replay of the All-Ireland… the quietest man in the world!' Austin Flynn, a lifelong friend of John's concurred.

'For the inter-county player who was the least likely to be put off in a match, I have no doubt that all the players of my time would name John Barron, so it has always been a great regret of mine that John was put off in the All-Ireland final... John was everybody's No. 1 gentleman.'

The eagle-eyed reporters in the press box seemed to have observed the entire incident but, typical of reporting at the time, were reluctant to call out an individual for an infringement. In the opinion of John D. Hickey in the *Irish Independent* the only untoward incident in the game *'was caused by another player whose conduct escaped the vigilance of the referee, who did not seem to be as alert as in the drawn game between the sides'*. Billy Kelly's theory is that *'the reporters wouldn't mention who was sent off, so they wouldn't be called as a witness when the case came before the county board'*. The *Evening Herald* wrote that *'from the terraces it appeared the real culprit escaped the notice of the referee'*. Joe Sherwood in his 'In the Soup' column in the Evening Press went a little further and, in tune with the controversial nature of his writing, placed the ultimate blame on a Kilkenny player.

> *'A bit of a barney in the Waterford goalmouth in which eight or more players indulged in a mixture of all-in wrestling and fisticuffs. John and Dick restarted a little feud of their own in which some timely punches were exchanged in the clinches. And the referee couldn't do anything else but "retire them" to the sideline. But the culprit who started off the spark that led to the shindy got off scot-free. And he wasn't a Waterford player.'*

The general consensus was that there was very little to the incident. Martin Óg Morrissey recalls 'I don't think there was anything in that. That was handbags stuff. There was nothing in it at all.' John Barron himself even commented that they were sent off 'for very little' and Frankie Walsh felt that 'John Barron didn't deserve to get sent off'. Forwards like Larry Guinan were at the other end of the field and left mystified.

> 'I barely remember it. I was on that time, but I honestly don't know what they were sent off for. As I was saying before, the backs job was to keep out the forward and Dick Carroll, I remember was on him and they were tussling. Dick Carroll was obviously trying to get in and John was trying to keep him out. They were tussling at the end-line, and they ended up over the end line, as far as I remember. I would say if it happened on the '21'... none of them would be sent off but when the referee went to them, they were actually off the field at that stage from the struggle.'

'59: AN EYEWITNESS ACCOUNT OF HURLING'S GOLDEN AGE

The official reasoning was clarified in the referee's report captured in the Central Council Minutes on November 28.

> *'I refereed the All-Ireland senior hurling final, Waterford v Kilkenny. During the second half of this game, I sent John Barron (Waterford) and Dick Carroll (Kilkenny) to the line. Each of these two players dropped his hurley and struck each other with their fists. Otherwise, the game was played in a good hard clean sporting spirit.'*

Kenneth Wolstenholme was impressed by the efficient handling of the game by referee, Gerry Fitzgerald of Limerick. *'One thing I will never forget is the way the referee had two offending players shake hands before putting them to the line. It was a sporting gesture you would rarely see anywhere.'* As a result, both players were suspended for two months. John didn't play again until 1960, being replaced by Joe Coady and Freddie O'Brien in the league matches that followed the All-Ireland.

Waterford were awarded a free out for the foul on Ned Power. When the ball made its way as far as Tom Cunningham, he was brought down, and injury required him to be replaced by Donal Whelan. Waterford were well on top now and after several attacks, Mick Flannelly scored another point to put Waterford six points ahead, and Frankie Walsh stretched it further to seven. It was desperate times for the Kilkenny defence. Ollie Walsh broke out of defence and ran all the way to midfield with the ball. He was chased every step of the way by Larry Guinan. This was typical of the Waterford players' work rate. As Carbery described it:

> *'Waterford played just as well into the wind in the third quarter as Kilkenny did in the opening session. As I looked down field every man in the Waterford side seemed to me to be on the move. And they moved at a sparkling rate. They never dallied with the ball. John Keane and Charlie Ware had schooled them well. Where I thought Waterford were superior was in the speed and security with which they hit ground balls from all angles. With smooth easy swings they smacked that ball surprising distances and with great confidence and accuracy of direction. As a team the winners looked an efficiently schooled lot, and obedient too. In a word, they played model hurling on Sunday, particularly near the end, when every man co-ordinated.'*

As the game neared the end, Kilkenny started going for goal instead of points, causing nervous moments for Larry Guinan.

'59: AN EYEWITNESS ACCOUNT OF HURLING'S GOLDEN AGE

'I remember they got a 21-yard free at one stage. It was near the end, and we were winning well... I was petrified, Christ they might get an oul goal here... knowing their luck. Who took the '21' was a foxy lad from Tulloroan. What he did was he just lifted the ball and tipped it over to the full-forward... Dwyer. Dwyer struck the ball but some of the lads saved it. It was a brave thing for your man to do, to just flick the ball instead of going for the goal.'

Frankie Walsh, playing a captain's part, scored the final point and Waterford had won, 3-12 to 1-10. The full-time whistle unleashed a torrent of emotion for all concerned. Jackie Condon, recalling it in 2021, still becomes emotional at the memories of that instant. His voice cracked as he told me:

'Winning the match mattered to me... the rest of it wasn't special. That was the pinnacle... it was just unbelievable. I leapt up in the air. I couldn't believe we were after doing it. It was the pinnacle for me... everything else was going to be downhill. It was unbelievable... unbelievable. It was just unbelievable. It was such a treat to win it. I just couldn't put words to it. It was just unbelievable... I was over the moon.'

In a couple of simple phrases, Martin Óg Morrissey also recalls the defining emotions of that moment.

'I played my heart out. We came out victorious.'

There was pure unbridled joy amongst the Waterford supporters on the pitch. As the match ended the players were mobbed by jubilant supporters. Jackie Condon recalls 'The crowd came on the pitch, and they were all digging you in the back. You were in no condition to be belted on the back. They'd be knocking the wind out of you and you on your last legs. It was all great stuff... they were just as enthused as we were. They were just over the moon. It is amazing how big a thing it was.' Some players were lifted onto the shoulders of their fans and Martin Óg Morrissey recalls 'Wattie Morrissey and young Micheal Gallagher threw me up on their shoulders.'.

Family members sought each other out. Sean Power, Seamus' brother, found him on the pitch and they embraced. 'It was everything,' said Sean recalling the emotion of the moment. 'Our mother had travelled up. A sister came home from England. We had lost our father the year before. I said to Séamus "You managed Clohossey". He just nodded "I had to..." That

Frankie Walsh raising the Liam MacCarthy Cup

◆

Frankie Walsh with President of Ireland, Éamon de Valera, and GAA President, JJ Stuart.

◆

was a crucial battle on the day. In a further twist to the family tale, Sean represented Wexford and won an All-Ireland medal in 1960. Surely it is a unique achievement for brothers to win All-Irelands in successive years for different counties.

The Waterford and Kilkenny teams stayed on the pitch while Frankie Walsh went up into the new Hogan Stand for the presentation. Martin Óg recalls 'We were out on the pitch… we waited below at the end of the stand. At that stage you didn't go up in the stand and around and down'. Larry Guinan recalls the pride he felt at seeing his great friend about to accept the cup.

> 'I think we were on the pitch when Frankie got the cup. I can't even remember Frankie going up on the stand. I remember looking up alright waving to him. He was something else. Frankie was a great captain... he was only 22 at the time. For the replay I was 21. He was a great captain... he played as a captain as well.'

Eddie Keher recalls that 'Kilkenny would have stayed on the pitch, a good way back. The Waterford supporters would be crowding around on the field'. Up in the stand, Frankie was not alone. His mentor and the driving force behind the team, Pat Fanning was with him every step of the way. Pat recalled in 1984, the 25th anniversary of the win:

> *'The replay is history, the supreme moment in my lifetime in hurling. This time there was no mistake, no last-minute effort at saving the day. This time it was Waterford rampant, unbeatable, surging to the greatest of hurling victories. Here were men, tested as few men had been tested, and they had come through in the manner of champions. The planning, the training, the sacrifice had paid off. Waterford hurling had come into its own. Frankie Walsh, hero of the hour, receiving the MacCarthy Cup from GAA President, J.J. Stuart, and chatting with the President of Ireland, Eamon de Valera, are others of my cherished moments of the day.'*

Frankie was asked for the rest of his life about this moment. In Conor Power's book he remembered:

> *'I was trying to get my thoughts together to see what I'd say. I didn't say very much. I don't agree with all this speech-making. All the county wants, and all the captain wants to do is to get the cup and show it to the supporters.'*

In speaking to Brendan Fullam, he claimed not to remember what he said in his speech.

'59: AN EYEWITNESS ACCOUNT OF HURLING'S GOLDEN AGE

He was so overcome with emotion and excitement that *'Dr. J.J. Stuart, President of the GAA, had to lift the cup with me'*. Frankie's son, Peter, tells a story from his mother.

> 'After being presented with the cup, Frankie was down on the field and he hit a fella on the head with the cup. Yer man was pulling and dragging him, and he got fed up with him… and he hit him a flog with the cup on the top of the head. That would be him. There was only so far you could take him… and then he'd fight.'

> Kay Grimes – 'He never came across to me as being any way violent off the field.'

> Peter Walsh – 'Oh yeah, he'd be narky out!'

> Phil Fanning – 'Frankie wasn't called the Nettle for nothing.'

There were also a few testy words exchanged between Jackie Condon and Denis Heaslip following the heat of battle.

> 'I remember going out the second day and Denis Heaslip was playing on me. He was a small little fella. By Jaysus… he wasn't going anywhere the second day. I went to go shake hands with him after the match. I said "Good luck." "You're an oul cur," he said. "Have it any way you like," I said, "as long as we won the match". I gave him a rough time I suppose.'

Martin Óg remembers the hysteria after the game.

> 'To tell the God's honest truth… to say you've seen fellas kissing one another, I remember coming out of Croke Park and met two workmates from Ferrybank which everyone knows is the hot-bed between Waterford and Kilkenny. I really thought they were women the way they were kissing me! The feeling of victory, there is absolutely nothing like it… you'd be walking on cloud nine.'

Not everyone was able to celebrate immediately. Tom Cunningham was on another trip to hospital.

> 'I suffered a half-accidental injury that forced me to retire. Jim 'The Link' Walsh was

'59: AN EYEWITNESS ACCOUNT OF HURLING'S GOLDEN AGE

full-back for Kilkenny. I think he hit me in the back of the head with the hurley, something like that anyway. It wasn't a clash anyway... it was an off the ball thing. I got injured. There was no doctor with the team. The practice at that time was if you got cut and it was bleeding, you'd be sent to the Mater Hospital for stitching. I visited a few hospitals! I stayed for the end of the match. You'd have to wait for the hackney driver to bring you to the hospital. Getting stitched then was a common thing... it wasn't unusual for fellas to end up with stitches. I missed the final whistle and the presentation of the cup.'

The players were rightly pleased with their own performance. Having gotten over the novelty of playing in Croke Park in the draw, players like Jackie Condon were more relaxed in the replay.

'The second game we had no bother with them. That game I was very relaxed. I won't say I had a great game, but I had a solid enough game... I was happy with my game that day. There are some days you go out and for whatever reason the game doesn't work for you. It worked for us that day and the team was working as well. If you get the ball in the half-back line and you fire it down in front of Frankie Walsh, you expect him to get it and score. That was all working well.'

Eddie Keher pointed out that the winning full-back line made all the difference.

'The full-forward line went to town in the first match, so you can imagine the full-back line in the replay were fairly geared up not to let those lads get a chance.'

Key to that line was Joe Harney who got the better of goal-scorer, Tommy O'Connell in the replay. The *Irish Press* described Harney's defence as *'masterly'*, especially in the second-half. Joe modestly deflected this praise.

'Austin Flynn and John Barron were top-class defenders and they helped me greatly during the course of the two games. Mick Flannelly, Tom Cheasty and Tom Cunningham scored brilliant goals... and Martin Óg Morrissey was a horse of a man in the half-back line, while Seamus Power and my friend Philly ruled the roost in the middle of the field.'

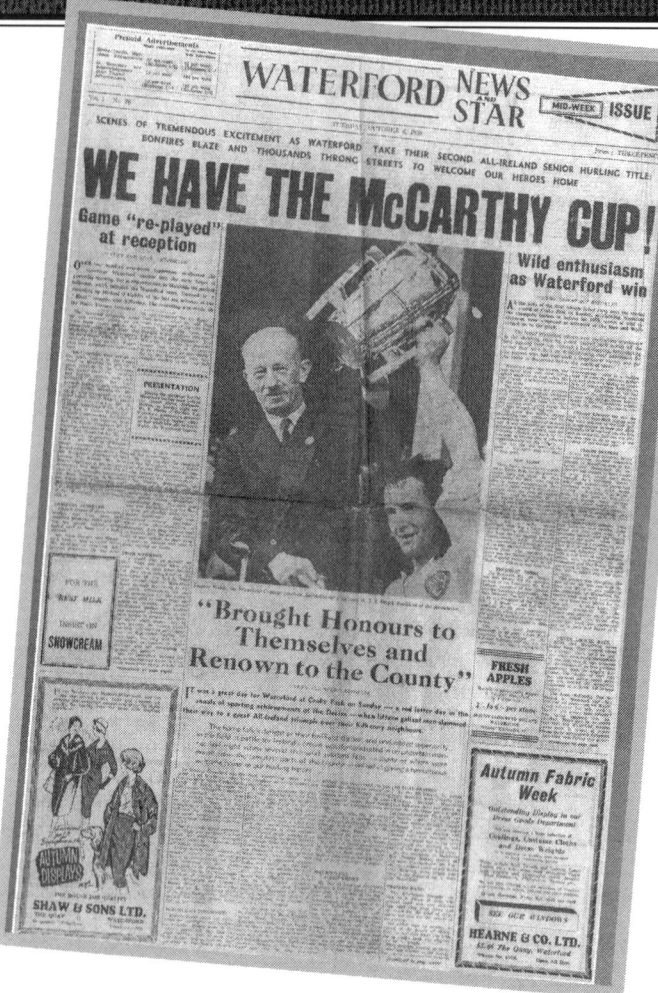

Front page of the Waterford News and Star newspaper

◆

Newspaper giveaways – a supplement with the Waterford News and Star and a team photo with the Munster Express

◆

'59: AN EYEWITNESS ACCOUNT OF HURLING'S GOLDEN AGE

While some Kilkenny supporters felt that O'Connell was being manhandled, he had no complaints when quoted in Joe Cody's book, *The Stripy Men*.

> 'It was a hard game. The Waterford backs were tough but fair. I have no complaints at all on that score. We were beaten because we lost the battle out the field and so the forwards didn't get enough of the ball. That was down to the fact that the team had to be realigned immediately prior to the game when Mick Brophy was forced to withdraw.'

John D. Hickey writing in the *Independent* the morning after the replay provided a comprehensive summary.

> 'As one looks back it is an inescapable conclusion that Kilkenny were so taken out of their stride by Waterford's first half recovery that they were upset. Subsequent events bore out the theory, when the black-and-amber-jerseyed brigade fell to pieces in the closing stages. Kilkenny's reputation for pulling chestnuts out of the fire kept the game alive, but in the end, they were caught in a cauldron from which all their great hurling craft could not devise a means of escape. Kilkenny were well and truly beaten by a team of superior craftsmen whose greatest attribute on this occasion was their refusal to panic in the face of peril. Waterford started like a side possessed by the jitters, but they recovered admirably from their most inauspicious start and then, early in the second half, they hammered nails in the Kilkenny coffin when they showed how chances should be snapped up.'

Frankie Walsh's performance in the replay saw him win the Sports Star of the Week award in the *Irish Independent* on the Friday following the final.

While television ownership was still a rarity, the final was shown on BBC television on the Wednesday after the final. The *Sportsview* programme at 8.45pm showed edited highlights to a prime-time audience across the UK. The filming of a hurling match had presented unique challenges to the cameramen due to the speed of the moving ball. The commentary was again by Kenneth Wolstenholme, who seems to have developed a real liking for the sport. Despite the fact that he had tipped Kilkenny to win in the national press, he was happy that the best team won the replay. 'It was a tremendous game and I enjoyed it immensely', he was quoted by the *Evening Herald*. 'Even though my team did not win, I was not at all disappointed in the game. If anything, both teams played harder than they did in that very exciting first meeting.'

'59: AN EYEWITNESS ACCOUNT OF HURLING'S GOLDEN AGE

Looking back on the 50th anniversary of the win, Pat Fanning's reflection is an apt summary.

'This was a different Waterford team. This was a steely Waterford team. This was a team of, if I may say so, intelligent men with a great regard for themselves and a true appreciation of their own qualities. They came out the second day a more complete team because of their experience and not a thought even in their innermost selves that this could end in other than a victory. That was the day of days. They were superb and those All-Irelands with Kilkenny, they rank with the best of the era.'

Waterford were worthy of the 3-12 to 1-10 win, although an eight-point victory was unexpected by supporters. The *Munster Express* ran a forecast competition leading up to the replay and asked readers to predict the score of the match. Nobody managed to predict the exact score line in goals and points, but three entrants split the £20 prize as they correctly predicted a 21-point to 13-point win for Waterford.

Not that any Waterford fan really cared, they were too busy celebrating!

8

THE CELEBRATIONS

The game had taken its toll in injuries and the first stop for some of the players after Croke Park was the Mater Hospital. Phil Grimes had an x-ray and was found to have broken his finger. That incident happened 10 minutes into the game, but he still played an outstanding part in the following 50 minutes. Tom Cunningham had a head injury, and he remembers that 'I got split by The Link Walsh and had to go to the Mater to get stitched'. Further stitches were required by Tom Cheasty for a facial injury. While others were recovering from the intensity of the physical battle, Jackie Condon needed some time to absorb what had just happened. The enormity of the win was just starting to sink in.

> 'When I got out to the hotel I fecked off for a walk. I went off up around Malahide. I went off on my own, off up the beach… and went away for hours. I just got away from it and let it all sink in. It was just brilliant… brilliant.'

There wasn't much time to dwell on the achievement as the Waterford public wanted to celebrate with their team. By 7pm, the players were in the Ballroom of the Grand Hotel, Malahide for the Waterfordmen's Association reception which they had been planning for months. The secretary of the Waterford Reception Committee, Matt Maloney, felt it was worth the wait. 'Beating Kilkenny is worth two All-Irelands,' he enthused. The event had its formal elements. The menu was in Irish and had the team line-out on one side and the menu on the other side. There was an array of special guests including Paddy O'Keeffe, Secretary General of the GAA, and Dr J.J. Stuart, President of the GAA. They were hosted by Sean Feeney, the chairman of the Waterford Men's Association and Ned Daly, the assistant secretary. The Dungarvan Observer captured the mood of the night.

'59: AN EYEWITNESS ACCOUNT OF HURLING'S GOLDEN AGE

'One of the features of the happy event was a recording of Michael O'Hehir's broadcast of the game, which was punctuated by lusty cheering as the score hungry Waterford forwards hit up their very convincing winning total. Afterwards a film of the previous game was shown in slow motion.'

Tom Cheasty was always unhappy with O'Hehir's pronounciation of his name. Years later, when working together on a TV advertisement, Tom approached him and said 'The first thing now is to get my name right. I'm Cheasty… not Cheesty'… just like there is no a in cheese'. The menu consisted of soup, salmon or chicken and ham with peas and creamed potatoes, trifle, and coffee. After dinner a series of speeches was given by the President and Secretary of the GAA, the reception committee, the Waterfordmen's Association, and Canon Walsh who was representing the Bishop of Waterford. Canon Walsh, in congratulating the officials, recognised that 'Pat Fanning is the soul of inspiration to the team. I would also like to thank John Keane who guided the Waterford team'. Pat Fanning completed the formalities when he spoke on behalf of the team.

> 'The Waterford hurlers can bask in glory today for a short time and then they must get down to work again. Other things remain to be done. This Waterford team has not come out of nowhere. It had its beginning in Fermoy about four years ago when they were defeated. Then we began to realise that if they were properly trained and nurtured, they would win an All-Ireland. Any county that has featured in three Munster finals in three years and reached two All-Irelands and shared equally in both and reached the National League final has not come out of nowhere. The Waterford team has taken hard knocks in the spirit of true Irishmen and sportsmen, and it is that spirit that brought us out on top on Sunday. I would like to pay tribute to all those who handled hurleys down through the long lost years when there was no sign of reward.'

Frankie Walsh was presented with a statue of a hurler by P.N. Phelan, the first of many awards and mementos he would receive on behalf of the team in the coming months.

Waterford people gathered from all over Ireland for the celebration and they were joined by a party of 30 from London. The win had big impact on our exiles in the UK as will be seen from later celebrations. For the group of players who had trained so hard and won Waterford's second All-Ireland it was time to relax and have some fun amongst a group of 400 supporters. With an average age of less than 26, this was a group of young men who had achieved their ultimate goal. The players from the city were generally a little younger and had an average age

'59: AN EYEWITNESS ACCOUNT OF HURLING'S GOLDEN AGE

of just 24. As Jackie Condon remembers 'The lads were all up for blackguarding and laughing. It was great stuff'. Martin Óg Morrissey agrees 'We had a good night that night. We had a right set-to… plenty of beer'. Tom Cunningham recalls that the game had taken its toll on some of the players.

> 'I know Austin Flynn wasn't feeling very well at the function that night. I remember he told me that. I was bunking with him. He said Paddy Kenneally looked after him. He was the treasurer of the County Board at the time.'

Some of the players could have required even more treatment than Austin, depending on how one particular incident turned out that night. Bearing in mind it was October 4 or, more precisely, the early hours of October 5, it wouldn't seem to be the obvious time to sample the delights of the Malahide Estuary. In a case of the blind leading the blind drunk. As Larry Guinan remembers.

> 'Seamus Power, Duck Whelan, Taylor O'Brien, myself and someone else… we went out into the river in Malahide at four o'clock in the morning… 4 o'clock in the morning and we out in the river trying to swim!! Out swimming as drunk as lords!'

Luckily, there was somebody present who could prevent the escapade from going badly wrong. Freddie O'Brien takes up the tale.

> 'I wasn't drinking at the time, so I said I better go out. We were out in the dark in Malahide. We were in shallow water, but we were in unknown water… that was the danger. You could walk out for half a mile and be alright or you could walk out 10 yards… and be gone down a hole. We were all able to swim but if one got into difficulties there was a major problem. It was a struggle to keep Seamus at bay, but I did.'

This seems to be an understatement from Freddie as Larry recalls.

> 'Powerie was nearly drowned. Taylor O'Brien was wicked brave… he went out and bloody well got him.'

Martin Óg agrees that the consequences could have been much more serious.

Pat Fanning and Frankie Walsh during visit to Jacob's.

Tea and biscuits for the team during their visit to Jacob's.

Mayoral reception in Waterford – Frankie Walsh, Declan Goode and Pat Fanning at City Hall.

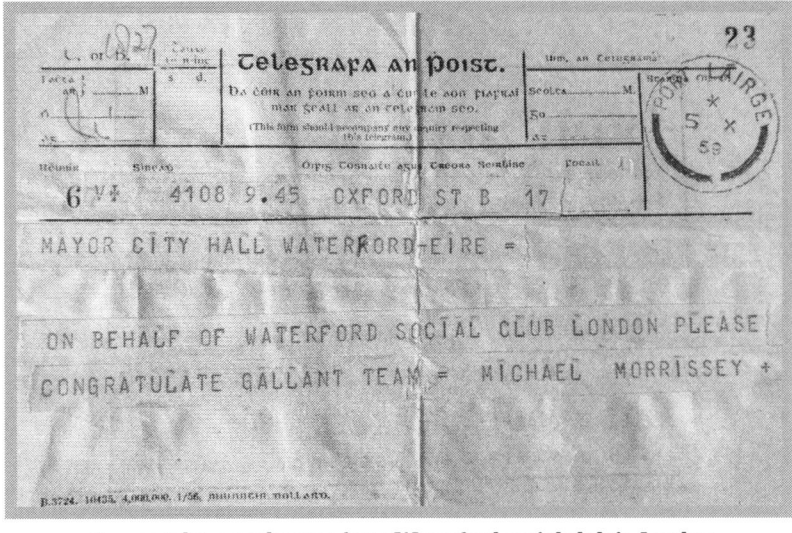

Congratulatory telegram from Waterford social club in London addressed to the Mayor of Waterford.

'59: AN EYEWITNESS ACCOUNT OF HURLING'S GOLDEN AGE

'Only for Taylor was there... Seamus was gone for the milk. He pulled him in out of it. He'd have drowned only for Taylor O'Brien.'

Having survived their late-night swim, the players were finally slowing down. Larry Guinan collapsed into his bed for a well-deserved sleep. This gave his teammates the opportunity for more fun. As Martin Óg describes it:

'When Guinan to bed, we went into Jack Furlong, our masseur, and I got a bandage from Jack. I went down to the kitchen and got tomato juice and put tomato juice on Guinan and put the bandage on him. When he woke up at 7 o'clock in the morning, he looked down and blood was coming out through the bandage on his chest... he nearly died!'

Larry takes up the story.

'The next morning... sometime early in the morning, I woke up and I was all bandages and everything. I was blood all over. What they were after doing during the night, they were after putting bandages around me and putting sauce or something on me. I didn't know what had happened.'

Freddie O'Brien recalls that tomato sauce wasn't the only item to disappear from the hotel kitchens that night.

'Martin Óg got salmon and mayonnaise in his early days somewhere. Everywhere we would go to, he used be looking for salmon and mayonnaise. So, it was in the early hours of the morning we went down to the kitchen and raided the fridge... and Martin Óg got his salmon.'

The celebrations had begun in earnest and as Matt Maloney, secretary of the Waterford Reception Committee said, 'You may think this is something, but it is nothing to what will happen in Waterford tomorrow'. Padraig O'Maoleathaigh of the Waterfordmen's Association looked further ahead.

'Apart from the adults of the city, probably 8,000 young kiddies will be getting in your way tomorrow night. Those little children are the very fellows that are looking up at you for example. Your influence on them will do more for hurling than anything else.'

RECEPTION AT GUINNESS AND JACOB'S

The atmosphere in the Kilkenny camp was naturally more subdued, but the Kilkenny team and mentors were complimentary of Waterford, even in defeat. At the Hollybrook Hotel, Clontarf, secretary, Paddy Grace said:

> 'We are quite happy about our display though naturally disappointed that we did not win. But we are glad it was Waterford that beat us because they have tried so long and so valiantly for All-Ireland honours.'

As the Waterford team left the hotel the next morning Frankie Walsh spoke to a journalist from the *Evening Herald* and commented that *'most of us feel more excited now than we did immediately after the match'*. Both teams visited the Guinness Brewery, where they were guests for lunch. These days, the winning team will bring the Liam MacCarthy Cup to Crumlin Children's Hospital but at the time it was common to go to the Guinness Brewery, the Jacobs biscuit factory, or the Player Wills cigarette factory. As Jackie Condon describes it, 'It was all part of the scene' at the time.

Larry Guinan remembers the event and has happy memories of it.

> 'I was more than surprised and happy that, believe it or not, the Kilkenny team were there with us at Jacobs and Guinness. I remember Ollie Walsh… he was a lovely fella, we became great friends afterwards. I remember him in particular when we were in Guinness and we were having a good time and enjoying ourselves, I needn't tell you. Ollie Walsh was one of the fellas who was all "fair play to ye and good luck". That Kilkenny team was gracious in defeat.'

Johnny McGovern also remembers those visits fondly. 'After the All-Ireland both teams would be invited over to Guinness' Brewery. We used to meet them all there and get to know them'. A brewery was probably a useful place to host a reception for the players who were feeling the ill effects of the night before. Strangely, it wasn't just pints of Guinness that were in demand. Martin Óg recalls drinking gin and tonic ,and Freddie O'Brien remembers 'some of the boys started to drink the barley wine which was on the go at the time. It was tough stuff, it would f****n' flatten you'.

The Kilkenny team left for home on the 6pm train from Kingsbridge. On arriving home,

'59: AN EYEWITNESS ACCOUNT OF HURLING'S GOLDEN AGE

Eddie Keher recalls a funny story about Tommy O'Connell who had scored three goals in the first match.

> 'Tommy was young, only 19, and he worked in the golf club in Kilkenny. A friend of his, Gus Carey was a member. He was a wit, and a legend in Kilkenny for the one-liners. You could tell stories about him till the cows come home. Gus was very proud of Tommy scoring three goals in the drawn match. The lads in the golf club were rising him after the replay. Someone said "Well, how did Tommy do?". "Jaysus", says Gus, "I think De Valera saw more of the ball then Tommy!" De Valera was nearly blind at that stage!'

RECEPTION IN WATERFORD

The plan was for the champions to arrive back in Waterford in time for their parade through the city, starting at Sallypark at 7.15pm. Many supporters waiting on the Quay believed they had arrived in by train, but the team had travelled by car from Dublin. Even that journey was eventful for some of them, and Larry Guinan was again in the middle of the action.

> 'We got back in cars. Wattie Morrissey was driving us. I remember coming back in the car. Wattie was an awful man for turning around when there was an argument between us... Wattie would have to butt in, and he'd always turn around. It was dangerous while he was driving the car... turning around to interfere. This Kilkenny fella was coming from Waterford, and he was going to Kilkenny to meet the Kilkenny team. Just outside Mullinavat, Wattie swerved around the corner. He was in the wrong... he went around the corner and yer man swung the car and went over a ditch and Jaysus... he destroyed his car. We came on into Sallypark and got on the truck.'

While that Kilkenny man had good reason to be upset by the Waterford team, old animosities between Waterford and Kilkenny supporters surfaced. On arriving in Waterford Larry continues.

> 'There was a few potatoes or something thrown at us from people in Sallypark, I remember.'

Taking up this theme, Michael 'Jinx' Walsh recalls:

> 'I was down at the bridge. There was war that night. A fella on a cattle lorry crossed

'59: AN EYEWITNESS ACCOUNT OF HURLING'S GOLDEN AGE

over the bridge and he had a Kilkenny flag and apparently the Guards stopped him. Somebody tore him out of the cab, and he got a couple of punches. They were tough times.'

The team gathered in Sallypark and transferred onto the back of a lorry. In an interview in 2017, Austin Flynn could still relive the reception and recalled 'the rattle of the lorry as it made its way across Rice Bridge'. They were accompanied by bands from the city and there was a torchlit procession along the Quay to the City Hall. Organisers hadn't adequately anticipated the size of the crowd and it became chaotic. Freddie O'Brien remembers 'It was an amazing sight. I was hoping we wouldn't repeat 1948 when somebody was killed'. Martin Óg agreed 'The truck was only barely able to move. It was lucky there wasn't 20 or 30 people killed that day'. Pat Fanning was able to get his teenage son a place in the parade. Phil recalls 'I was fortunate that I was up on the lorry going down the Quay. The excitement was unbelievable. You had to get up and hang on'. Not everyone joined in though. Jackie Condon remembers 'I wouldn't get up on the truck. I walked... I don't like flaunting myself, so I walked over the bridge. I didn't get up on the truck and I had to walk all the way to the Town Hall. The crowd all fell around the place. They all thought I was drunk or something. A lot of people recognised me'. Tom Cheasty summed up the importance of the event 'It was great for the people of Waterford, coming back to the city and to a great reception". Larry Guinan still expresses a boyish enthusiasm at the memory 'Oh boy, it was fantastic coming down the Quay!'. Pat Fanning expressed what it meant to him, and all Waterford hurling people.

> 'A magical scene, entering into Waterford. The people were packed into Sallypark and all the way across the bridge and down the Quay. It was an eruption, an indication of what an All-Ireland win means to a hurling county and, mark you, Waterford is a hurling county as proud as any of them and as good as any of them. The reception in the City Hall was a terribly emotional thing and very significant and demonstrated the degree to which people were affected and the degree to which the county responded to this effort. Remember this was repeated time and time and time again in Dungarvan and Capppoquin, and Ballyduff and Tallow, and in every place in the county as the cup went around. As if a people had refound its spirit and felt they were now entitled to walk in the company of hurling men.'

The *Munster Express* estimated that there were 20,000 people present, which represented two-thirds of the city's population.

'59: AN EYEWITNESS ACCOUNT OF HURLING'S GOLDEN AGE

'In ever increasing volume, the cheering continued unabated along the entire triumphal route, reaching its deafening crescendo as the lorry containing the victorious players and GAA officials came to a halt outside the Municipal Buildings and, individually, they literally had to fight their way through the heavy press of staunch admirers. An augmented force of Gardai and a small army of stewards, supplied by local Gaelic organisations, did all they could do to regulate this unprecedented, excited crush of people, but, numerous as they were, they found themselves faced with an almost insurmountable task. That they did eventually succeed in keeping open a passage to the ship's gangway which had been set in place outside the main entrance to the City Hall is a fine tribute to the good-humoured efficiency with which they did their very difficult job.'

Martin Óg recalls 'We went down to the Town Hall for a Mayoral reception. The Corporation officials and the councillors were all there'. The reception was due to start at 8pm but inevitably was delayed as the lorry crawled down the Quay. As there isn't much room in the Council Chamber, the proceedings were broadcast by loudspeaker to the crowds on The Mall. In a classic piece of Waterford folklore, one speech stood out. Jackie Condon describes it well.

'The councillors were spoofing off. The Bully Man came out to give a speech. He said, "I know John Keane, he captained the 1948 team". He didn't, it was Jim Ware. Then he went on to say, "Waterford is not only the best team in Ireland, they are the best team in Europe!!". That brought the house down.'

The Mayor, Alderman Dick Jones, presided over the Civic Reception. There is no balcony out on to the street, so the players were each brought to the window, starting with Frankie Walsh, and introduced to the crowd below. After the formalities, there was a victory ceili scheduled for the Olympia Ballroom at 9 o'clock. There, the team was greeted with a fanfare by the St. Patrick's Brass Band. The excitement continued into Monday. Rue Colbert, a young hurling fan at the time recalls the excitement amongst his classmates.

'I had school the next day and my father had work. He was working in Clover Meats with Martin Óg and he was delighted because at that time half of Clover Meats were from Kilkenny. There used to be wicked slagging and wicked rivalry. I went to Mount Sion and I remember them bringing the trophy to the school. All the Mount Sion players were there... it was a great thing. We were told to go into the playground and when the cup came, we were cheering and, better still... we got a half day, which was unknown in those days. Tom Cheasty was my man of the match. About six years later I was playing junior hurling for Gael Óg and I played against him.'

Mount Sion wasn't the only school visited and photos appeared in the newspapers from the Manor School and the new Christian Brothers school in St. John's Park. Players visited their old schools or the schools in their parish. Humphrey Kelleher, who later played for Waterford and managed the Dublin hurlers was a seven-year-old student in Abbeyside National School at the time.

'When I went to school in Abbeyside, every day we passed Austin's house in Murphy Place. I have a photograph of them bringing the cup into the school. Michael Foley (a selector on the 1948 team) and all the teachers were lined up. I remember that day when they came to the school with the cup. Tom Cunningham, Duck and Austin came... that was a big big day, about a week after the final.'

DUNGARVAN AND THE COUNTY

While the reception in Waterford City was a highlight for the city-based players, they equally enjoyed touring the county with their teammates from clubs in the county and Freddie O'Brien remembers 'We went all over the county with the cup'. The first event was on the Monday night in Dungarvan. The Dungarvan club hosted a homecoming reception with a parade through Abbeyside and the town, a monster céilí in the town and a meal for the team in the Devonshire Arms Hotel. Tom Cheasty recalled 'I remember going up to Dungarvan and we had a great old time'. Michael O'Connor recalls the excitement in the west of the county.

'In Dungarvan my memory is that we came into the Square on the back of a truck. That was really exhilarating for us all. It was such a wonderful occasion. In that period there was no soccer, or golf, or television. There were incredible scenes. The local interest was unbelievable. We came up to little Cappoquin and it was similar... we were up on a truck. That was fantastic.'

Tom Cunningham recalls:

'We did a tour with the cup. We went to Dunhill, Kilmacthomas, Cappoquin, Lismore, Ballyduff... all the main clubs at the time and particularly the clubs that had a player on the team.'

'59: AN EYEWITNESS ACCOUNT OF HURLING'S GOLDEN AGE

Martin Óg remembers the royal treatment they received.

'For more than a fortnight, we were going out every night. We were in Dungarvan, Cappoquin, Lismore, Dunhill... every place. It was out of this world. We were treated like kings... we were feted all over the county.'

Larry Guinan also remembers the different events.

'We went to Dungarvan, we went to Lismore, we went to Cappoquin, Kilmacthomas... we went all over the place. Everywhere we went we were heroes.'

Martin Óg and Larry are still telling tales about the celebrations to this day.

'We went to Dungarvan another night. We went into the hotel and Austin Flynn's aunt had the Shell House. He asked of we'd like to come over and have a look at it. Guinan and myself were after polishing off a couple of bottles. We walked outside the door to go to the Shell House and ... the air hit him! We didn't see the Shell House that night.'

The relentlessness of the schedule is emphasised by the fact that Waterford played a league game against Wexford in the Gaelic Field on the Sunday following the All-Ireland. It was the opening of the 1959/60 league campaign and amazingly, Waterford managed a 15-point victory. Martin Óg recalls that as being the precursor to two different events that same evening.

'The following Sunday we played Wexford in the league in Walsh Park. That was the night we went to Dunhill, I think. After the game, we had a feed down in the Brewery. The feed was supplied by the Tower Hotel. I was sitting down with my drink in front of me. A chap I went to school with was working in the brewery... Karl Cummins. He came over and said will you have another drink. "I don't feel like it, Karl", I said. He said there was another drink there... a thing called barley wine, would you like to try it? He came back with a pint glass of barley wine in his hand. It tasted lovely! When we were finished there, we went out to Dunhill for another feed!'

Jackie Condon found it all to be a little overwhelming in the end. While the players really appreciated the attention and enjoyed celebrating with the supporters, it was a merry-go-round that lasted for several months.

> 'There were all sorts of dos. I remember going out to Kilmacthomas one night for a do (a céilí in Hill's Hall sponsored by the Newtown and Ballydurn clubs). They had a dance and a big meal there. This was replicated all over the county... we were on the go like you wouldn't believe. You get a bit tired of it eventually and you have to start saying "I can't go here, I'll go there". You were getting all these invitations, proper invitations. I must say it was nice. That gave you a bit of a big head as well. It made you think you were something special.'

MEDAL CEREMONY

The All-Ireland medals were presented to Waterford's representative at Central Council, Charlie Ware, at a meeting in Croke Park on November 28, 1959. It wasn't until January of 1960 that the team received them from GAA President Dr J.J. Stuart, as Tom Cunningham recalls.

> 'The presentation of the medals was at the Majestic Hotel in Tramore. It was there that the actual medals were presented because you wouldn't get them until months afterwards. They'd be gone rusty by the time you'd get them!'

Also present were Paddy O'Keeffe, General Secretary of the GAA, the Mayor of Waterford, Dick Jones, S. O'Giollain, City Manager, and Canon Walsh on behalf of the Bishop of Waterford. For most of the team, like Jackie Condon, the presentation of the medals was just a formality and an excuse for a good night out.

> 'I remember getting the medals. I brought the wife with me... we were only courting at that stage. She was out there with us and really enjoyed it. We had a great night out there in the Majestic. Pad Joe Penkert from Ferrybank, who used to drive the team around, we had him to drive us home.'

However, for Freddie O'Brien, it was the start of a long and frustrating process.

> 'The medals were given out in Tramore at the Majestic. There were 20 medals, 20 Munster medals and 20 All Ireland medals. The only three players who didn't play in the championship were Paudie Casey, Joe Coady and myself... I was the youngest

C. L. C. G.
Coiste Connbae Portláirge

Fleaḋ
I gComóraḋ Craoḃ na h-Éireann

in Ostlann Majestic, Trá Mór

24 Eanar, 1960

Céad míle fáilte romat

Sláintí	Séire
Éire	Grapefruit Cocktail
Cumann Luith-Chleas Gaedheal	Creme of Celery
	Consomme Julienne
Na h-Iomanaithe	Fried Filet Plaice
Na h-Aíonna	Roast Chicken and Ham
	Sage and Onion Dressing
	Mixed Vegetables
	Creamed and Duchess Potatoes
	Plum Pudding ; Brandy Butter
	Charlotte Russe
	Tea or Coffee

Medal ceremony menu

◆

All-Ireland winner's medal (front and back)

♦

Tom Cheasty's medal collection: Top (All-Ireland 1959), Second row (Munster 1957, 1959, 1963), Third row (League 1963, Oireachtas 1962), Bottom (Railway Cup)

♦

'59: AN EYEWITNESS ACCOUNT OF HURLING'S GOLDEN AGE

member on the team. What did they do? They drew for the medals... and I lost out. I was never so upset and disgusted in all my life... the hurt. The one medal that you were going to see in your lifetime. It went on from there.'

To explain in more detail, the team through the Munster Championship was unchanged. The first XV were Power, Harney, Flynn, Barron, Lacey, Morrissey, Condon, Power, Grimes, Guinan, Cheasty, Walsh, Ware, Whelan and Kiely. Mick Flannelly came on as a sub against both Galway and Tipperary entitling him to a sixteenth medal. Tom Cunningham came on as a sub in the Munster final against Cork entitling him to the seventeenth medal. Heading into the All-Ireland final and replay, that left four players on the panel who had not yet played a minute of hurling – Paudie Casey of Ballygunner, Joe Coady of Erin's Own, Michael O'Connor of Capppoquin, and Freddie O'Brien of Mount Sion. Unlike the other three players, O'Connor was only listed in the panel for the Munster final, while Casey, Coady and O'Brien had been listed as subs in all of the games. Freddie describes what happened from his viewpoint.

'Micky O'Connor was on the team in '57, I would have ran against him in sports in athletics... I think he was a Munster 100 yards title holder. He got TB in '58 and I was one of the few hurlers in Waterford who went out to see him in Ardkeen. In '59 he became a selector, so we got to the Munster final and didn't he make himself available on the team. So, we went up to Dublin and played the All-Ireland. He was fully togged out. He went on that day in the All-Ireland final. He played five minutes of hurling for Waterford in 1959 and he received a Munster and an All-Ireland medal. I had given the whole year of commitment to the team. I was very hurt... and I am still hurt over it.'

Tom Cunningham remembers the incident in a similar way.

'Micky O'Connor was a selector as well. He got TB after the '57 All Ireland. He was based in Ardkeen for months and then he came back playing. He was nominated as a selector. He'd have been a fine half-back if his health held out. On the minor team he started off as a half-forward and on the senior team he became a half-back and that became his natural position. He came on for Mick Lacey in the final for a short time.
'They used to only get 20 medals at the time. They gave medals to anyone who played in any championship game. Micky O'Connor got his medal on the basis of playing in the final.'

'59: AN EYEWITNESS ACCOUNT OF HURLING'S GOLDEN AGE

While Freddie was upset at what happened at the Majestic Hotel, this was compounded by further failures by the County Board to rectify the situation over the years.

'There is an issue with me, the County Board and the GAA and it is still ongoing after 62 years. I was told that night that they had drawn for the medal... and they were all apologies that because none of the three of us had played in the championship. They presented me with a replica All-Ireland medal in Casement Park in Belfast when we went up to play Antrim. They told me that at that time they had no bother getting the Munster medal but couldn't get the authentic All-Ireland medal. I looked and looked... and looked and continued to look, and I'm still continuing to look for a medal. That was 1960.

'In 1969 I played with Butlerstown, I was going in to play a junior football final in Dungarvan and Declan Goode called me. "Freddie, I have that medal for you," he said. Now, listen to this... I took the gold medal, and the minute I saw the pattern of the medal, I knew it wasn't the real thing. I said thanks to Declan, and I looked at the back of the medal and what was it for.. the All-Ireland in 1963. I think my brother Fintan was on the panel and F. O'Brien was on the back of the medal. I was Fred and he was Fintan... and that's all it said. I took it anyway.

'In 1971 I was going down Mattie's Hill and a dog ran across the road. Who was in front of me only Pat Fanning and he stopped to avoid killing the dog and I ran into the back of him. He came out to the house, and we spoke about the accident. I said, "By the way Pat, I have a medal here, it was supposed to be a Munster medal... I got it from Declan". He said "Give it to me and I'll get you the right one". I said "No, get me the right one first". That's 1971... and this is 2021. That's 50 years ago and I am still waiting for that Munster medal.

'That is two medals I had then... one in Casement Park and one from Dungarvan. In the Centenary year I continued to look for the medal and Dick Roche, an Ard na Greine man, who played on goal for Waterford, rang me and said "Taylor, I have that medal for you". I said, "What medal?" He said, "The All-Ireland from 1959". 'Ah, Jaysus, Dickie... you're codding me," I said. "No," he said, "I have it... a gold medal." That was three medals I had. They made up a replica as well, but it wasn't an authentic medal. I don't know was it silver with gold plate or a gold front.

'I continued to look for the Munster medal and the All-Ireland medal. Time went by and I used to give out the medals to fellas here. They used to ask the question in the pub "What Waterford player has three All-Ireland medals?" Nobody could ever think of it. Nobody knew. They would bet a fiver, or a tenner and I'd give them the medals to go to the pub. I gave them to someone, and I brought them home and I left them in the kitchen. I had a fella rob the f****n' medals.

'I still continued to look for the medals. I'll be 83 in April. When I was 80, didn't my family buy me another replica medal. It wasn't authentic either. It was silver with gold plating. I accepted that and I appreciated what they had done but I wanted what I was entitled to.

'So, I continued to fight. Pat Flynn in Passage was secretary. My son, Ray got onto him about it. I had written to Croke Park several times and they were trying to pull the wool over my eyes. They said they didn't have the information in the archives. Irish society boy... they'll tell you lies to beat the band.

'Anyway, last January 12 months, awards were given out to the remaining players, and I got the original All-Ireland medal that night. They were giving out trophies to the hurlers and footballers... young player of the year and that kind of thing. I got the medal that night. It is the genuine article. That was five All-Ireland medals I had.

'I'm heading towards Christy Ring territory!'

Tom Cunningham was pleased to see Freddie finally get his All-Ireland medal.

'There was a function last year and Freddie was always and forever complaining about the medal. At this 60th reunion, Freddie was called up, he was presented with the real All-Ireland medal. He made a bit of a speech at the function saying that when he won the All-Ireland in 1959, he was presented with an Antrim County Hurling medal. I think that's what he said... or words to that effect. That bothered Freddie for years. He felt that Mount Sion could have done more to get him a medal. I think you could have got extra medals at the time. Now you can get 30 or 40 of them... there is no limit on them. At that time, they were limited to 20. Freddie felt very hard done by.'

That view is confirmed by Freddie:

'I was very very disappointed and amazed that two prominent Mount Sion men were on that selection committee and that they agreed for that to happen with Mickey O'Connor. No way should Mickey O'Connor have got a medal. In the old dressing-rooms in Walsh Park, Mickey O'Connor came to me and apologised over not getting the All-Ireland medal. He said "You are young yet... there's plenty of years in you".

'59: AN EYEWITNESS ACCOUNT OF HURLING'S GOLDEN AGE

You'd think that Waterford were getting medals every day of the week.'

While he accepts Freddie's cause for grievance, Jackie Condon also took the opportunity to rile him about it.

'Freddie is a good oul butty of mine… I was always friendly with Freddie. He had genuine cause for grievance. They gave the medal to Mickey O'Connor. Mickey had been in hospital with TB a year before the match and he got the medal and caused Freddie to be twice as annoyed. Any time I used to meet him I'd say, "Now Freddie, don't talk about that medal". He used to be giving out yards about it. All his life he is giving out about it. I never thought he'd be so upset about it. It really hurt him. Somebody sold a Tipperary All-Ireland medal in America, and they got a fortune for it. I was blackguarding at home with the wife saying "Jaysus, a Tipperary medal… sure they have heaps of them, a Waterford All Ireland medal would even be more unique. I'd get twice as much money for it".

'I never saw the medal since… the wife hid it on me! She's afraid I'd sell it.'

Billy Kelly of Erin's Own had an insight into the thoughts of the selectors, as his clubman Jim Ware was part of the committee. He relates that Jim Ware wanted Michael O'Connor to play. With his proven experience in the half-back line, he was an obvious calming experience, particularly in the heat of the closing stages of a Munster or All-Ireland final. Outside of the usual slagging between teammates, Larry Guinan appreciated the efforts made by O'Connor to return to hurling.

'Michael O'Connor, given what he went through with his health prior to 1959, he earned that Celtic Cross more than the rest of us did.'

In an unusual parallel, Michael O'Connor also had medals stolen.

'All of my medals were stolen 15 years ago. We were cleaned out one night. We went into town and people broke into the place and stole everything we had. We got onto the GAA at the time… and they replaced them.'

Thankfully, all the players are now in possession of their All-Ireland medals, or at least their wives are, but Freddie is still waiting for that Munster medal.

PRESENTATIONS TO PLAYERS

In the months following the All-Ireland win, the players were presented with gifts by their clubs, their employers, their neighbours, and various local groups. Every week, there was another photograph of such a presentation on the local newspapers. The gifts ranged from the traditional canteen of cutlery received by Tom Cheasty from the Ballyduff club to the gold watches their colleagues presented to John Kiely (Dungarvan Co-Operative Creameries) and Jackie Condon (Hearne's Cabinet Factory) as he recalled recently.

> 'When I was playing, I was working in Hearne's cabinet factory. Shortly after the All-Ireland I left that and went out into business on my own. I still have that gold watch from Hearne's… that was a nice gesture. All the guys chipped in for that.'

As Ireland entered the 1960s, anything electric was seen as very modern and that is reflected in the choice of gift Clover Meats presented to their staff. Two Waterford players (Martin Óg Morrissey and John Barron) and two Kilkenny players received electric razors from their employers to mark the occasion, while Austin Flynn received a portable radio from the yard staff and lorry drivers at the County Council.

As captain, Frankie Walsh received more than anyone else. For example, when the De La Salle club presented a trophy to their own John Barron, Frankie was given one too. Similarly, when staff at the GPO presented their colleague Seamus Power with a watch, Frankie was also given the same. In return Frankie and Seamus presented Postmaster John Power with a signed hurley.

The only example of a presentation to the entire team appeared to be a set of shirts and ties gifted by the Blackrock Trading Company in Dublin.

CELEBRATIONS IN LONDON

The All-Ireland win prompted congratulations from all over Ireland but also from Waterford associations further afield. Michael Morrissey of the Waterford Social Club in London sent a telegram to the Mayor at City Hall on the day of the homecoming. In March 1960 Frankie Walsh and Pat Fanning brought the Liam MacCarthy Cup to London to celebrate with the Waterford diaspora in the city.

It was the final location to be visited and it brought an attendance of 700 to an event in the Town Hall of the Royal Borough of Kensington. The visit was organised by the Waterfordmen's Association of London, the chairman of which was Ted Flynn, a former inter-county hurler from Dungarvan who now held the position of Councillor for Hammersmith. The secretary

'59: AN EYEWITNESS ACCOUNT OF HURLING'S GOLDEN AGE

was Jim Griffin from Waterford City and between them, they arranged the event. The guests from Waterford were led into the hall with the Liam MacCarthy Cup by the girls of the London Pipe Band.

Celebrating in London: Willie Barron, Pat Fanning and Fr. Michael Ryan.

Sláinte poster

Smithwick's poster

'FREDDIE IS A GOOD OUL BUTTY OF MINE... I WAS ALWAYS FRIENDLY WITH FREDDIE. HE HAD GENUINE CAUSE FOR GRIEVANCE. THEY GAVE THE MEDAL TO MICKEY O'CONNOR. MICKEY HAD BEEN IN HOSPITAL WITH TB A YEAR BEFORE THE MATCH AND HE GOT THE MEDAL AND CAUSED FREDDIE TO BE TWICE AS ANNOYED. ANY TIME I USED TO MEET HIM I'D SAY, "NOW FREDDIE, DON'T TALK ABOUT THAT MEDAL". HE USED TO BE GIVING OUT YARDS ABOUT IT. ALL HIS LIFE HE IS GIVING OUT ABOUT IT. I NEVER THOUGHT HE'D BE SO UPSET ABOUT IT. IT REALLY HURT HIM. SOMEBODY SOLD A TIPPERARY ALL-IRELAND MEDAL IN AMERICA, AND THEY GOT A FORTUNE FOR IT. I WAS BLACKGUARDING AT HOME WITH THE WIFE SAYING "JAYSUS, A TIPPERARY MEDAL... SURE THEY HAVE HEAPS OF THEM, A WATERFORD ALL IRELAND MEDAL WOULD EVEN BE MORE UNIQUE. I'D GET TWICE AS MUCH MONEY FOR IT".

'I NEVER SAW THE MEDAL SINCE... THE WIFE HID IT ON ME! SHE'S AFRAID I'D SELL IT.'

JACKIE CONDON

9

REST OF IRELAND

Similar to the Goal Challenge of recent years, there was an annual tradition of challenge games in the 1950s, pitting two representative selections against each other, although the format was tweaked regularly. Donal Whelan was one of the few Waterford players to attend university when he studied in UCC. His success in the Fitzgibbon Cup competition led him to be selected as captain of the Combined Universities team to play against an Ireland XV in 1955. This was the only year in which the Universities won. In an era when few players went to college, the students were usually overrun by the more experienced inter-county selection. In later years, the format settled on the All-Ireland champions playing a Rest of Ireland selection. In 1959, Tipperary played The Rest at Thurles in front of 8,000. The selection committee for the Rest of Ireland team chose Seamus Power, Martin Óg Morrissey and Donal Whelan, with another Waterford man, Jim Fives, as captain of the team. Some of the players didn't take the games very seriously, including Tipperary captain, Tony Wall.

> 'They were obscure little matches, and nobody gave a s**t about them. You went up and you did your best on the day and if you were beaten... so what. It didn't matter one way or another. It wasn't the same as Cork in the Munster final.'

His Tipperary teammate, Donie Nealon felt the same way.

> 'There wasn't great intensity in the matches. They were more like a challenge. Really, there was nothing only pride at stake.'

Martin Óg on the other hand was taking it seriously.

'59: AN EYEWITNESS ACCOUNT OF HURLING'S GOLDEN AGE

'It was a serious match, as far as we were concerned. In 1959 we played Tipperary. Johnny McGovern was playing left half-back and I was playing left full-back. He was on Donie Nealon... and Donie was fast. The first ball that they went for, Nealon got the ball and went around McGovern... and I had a go at him. I could see that the way McGovern was playing on him that he was only there for a day out. The second ball that Nealon got, he came around McGovern and I hit him a rattle... and I turned to McGovern and said, "You can hurl him now".'

Seamus Power also enjoyed matching his skills with the best in the game but without the pressures of the championship.

'Players outside of Waterford in that period who I admired most were of course Christy Ring, the greatest of them all, and Paddy Barry of Cork; Pat Stakelum and Jimmy Doyle of Tipperary; the Rackards and Ned Wheeler of Wexford; and Sean Clohessy and Ollie Walsh of Kilkenny. In these games you could hurl with freedom and abandon. You wanted to win, but if you lost you didn't suffer the disappointment and sense of loss that you felt after a Munster final or All Ireland defeat.'

On April 10, 1960, it was Waterford's turn as champions to host The Rest. Nine thousand spectators attended the Gaelic Field in Waterford for the annual representative game. According to the *Irish Independent*, the emphasis in the first-half *'was on exhibition rather than all-out endeavour'*. The Rest of Ireland team played into a wind of near gale force and still managed to lead 2-5 to 0-6 at half time.

Waterford came out strongly in the second-half and even though they *'lacked the services of Frank Walsh of their selected side, performed so magnificently that one is compelled to venture the prophecy that the side which beats them will win the 1960 All-Ireland'*. Waterford scored a goal and a point in the first four minutes of the second-half to bring them back within a point. Seamus Power and Philly Grimes were dominating in midfield, and it was only the performances of Ollie Walsh in goal and Jimmy Doyle in the forwards that kept the scores close. Austin Flynn was full of admiration for Doyle's performance.

'Jimmy Doyle was an exceptionally talented and skilful hurler with an amazing hurling brain which enabled him to be constantly drifting into a position where he anticipated the ball to arrive. I have a vivid recollection of one such incident in a match in Walsh Park when Waterford, as All Ireland champions, were playing the

'59: AN EYEWITNESS ACCOUNT OF HURLING'S GOLDEN AGE

Rest of Ireland selection. The ball was coming off the arc between our centre-back and their centre-forward. Jimmy drifted across to the wing. Three hurleys were reaching for the sky. Jimmy was a split second faster... managed to trap the ball on the bas of the hurley, control it, hop it twice on his stick as he distanced himself from the other players... and then send it over the bar. I still remember that moment as if it was yesterday... it was hurling magic... with the supreme artist showing his skill.'

Remembering the same performance, Larry Guinan recalled Doyle's brilliance.

'Jimmy Doyle of Tipperary was the best I played on. Jimmy was a lovely hurler... he got a fair few goals off me at one stage in Ferrybank in a tournament. I never played on Ring so I wouldn't know, but Jimmy Doyle was the best I played on.'

Doyle scored all eight of The Rest's points, four from play and four from frees but Ollie Walsh was considered *'the real Saviour'*. His understudy on that day was Jimmy Gray of Dublin who, despite not making his Irish debut for another two years, still enjoyed the occasion.

'I was a sub that day. It was a good experience to meet so many different fellas from different counties.'

Guinan and Whelan managed to breach Ollie's goal once each but were denied on several other occasions. Christy Ring, who had carried a hand injury into the game, had to be replaced by Jimmy Smyth of Clare. Ring was marked by Freddie O'Brien, who won the battle on this particular day.

'We played the Rest of Ireland, and I played on Christy Ring that day. He was gone over the top... so it was no great achievement at that time. He was tough... he was small and low to the ground. He was tough and hard to knock about. He'd hit you a clatter... but at that time if you got a bang, you'd give another one back... on the quiet. He was tough to be on. He codded me in a club match up in Limerick... he ran out for a ball, and I thought I had him covered... *He's not going to get past me now.* He let the ball land on the hurley and hopped it on over my head... and ran around me like a ferret. He made me look foolish the same day. I said I wouldn't let it happen again.'

'59: AN EYEWITNESS ACCOUNT OF HURLING'S GOLDEN AGE

No matter how Ring played, it was still an honour for Johnny McGovern to play with him.

> 'We played down in Waterford. Christy Ring was playing that day. It was a big honour to play with very good players like Christy Ring. I appreciated it.'

The Waterford team were winning their battles all over the field… Flannelly over McGovern, Cheasty over Bohane, Austin Flynn over Billy O'Dwyer, and John Barron over Paddy Barry. Martin Óg was impressed with John Barron's performance as he rated Barry highly.

> 'Paddy Barry was my toughest opponent. He was a big man, but he was a good hurler and a big strong man into the bargain. He reckoned he was as good as Christy Ring.'

The *'legitimate devil of Jackie Condon's hurling'* was also praised in the *Independent*, which would really please Jackie. With 13 minutes to play, Waterford drew level. The big local crowd got behind the champions and it seemed they would go on to win the game, but another Doyle point levelled the game with six minutes to go. A fourth free from Grimes edged Waterford ahead but Doyle's fourth free tied the match at the death. Most players were content with the result. Just like the All-Ireland final, Martin Óg grabbed a souvenir.

> 'I have the ball inside from the game against the Rest of Ireland in the Sports Field. I also have the ball from the '59 All-Ireland final. I just wound up with them in my hand and that was it… they were mine.'

Also similar to the All-Ireland, Tom Cunningham ended up in hospital, but for an unusual reason.

> 'It ended in a draw. I always remember Larry Guinan… he was the only fella ever to split one of his own team. He split me and I had to go to the Infirmary. The ball was falling in the square, and he was pulling, and I was trying to pull… and he connected with my lip… that's all I know! I remind him of that from time to time when I meet him.'

Programme for Waterford v Rest of Ireland match

◆

Team sheet for Waterford v Rest of Ireland match

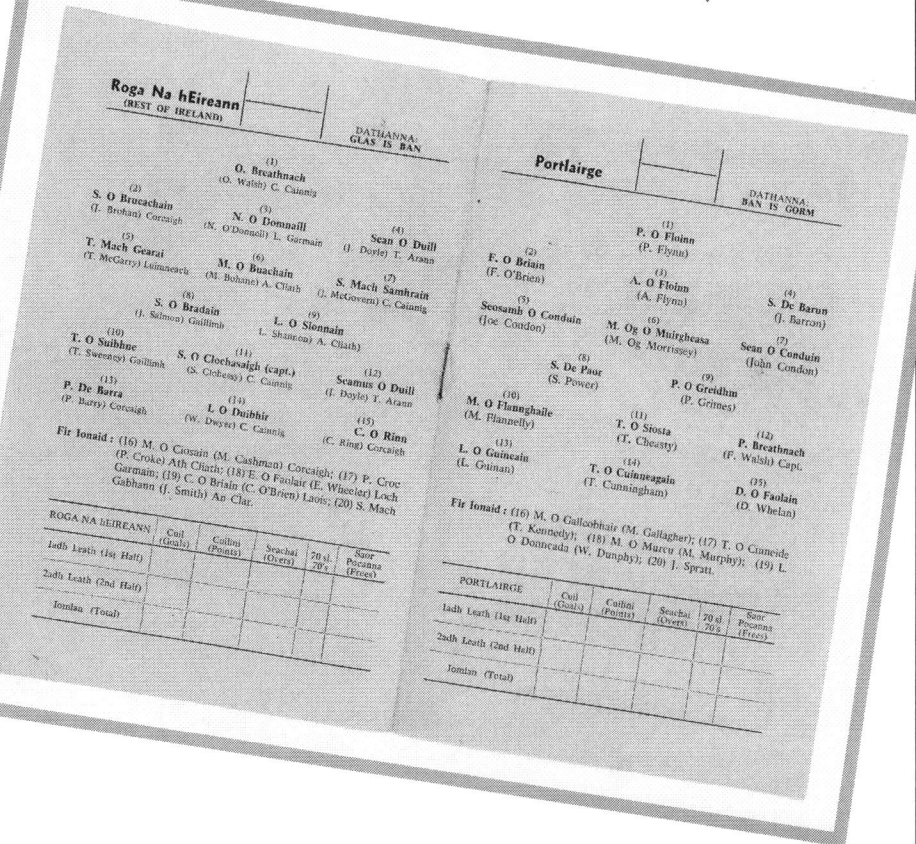

◆

Waterford team: Back - Freddie O'Brien, Donal Whelan, John Barron, Jackie Condon, Joe Condon, Martin Óg Morrissey, Percy Flynn, Tom Cunningham. Front - Mick Flannelly, Larry Guinan, Austin Flynn, Philly Grimes, Tom Cheasty, Tom Kennedy, Seamus Power.

✦

Ireland team: Back - Mick Bohane (Dublin), Paddy Barry (Cork), Christy Ring (Cork), Sean Clohessy (Kilkenny), John Doyle (Tipperary), Nick O'Donnell (Wexford), Ned Wheeler (Wexford), Ollie Walsh (Kilkenny). Front - Billy Dwyer (Kilkenny), Johnny McGovern (Kilkenny), Larry Shannon (Dublin), Joe Sammon (Galway), Jimmy Brohan (Cork), Tim Sweeney (Galway), Jimmy Doyle (Tipperary).

✦

Trophy presented to the players following the Rest of Ireland match

✦

10

WEMBLEY STADIUM

There is a long history of hurling being played in London, stretching back to the end of the 19th century. Notable GAA figures such as Liam MacCarthy and Sam Maguire were prominent in the London organisation and there were always strong ties to home. This was enhanced by regular meetings between teams from Ireland and those in Britain on the Easter, Whit Weekend, and August Bank Holidays. At the earlier times of year, the weather was good, and the championship had not yet started, allowing teams to travel. Unfortunately for some, in the days of knockout hurling, their championship was finished by August. The bank holiday weekends also gave supporters more time to travel from the industrial centres of the north to London where regular events were hosted in Woolwich, Herne Hill, and Mitcham.

WEMBLEY TOURNAMENT

With the increasing number of Irish people moving to Britain to work in the construction industry after the Second World War, these GAA matches were proving increasingly popular so in 1958, the London County Board rented Wembley Stadium for the first in a series of annual games. Secretary of the London Board, John Dunne, described the booking of Wembley Stadium as 'The greatest challenge ever faced by the GAA in London' even though it came at the same time as their purchase of additional land in New Eltham at the huge cost, for the time, of £15,000.

The eagerly anticipated event was boosted by a strong advertising campaign within the Irish community where posters were placed in dance-halls, churches, local shops, pubs, and restaurants. Posters were also sent to the other County Boards in Britain to encourage fans to travel to the matches. The opening games saw the All-Ireland hurling champions, Kilkenny, beat Clare by 6-10 to 5-7 and in the corresponding football match, Galway played Derry. The crowd was a creditable 33,240 considering there was a bus strike that weekend and the many

'59: AN EYEWITNESS ACCOUNT OF HURLING'S GOLDEN AGE

of the forecasted 50,000 supporters couldn't get to Wembley. Donie Nealon recalls 'There was 40,000 or 45,000 at the matches. They'd even come down from Glasgow and Edinburgh'. One reminder of home that had a huge impact on the crowd was the appearance of the Artane Boys Band. Unfortunately, they didn't get to play *Amhrán na bhFiann* as the protocol was that when a foreign anthem was played, *God Save the Queen* would also have to be played. Instead, it was replaced by *Faith of our Fathers* and *A Nation Once Again*.

As a first attempt, it was major PR coup for the London Board and while it wasn't a big financial success, it helped establish a tournament which ran until the mid -70s. John Dunne summed up the first running of the tournament by saying 'Financially, we may not have gained much, but money could not buy the prestige we won at Wembley Stadium on Saturday'. Despite the downplaying of the finances, the board still made a profit of £2,156, which would have provided a useful deposit for the investment in Eltham. There were 79 press correspondents accredited for the games. Several British newspapers reported on the novel event and positive commentary was published in *The Daily Telegraph* (whose reporter described hurling as 'hockey with the lid off'), *Daily Express*, and most notably the *Daily Mail*, who praised the Irish athletes.

> 'To every British soccer man who has shirked a tackle, a heavyweight who has ducked a fight, a batsman who has sulked over a decision, I commend the spirit, sportsmanship and guts of the sixty Irishmen who took part in Saturday's Gaelic Games at Wembley Stadium. Yes, these tough men of Ireland could teach our sportsmen a few things about the way to conduct themselves before a crowd who pay to be entertained, not to be treated with displays of petty temper.'

The success of the event boosted the London GAA scene in several ways, most importantly the creation of 12 new clubs who joined the association in 1959. It was decided to run the tournament as an annual event and in its second year Kilkenny qualified again but were beaten by Cork (7-9 to 3-8), this time in front of 32,000. With public transport running normally, this attendance was disappointing, with some blaming the absence of Christy Ring on the Cork team as a contributory factor. Receipts were down by £700 and there was a suggestion that the qualifying games be scrapped and that the two most popular or attractive teams be selected to travel. In particular, the Kerry footballers were mentioned as ideal participants.

More dramatic calls to abandon the tournament were swept aside for fear of bad publicity reducing crowds in later years. From a publicity point of view, the 'Wembley at Whit' event was positive, although the novelty was gone and in the British press only the *Daily Express* even mentioned the match. The decision to continue the tournament gave Waterford the chance to compete for a place in the 1960 final.

QUALIFYING

The teams that were invited to participate in the Wembley Tournament were put in a hat and drawn randomly for the semi-finals. In their tie, Waterford played Cork at the Gaelic Field in Waterford on March 27, 1960. They eased to a comfortable victory on a scoreline of Waterford 5-9, Cork 1-5. Waterford were close to full strength, with strong replacements such as Percy Flynn for Ned Power, Freddie O'Brien for Joe Harney, and Donal Whelan retaining his place in the absence of John Kiely. However, Cork were fatally weakened by the loss of Christy Ring, with a serious hand injury, along with Brohan (who had been injured while on Railway Cup duty with Munster), Gallagher and Murphy. With a strong breeze at their backs, Waterford dominated in every position. Tom Cunningham scored the opening goals. Two more goals followed in quick succession in the 19th and 20th minutes and were deemed by the *Cork Examiner* to be *'soft enough, but the other three were worked brilliantly all the way'*. Waterford led 3-5 to 1-1 at half-time but the Cork forwards disappointed in the second-half when they only managed three points with the wind advantage. Best for Waterford were Donal Whelan, who finished with three goals, and Tom Cunningham who scored two.

After the game, there was still scepticism amongst Waterford supporters of the quality of the team's hurling as All-Ireland champions. It was claimed that Cork were not interested or trying hard enough. In the *Waterford News & Star*, Pat Fanning put the situation in perspective as he wrote *'Let them go to Wembley – they have earned that – let them travel to America – they deserve it – but let them never lose sight of the fact that their primary purpose and duty is to win honour for the Decies on championship fields at home'*. Once again echoing the rivalry with Kilkenny, he ends on the phrase *'Let there be no pause now until September comes and the mantle of champions rests again on the right side of the Suir'*. It was also Kilkenny who would be the opposition at Wembley. In the other semi-final they beat Dublin by 7-7 to 2-7.

BUILD UP

A full-strength team was named, but at training on the Wednesday before the Wembley final many of the players were not at their best. Several were reported to be 'a little sluggish' having received their vaccinations for the upcoming U.S. trip. Jackie Condon and Martin Óg Morrissey were among those most affected. Morrissey is reported to have spent a week in bed under medical care, while Condon's arm was very sore. Frankie Walsh, and, to a lesser extent,

'59: AN EYEWITNESS ACCOUNT OF HURLING'S GOLDEN AGE

Tom Cheasty, were said to still look 'a little washy' after their vaccination. Joe Condon was also ill and missed some club engagements as a result. On the plus side, Ned Power returned in good form from an illness which it had been feared would rule him out for 1960; Joe Harney had just come back from injury; and Seamus Power was playing through a leg injury. With question marks over half of the Waterford team, Kilkenny were correctly the bookies' favourites. The selection mirrored the All-Ireland replay team with Joe Condon replacing Mick Lacey and Donal Whelan replacing John Kiely.

As a staunch supporter of the 'Ban', it must have been a strange experience for Pat Fanning to attend a match at Wembley Stadium. In his preview of the game in the News & Star, he pointed out the opportunity the event presented to publicise the game more effectively than the brief clips of the All-Ireland on BBC's *SportsScene* the previous October.

> *'Present too will be the great, smug, insular British Press. These men will come to scoff; their pens dripping poison will be poised to paint fantastic word pictures of the comical Irish and their strange pastimes. It is within the compass of Waterford and Kilkenny, of Down and Galway, to rout the scoffers, to turn their jeers to cheers and prove even to the most prejudicial that Irish games, played by Irishmen, are unsurpassed in the world of sport. Our Waterford boys can best achieve this object by producing their best form, that form which, even in a matter of seconds on television last year won commendation from all sides.'*

ARRIVAL AND RECEPTION

The opportunity to play at Wembley was attractive for all the players and for many of them it was their first time out of the country or on an aeroplane. The flight was Tom Cunningham's abiding memory as he told me 'I remember the Wembley trip to the extent that it was my first time on an aeroplane, but I have no recollection of the match at all'. It was a similar experience for the younger Kilkenny players. Eddie Keher recalls that 'We travelled separately to Waterford, not on the same flight. At that time, each county board made their own arrangements. It wasn't London who were inviting us over and arranging it. The county boards did their own thing and Kilkenny would have done their own thing'. Seamus Cleere remembered it vividly as it was his first flight, but also for the significance of the visit.

> 'It was my first time in a plane. Imagine going from the Ring in Bennettsbridge to a city like London on an aeroplane... and then to come home and talk about it. Thousands of Irish emigrants made their way to see the games and to welcome the players. When

Waterford and Kilkenny teams parade around Wembley Stadium

Studio portrait of Larry Guinan and Frankie Walsh

'59: AN EYEWITNESS ACCOUNT OF HURLING'S GOLDEN AGE

money was tight, and jobs were valuable, it was amazing how the Irish responded to the visits of their sporting heroes among them, from so many miles away. I suppose you could say that it brought home to us what the Irish Diaspora really meant.'

Johnny McGovern agreed and emphasised the importance of the GAA as a hub for Irish families.

'It was a great meeting place. When we were playing matches, we would have lads who had emigrated from here and we'd all meet afterwards. There used to be a big crowd from all over the country. A lot emigrated from Bennettsbridge to England around that time. Full families went over, and they'd all be at the match.'

The Waterford team left Dublin Airport on a special Friendship Flight on Friday evening. Travelling with them was His Grace, the Archbishop of Tuam, who was making the trip as a guest of the London GAA. He would throw in the ball for the football game and be the principal speaker at the banquet in Wembley following the matches. At London Airport, the team was welcomed by Jim Mullarkey, chairman of the London County Board and by Ted Flynn, chairman of the Waterfordmen's Association.

From the moment of their arrival, the Waterford team were in demand. They were also met by a group calling themselves the Waterford Social Club who had invited them to attend a function on the night before the game. As the Waterfordmen's Association was the more recognised body, affiliated with the County Associations of Ireland, they were seen as 'the official organisation of our people in London'.

Having registered at their Russell Square Hotel, a special coach was provided by the Waterfordmen's Association, and they were driven to Hammersmith and 'into a scene of jubilation and enthusiasm that beggar's description'. On the arrival of the team and officials, chairman Ted Flynn mounted the stage and ramped up the excitement by cutting the music to announce to the cheering crowd that the entire Waterford team were soon due to enter the hall. After the formalities came the big reveal as Frankie Walsh led the players from an adjoining room to a reserved space in front of the stage. As each man appeared, he was introduced by Pat Fanning. The newspaper report captures the scene *'pandemonium reigned. This was the moment our exiles had waited for; this was the purpose of their coming together. They broke ranks, making for their heroes'*. Buoyed by such a positive reception, the travelling party had an enjoyable night. It was probably not the ideal preparation for a match the following day, but it was an indication that this was part of the victory lap from 1959. To the Waterford diaspora, it was a chance to celebrate the great victory of the previous October while at the same time hoping for a repeat of the classic 1959 All-Ireland final.

THE MATCH

The *Evening Herald* set the scene for the match nicely. They described *'the mammoth stadium presented a colourful scene with the ladies in their summer finery and the men in their shirt sleeves basking in the brilliant sunshine and over it all the Irish flag flying proudly from the famous turret'*. As the teams marched around behind the Dagenham Girl Pipers Band, the players were able to take in the scene. The Artane Boys Band who had featured in the previous years had been replaced as a cost-cutting measure. The £600 it cost to fly them to Wembley on a chartered plane was deemed excessive by the London Board, who also managed a reduction of printing and programme costs by some £400. The crowd of almost 30,000, who had paid between 5 shillings and 30 shillings for their tickets, seemed quite small in such a large stadium. It is a memory that stuck with Joe Condon who described the setting.

> 'It was a vast place. The day we played there it seemed like there were only 17,000 or 18,000 there. You wouldn't see them. It was strange… it was so big.'

On the Kilkenny team, Seamus Cleere had the same observation.

> 'I mean Wembley was enormous. Its capacity was 100,000 and even though there were thousands from all over England, they still looked very small inside the place. I remember playing against Waterford and I was marking Mick Flannelly. I thought the pitch was wider than Croke Park, and there was a three-foot pailing around it… I don't know what that was for, but I remember Mick raced out to the sideline for a ball, and he careered on towards the pailing. He tried to jump it… but he fell over it. If 'twas a horse race, you could say that he fell at the first!'

Waterford started well and within nine minutes they had a five-point lead. Kilkenny started to find their feet and with Mick Brophy and Paddy Kelly performing well in midfield, they reduced the deficit to three points after 21 minutes. After Ned Power in the Waterford goal had saved from Denis Heaslip, Phil Walsh burst in and scored with an unstoppable shot. Kilkenny were on a roll now and Heaslip scored their second goal to take a three-point half-time lead, 2-08 to 0-11. The excitement of the day was infectious, and Joe Condon remembers one Waterford supporter's attempts to get closer to the action.

'59: AN EYEWITNESS ACCOUNT OF HURLING'S GOLDEN AGE

'An uncle of mine was there and he said, "Who's the fella that ran out on the field?". You couldn't get straight out on the field... but this fella got out over the wire. He was hanging up by the legs of his trousers. He was a quare fella. It turns out it was John Meany's brother who was living in England... he tore off and he fell down onto the field and got a huge cheer. My uncle said, "It was over to you he ran!".'

In the second-half, with Ollie Walsh at his brilliant best, Kilkenny were never seriously threatened. He made multiple saves from the Waterford forwards keeping them to just two goals in the game. Waterford's scorers listed in the national newspapers included Seamus Power 1-2 and Larry Guinan with 1-1. Larry Guinan strongly objects to this piece of 'fake news'.

'I scored two goals. I scored 2-1. The newspaper must have been wrong. Somebody got one of my goals.'

This was a regular occurrence in the days before multi-camera TV coverage and instant replays. If a goal was not clearly taken or emerged from a group of players, the journalists would have a brief conference in the press box to nominate the scorer. In this case, Seamus Power was rewarded for Larry's work. In his book on Christy Ring, Val Dorgan wrote:

'Ring once said to me that he would like to see all the GAA writers seated in different parts of the field and then write their reports without consulting each other. He was convinced there was complete collusion between sportswriters. On many occasions he had noticed the same mistake in all the match reports.'

Dorgan, a journalist, responded by saying 'There is collusion in the press box, but, among the specialist GAA writers, this co-operation is almost entirely confined to checking the facts'. Considering the lack of technology at their disposal, the journalists did a pretty good job of covering the detail of the games at the time. How difficult it must have been to distinguish the last man to strike a ball in a dusty square on a summer's day when the ash was flying.

The other influence that Ollie Walsh had on the game was to start attacks direct from his long puck-outs. Chief amongst the beneficiaries were Phil Walsh who scored 3-2 and Denis Heaslip who grabbed 3-4. John Barrett in the *Irish Press* reported *'On this day of victory for the Leinster champions, Kilkenny, how the crowd loved Ollie Walsh. Two years ago, the eagle-eyed*

'59: AN EYEWITNESS ACCOUNT OF HURLING'S GOLDEN AGE

goalkeeper won the exiles' hearts and warm admiration with a brilliant display. But it was nothing to the hour of supremely spectacular, coolly courageous saving he did yesterday'. Mick Dunne in the same newspaper reported *'The hurling was as good as you could wish for. After Waterford's early burst, Kilkenny turned in a display of quick incisive ground striking that shocked the All-Ireland champions, whose persistent search for goals was surprising in face of the incredible goalkeeping of Ollie Walsh'.* Martin Óg Morrissey also credits Sean Clohessy with a man of the match performance.

> 'Sean Clohessy beat us that day… he had a whale of a game that day. Heaslip was a lovely fast hurler… Keher was outstanding too. Clohessy started at centre-forward but when he moved out to the middle of the field, I thought he won the game for Kilkenny from there.'

Eddie Keher's performance yielded seven points and the final score of 6-16 to 2-16 was never in doubt. Reflecting on the experience of playing at Wembley, players from different counties share similar views. In general, Larry Guinan summed up the day by saying:

> 'I enjoyed playing at Wembley, but I always said after that I'd prefer to play on Thurles. Thurles, to me, was a finer pitch and a nicer pitch to play on than Wembley. The soccer lads wouldn't like that now but that's the way I felt anyway.'

Jimmy O'Brien could see why Larry would prefer Thurles over Wembley and even over Croke Park.

> 'I played there a few times. You'd think it looks perfectly level, but it wasn't. There were dips in it… the same as any field, then anyway. I only played in Thurles once or twice, but it is a great ground for summer hurling. Croke Park is different… slower. It wouldn't have suited Waterford, but it would suit Kilkenny.'

The small pitch was a factor as Joe Condon recalls.

> 'The pitch was shorter. It wasn't played as a normal game… it was mostly puck outs down to the corner-forwards. Ollie Walsh and Ned Power could puck the ball the length of the pitch so there was very little play in it.'

Martin Óg Morrissey picks up the topic of the surface which, while far more suitable for soccer than most pitches of the time had its drawbacks for the hurlers.

> 'The grass was very short. It didn't suit our type of hurling.'

There had been talk in the *Irish Press* of *'killer turf'* at Wembley not being suitable to Gaelic games and causing injury, but no problems had been encountered for three years and there were no substitutions made in the hurling match. For Joe Condon, it reminded him of his days playing street hurling.

> 'I found that the grass was cut to the bone, whereas here you'd have a little bit of grass to get under the ball. It was like playing on the road.'

One area in which there were no modifications were the nets. Donie Nealon recalls the confusion and the messing, typical of an exhibition match.

> 'They would still use the soccer nets. The ball would go through them, and the Kilkenny lads would be saying 'That was wide... it came in the side of the net!''

AFTER MATCH

The Waterford team were getting changed after the game when, accompanied by a Wembley official, they were visited in their dressing-room by the Archbishop of Tuam who congratulated them 'on their sporting display which was a credit to all of them'. Following the games, the four teams (the hurlers of Waterford and Kilkenny and the Down footballers who had defeated Galway) and distinguished visitors were the guests of the London County Board at a banquet. Some 400 guests attended. Kilkenny and Down received their prizes at the banquet. As Donie Nealon remembers 'We used to get small silver cups. I had three of those little cups'.

SEEING LONDON

There wasn't much time for the players to get to see London. Having had the Waterfordmen's reception on Friday, and the match and banquet on Saturday, it really only left a couple of hours to relax. Eddie Keher recalls 'Some of the Kilkenny team would be meeting relations and they would take them out for a day. I remember a number of us went to Madame Tussaud's, probably the next day. We were only there a couple of days. I don't know about other teams but from our team that year, very few of them drank, maybe two or three, but the rest of us were not drinkers so we weren't heading for the nightlife.'

'59: AN EYEWITNESS ACCOUNT OF HURLING'S GOLDEN AGE

From the Waterford team, the Condon brothers, Joe and Jackie, played together in the half-back line. Another brother, Mick, was living in London so they took this golden opportunity for a family reunion, slipping away from the banquet as early as possible. As Jackie described, 'Joe was at Wembley with us. We had a brother over there and we went to visit him. The memory I have is of meeting the brother, Mick, after the match and he took us off down to his local pub. We had a bloody great time. We weren't with the rest of the lads at all for that reason. We were just with them coming back home again'. Joe's memories are of the number of Irish people, particularly those from Waterford, who had descended on London for the weekend.

> 'Waterford fellas that wouldn't be able to get home for the All-Ireland or other matches... they came from all over the place. London was full of Waterford fellas because it was advertised that the Waterford team would be appearing. We went this dancehall... La Bamba I think was the name of it, in Kilburn. I had a couple of brothers working in England at that time. We met up with our brother, Mick and he came with us to the dance and brought us around. They kept saying to me "Do you know him?" They came from all over England, fellas you'd only see going to school, you'd see them down around Doyle Street... they were all over there.'

FUTURE OF THE TOURNAMENT

While the Wembley Tournament was only three years in existence, there were still questions as to whether it would continue. The attendance for the 1960 game of just under 30,000 was the smallest of the three Wembley games and while the profit of £1,300 was higher than the previous year, this was achieved not by greater receipts but by reducing expenses. In London on the Saturday night there was some talk that the small profit from such a huge undertaking was not worth the risk, but London officials were adamant that the games at Wembley must continue.

Pat Fanning in the *Waterford News & Star* reflected on the trip.

> 'It is wonderful to witness a gathering of the Gael in this renowned stadium and I pondered the fact that a few short years ago the London Board would not contemplate so ambitious and costly a venture. Now an established feature of London's Gaelic year, it furnishes a fine picture of the status and importance of our games in England and of the initiative and intelligence of the men who control them. Wembley is a most impersonal place, unlike Croke Park, but the faces and voices there on Saturday were friendly and familiar.'

'59: AN EYEWITNESS ACCOUNT OF HURLING'S GOLDEN AGE

The games continued at Wembley. With increased promotion, the 1961 and '62 matches attracted crowds in excess of 40,000. By 1964, television coverage and increased ticket prices helped place the event on a sound financial footing and secured its future. The event extended to fill the weekend, with the visiting counties playing each other on Saturday at Wembley and taking on a London selection at New Eltham on Sunday. In the 1970s, with an increasingly busy fixture list, the Wembley Tournament along with the Railway Cup went into decline, with the last tournament hosted in 1975.

COMING HOME

Early on Sunday afternoon, the Waterford team boarded a bus to take them to London Airport. The flight home was eventful. As bad weather was forecasted, the cabin crew made every attempt to ensure their inexperienced passengers would be safe. Freddie O'Brien recalls their instructions.

> 'I remember Wattie Morrissey, he was the hurley man that time. In the plane, we were told to fasten our seat belts. They were modern seat belts and Wattie couldn't fasten it… so he put two big knots in it. The air hostess said "You can't do that… you'll have to put it on properly… or you won't be able to open it". "Oh bejaysus, I'll open it," he said.'

Jackie Condon picks up the story there.

> 'The plane met a thunderstorm. I looked over and Wattie Morrissey was on the other side of the aisle and there he was with the rosary beads out and he praying away. All I could do was curse and swear. This was the first time I was up in an aeroplane. I said, "I effing well knew this would happen when I go up in one". We were lucky to get out of the bloody thing. They were all kissing the ground when they got out of it.'

Thankful to be on solid ground again, there were only the formalities to clear before the journey home to Waterford, but their adventures were not finished, as Jackie Condon continues:

> 'We went in anyway… and up to customs. There was a little fella there… he was about four foot nothing, a right little weasel of a fella. He said, "Open up the bag, have you anything to declare?" I said "No, I have nothing to declare", but I had a suit that the

'59: AN EYEWITNESS ACCOUNT OF HURLING'S GOLDEN AGE

sister who had been in London had made for the husband, Tom Heffernan. She had to come home without it, so she asked me to pick it up. He pulled open the thing. "Made in London," he said, 'You have to pay duty on that"... and he went on about it. He annoyed me so much I just caught him and said "Listen, I'm in no humour for you"... and I fired him back in again. Next thing, two fellas came out, and I was marched in the back. I reckon if it wasn't for Pat Fanning that day, I'd still be in jail. The plane nearly after crashing... and we still had to go through customs. Anyway, they took the suit off me, and you should hear the sister when I came home... oh Jesus! They fined me, but the GAA paid it.'

Most of the team didn't have time to reflect much on their trip to Wembley as they went straight on to New York the following week. In the weeks after the game, Joe Condon recalls being the envy of some other soccer supporters.

'It was just nice to say you were over there. We were in a pub in Ballylaneen a few weeks later. Yer man O'Neill, the poultry farmer... he was into the soccer big-time. Tom Cheasty, the builder, was friendly with him. He said to Tom "Do you know where I was recently?" he said, "I was over at the Cup final". "Were you?" said Tom. "I walked across the field," he said. He took out a matchbox and said "Do you see that? That's grass off the field!" I said, "Sure, I played there a couple of weeks ago!"'

In later years, Larry Guinan was regularly able to confound soccer supporters by asking them to name the Waterford man who scored two goals at Wembley.

Ned Power souvenir
calendar

◆

Cuchulainn annual 1959
◆

11

NEW YORK CITY

Visits of hurling teams to the USA was a regular affair stretching back to the original 'American Invasion' in 1888. In addition to visiting teams, individual hurlers often spent time in America and played for local teams. Most relevant to this story is the time spent by Philly Grimes in New York from 1948 to '50. Having played in the semi-final of the Munster Championship for Waterford against Clare, Phil left for New York before the final against Cork. His move denied him the opportunity to have been on both Waterford All-Ireland winning teams. In a Munster Express interview Phil recalled:

> 'I had a marvellous three years. I stayed with an uncle in Brooklyn and worked in the construction business. I hurled with the Tipperary side in the company of many fine players, notably Terry Leahy.'

He took up the story in an interview with Brendan Fullam, reproduced in Giants of the Ash.

> 'When I arrived in New York the first thing that struck me most was the standard of play in both hurling and football... which was so high. The dedication of the players and officials was great. They would have to travel long distances to get in one hour's practice... maybe one or two hours by train. Some of the prominent players that played in New York were Terry Leahy and Steve Kelly of Kilkenny, Joe Looney of Cork, Des Dooley and Sean Craven of Offaly... and, of course, the Galvin brothers of Waterford.'

The high standard was emphasised when he played with New York in the 1949/50 National

'59: AN EYEWITNESS ACCOUNT OF HURLING'S GOLDEN AGE

League final against Tipperary in New York. Terry Leahy had a great game on Pat Stakelum, but it wasn't sufficient to carry the day for New York, who lost by just two points, 1-12 to 3-4. It stood out in Phil's memory though.

> 'A highlight was playing for New York against Tipperary in the Polo Grounds in 1949. That was a marvellous Tipp side... including Jimmy Kennedy, Tony Reddan, Pat Stakelum, Tommy Doyle and so many others, but we ran them to two points in the first of the 'away' league finals.'

Phil enjoyed the GAA scene in New York, in particular the field days in support of county associations that were held every Sunday and the many Irish who would assemble in John 'Kerry' O'Donnell's bar in Gaelic Park after the game. Luckily for Waterford hurling, Phil returned to Ireland in 1950 and was a driving force behind the teams of the 50s who ultimately became champions in 1959.

Interviews with other players of the time emphasise the attractiveness of a New York visit. Jimmy Brohan, Cork and Munster corner-back, was lucky enough to experience a visit and has interesting memories.

> 'A trip to New York was huge at the time. I got a trip in 1957... there was a special invitation to the All-Ireland finalists from the year previous and it was Cork and Wexford that went out that year. We played two games in Gaelic Park... it was only a bit of a dive really. There was very little grass on the field. All they were interested in was selling beer. John Kerry O'Donnell owned the place... he was a representative for Ballantine Beer at the time. I have a photograph here of a fella standing at a table with a big placard saying, "Subscriptions taken here for the IRA".'

ST. BRENDAN'S CUP

By 1959, the winners of the National League qualified for the St. Brendan's Cup against New York. In addition to the league final defeat to Tipperary, there was double disappointment for Larry Guinan in missing out on a dream trip.

> 'It was a wicked disappointment losing the league final. I mean at that time to go to New York was something you'd have to save for... for months, maybe years for. It was a trip of a lifetime.'

'59: AN EYEWITNESS ACCOUNT OF HURLING'S GOLDEN AGE

Some commentators felt that Waterford had 'fallen prey to the American bug' but the defeat of Tipperary in the Munster semi-final banished the disappointment.

PROPOSED WATERFORD TOUR

The proposed culmination of eight months of celebrations of their All-Ireland victory was to be the Waterford team's tour of New York in June of 1960. Having just returned from the London Tournament final at Wembley Stadium, a visit to New York would be their most exotic reward yet for winning the championship. Intercontinental travel or even air travel was not commonplace in 1960 and, apart from Phil Grimes who had spent time living in New York, none of the travelling party had ever been to the USA.

A quick look at the prices of Aer Lingus flights at the time shows the return fare between Shannon and New York to be £149 and 5 shillings. This was £6 cheaper than the equivalent flight to and from Dublin which, when multiplied by a 23-man travelling party, might have driven the choice of route. After all, the average weekly wage in 1960 was £7 and 15 shillings so a saving of £138 was approximately four months' wages. It is also interesting to note that the single fare of £58 was classed as an 'emigrant fare', starkly underlining the emigration issue of the time.

The idea of a Waterford tour to New York was being suggested almost immediately after the All-Ireland win. While nothing official had been confirmed by Waterford, New York or the Central Council, Paul Russell writing in the *Sunday Review* on November 29, 1959, mentions a contact by Frank Ryan, the famous tenor from Tallow, Co. Waterford, with the New York GAA governing body while he was performing in concert in the city. The suggestion for a Waterford tour may have been Ryan's own idea but, as a close friend of Larry Fanning, former Mount Sion and Waterford hurler, manager of the Theatre Royal, and brother of county chairman, Pat Fanning, it seems likely he was working on behalf of the Waterford County Board.

The initial approach to the New York GAA board seems to have been well received and they said 'We should be delighted to have a visit from Waterford, and we think that they would be a tremendous crowd-puller over here, but they must get the ok from the authorities at home'. This approval was far from guaranteed as the GAA had decided at their 1959 congress that only the National League winners should travel to New York to contest the St. Brendan Cup final and that no games other than these official ones would be permitted during a three-year cycle running from 1959 to '61.

'59: AN EYEWITNESS ACCOUNT OF HURLING'S GOLDEN AGE

ARRANGEMENTS

In January of 1960, a request was sent by Patrick Kenneally of the Co. Waterford Association in New York, via the Secretary of the New York GAA, Tom McGuinness, to the GAA Central Council to allow a tour of New York by the Waterford hurlers in May 1960 to play a two-game series. As the 1959 congress had already ruled on the matter, the secretary of the GAA, Pádraig Ó'Caoimh, responded that no action could be taken at that time. A decision would have to wait for further discussion at the 1960 congress. This meeting took place at the Gresham Hotel on April 17, 1960, with Waterford represented by Michael Vincent O'Donoghue, a former chairman of the Waterford County Board and president of the GAA from 1952 to '55. O'Donoghue, ironically, had in the past been very vocal in his opposition to GAA tours of the USA. He had been particularly outspoken against the holding of the 1947 All-Ireland football final between Kerry and Cavan in New York, arguing that it would encourage emigration.

After much discussion, it was agreed that *'In conformity with established policy re unofficial tours it was the decision of the Congress that permission be granted on condition that the tour be under the direct auspices and sponsorship of the New York GAA and that it conform with existing regulations pertaining to official tours'*. While this was good news for the Waterford hurlers, there were still some obstacles to be overcome. First, the costs of the tour (including a payment of $30 to players which would include the cost of their transport to Shannon Airport and other incidentals) would have to be raised in New York. Also, travelling parties usually only included three officials, the chairman and secretary of the Waterford County Board (Pat Fanning and Declan Goode), and the county's representative on Central Council (Charlie Ware). The proposal from the New York side was that the team trainer, John Keane of Mount Sion would replace the Central Council representative, Charlie Ware of Erin's Own. That was too sensitive a battle for anyone to take on, so both men were listed to travel.

Under normal circumstances, Pádraig Ó'Caoimh, as GAA secretary, would usually accompany the travelling party. Due to the sensitive nature of the case, he decided to sit it out and hand over responsibility to the New York and Waterford County Boards. Central Council minutes confirm that *'It was the view of the officers that while New York GAA is accepting responsibility for the control and financing of this tour, the Central Council can only look upon it as an unofficial one. Such being the case the Secretary had decided not to travel and recommended that Pat Fanning, Chairman of the Waterford Board, would sit in on all discussions and decisions'*. With the New York County Board now tasked with arranging the tour, Paddy Kenneally of the Co. Waterford Association was appointed 'Tour Chairman' and faced with the task of fundraising and sponsorship to underwrite all of the costs. Back in Ireland, the Waterford County Board

'59: AN EYEWITNESS ACCOUNT OF HURLING'S GOLDEN AGE

called a meeting for Friday April 22 and, within a week of congress, the detailed planning had begun. Waterford county secretary, Declan Goode was able to provide a list of the travelling party to their U.S. hosts within three days. In a letter to Paddy Kenneally, he announced the following travellers:

Officials: Pat Fanning (Co. Chairman), Charlie Ware (Ard Comhairle), Declan Goode (Co. Secretary), John Keane (Trainer).

Players: Ned Power, Joe Harney, Austin Flynn, John Barron, Martin Óg Morrissey, Jackie Condon, Seamus Power, Phil Grimes, Mick Flannelly, Tom Cheasty, Frankie Walsh, Larry Guinan, Tom Cunningham, Donal Whelan, Charlie Ware, Joe Coady, Freddie O'Brien, Paudie Casey, Michael O'Connor.

The qualifying criterion for inclusion in the panel to travel was that they must have been part of the All-Ireland panel. This meant that Joe Condon, who was now featuring regularly in the team, was not part of the tour. Others who got to travel to Wembley, such as Percy Flynn, Bill Dunphy, Tom Kennedy, and Mick Gallagher, did not qualify either. John Kiely 'did not wish to travel, declaring that his All-Ireland medal was all that he wanted out of hurling'. Mick Lacey was particularly unlucky to miss the trip. *Gaelic Weekly* newspaper on April 9, 1960, reported that *'Mick Lacey, the Waterford All-Ireland hurler, is at present suspended for attending foreign games'.*

At this point the plans were based around departure from Shannon Airport on May 16 with the intention of leaving New York not later than May 31 to allow time to get to London for the game at Wembley. As this only allowed a month for all arrangements, it did not prove to be possible so, in a phone call between Pat Fanning and John 'Kerry' O'Donnell, president of New York GAA, in the early hours of April 29, the tour was postponed until June, with matches scheduled to take place on the Sundays of June 12 and June 19. The GAA Central Council were putting pressure on Waterford that the tour should not impact on their preparation for their Munster Championship opener on June 26. In a letter to New York on May 1, Declan Goode noted that 'having considered all aspects of the situation and mindful of the fact that the matter was urgent, we did not seek a postponement of the Galway game'. In an upbeat prediction of the game, he stated 'We will come home, beat Galway, and lay another of those mythical American bogies'.

By May 16, most of the arrangements were in place and in a wrap-up letter to Pat Fanning, Pádraig Ó'Caoimh commented on some of the final requirements. It seems that

'59: AN EYEWITNESS ACCOUNT OF HURLING'S GOLDEN AGE

the GAA secretary had a direct line to the Passport Office and was able to inform the county chairman that Charlie Ware's passport had been issued the previous week. However, while Tom Cheasty's application had not yet been received, his new passport would be issued within a day of receiving the application. He had also been in touch with Aer Lingus to forward 23 vaccination certificates to Declan Goode, who was responsible for all the travel arrangements, as these would be required by the American Consul in Cork along with a valid passport and extra passport photo. Their final requirement was 'a letter from a priest or employer stating that the member's normal domicile is in Ireland where he is employed and that he will be returning there at the end of the tour'.

At that time, visitors to the U.S. were required to have smallpox vaccinations. These were administered in two stages by the team doctor, Milo Shelley, on May 17 and 20. Martin Óg Morrissey recalls the preparations.

> 'I remember the injections that we got here before we went to America... I spent a week in bed with it. One of my arms was the size of a small saucer... the size of the scab that was on it. The rain washed it off and there was one of the New York fellas saw it and said "Jaysus, what happened to you?" and I said that was the injection I got from the doctor before I came out. "What butcher did that to you?" he said. I remember we had to go to Cork to collect our visas. I got out of the bed, and I was in the car with Frankie Walsh and when we got down to Cork, he said "You're not going in there for that visa, I'll get your one. You see that pub over there?" He handed me two tablets and he said, "Go in there and get a brandy and ginger ale... and take those two tablets and then come back to the car and wait for us".
>
> 'I went in and got the brandy and ginger ale, took the two tablets, and came back to the car... and fell asleep... BANG! Out like a light I went. They came back about an hour after and woke me up. Jaysus, I felt great! We were in the car coming out of Cork and we passed the Metropole Hotel. I said to the driver "Pull over there, I'm going in for a feed... I'm starving". There was a member of the County Board in the car with us and he said, "Who's going to pay for this?" "The County Board will pay," I said, "Come on!" We had our dinner, and the county board did pay.'

The visa took up a full page in the players' passports and was valid for four years. Immigration officials wrote the reason for entry as 'taking part in hurling games'.

In New York, the local Irish American weekly newspapers began their advertising campaigns and the build up to the game was featured in the *Irish Echo* and the *Advocate*. A man of many talents, Offaly-born Paddy (PJ) Grimes was the president of the *Irish Echo* and also of the Grimes Travel Agency, 'Travel Agent of the Gael', both of which operated from the same address at 1849 Broadway. In addition to the making all the travel arrangements and acting as fundraiser and treasurer, he was heavily involved with Tour Vice Chairman Jim Cotter in the marketing of the tour through the *Irish Echo* newspaper, selling tickets, printing the programme, and even providing financial support.

With everything in place in New York, the organising committee eagerly awaited the arrival of the group from Waterford.

UP IN THE SKY

On Tuesday June 7, at a brief ceremony at Mount Sion, the travelling party was presented with a set of hurleys by Messrs. Swift of Waterford. Many of these hurleys were destined for groups of exiles in the U.S. and they added significantly to the weight of luggage being stowed. Each player also received a wallet engraved with their initials. The players from the eastern part of the county set out by bus to Shannon accompanied by a couple of rogue supporters, Michael and Charlie Dowling. They were cousins of Charlie Ware and nephews of Charlie Ware Snr, and they travelled with the team to wave them off at Shannon. Michael Dowling was only a teenager at the time, but he went on to become secretary of Erin's Own for many years. He recalls that 'We got on the bus, Charlie and myself… down at Kenneally's. They were travelling on a Kenneally's bus, and I clearly remember going up to Pearse Park to pick up Joe Coady. He came out of his house with his gear, onto the bus… and off we went'. They were joined in Clonmel by players from the western part of the county who had driven from Dungarvan, and the mood was one of high spirits and excitement at the adventures to come. It wasn't long before a sing-song broke out and Michael remembers that 'Declan Goode was on the bus. His party piece was On The One Road which he performed with gusto as they drove westward, a theme tune for the entire endeavour.

When they arrived at Shannon, the group were not all allowed through to the boarding area, so a group photo was convened in the lobby. The bus travellers were joined by other well-wishers who had travelled separately, among them a group of ladies including Biddy Gallagher, Maura Fanning (Pat's wife), Lily O'Neill and Maureen Hayes. 'They travelled on their own because there wouldn't have been an awful lot of space on the bus for all the gear and everyone', which must have been a relief to the ladies. Once the travelling party had been waved on their way, it was time for a more subdued journey home. Michael recalls that 'Brother Keane was on the bus, and he came home with us. I think there was only four of us on the bus coming home. That was the driver, Seamus Wells, God rest him, Charlie, myself,

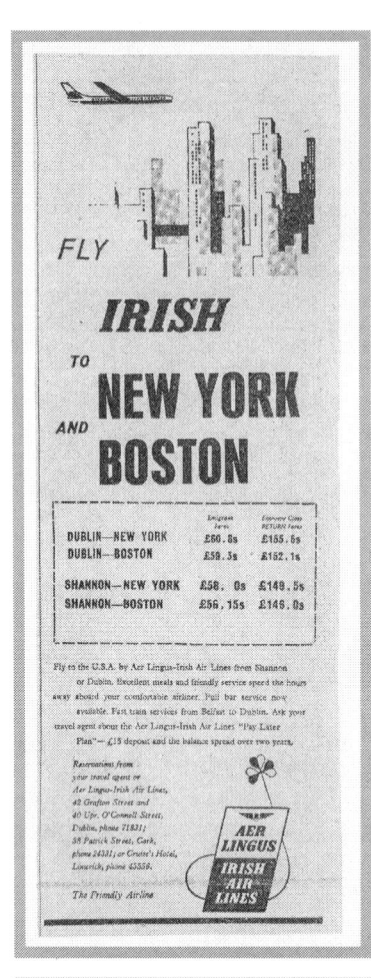

Pricing for flights to New York

✦

The official touring party of 19 players and 4 officials: Back - Martin Óg Morrissey, Joe Coady, Jackie Condon, Charlie Ware, Joe Harney, Freddie O'Brien, Michael O'Connor, Ned Power, Larry Guinan. Middle - John Keane, Tom Cheasty, Philly Grimes, Paudie Casey, Donal Whelan, Austin Flynn, John Barron, Seamus Power, Charlie Ware Snr. Front - Mick Flannelly, Pat Fanning, Frankie Walsh, Declan Goode, Tom Cunningham.

✦

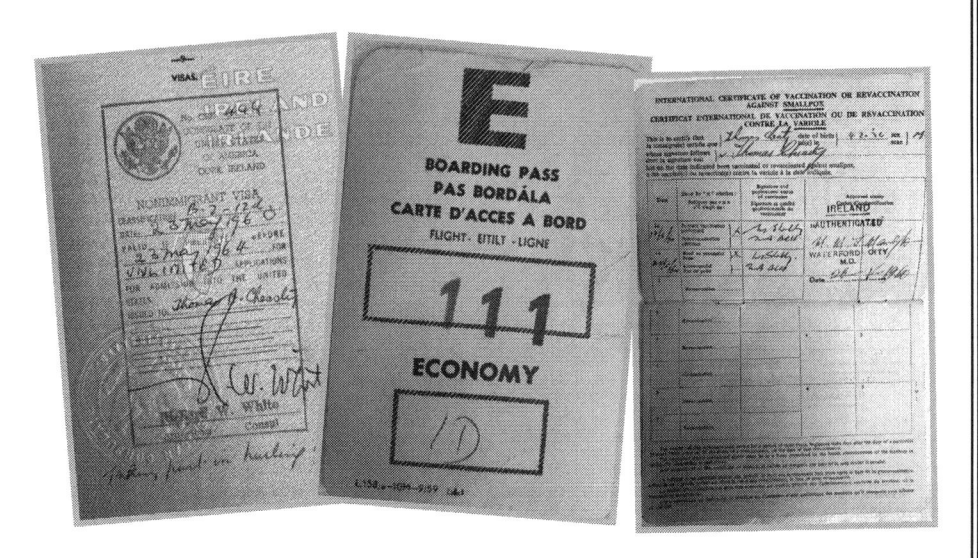

Tom Cheasty's documents: US Visa for the purpose of 'taking part in hurling games', Boarding pass for flight 111 from Shannon to New York, Smallpox vaccination card, signed by Dr. Milo Shelley.

◆

Touring party and supporters at Shannon Airport before departure for New York.

◆

'59: AN EYEWITNESS ACCOUNT OF HURLING'S GOLDEN AGE

and Brother Keane'.

With fewer direct flights at the time, the route of flight 111 to New York was from Shannon to Boston and onwards to New York. The first report of the trip to be published in the *Waterford News and Star* focused heavily on the flight itself, something we may take for granted today but as novice travellers, they admitted to being 'just a little apprehensive'. The boarding, taxi, safety demonstration, take off, receding coastline, pilot announcements and meals were all described with the detail of 'people enjoying a new experience'. Jackie Condon recalls the flight.

'The plane to New York went out at midnight and you wouldn't believe the wind and the rain. We went out to the plane… and they had to drag Tom Cheasty on it. He didn't want to get on… I didn't blame him. I was a bit nervous getting on myself. We got on it anyway and I was sitting at the window… and Paudie Casey was just out from me. The plane was a Super Constellation, a big four-engine aeroplane and she needed an awful lot of runway to take off. She was going down the runway and Paudie said to me "Is the feckin' thing gone up yet?" "No, it's still on the runway." "Are you sure?" "Tis still on the runway!" "Ah, for Jaysus sake… it would want to be taking off soon."

'It looked like the plane would take forever to get off the group but up she went, slowly… slowly, crawled up… and out over the sea. We weren't up only 10 minutes and there was a beautiful moon, and you could see all the fishing boats down in the water… it was magnificent. They gave us pillows to lie back and go asleep because of the long journey. The plane went into a cloud bank, and it was like it was gone into water. The propellors ploughed up the clouds. Jaysus, every fella was sitting up… no sleep, and all the tables gone down.

'Seamus Power was going up and down the middle of the plane, in the horrors, singing *I like New York in June, what about you?* We were at a do for the team down in the Granville years later. I was sitting next to Seamus Power… I used to love Powerie. He had his son with him, and I was chatting to the son, and I was telling him about the singing in the aeroplane. Powerie came down to me later in the night and he said "You don't be telling tales out of school!" He didn't want the young fella to know anything about that end of it.'

Tom Cheasty admitted to his fear in a letter home to his parents from New York.

'Just a few lines to let you know that we all arrived safely here this morning at about

'59: AN EYEWITNESS ACCOUNT OF HURLING'S GOLDEN AGE

7 o'clock American time. I suppose if anything happened you would have heard by now. In all we were about 12 hours up. It was a great relief to have it over us. We had plenty of room on the plane... we had pillows and rugs and two or three seats each to stretch out on. A few of the lads got a little sleep but I did not get any myself as there was too much noise and shaking.'

Martin Óg recalls others' trepidation, but it didn't prevent him from his love of salmon dinners.

'I remember they were serving the grub on the plane... and it happened to be salmon. Tom Cunningham was tensed up and couldn't eat it, so I ate his and mine... no bother at all.'

In the early morning of June 8, the no-smoking signs were illuminated on the Aer Lingus Super Constellation, St. Brigid, and the travellers arrived in Boston. As in-transit passengers, they were confined to an airport lounge but several of the party made use of the public phones to contact friends and relatives in the Boston area. Landing at New York's international airport, Idlewild (later renamed JFK), at 7.30 in the morning, the team busied themselves with retrieving their luggage and a cargo of 'more hurleys than we could use in a couple of years hard hurling'. Their passage through the formalities of the airport was smoothed by Paddy Grimes, travel agent for the tour. The party was welcomed by Paddy Kenneally, himself an exile from Ballinameela of 40 years standing, the driving force behind the tour and Tour Chairman.

Tom Cheasty had his own welcoming committee consisting of an NYPD cop and an FBI man.

'I got a real surprise at Idlewild Airport. When I came through customs two men came up to me an introduced themselves as Geoffrey and Sigh (this is the way it is pronounced anyhow) Cheasty. They introduced themselves as my cousins and insisted on driving myself, Joe Harney and Donal Whelan into the hotel... showing us around as well on the way. I must say they are really nice people. I might mention that Geoff is an FBI man or something like it.'

The team were treated as VIPs and had breakfast in the airport restaurant as the guests of Irish International Airlines (Aer Lingus) and afterwards were gathered outside for

Touring party being welcomed to New York at Idlewild Airport

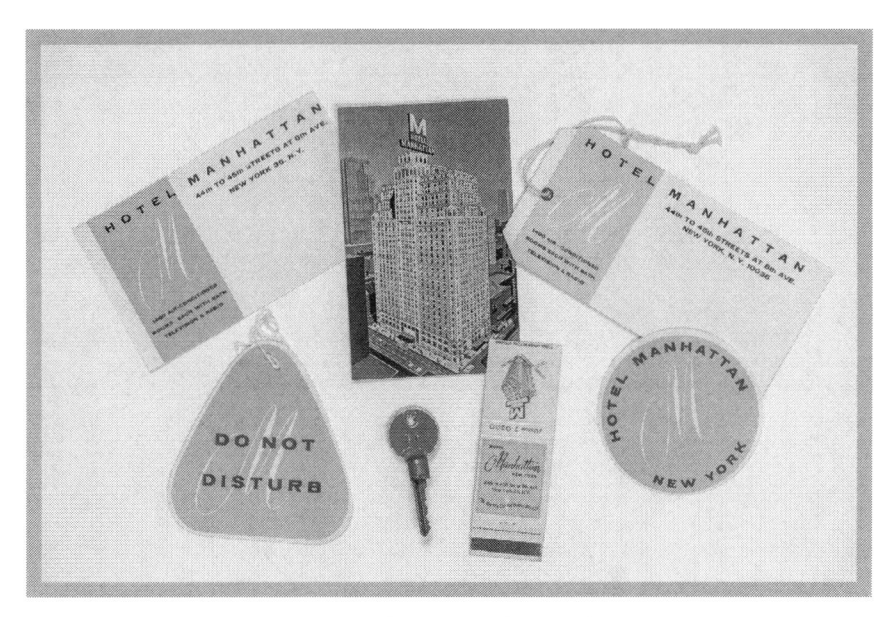

Manhattan hotel souvenirs

Room service menu

After mass with Cardinal Spellman outside St. Patrick's Cathedral

photographs and interviews with local journalists. Despite the long journey, Pat Fanning reported to the press that the team was in good shape. When the players were questioned by the *Irish Echo* reporter 'a sampling of their opinions on the outcome of Sunday's game at Gaelic Park elicited a victory complex and a wish to see the much-talked-of Bohack Cup and replicas, the prize for the winners. Apparently, they intend to bring it back to Waterford. John Keane was already making enquiries of the facilities available for a good workout Thursday and Friday'.

The 45-minute trip from the airport by bus to their hotel was almost as exciting as the flight had been. The Manhattan Hotel on 44th to 45th Streets at 8th Avenue was in midtown Manhattan which brought the party 'through wide streets made narrow by the high buildings that went up and up until they seemed to scrape the sky'. Those first sightings of Broadway and Times Square readied the team for their hotel, the old Lincoln Hotel, recently rebuilt, standing 28 floors high. Each of the 1,400 rooms had air conditioning, private bath, telephone, television, and radio, quite an upgrade on standard living conditions in Waterford at the time. There was not much time to settle in though and almost immediately, friends and family members began calling on the players.

Despite having travelled overnight and already attended a welcome breakfast and press conference, the party had their first official reception at 1pm on the day of arrival at their hotel. Among those at the head of the table was John 'Kerry' O'Donnell, president of the New York GAA, who contented himself with a formal welcome to the party and told the players to 'ask when they wanted anything and to insist that they got all that was coming to them'. The Waterford party felt there was initially a little distance between them and O'Donnell which would need to be bridged. As owner of Gaelic Park, O'Donnell had been instrumental in arranging the financing of the tour. Despite his gruff manner, he took a practical approach to these tours and was in favour of them. He was later quoted as saying 'It's a grand thing to have teams come here, and equally for our lads to go home. After all, what is in the game? It's an amateur game and if you can't get a trip out of it for the top team or look forward to it, then I think it takes away something from our game'.

Along with others of the Irish diaspora from a range of organisations such as politicians, police officers, journalists, priests, lawyers, and diplomats (including John J. Conway on behalf of the Irish government), there was also William J. Kent Jr. president of H.C. Bohack. This chain of grocery stores gave their name to the Bohack Challenge Cup which they had sponsored along with individual miniatures for the players of the winning team. In the early descriptions of this sponsorship, the cup was to be presented to the team which was successful in the aggregate score of the two games. This approach was planned to give the second game all the competitiveness of the first and maintain interest through the series. However, this American-style innovation was shelved as the Waterford team's schedule now only allowed for one appearance on a Sunday, the traditional day out for the Irish at Gaelic Park, and so the Bohack Cup was awarded to the winners of the first game on Sunday June 12.

After the reception, the players were briefed on the detailed plans for the tour at Room 532, the Tour Committee's office at the Manhattan Hotel. They were free to do as they pleased, provided they informed the committee and received their approval. While some of the players finally succumbed to the exhaustion of the previous 24 hours, a few set out to see something of New York. Paddy Kenneally and his team based themselves at the hotel and the advertisements for the upcoming matches in the local press directed supporters to the Manhattan Hotel to buy tickets. Tickets were prices at $2, $3 and $4 and were also available at Gaelic Park on the Sundays leading up to the game. Ticket sales were expected to be brisk and 'an expected throng of 15,000 people will cram into every seat and vantage point of Gaelic Park to see the champions of Ireland clash with New York's best hurlers'.

Anticipation was high amongst GAA supporters who had tuned into the two All-Ireland final matches on local radio station WNYC the previous autumn. The players were household names and *'truly a team of champions'*. The local press used some terminology that may have been unfamiliar to the visitors with Seamus Power being described as 'the clutch player of the team' probably due to his last-minute equaliser in the drawn final. Martin Óg Morrissey was also highly praised, but his name caused some difficulties, and he was variously referred to as Martin Morrissey or Martin Oge Morrissey. Despite their illustrious opponents, New York were confident of victory and the Irish Echo GAA correspondent reported that the New York team *'has trained well and will lack nothing in eagerness and incentive. Their mentors are highly confident of victory and this corner picks them to win'*.

HOTEL MANHATTAN

With almost two weeks in New York and only two games to play, the Waterford group had plenty of free time to enjoy their impressive surroundings. Having just experienced London a week earlier, Charlie Ware Snr. was so impressed he wrote home that 'New York is a wonderful city' and that 'London is a wash-out when compared to New York'… and is only 'a village' in comparison. The hotel was certainly impressive. John Barron reported back to his family that the players had spent the first half hour in the hotel riding the escalators and elevators in awe of their new surroundings. The hotel itself provided lots of opportunities to spend their dollars and the exchange rate was favourable to the Irish party with the punt being worth $2.75. A laundry list from the hotel gave an indication of how prices have changed since 1960. A shirt could be cleaned and starched for 50 cents and a silk dress dry cleaned for 75 cents. Fashions have also changed. A collar could be laundered individually for 15 cents and a handkerchief for 12 cents. Pyjamas cost 60 cents to clean, but an extra 15 cents if they were silk. John Barron's son, John, joked that 'Dad was in trouble so… he only used silk pyjamas!'. The laundry itself was done by the Metropolis Laundry, just around the corner on W 46th Street.

Tom Cunningham recalls that each of the players had a roommate.

> 'I was bunking with Austin Flynn in New York. He had a lot of friends from Abbeyside who were living in New York. When he was going to visit them, I'd go along with him. I had only one relation in New York, a first cousin of my mothers. That's the only connection I had. She invited us to tea.'

The breakfast menu for the Hotel Manhattan would also make modern-day travellers to New York jealous. Two poached eggs on toast only cost 85 cents while a Danish pastry could be had for only 35 cents. Long before hurling squads followed special nutritional advice, the Waterford group could enjoy a low calorie, high protein breakfast which was advertised for $1.40. It included one egg (any style), toast, orange juice, coffee, and the 'new protein cereal', Special K. For those who really felt like taking advantage of their expense allowance from the County Board, breakfast could be delivered as room service, with the 85-cent breakfast costing $1.75 in your room. As Frankie Walsh recalled 'We had a meal allowance and a laundry allowance. The Waterfordmen's Association looked after us brilliantly'. The organised meals followed the same format as in Ireland to the extent that Tom Cheasty recalled that 'We were there on a Friday. Just imagine… the waitress came in and said "Ye are Irish, you must have fish for your dinner".' Jackie Condon remembers that the players used the food allowance to find cheaper diners in the area of the hotel.

> 'We got $100 each to feed ourselves. Paudie Casey and myself went into this restaurant across the road from the hotel. These girls were going around, and they had these see-through plastic coats on them and very little else on underneath it. Jaysus… we didn't know where to look. Everything was a culture shock.'

MATCH BUILD UP

Sunday June 12 was the date of the first game between Waterford and New York and it started with 10 o'clock mass at St. Patrick's Cathedral on 5th Avenue, followed by a reception with His Eminence, Cardinal Spellman. Met at the main doors, the Waterford group were escorted

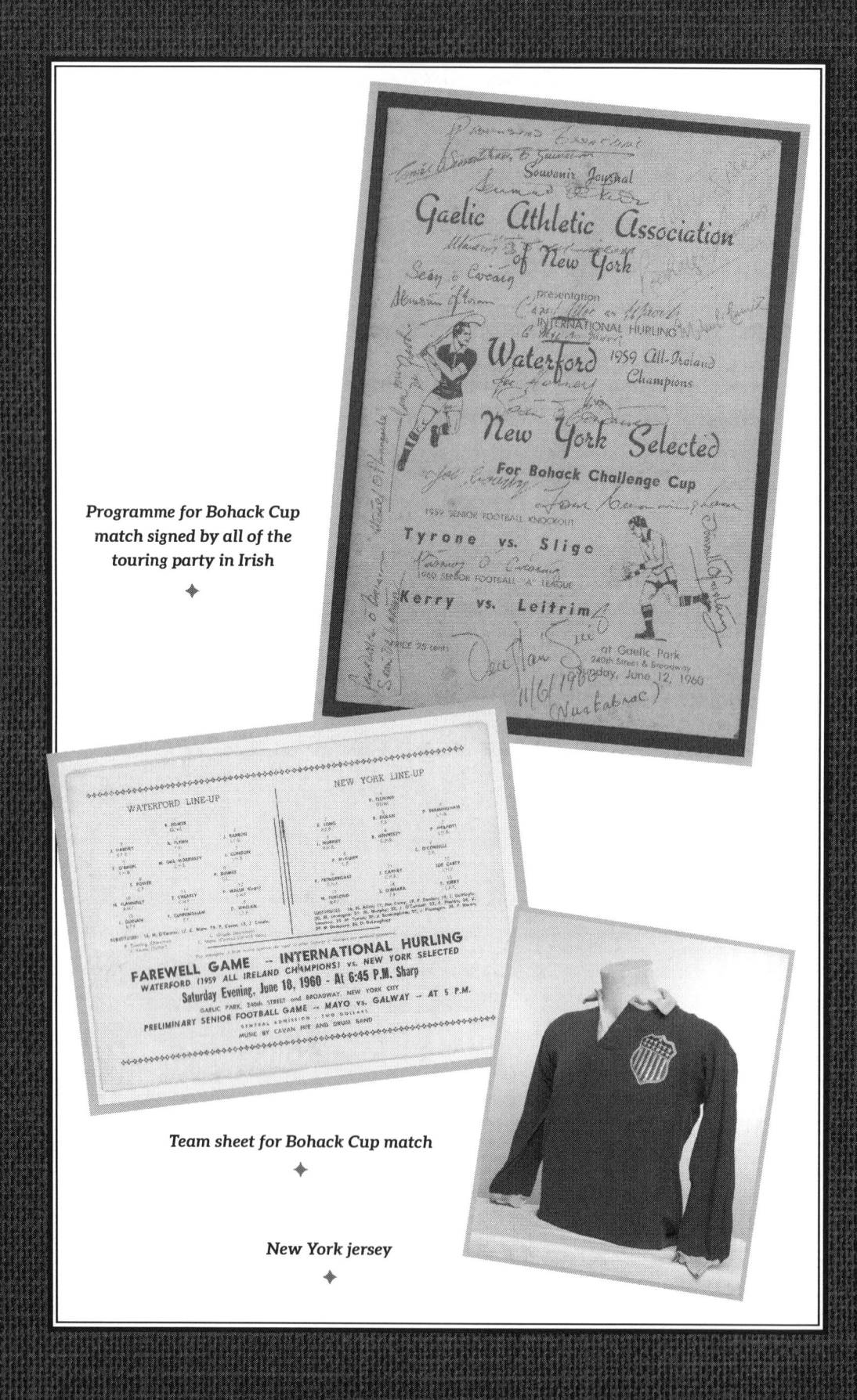

Programme for Bohack Cup match signed by all of the touring party in Irish

◆

Team sheet for Bohack Cup match

◆

New York jersey

◆

down the centre aisle to special seats close to the altar rails. The Cardinal, Bishop Flannelly, and priests strode in procession to the high altar. When it came to the announcements, delivered by Monsignor O'Flaherty, the presence of the party of athletes from Ireland was announced to the congregation. On behalf of His Eminence, he wished them a pleasant stay in New York. After mass, there was the procession of the Cardinal to a spot in the Cathedral grounds where each member of the extended Waterford party was introduced and kissed his ring. This included Mick Flannelly's uncle, Larry, who was visiting from Boston, and Pat Fanning's cousin, Jim Stubbs, of Morgan Street. His Eminence had received and spoken briefly to about 30 of the extended group when he asked with some humour 'How many have you in a team?'. Then, with 'the typical American's regard for the press', he posed for photographs.

At around noon, as the squad set out on their 15-minute walk back to the Manhattan Hotel, the sky darkened ominously, and it started to rain. This was no ordinary summer shower and, over the hours ahead, it led to some of the heaviest rainfall seen in New York for several years. The effect on the relatively poor surface of Gaelic Park, particularly following a curtain-raising football match, was to be expected and the day's headline hurling match went ahead in what was described as 'flood and mud and discomfort'. There were even fears that the match may have to be cancelled. The first impact of the weather was on the attendance. 1,500 tickets had been sold in advance, but it would have been expected that most supporters would pay at the gate. A total attendance of 5,000 was a tribute to the drawing power of the Waterford team, but also a financial catastrophe for the organising committee.

The New York team were no pushovers, even for the All-Ireland champions, as they proved many times in the late 50s and early 60s. Pete McDermott's men were reported to have been training extremely hard for this game under the Offaly man and his assistants, Mickey O'Connell and Mike Cody. This was underlined by a notice in the *Irish Echo* which appeared as soon as the tour was approved for the earlier dates in May.

> 'Selected players are being urged to note the impact which the results will have on N.Y. hurling in general and are being requested to prepare conscientiously for May 22nd. Since the training period for the coming Waterford game must be completed in three weeks, no absences from training will be permitted. Trainer Mickey O'Connell has announced the training schedule as follows: Tuesday and Thursday evenings at 6pm; Saturday at 2pm; and Sundays at 12 noon. Where possible, competitive games will be played at the Sunday sessions.'

In a postcard home, Charlie Ware described how the Waterford team were to train on the

'59: AN EYEWITNESS ACCOUNT OF HURLING'S GOLDEN AGE

evening of June 9, 'when the sun goes down', and that the New York team were 'training three hours every day and they are bent on winning'. This may be an exaggeration, but it does square with the New York approach of train hard, play hard and echoes the comments made about their training and general play at the time of the St. Brendan's Cup final against Tipperary nine months earlier. In a letter home, Tom Cheasty noted that 'the pitch here is very small and hard. They say it won't suit us so don't be surprised if we are beaten'. Waterford were ready though and lined up with their full All-Ireland-winning team with the exception of Mick Lacey and John Kiely.

The line-up for the Bohack Cup game was:

- Ned Power
- Joe Harney
- Austin Flynn
- John Barron
- Freddie O'Brien
- Martin Óg Morrissey
- Jackie Condon
- Seamus Power
- Phil Grimes
- Mick Flannelly
- Tom Cheasty
- Frankie Walsh
- Larry Guinan
- Tom Cunningham
- Donal Whelan

Subs: Charlie Ware, Michael O'Connor, Joe Coady, Paudie Casey

The New York team was named a week in advance and included players from all parts of Ireland, lined out as follows:

- Patrick Fleming (Tipperary)
- Kevin Long (Limerick)
- Brendan Dolan (Offaly)
- P. J. Bermingham (Offaly)
- Johnny Murphy (Tipp)
- Brendan Hennessey (Kerry)
- Pat Philpot (Cork)
- Paddy McGuirk (Cork)
- Christy O'Connell (Clare)
- Ray Prendergast (Limerick)
- James Carney (Clare)
- Joe Carey (Tipp)
- Michael Furlong (Offaly)
- Sean O'Meara (Tipp)
- Pat Kirby (Clare)

Subs: 16. Norman Allen (Dublin), 17. Jim Carey (Tipperary), 18. Peter Doolan (Cork), 19. Tom Guilfoyle (Clare), 20. Mick Lonergan (Tipperary), 21. Martin Murphy (Galway), 22. James O'Connell (Kerry), 23. Paddy Phelan (Kilkenny), 24. Vincent Sammon (Clare), 25. Mick Tynan (Limerick), 26. J. Bermingham, 27. James Flanagan (Clare), 28. Paddy Hearne (Dublin), 29. Martin Dempsey (Galway), 30. Dave DeLoughery (Kilkenny).

The *Advocate* newspaper was quick to comment on the listing of 15 substitutes on the New

'59: AN EYEWITNESS ACCOUNT OF HURLING'S GOLDEN AGE

York side. In their 'Dolan's Corner article', he commented:

> 'For the life of us we fail to understand why the New York selectors have named a second fifteen hurlers as subs. We were under the impressions that the new Gaelic Athletic Association of Ireland rule changes governed Gaelic football and hurling teams both at home and abroad to only three substitutions. It is most unfair to the fifteen men on the side-line. Why not let the second 15 meet Waterford in the replay on Saturday evening, June 18th?'

As the game got closer the list of subs was reduced to just seven – Sammon, Carey, Dempsey, Phelan, Allen, and Guilfoyle. Strangely, there was a new man added in Devlin from Cork, while eight others lost out. The line-up placed Tom Cheasty and Brendan Hennessey in opposition, both players from Ballyduff, one in Waterford and the other in Kerry. Brendan Hennessy was well known to Eddie Keher from his years of colleges hurling.

> 'New York would have had a lot of emigrants at that time. A lot of fellas were emigrating to America and New York particularly. They would have had a strong team from all over the country. I remember particularly Brendan Hennessy from Kerry. In our first All-Ireland Colleges final he was with St. Flannan's of Ennis that year in 1957. He was one of the outstanding hurlers of the time at college level. Obviously, as a Kerryman he wasn't being noticed at the inter-county level, but he certainly was in New York. He was one of the main players over there. He was one of the lads I remember from our matches. Pat Philpot was another name.'

Philpot had played for Cork in the All-Ireland final of 1956 and was one of the more prominent New York players. Donie Nealon describes him as 'a beautiful hurler' but he was best known in Waterford as the player who had broken Frankie Walsh's skull in his Waterford debut. However, by 1960, Frankie had obviously forgiven any previous transgressions. His son, Peter confirms that 'he met Philpot in New York after. They met and had a drink'. Phil Fanning recalls that 'Frankie gave me the impression that yer man was very apologetic, and they had a few drinks. Every time he went to New York, he saw him'. Jackie Condon was present and remembers the occasion.

> 'I knew of Philpott. He was the Cork fella. We went out for dinner with Philpott... we sat down to dinner, and it was lovely, I really enjoyed it. We were in the restaurant

'59: AN EYEWITNESS ACCOUNT OF HURLING'S GOLDEN AGE

at about 1 o'clock in the morning. It was a 24-hour day in New York.. you wouldn't go to bed at all, up all night. Everything was just normal in the middle of the night.'

Martin Óg Morrissey recalls that 'The New York players were all new to me. They had players from Tipperary and other places… and a fella called 'Loose Ball' Allen from Dublin. In speaking to players in other counties, they may have gotten more information on the New York panel. Tony Wall still remembers some of them well.

> 'There was a fella called Carey from Tipperary out there. He had been banned for life at home here in Tipperary. They had a fella called Carney who was a Clare man... he was a great hurler. He had played with Clare before he went out. He was a big, long fella… a formidable centre forward. I was glad he was over in New York and that he wasn't at home playing with Clare. I was up against him. He was two or three inches bigger than me, and he had a big, long stride. Jaysus, he was a formidable hurler. Johnny O'Meara played with Tipperary before he went out… he was a fine lad, a fine fellow. He had been out with us in visiting New York with one of the teams and he had played with Tipperary in New York earlier in the 1950s. Then he got a job in New York, and he was playing in New York. He was a handy player… a good hurler.'

Donie Nealon remembered many of the players, particularly those with a Tipperary connection or those whom he had played against in colleges or inter-county hurling.

> 'Seán O'Meara won a league afterwards with Tipp and played for Munster. He was from Lorrha, and he'd go back and forward between Tipperary and New York. He was a great athlete.
>
> 'Pat Philpot, he was some hurler. He was on the team that lost to Wexford in 1956. He was a smashing guy but, you know… he disappeared in New York. He played for a couple of years with New York, and nobody knows what happened him after that.
>
> 'Ray Prendergast from Limerick was in Flannan's with us. He was a flyer. His father was a guard from the midlands, and they were living in Clare, He was a couple of years older than me. Great runner as well.
>
> 'Joe Carey. I knew him well. Jim Carey and himself were brothers.
>
> 'Pat Kirby. He was a great handballer.
>
> 'Johnny Murphy played for Tipp in the first round of the championship in 1958. He was from Cashel.

'59: AN EYEWITNESS ACCOUNT OF HURLING'S GOLDEN AGE

'Brendan Hennessy was a marvellous player. He was in Flannan's as well. He had a brother Michael... he played for Kerry before he went to America.

'Brendan Dolan. I think he was a great rugby player as well.'

The New York style of play was even tougher than that seen at home. Martin Óg Morrissey has a theory which explains it. 'The hurling out there was different to the hurling here. It was a lot tougher... they were a tough bunch. They were like all Irish men when they went away. They had to show that they were tough'. Tony Wall is a little more pointed in his description. 'It was a rougher style of hurling in New York. There was a crowd of f****n' hatchet men out there.'

BOHACK CUP FINAL

Throw in was at 3.30pm but the game was preceded by a local senior football match, Sligo beating Tyrone in the 1959 Senior Football Championship Division B decider. Considering the awful weather, the football opener cannot have done much for the condition of the playing surface. Martin Óg Morrissey recalls the conditions.

'The first day we played it pissed rain. I'm not joking you; I never saw rain like it before or after. They were taking photographs of the team before the match... and they were using flashbulbs at 3 o'clock in the day. That will tell you how heavy the rain was. I had to throw away my togs afterwards... I couldn't get the dirt out of it. I never saw anything like it. Gaelic Park was a bit small, and it was tight. The grass was scarce enough before the match... there was no grass there after the match. It was a waste of time playing first time hurling, the way we played, on that. We probably would have beat them on a normal day, but it wouldn't suit us at all on a day like that.'

The players were *'ankle deep in water in many parts of the flooded field, hurling was lowered from the matchless game of skill to a sort of combination field hockey, water polo and golf'*. When the ball hit the ground, particularly in either goalmouth, it stopped in the puddles which were compared to *'miniature lakes'*, leading to a lot of wild swinging from both sets of players. The New York team were bigger and stronger and were better suited to the conditions. There was no place for Waterford's fast-moving ground hurling on the day. Phil Grimes was singled out in the *Irish Independent* for his *'spectacular performance'*, but the forwards struggled *'to make any worthwhile headway against the devastating but legitimate pulling of the New York defenders'*. Only four Waterford players managed to score, while New York dominated with five goal scorers (O'Meara, Kirby, Carney, Murphy, and Furlong).

Jack Dempsey souvenirs

✦

Larry Guinan, Ned Power, Austin Flynn and Donal Whelan meet Jack Dempsey. Also included is Nellie Greaney, wife of Pat 'Fox' Greaney from Dungarvan.

✦

Jack Dempsey postcard.

✦

Jack Dempsey postcard, inscribed to 'Phil (Grimes), Good Luck Pal'

✦

'59: AN EYEWITNESS ACCOUNT OF HURLING'S GOLDEN AGE

The first quarter was all New York despite losing full-back Dolan (replaced by Jim Carey) through injury. Sean O'Meara, the former Tipperary player, opened the scoring in the first minute with a goal and Carney soon followed it with a point. After that, New York were never behind throughout the game. Frankie Walsh scored Waterford's first point in the third minute. Carney pointed again in 7th minute and soon after he centred to Furlong for New York's second goal. Kirby scored a goal in the 13th minute putting Waterford three goals behind. After 15 minutes, Waterford had their first lucky break with a Walsh goal direct from a free. O'Meara edged New York further ahead but Waterford were now coming into the game. A second Walsh point and a goal by Larry Guinan from a Tom Cheasty pass after 20 minutes brought the score to 3-3 to 2-2. The resurgence died in the mud though and there were no further scores in the remaining 10 minutes of the half.

O'Meara opening the scoring in the second-half with a goal, but Waterford were not giving up. Seamus Power pointed from midfield and a goal for Mick Flannelly, after a skirmish in the goalmouth, brought Waterford in range again. With 20 minutes to go, they must have felt they had the beating of New York. However, apart from another long-distance point from Seamus Power, New York dominated the rest of the game with points from Hennessey, O'Meara, Philpot, and Murphy, in that order. Martin Murphy had a shot which slipped past Ned Power for a goal and Carney scored New York's sixth goal with eight minutes to go. Near the end of the second-half, Lonergan replaced O'Connell and Paddy Hearne replaced Sean O'Meara, but not before he scored New York's final goal.

O'Meara had been the hero of the hour for New York as he scored 3-2 of their total, with another former Tipperary player, Jim Carney, adding 1-2. For Waterford, Frankie Walsh had to be substituted having received a cut behind his left ear which required six stitches. Waterford's best player was deemed to be Seamus Power at midfield. The *Irish Echo* described his performance as *'the outstanding hurler of the day. His control of the slippery sliothar, his deft striking, his keen desire and unflagging attempts to rally his team in the face of apparent defeat all bore the marks of a great hurler and competitor'*.

In the end, New York ran out 7-7- to 3-4 victors. Pat Philpot, the New York captain accepted the Bohack Cup, made of sterling silver and reported to be worth $2,000, from Paddy Kenneally. With some hyperbole, the *Irish Echo* announced *'It can truly be said that New York now are World Champions of the hurling scene. That's a big title but who else can they beat. It was a thorough and complete victory'*. The individual miniatures of the Bohack Cup for the winning players were presented at a final celebration of the Waterford tour at Gaelic Park after the second match on Saturday evening.

Most reports of the game emphasised the foul weather. The *Irish Independent* ran the

'59: AN EYEWITNESS ACCOUNT OF HURLING'S GOLDEN AGE

headline *'New York Swamp Waterford on Quagmire Pitch'*. They noted how the torrential rain fell throughout the game and *'the ball was often lost in pools of water'*. They suggested that the game would have been postponed had it not been for Waterford's tight schedule. The Cork Examiner ran a similar headline *'Downpour Washed Out All-Ireland Champions Hopes'* and emphasised that Waterford had been well beaten by New York.

Pat Fanning was sent out to the waiting reporters to discuss the game. To the *Irish Echo* he explained that *'Waterford hurlers are known as "top of the sod" men and in the quagmire that was Gaelic Park, the game could not be considered a real test of hurling'* but, at the same time, he was strong in his praise of the New York selected team and the officials of the New York GAA. However, the *Irish Echo* had a valid response, making the point that *'It could have been said before the game that the visitors would fare better on the wet pitch... seldom do any of the home clubs here play in wet weather, while in Ireland only the severest of weather forces postponements. But it looked the other way as New York seemed to revel in the mud'*. The reports sent back home were similar with the *Examiner* quoting Fanning at the end of their report as saying *'to say the weather ruined our game is putting it mildly. New York are a good side, but I think we can beat them next time'*. In the *Waterford News & Star*, in his own column as 'Deiseach', he commented that *'The hurling was tough, rough perhaps by our standards, but not dirty'*. The New York newspapers agreed that *'taking everything into account it was a tremendous exhibition of a fine manly game with many hard knocks on both sides'*. The small pitch, bad weather, mud, pools of water underfoot, and tough hurling led to quite a few injuries to the extent that Jackie Condon and Frankie Walsh were unavailable for selection in the second match six days later. Jackie Condon recalls the treatment he received.

> 'I got injured in New York. I got a knee in the thigh... a dead leg. I was alright walking, but that thing takes a week or more to go away. When you are coming down the stairs, you can't bend the knee and you look worse than you are really. The American fellas saw me coming down the stairs and said, "What's wrong with you?" I said "I have a dead leg after the last match." They said '"Did nobody do anything about it?" Jaysus, they went after Pat Fanning and read him the riot act. So, I was brought to hospital, and they had a big bath of hot water... and I was getting dunked up and down in it and these masseurs working on me. Sure, they got the leg right in no time.'

New York also had their share of injuries. One player suffered a broken jaw while another received 11 stitches for a cut over his eye. The *Advocate* commented that having played in such awful weather conditions, Waterford should have no trouble in winning the championship on their return home as surely nothing their opponents could throw at them would equal their New York debut. They also expected that Waterford had a good chance of turning the tables in the second game.

In general, the players were not too disappointed. As Tom Cunningham reflects *'We were beaten by New York who had a tough team at the time, but we weren't totally interested in the match'*. There were also the sights and the nightlife of New York to enjoy in the week leading up to the second match.

JACK DEMPSEY'S RESTAURANT

Perhaps it was playing to a stereotype or an attempt to win market share with the Irish residents of New York, but Rheingold, Ballantine and Schaefer beer companies all placed adverts in the New York Irish newspaper, the *Advocate*, to offer a *'céad mile failte'* to *'Ireland's finest hurlers – the Waterford 1959 All-Ireland Hurling Champions'*. A few of the local beers may have been consumed on a night out at Jack Dempsey's Broadway Restaurant in the Brill Building on Times Square (at Broadway between 49th and 50th streets), owned by former world heavyweight boxing champion Jack Dempsey. After a tough afternoon at Gaelic Park, the Waterford group returned to their hotel and Freddie O'Brien remembers the short walk to get to the restaurant that evening.

> 'We were staying in the Manhattan Hotel. Jack Dempsey's restaurant was only a block or two away… it was quite close, walking distance. I remember somebody ordering bacon and cabbage whenever we went in for a meal and he was amazed that he got it.'

Jackie Condon recalls arriving at the restaurant. 'We went into Jack Dempsey's and Declan Goode said, "Put them up there Jack, the name is Goode!" Dempsey was often on hand to greet guests, sign autographs and pose for pictures and he didn't disappoint that night. Tom Power, Seamus' son tells 'One of the stories from New York is that they visited Jack Dempsey's bar. My father would always have said that Philly was the best person he saw to box on a field. At that time, it was a different era… people would drop the hurleys and box. He said Philly would have made a boxer such was the quickness of his punches. They were in Jack Dempsey's Bar and they met Jack Dempsey and they got photos with him. Dempsey said, "Seamus is the second-best boxer I ever met, Philly is the first".' This is the borne out by the postcard Phil had signed by Dempsey which is still in his family's possession. Photos from the night include Dempsey with Joe Harney, Paudie Casey, Tom

'59: AN EYEWITNESS ACCOUNT OF HURLING'S GOLDEN AGE

Cheasty, John Keane, Jackie Condon, Larry Guinan, Ned Power, Austin Flynn, and Donal Whelan. Larry Guinan still has a photo from this dinner on display in the office of his tyre business in Waterford and Ned Power brought back a miniature pair of boxing gloves with a printed Jack Dempsey signature.

Many years later in an interview reflecting on his career, Tom Cheasty remembered the occasion fondly.

> 'Playing with Waterford gave me a chance to see some of the world. When we played in America, we were invited to attend Jack Dempsey's pub. The bouncer on the door asked if we were 'in for a drink or a fight?', that's how imposing some of our players were. Boxing was a big hobby of mine and I loved to watch Sugar Ray Robinson, Cassius Clay and the 'Brown Bomber' Joe Louis. Sometimes you can compare hurling with boxing. A good hurling team never lies down when they get hurt... like a top-class boxer you must bounce back, or you have no business in the sport.'

EXPERIENCING NEW YORK

Austin Flynn recalled that 'We travelled to New York as a team in 1960 and it was amazing how the visit brought so many Waterford people together in New York'. Tom Cheasty had met long lost cousins but also had plans for a side trip to Boston to see other family. Over the first weekend, Charlie Ware was visited by his cousin, Lillian who lived in Rhode Island but travelled to New York to meet their Irish relations and see the match. Day trips and activities were arranged for the players, but they did not need to go far to be impressed. Mick Flannelly recalls being collected by Waterford man Billy Griffin and that 'to be going down through Manhattan in an open top car, it was another world!' Billy was heavily involved in the Waterford Association of New York and had emigrated to New York in the late 20s. His nephew, Des Griffin, explains that while in New York Billy met and married Kitty Fleming from Newport's Lane, which was just around the corner from his own home in Doyle Street. The only player with personal experience of New York was Phil Grimes so he took the lead on some expeditions. Martin Óg Morrissey enjoyed one in particular.

> 'Philly was after spending a couple of years in New York and he brought us around to the different places... Coney Island and to where they played baseball. We went into the cage and put our cents into the machine, and it fired out balls at you like you were playing baseball. Ah, we had good craic alright. We had a baseball bat. I'm not boasting or anything, but I hit every ball that came out... I'm not saying I did a great

'59: AN EYEWITNESS ACCOUNT OF HURLING'S GOLDEN AGE

job with them, but I hit them anyway. If there were any of the New York Yankees around, I would have got a trial!'

Freddie O'Brien recalls the tougher parts of New York to which they were introduced.

'Philly's cousin took us out to Coney Island and down around the Bowery. Now the Bowery was a tough spot. In the Bowery there was fellas eating polish, drinking methylated spirits... anything that there was a taste of alcohol from. The policeman was telling us it was a tough place. If you go asleep with a feed of drink in you, you'd wake up and your coat could be gone... or your trousers or your shoes. They were all living off of one another down there.'

This was confirmed by Martin Óg Morrissey who was part of this unsuspecting 'gang'.

'On the way back home, Guinan was out in front of us on his own staggering along. A fella came out of a doorway and said to him "Give me a dollar and a half for a cup of coffee"... yer man was looking for a fix. I got friendly with two Americans in Clover Meats who had served in the U.S. Forces a couple of years after and I told them we went down through the Bowery and they said, "How many of ye were in it?" and I said there were about 30 of us. "I don't believe you," he said. There were gangs in all the different parts of the cities and if they saw a gang like that coming in, they would think they were a gang trying to take over their patch and there would be a big row. We walked there and back and there was no disturbance.'

There were also tours of the city organised for the group. Jackie Condon remembers a boat ride around New York which emphasised the vast scale of the city.

'We saw an awful lot of New York. We were brought on a boat trip around Manhattan Island. Yer man was going "The Brooklyn Bridge is the longest bridge in the world... the highest this and that... the Colgate Clock is the biggest clock in the world". I was standing with Duck Whelan and Duck said, "and he has the biggest mouth in the world". Yer man heard him.'

Tom Cunningham recalls seeing the sights of New York.

'59: AN EYEWITNESS ACCOUNT OF HURLING'S GOLDEN AGE

'It was about seeing places, looking up at the skyscrapers, going to the big stores like Macy's. They were all new to us. Philly Grimes had been in New York, but it was different to the rest of us. We went up on the Empire State Building. It was a unique tour.'

That moment was captured on camera by some of the players with an official souvenir photograph.

From such a unique trip, families at home expected to receive presents. The officials with the team, Charlie Ware Snr, Declan Goode and Pat Fanning, all reported shopping in Macy's department store. Declan also bought jewellery for his wife and Charlie bought jewellery for his wife and three daughters. One of those daughters, Mary Ware, commented that 'They were brave men to go buying jewellery for so many women'. Mick Flannelly's next-door neighbour in Griffith Place, Michael 'Jinx' Walsh remembers Mick bringing home a treasured souvenir.

'Mick Flan brought back a radio... a solid-state transistor radio in a white box and it was red in colour. It was battery operated. I remember sitting down above in the field, up on the hump, as we'd call it, it was grassy then, watching a match and we were listening to another match from Croke Park on the portable radio, and so were a load of other people. That was always kept in the white box. When he'd be finished using it, it would be put back into the box. He was a great man for method. I always remember the radio... it was absolutely beautiful.'

Mick was generous with his presents too and brought home 'a little statuette of the Empire State Building with a thermometer on it' to his neighbour Mrs. Walsh. It was displayed on the mantlepiece and was still there when the family left the house 30 years later. Ned Power brought home a model of the Statue of Liberty. It was so precious to him that he wouldn't part with it, despite requests from his son Conor.

Charlie Ware, in a postcard home to his sister, described going to see Ben Hur at a cinema in Times Square. He described it as 'just marvellous, it started at 8pm and did not end until 12'. A racing enthusiast, he also reported to another sister that he planned to go to the Belmont Races that Saturday but that he would miss her 'to give him the horses'. It was an ideal week for a horse racing fan to visit New York as it coincided with the 92nd running of the Belmont Stakes, the third and final leg of the Triple Crown. The race was won by a horse with the portentous name of Celtic Ash. Ned Power also sent postcards home to his fiancée

'59: AN EYEWITNESS ACCOUNT OF HURLING'S GOLDEN AGE

Gretta with views of Times Square, the Statue of Liberty, and the Empire State Building. The young and single Freddie O'Brien recalls seeing some of the New York nightlife.

> 'Philly Grimes cousin was out there at the time. He was a policeman and he brought us to all the hotspots. I met a girl there and I went out with her a few times… her name was Fleming and her brother played football with Tramore. She took me to Radio City. It was a massive place. I saw this big limousine coming up out of the pits and onto the stage and I had to ask myself "Am I in the real world at all?" We went to Harlem another night… it was an Irish fella who had a restaurant there.'

Jackie Condon saw some of the seamier side of the city and wasn't impressed.

> 'There were lots of things in New York that were very unsavoury. There was one day we were walking down the street and this young black fella came running out of a shop. The guy came out after him shouting "thief! Thief" He went down the subway and two policemen ran after him and had their guns going. They shot at him on the steps of the subway… it was horrendous stuff. You didn't know where you stood with the police. They were all scared or something… they'd shoot you as quick as they'd look at you. When we got there first, they took us in for a speech. They advised us "We know you are all tough guys but if someone puts a gun in your back, put your hands up in the air and give them your money. Don't attempt to have a go at them". You were warned in that way.'

Jackie didn't think he could ever live in New York and, on balance, Freddie O'Brien agreed.

> 'I don't remember much about the matches… more about the good times in New York. It's a fine place… a lovely place, but I don't think it would be my cup of tea.'

The group acted as ambassadors everywhere they went. Cementing links with fellow members of the association, the Waterford officials were keen to share information with their counterparts. Austin Flynn remembered (in Brendan Fullam's Decades of Stars) that 'During the visit, Pat Fanning addressed what would be the equivalent of a county convention in Ireland. He made us all feel proud… he made you feel proud of being from Waterford. He was a wonderful ambassador for the game'. These friendships survived beyond the trip and Mattie Lonergan, who was very generous with his time, made a reciprocal visit to Waterford

Tom Cunningham, Seamus Power, Larry Guinan, John Keane and Jackie Condon at Gaelic Park.

in October with his new bride, Eileen. He was also tasked with hand carrying a batch of souvenir programmes for the Bohack Cup match to Mr. Crotty of the Kilrossanty GAA Club for distribution throughout the county. The unexpectedly low turnout for the match meant that too many were printed. As these were not to be resold, they were overwritten with a note that said, 'Not for sale'.

MATCH DAY 2

Rather than getting to play a second match the following Sunday, which, weather permitting, would have attracted a large crowd, it was scheduled as a Saturday evening throw-in which was variously advertised as starting at 6.45pm sharp, or 7.30pm. As Sunday was the day most Irish people had free from work and their routine was to gather at Gaelic Park, the Saturday night fixture limited the attendance to only 5,000 and put further pressures on the financing of the tour. Waterford lined out with two changes, with Joe Coady and Charlie Ware replacing Jackie Condon and Frankie Walsh.

- Ned Power
- Joe Harney   • Austin Flynn   • John Barron
- Freddie O'Brien   • Martin Og Morrissey   • Joe Coady
- Seamus Power   • Phil Grimes
- Mick Flannelly   • Tom Cheasty   • Larry Guinan
- Charlie Ware   • Tom Cunningham   • Donal Whelan

Subs: Micky O'Connor, Paudie Casey, Frankie Walsh, Jackie Condon

There were several changes to the New York team and the local view, as voiced by the Advocate newspaper, was that *'Waterford was playing against New York's second string in the second-half. However, even New York's second line was enough for the 1959 All-Ireland senior hurling champions'*. The New York team was:

- Patrick Fleming (Tipperary)
- Kevin Long (Limerick)   • Jim Carey (Tipp)   • P.J. Bermingham (Offaly)
- Johnny Murphy (Tipp)   • Brendan Hennessey (Kerry)   • Pat Philpot (Cork)
- Paddy McGuirk (Cork)   • Christy O'Connell (Clare)
- Martin Murphy (Galway)   • James Carney (Clare)   • Joe Carey (Tipp)
- Michael Furlong (Offaly)   • Sean O'Meara (Tipp)   • Pat Kirby (Clare)

Subs: 16. Norman Allen (Dublin) for O'Connell, 17. Vincent Sammon (Clare) for Fleming, 18.

'59: AN EYEWITNESS ACCOUNT OF HURLING'S GOLDEN AGE

P. Guilfoyle (Tipp) for Carney, 19. Ray Prendergast (Limerick) for Murphy, 20. Paddy Phelan (Kilkenny) for Long.

Better weather led to a freer flowing and more even game. A clash of styles was evident with Waterford trying to play their usual ground hurling game and play short hand-passes. This often resulted in a loss of possession as the *'hard swinging New Yorkers ... wasted no time in such trivialities. In the air or on the ground, New York took their swing, hit or miss and they seldom missed'*. After only two minutes, good combination play by Grimes and Cheasty put Guinan through for a goal. New York responded quickly and they opened their scoring with a point from Carney, quickly followed by a free by Martin Murphy, which he initially mishandled but pointed from the ground. Guilfoyle was called upon to replace the injured Jim Carey and after eight minutes a Carney free brought New York level. The teams proceeded to exchange points – Flannelly from play followed by Philpott from a free; Grimes followed by Carney. The decisive exchange of the first-half came just before half-time when errors in the Waterford defence allowed Furlong in for a New York goal. Once again, good play from Grimes set up Guinan for a point, leaving the half-time score at Waterford 1-3, New York 1-5.

Freddie O'Brien recalls that first-half:

> 'In the second game a fella by the name of Carney from Clare was playing centre-forward for New York. Martin Óg wasn't a tough hurler but a very very skilful hurler and very fast over a short distance but once he went beyond 30 or 40 yards, he got a bit lazy about it. This fella Carney was rough and robust... and he was handling Martin Óg, so they put me out centre-back that day. There was a man I met... he'd be a grandfather of Calum Lyons on the Waterford team at the moment. This man was resident in New York. I spoke to him a lot and we hit it off. I was quite friendly with him on the trip. They have a shot of me from a cine camera.'

That cine camera footage is only three minutes long but gives a real insight into the tour. The photo in question showed Freddie on the sideline at half-time, smoking a cigarette. His bandaged left arm a result of the vaccinations received before travelling.

The second-half started with New York playing most of their substitutes from the week before, the most notable change being to replace goalkeeper Fleming with Clare man, Vincent Sammon. Grimes re-opened the scoring with a point. New York's hard work led to a period of dominance from which they seemed unlikely to be caught. A point from O'Meara and goals by Murphy, O'Meara, and Furlong from his boot, with only a point reply from Grimes gave

'59: AN EYEWITNESS ACCOUNT OF HURLING'S GOLDEN AGE

New York a 10-point lead with just 11 minutes remaining.

Waterford steadily made their way back into the game, first with a goal by Cheasty. A shot from Phil Grimes was saved by Sammon but Charlie Ware nipped in to score a goal. Then, a point from Martin Óg Morrissey reduced the gap to just three points in the dying seconds. Then came the decisive moment of the match. Having been awarded a free, Donal Whelan's strike was blocked but the ball deflected to Phil Grimes who steadied himself on the 21-yard line. The former New York player drove the ball through a packed goalmouth to equalise with a goal in last play of the game. The Bogue clock signalled full-time before the ball was in the New York net, but the referee, Jimmy O'Grady, decided that the score should be allowed. There was confusion for the supporters as reported by the Irish Independent. When the ball crossed the line, *'an umpire reached for the flag to signal goal, but it was snapped from his hand by New York player, Pat Philpot, and the score was not recorded by the scoreboard operator'*. It was reported that there was a mix-up in the setting of the clock at the start of the second-half and the referee, Jimmy O'Grady of Limerick, even allowed a puck out after the goal and then whistled full-time.

After much confusion, it was announced to the crowd that the match was a draw. To help explain the confusion, it should be noted that a Bogue clock was in use at Gaelic Park at that time. This was an electrically operated, single-hand clock which was used to count down the 30 minutes of each half.

The crowd would have automatically turned to the game announcer for guidance. John 'Lefty' Devine had been commentating from the sideline at matches in Gaelic Park since 1947. He was there to *'pick out the team players and those that perform during the progress of the hour, to identify them as they make their play'*. This American innovation was in place during the 1960 tour and would have been at the front-line of reporting at the game. It would have fallen to him to announce the final score of the match to the crowd, the first ever draw in an international hurling challenge.

Martin Óg Morrissey remembers Devine.

> 'There was a fella commentating on the match there. I remember him saying that... "It is water polo we should be playing here today". He was commentating for the spectators that were there.'

Another new feature at Gaelic Park which was introduced in 1960, just before the Waterford tour, was a GAA Roundup broadcast over the speakers from RTE's Seán Óg Ó Ceallacháin, although similar to Martin Óg, he reverted to being Seán O'Callaghan in his

American advertising. This broadcast was a recording of his Raidió Éireann show Gaelic Sports Results recorded with the advantage of the five-hour time difference and replayed after the local games were finished. A final innovation that must have been appreciated by the players injured during the game was the medical support. Tony Wall, in his book Hurling, drew attention to this.

> 'I might mention here that we could well adopt the practice which obtains in Gaelic Park, New York. There a doctor is on duty every Sunday in a medical hut beside the pitch, and players can get proper treatment and be back in the fray in a few minutes.'

The press reporting on the match later singled out the performance of Phil Grimes who, according to the *Irish Independent*, saved Waterford from being overrun *'by the power and glory of his game, first at midfield and in the closing stages when he stepped up to the attack to transform a previously inept forward division'*. A New York friend who accompanied the reporter to the game asked, 'Do you folks at home regard that boy as the Babe Ruth of the hurley game?', rehashing the often-used comparison to the baseball superstar. The *Examiner* described the last-minute draw as a *'face saver'* for the tour but to most observers it was felt that, on the run of play, the 4-6 to 4-6 draw was a fitting end to the game and the tour. To celebrate, the tour committee and New York GAA hosted an official farewell dinner and dance at Gaelic Park's Pavilion after the game.

TOUR REVIEW

The timing of the team's homeward journey was partially dictated by the high level of bookings on eastbound flights. It wasn't possible to secure 23 seats on the Monday flight to Shannon or Dublin, so the return was set for Sunday 19. Having departed on Sunday, the team arrived home from New York on Monday, June 20 allowing them just five days to prepare for their successful championship opener against Galway the following Sunday.

The tour was judged to have been a huge success, particularly in fostering close relationships with the Waterford diaspora in New York and as a team building event for the players. The first opportunity to review the events of the previous week came at the Waterford County Board meeting of June 24 where Pat Fanning made a formal statement on the American trip. He opened by reporting that the tour had been 'an outstanding success, and it is so regarded by our hosts, the Waterford men resident in New York, despite the financial loss (estimated at $5,000) suffered by them. In this connection, the Board will be pleased to learn that the personal loss suffered by the guarantors of the tour will be met in full as the result of special

'59: AN EYEWITNESS ACCOUNT OF HURLING'S GOLDEN AGE

field days arranged for Gaelic Park, New York'.

As a cultural exchange, the tour was a huge success. In his closing remarks to the County Board, Pat Fanning stated, 'I learned a great deal from this visit to New York, and my hope is that relations between us and them will grow more and more cordial, and that tours – by our hurlers and footballers, to New York, and by the New York boys to Ireland – subject to the sanction and control of the Central Council or congress, will for long provide a bond between our people at home and those overseas'.

In turn, Paddy Kenneally's closing words in his review letter echoed those of many exiles when he said 'The good wishes of ever so many here go to all of you every day, not for hurling success so much, although that is important too, as for your health, happiness and good living in the homeland. Stay there good friend for all your days – keep the kids beside you. You'll find towards the end that Ireland for an Irishman is still the closest place on earth to Heaven'.

EPILOGUE

1960 TO 1962

After the highs of 1959, Waterford struggled for a couple of years. It is understandable that in the midst of their All-Ireland celebrations the team had mixed form in the league of 1959/60. Incredibly, just a week after the All-Ireland final, Waterford beat Wexford by 15 points. Just three weeks after the success against Kilkenny, the teams met again in a league match in Nowlan Park and played out a 4-6 to 4-6 draw. The momentous year of 1959 came to a close with a return to Croke Park in December, where the team suffered a 3-10 to 1-9 loss to Dublin. Dublin's goalkeeper on the day, Jimmy Gray, remembers the game.

> 'We played Waterford in the National League after the All-Ireland, and we beat them. We usually played them in the league, but they normally beat us. The celebrations must have told on them.'

For completeness, it is worth noting that Waterford were beaten 6-6 to 5-3 by Cork at the Gaelic Ground in Waterford on February 28, 1960, and finished out the 59/60 league campaign with a trip to Antrim where they had an easy 7-7 to 1-2 victory at Casement Park. Freddie O'Brien laments the loss of that famous old ground… 'look at Casement Park now, totally obsolete and overgrown'. His other memory of that visit to the north brings up an unusual episode in Belfast's social history.

> 'This is more history. I brought up bread from Dublin that time to Belfast because there was a bread strike up there. I had a cousin in Dublin who had a friend in Belfast, and they had no bread… I brought up a couple of large pans.'

Waterford finished fourth in Division 1A, behind Cork, Kilkenny and Dublin, with Cork qualifying for the league final where they were beaten by Tipperary.

Waterford's reign as All-Ireland champions survived the distraction of the trips to London and New York. Within a week of their return from New York Waterford beat Galway by 9-8 to 4-8 in their opening championship match of 1960. They went on to play Tipperary in the Munster Championship semi-final in Limerick on July 17th, but Tipperary gained their revenge for the hammering of 1959 with a 6-9 to 2-7 win. The champions of '59 had been dethroned and Wexford went on to take their crown in the All-Ireland final against Tipperary. Waterford reached the Munster final in 1962, when they were again well beaten by Tipperary. It is an image from the semi-final match against Cork that keeps that year alive in the memories of Waterford supporters. Ned Power was photographed jumping to catch a ball while Christy Ring followed through and collided with Tom Cunningham. An iconic image, it has featured on the cover of books such as Conor Power's biography of his father, Ned, and Liam O'Donnchu's *Semple Stadium, Field of Legends*. It has even been reproduced as a statue outside Tallow. The third Waterford player in the photo is Austin Flynn, all three players alumni of Dungarvan CBS. Ned was the oldest, Tom a year below and Austin a couple of years below again.

1963 FINAL

Waterford's win in 1959, following their narrow loss in '57 gave supporters every confidence that this pattern would be repeated. Pat Fanning wrote:

> 'With the same will to win, with equal and sustained concentration on victory and with that zeal and unity of purpose, without which there is no success, 1959, far from being the end can be made the prelude to an era of undreamed glory for the Decies.'

Despite a couple of years without success, his prediction appeared to come true in 1963 when Waterford won the league, Munster and Oireachtas titles. However, they failed to beat Kilkenny in the All-Ireland final. They could claim to be somewhat misfortunate as Tom Murphy of Kilkenny recalls.

> 'I had gone up with Ned Power for a ball earlier and he'd landed on his shoulder and broken a rib. That's why he wasn't able to get down to it for my second goal.'

Power being replaced by Percy Flynn at half-time might have been a partial excuse, but it didn't stop the forward line from firing as Fr. Tommy Maher remembered.

> 'It was indeed a great feat for Waterford to score six goals against Ollie Walsh.'

Martin Óg Morrissey expressed his disappointment with not making those six goals count.

'59: AN EYEWITNESS ACCOUNT OF HURLING'S GOLDEN AGE

'There are not many teams that can say that they played in an All-Ireland final, scoring 6-8 and still losing. We should have been all shot after failing to win that game to be honest with you.'

Philly Grimes discussed the same topic with the Kilkenny players when they met at a reception at the Guinness Brewery the next day.

'If somebody said to us before the match that we'd score six goals on Ollie Walsh and still lose, we wouldn't believe it.'

Kilkenny's tactics helped in that game. Johnny McGovern played on Martin Óg that day and remembers the influence of Fr. Tommy Maher.

'I played on Martin Óg in 1963. He was a very good hurler, a fine striker of the ball. I remember Fr. Maher in training coming up to the game. I wouldn't have been a centre-forward... I only played there when the Bridge had more backs than forwards. Fr. Maher was trying to get me to come out in front of the man and bring the ball down in front of me and just get it on the ground. I had Heaslip on one side and Keher on the other... inside was Tommy Walsh and Tommy Murphy. The plan was to get the ball on the ground out to those.

'We were doing that in training, and they knew that if I won a ball I was going to hit it on the ground and they could be moving out for it. It worked alright for the first half hour... they got a good lot of scores. In the second half hour, Martin Óg Morrissey came out in front of me and caught every ball! He drove a couple of long balls into the square and there were goals got from them. I had thought I was doing fairly well but he got out in front. Oliver Gough was a sub for us. It was decided to bring him in. He was a very fit lad, and he might get out in front of Martin Óg. We won anyhow. There were six goals scored against us which is hard to believe.'

Kilkenny had some excellent individual performances with Eddie Keher's 14 points the standout display, which Jackie Condon recalls with regret.

'In 1963, my brother Joe was the captain. They got six goals and eight points and lost the match. Eddie Keher was banging over points for fun. There was a chap on him, Jim Irish, a relation of mine from Ferrybank... and that was my position. That guy wouldn't have been getting those points if I was on him. We lost by a couple of points. If I had been playing that day, we would have won the match... I always said that to myself, but I was retired three years at that stage.'

The loss of players from the All-Ireland-winning team was a factor and Philly Grimes questioned the depth of the squad.

'I would say that we should have won maybe three All-Irelands at least between 1957 and '63. We won one, and a league and the Oireachtas... and played in some of the games generally recognised as among the best ever. It's a shame that we didn't add another to all that by getting another couple of All-Irelands. I always felt the reason we didn't win them was... you need a very strong panel, and I don't think we had enough strength in depth.'

Freddie O'Brien also felt he would have made a telling contribution had he been given the chance.

'They dropped me to bring on Mickey Walsh of Kilkenny. He was gone over the top, but he married Billy Mulcahy's sister. Billy Mulcahy was a staunch Mount Sion man. He would have been great friends with Seamus Power. He came on the panel, so I was booted off. He was nearly 30 at the time and I was only 24. When I was dropped, Eddie Keher got 16 points. The highest score that anyone ever got on me was 2-1 and it was a disaster for me that day.'

Even Ollie Walsh, despite conceding six goals, three of which were tap-ins from the edge of the square, made some saves from Seamus Power that should have been goals. Jimmy O'Brien thought that Waterford, no longer perennial underdogs 'were way too confident. I knew Waterford wouldn't win that match'. Tom Cunningham admits that there might be some truth in that.

'People say Waterford should have won more. Maybe, but it was very hard to get out of Munster. We might have been overconfident in 1963 for Kilkenny. Not us, the players... but the county. Kilkenny saw us coming, but no regrets.'

Waterford had been in impressive form, and they seem to have found the key to beating Tipperary, their biggest rivals in Munster at the time. In 1963 they beat them in the Oireachtas final (4-12 to 3-9), the league final (2-14 to 4-7) and the Munster final (0-12 to 0-9). Jimmy O'Brien particularly remembers the league final.

> 'Grimes and Power were two great hurlers. The league final that Waterford won in 1963... they were way behind Tipperary and every time the ball went in Tipp were getting a goal or a point. Grimes was left corner-forward and I was on the Hogan Stand on the other side of the field. Waterford got a free out at the corner flag and I saw Grimes going over... I said to myself *What in the name of Jesus is he going over there for?* The one thing they didn't need was a wide. He trotted across the field as if it was nothing and turned around... and stuck it straight over the bar. That took doing! It was psychologically one of the best points I ever saw scored... in every way. He believed in himself that he could do it. Then Waterford got back into the game and won it... a great game.'

1963 was just a bump in the road for Tipperary, who continued to refresh their team through the early 60s, winning four out of five All-Irelands. They added Roche, Gaynor, Keating and others, but Waterford failed to replace the team of '59. When they did, it was sometimes too late. Moving Philly Grimes, Seamus Power and John Barron to the full-forward line for 1963 paid dividends in winning three trophies, but Tony Wall's experience told him that these were only temporary measures.

> 'I started my career in the forward line, and it is much easier to move back to the backline than go up into the forwards. You are on to a loser if you are moving the back man up into the forward line when he gets old. That doesn't work.'

Sure enough, after the All-Ireland, the team required a complete rebuild and Waterford went into a decline during which they failed to win another Munster title for 39 years.

RETIREMENT

Throughout the 1960s the players from 1959 retired from playing. John Kiely retired from inter-county hurling shortly after the All-Ireland in '59 and didn't travel to either London or New York with the team in 1960. He had achieved the ultimate accolade after a long career. Michael O'Connor had a stellar career and considering his bout of ill-health, he too finished hurling with Waterford and went on to become a successful businessman, but continued hurling with his club.

'59: AN EYEWITNESS ACCOUNT OF HURLING'S GOLDEN AGE

'My job developed, and I had to say that I have to concentrate on our business. Everything I've done, I was proud of Cappoquin. I was born in Cappoquin and when I played hurling for Cappoquin... Jesus I played harder and harder than ever.'

Jackie Condon, on the other hand, was only 21 when he won the All-Ireland but stopped hurling over the following year and wasn't involved with Erin's Own in any capacity, to the regret of Michael Dowling.

'He didn't play for anything as long as you'd imagine he did, although he was some bit of stuff. With an All-Ireland medal he was entitled to a ticket for an All-Ireland final, but he never looked for one. He drifted away from hurling. When he got into business, he had other interests. How could Erin's Own not have made something out of fellas like that... to our shame!'

For most of the players, retirement came naturally with age, passing on their knowledge and experience to the next generation in the process. Austin Flynn and Duck Whelan certainly had a big influence on Humphrey Kelleher.

'I got the opportunity when I was 18 to play with them on the Abbeyside senior hurling team. I will always remember playing in goal on my debut against De La Salle in Walsh Park and God is in front of me, No 3... Austin! One of the subs was Duck. That would have been 1970. Austin was coming to the end of his hurling career, so he wasn't the quickest. A ball came in and I stopped it with my foot and I kicked it out to the right. As I kicked it... the full-forward who Austin hadn't kept out, pulled full belt on my ankle. I went down in agony. Austin saw me down on the ground and in choice language he said "Get up, get up... for f**k sake, the ball isn't cleared yet". It went out to the right and came back again. I went out to catch it at an angle and the corner-forward hit me down on the head. I went down on the ground... and I see Austin looking at me. At this stage I had the ball in my hand. I looked up at Austin and said "I'm not getting up this time!" I had to go off because of the ankle injury and who took my place in goal... only the Duck Whelan!

'Austin would want to win every time. I would have been quiet in the presence of greatness. You don't start shouting at your hero. He was the leader... he called the shots. You listened... you had no choice! It was a privilege to play with Austin Flynn.'

'59: AN EYEWITNESS ACCOUNT OF HURLING'S GOLDEN AGE

Most, like Freddie O'Brien, naturally drifted into retirement and other interests in the late 60s and early 70s.

'I stayed with the club. I had a bit of hip trouble in about 1967. I was working in St. Otteran's on shift work, and I was pushing on in years. I wasn't terribly old, but I found it difficult to get in adequate training. I felt it a bit awkward. The hip would be sore after a match. Later in life I said there were other sports to be looked into. I got into pigeons and shooting… and that took up a lot of my time. I went to Butlerstown but I never fell out with Mount Sion'.

This last comment is an indirect reference to Mick Flannelly. One issue that looms large in the minds of the players in the years after the All-Ireland win was the incident which caused Mick Flannelly to leave Mount Sion. John Flavin recalls Mick's impeccable pedigree at Mount Sion and his team spirit.

'Mick Flannelly's father, Matt Flannelly also won a handball All-Ireland medal in 1929. He was captain of the 1948 minor team. Pound for pound he was the best of the whole lot… he was a great man. He was small and light and fast, and I can tell you he brought me on big time. He'd be about 90 and I'm 82. For me, when I got on the senior team, he'd be telling me what to do and where to go. He was unreal… he was brilliant. I remember the first time I ever played for Mount Sion senior hurling team, I was only 17. We were at a tournament down in New Ross, playing for a suit length. Mick Flan was on the team… Ailbe Richardson played corner-forward. A fella called Joe Galway was playing for Bennettsbridge the same night. Yer man absolutely cut the head off him with five minutes to go and Ailbhe was carted off.

'John Keane was the manager of the team and he came down the line to look at who he had on the subs. He said "Seanie, c'mon!"… and I went out to play. There was only about two minutes to go and Mick Flan got the ball in the half-back line. He shouted at me to go run out to the left-hand side. I ran out and he hit the ball out to me. Galway, the guy who had done Ailbhe, took a swipe at me… but I was so light and so small that he missed me. I was gone and I went in and I scored the winning point. We won the match by a point. We got 22 suit lengths.

'Mick Flan was great. When I was on the team, I'd play right half-forward… he was centre-forward and Frankie Walsh was left half-forward. That was the Mount Sion half-forward line. He was great to me.'

'59: AN EYEWITNESS ACCOUNT OF HURLING'S GOLDEN AGE

John takes up the story of the Sunday evening in question when Mount Sion were playing a football match.

'Mick Flan fell out with Mount Sion. Danny Mahon was the captain of the team. He wouldn't go out and play because it was raining. At half-time when it got fine, Pat Fanning came into the dressing-room... we didn't know anything about it at the time. "I'm making a change," he said. "Danny Mahon is coming on,"... and he took off Mick Flan. Mick Flan... he was some man, and a great Mount Sion man. It was unbelievable... it was an absolute disgrace what they did to him. It was wrong. Pat Fanning was prone to doing some silly things, he done me as well (laughs)... So Óg tells me every time I meet him.

'I have no doubt they could have taken anyone off at half-time and none of us would have minded. If I was told... it wouldn't worry me. If it was hurling, I would be worried... but not football. They could have taken anyone out of the 15 off but to take Flan off was a disgrace. He used to love football and he was a good footballer even though he was a small man. He was very skillful.'

Freddie O'Brien is sorry he didn't walk off in protest.

'Mount Sion did the dirt on Mick Flannelly too. Danny Mahon was from Presentation Row... a nephew of Michael Cleere. They were playing Kill in a football semi-final, about 1963 or '64. Danny Mahon was at Norris' Corner, and somebody said to Danny "Are you going up to the match?" and he said "Ah, I don't know". He came along at half-time, and they took off Mick Flan... and put him in. I had great regard for Mick Flan. When I met him later, he had a bee in his bonnet with me. We were young and we were playing for Mount Sion, so we weren't going to walk off the field, but when I did get the chance to think about it... I was never so sorry I didn't walk off the field because of his total commitment to Mount Sion. The Flannelly family in general were totally dedicated to Mount Sion.'

Mick's move to another club is remembered by his next-door neighbour, Michael Walsh.

'Flan never played for Mount Sion or ever had any dealings with them anymore and then he joined Roanmore after that. That bitterness was there... I remember him telling me "I'll never play again".'

'59: AN EYEWITNESS ACCOUNT OF HURLING'S GOLDEN AGE

The topic was rarely discussed directly with Mick, as even close friends like John Flavin felt it was too sensitive.

> 'I never discussed it with him. I wouldn't like to bring that up because it wouldn't be the best topic. I did say to him early on, but in later years I didn't say anything to him. He used to come out on the bus... and I'd meet him for a stroll. I never heard anyone say anything bad about Flan.'

Many of the players stayed involved in coaching or administration at club, county or even national level. Coaching was becoming more structured and organised, and Humphrey Kelleher recalls Ned Power's involvement.

> 'With Joe Lennon, Jim McKeever and Tony Mansfield, Ned Power weas involved with the coaching initiatives at Gormanstown College in Meath. They were ahead of their time. It was the coach education that was novel.'

Ned developed coaching courses and helped transform coach education within the GAA. He also put his own skills to the test by helping Tallow to three county titles and even found time to encourage opposition goalkeepers like Humphrey Kelleher.

> 'When I was minor, our greatest rivals were Tallow... and Ned Power brought through that team. Being a goalkeeper when I was senior, Ned used to commend me if I had a good game. He used to give me encouragement as much as advice. I remember his walking around the goal in Cappoquin and he nodded to me after I made a good save. That spoke volumes from the main man... that nod to me meant a lot. He was a thorough gentleman, maybe too nice at times. We looked up to him... he was THE goalkeeper. Only Ollie Walsh and Ned mattered. Ned would always have time for you after the game, always with appreciation for good work.'

Ned, in turn, was full of praise for Mick Lacey who continued coaching for decades after his playing career.

> 'A good versatile player who could do a good job also at centre-back or midfield. He's still active and doing great work coaching.'

'59: AN EYEWITNESS ACCOUNT OF HURLING'S GOLDEN AGE

While several of the squad had success in training club teams, like Martin Óg Morrissey, none of them came to the fore as manager of the county team.

> 'Maybe a few of us from our team should have had a bit more in-put with the senior panels that followed after we retired. I know I had my year with the panel in 1983, but I'd have liked a bit more time with them. I think I'd a bit more to offer the county and I think my time with Glenmore and Ballyhale underlined that. I'd have liked to manage Waterford but that's all water under the bridge now.'

The players were often introduced to the administration of their clubs while still playing, as Michael Dowling of Erin's Own remembers.

> 'Charlie Ware stuck with Erin's Own through thick and thin… even when they were being beaten in play-offs and losers' groups. He was the club secretary for years.'

Phil Fanning, also points out Seamus Power's dedication to the club.

> 'Seamus did everything… the record he has in the club as chairman, treasurer, secretary for years… everything. He refereed a lot of inter-county games. He went to New York to referee a league final. When Seamus was refereeing matches, he would always give me a shout and I'd end up doing linesman or umpire. It was a good day out… always. He didn't bring me to New York though!'

Unusually, he was already secretary of the club in 1959 when he won the All-Ireland. His complete dedication to Gaelic games is further emphasised when you realise that in April of 1959, he was playing football for Waterford against Tipperary. A dual player, like most of the panel, he won four senior county medals for football along with his 13 hurling championships.

Tom Cunningham and Donal Whelan also dedicated many years to GAA administration. Tom was a selector for the county team and a Munster Council delegate from 1967 to '91. Donal was on the GAA's Central Council, and ultimately as a trustee of the association. Duck's rise to the top of the GAA administration is no surprise considering his family background but as Humphrey Kelleher remembers, it wasn't without baggage.

> 'Duck's father, Pax ran Fraher Field, named after Duck's grandfather… Dan Fraher. He ended up the Waterford representative on the Munster Council. It was your

natural progression to go into administration. It wasn't until 1975 that the family relinquished ownership of the Fraher Field.

'There was a political undertone to the club that we didn't really understand. We were surprised to hear that Duck was involved with the Claudia in 1973 when the IRA got guns from Gadaffi. They were being monitored by the British forces all along. By the time they came to Helvick, they were found out. Duck was on one of the boats. He had finished playing at this stage and was a teacher in Kilmacthomas.

'He was given a seven-year suspended sentence, and he was suspended from the school for seven years too. While he wasn't principal... there was no principal of St Declan's. Nobody put their name forward to take the position. When the seven years was up, he got his job back. They looked after their own. Being an All-Ireland winner at minor and senior... nobody was going to say boo to him.'

The last player to retire from hurling was Tom Cheasty. He had captained Portlaw to a senior county championship win in 1977, aged 43, and the Junior Championship win with his native club Ballyduff Lower in 1983 was only a few months shy of his 50th birthday. In the same year he cycled to the All-Ireland final as part of a fundraiser for Ballyduff. Nobody, including his wife, could talk him out of playing, under any circumstances.

'Portlaw went to play Pat Hartigan's team in Limerick in 1976. I got a call to tell me that Tom was in hospital in Limerick. I had seen the results on the television and the score was six points to four. I never knew until the 40th anniversary that Tom got a bang on the side of the head, and they thought he was dead... so they called off the match. That was why it was such a low score. He was in hospital for about a week and he still didn't stop hurling! There was no stopping him.'

The love of the game shines through in every interview with players of the time. Most followed Tom's approach and played for as long as they could because, as Martin Óg said 'Nothing really replaces the feeling of playing and winning once you've taken the boots off for the last time'. This approach was typified by 90-year-old Billy Kelly's comment, 'I hurled up to the last minute... I'm not so long after giving up!'

LEAN YEARS

Through the rest of the 60s, there were occasional flashes of brilliance to remind supporters of recent glories, such as Larry Guinan's performance in the 1966 Munster final.

'59: AN EYEWITNESS ACCOUNT OF HURLING'S GOLDEN AGE

'Guinan scored one of the best goals ever in a Munster final against Cork in 1966. Guinan was playing at left midfield... he gained possession around his own full-back line and set off on a breathtaking and beautifully controlled solo run that he climaxed by crashing a superb shot from 30 yards to the Cork net. They lost 4-9 to 3-9 to the Cork team which was led by Gerald McCarthy who later managed Waterford.'

Generally, though, the team was weakened by successive retirements of their All-Ireland winners and performances were poor. Success deserted Waterford and defeat became a habit, much to the disappointment of Seamus Power.

'Basically, our players lack that driving force and that fierce will to win which is so necessary and vital to achieve success in the inter-county sphere. While defeat may be our lot on occasions, it should never be accepted as inevitable.'

The extent of the lows was described by Raymond Smith in the *Clash of the Ash*.

'It would have been impossible to entertain the thought then that in the 1971-72 season they would have been battling to win promotion from the Second Division of the Hurling League – and failing in the attempt! It was a fall like this that made us conscious of the need to set the main resources of the hurling revival scheme directed towards bringing the real strongholds back to their former glory rather than extend the lines on too wide a front. Is it more important to have Mayo figure in an All-Ireland minor hurling final or see Waterford inscribe their name again on the MacCarthy Cup? For me there is only one answer to the question.'

Some of the '59 team were still involved as mentors and officials but couldn't force success from a weaker panel. Damien Tiernan interviewed team doctor, Tom Higgins, about Seamus Power's management of the county senior hurlers in 1978.

'I never saw anything like the manic atmosphere in the dressing-room. It was hell and fury stuff... lads hitting the table and shouts of "Go out and die for the jersey and leave your last drop of blood on the pitch". Seamus Power broke a hurley on the table and no one would give him another one as they knew it'd go the same way... so he battled on with the remnants and sent the lads out. It was like a psychiatric outpatient's unit... and I was told that was mild.'

'59: AN EYEWITNESS ACCOUNT OF HURLING'S GOLDEN AGE

Jim Greene, one of the best players of the 70s and 80s felt the depth of talent let the county down.

'In Waterford from 1968 to '86, there were only ever six or seven players each year good enough to compete with what the best other counties would throw at them. We never had a full deck and never showed enough intent to get it right. We didn't have the right underage structures either. As for coaching? The joke in Waterford was that coaches were for travelling in!'

While the passion was there, and pockets of talent, the success was missing. While struggling at senior level, minor and under-21 teams occasionally showed some promise for the future. Waterford lost to Kilkenny in the All-Ireland Under-21 final in 1974 at Thurles but fruitless decades passed, and it wasn't until Waterford won the under-21 All-Ireland in 1992 that a new era was finally kickstarted.

RESURGENCE

The 1992 win translated to a very competitive senior team in the late 90s. A strong crop of young players were to become the backbone of the Waterford team for the resurgent years to come. More than 30 years after 1959 each of these young players was still being compared to the heroes of old, not least by the men themselves. Martin Óg is well known for his sense of humour and self-confidence, and both are captured in this story told by his Waterford teammate and neighbour John Barron.

'I was walking through town... and I came across Óg. This would have been in the mid-90s. I said to him that I'd been hearing great things about young McGrath... Pat's son. Óg said "Ah, he's fine young player alright". The rumour was that Ken might even be better than Pat. "He might be alright, give him time." Then I pushed it a bit too far and said I'd heard he might be even better than Óg himself! Óg's response summed him up "Go way John... I'd bate him with me coat on!!'

As this team matured, 1998 was seen as a lost opportunity. Many Waterford fans felt that Kilkenny were there to be beaten in the semi-final and that an All-Ireland final against Offaly would have been an easier prospect than against the traditional counties of Cork, Kilkenny and Tipperary, or the physical strength of Clare, Limerick, or Galway. Having beaten Offaly in the 1992 under-21 All-Ireland, McGrath, Flynn, Hartley, and Browne would have relished the prospect of meeting them in the senior final. Either way, 1998 was a convincing return to the big time for Waterford and, while ultimately disappointing, gave encouragement to everyone, including Martin Óg Morrissey.

> 'I have to say that we were very unlucky in 1998 but I have to say that we could have reached a couple of finals during recent years... only for we made a number of mistakes in key games, and we never really learned from those mistakes because we kept on making them. It was terrible and to say it has taken 45 years to reach our next All-Ireland final... I didn't see that happening. We had some great teams over the years... teams that could and should have reached All Ireland finals... and probably even won them, but it wasn't to be.'

Since 1998, Waterford have lost 11 All-Ireland semi-finals and three All Ireland finals. With each advancing year, the glories of 1959 were left further behind, but the '59 winners are still remembered. They were always shown great respect by the hurlers of the day, as evidenced by Kathleen Cheasty.

> 'Tom was always interested in the matches. Just before the league final in 2007, Justin McCarthy dropped in a huge get-well card and every one of the players and the backroom team signed it. They beat Kilkenny in the final. Tom wasn't well enough to go to the match. Brick Walsh came down with the cup to Tom before he went into Waterford.'

Before every game at Croke Park, particularly All-Ireland finals, members of that squad would be contacted by journalists for their thoughts on the latest team to attempt to win a third title. For example, this extract from an interview with Martin Óg before the 2008 final was probably the peak of expectation.

> 'It's fantastic for the county... the type of hurling that Davy Fitzgerald had them playing in the first quarter of the game against Tipperary was unbelievable. I have no doubt that if we play that type of hurling against Kilkenny... the Liam MacCarthy Cup will be down on the Quay on Monday night.'

Even the most positive and upbeat of the players, Tom Cunningham, who remained close to the game and continued to follow the Waterford team finally gave up on attending games, but kept his sense of humour intact.

'59: AN EYEWITNESS ACCOUNT OF HURLING'S GOLDEN AGE

> 'We are still talking about it as the last All-Ireland... that is the sad part of it. I don't go to the matches now anyway because I wouldn't see too much of them. I listen to it on the radio with Kieran O'Connor and Fergal Hartley. I was going to matches up to the All-Ireland in 2008... that was a bad choice!'

For the next final against Galway in 2017, detailed interviews with Austin Flynn focused on his enjoyment of the modern game and his admiration of the current players.

> 'The bar is being raised the whole time. The strength, the speed, the fitness, the skill, the excitement... everything's faster. There's excellence on the field and excellence on the sideline. Hurling now is way... way better than it was in our time. There was an awful lot of dirty hurling in that time. Nowadays fellas are so fit and so fast they haven't time for the dirty. The fellas nowadays are so skilful, they're training seven days a week. I marvel at their skills.'

By the latest final in 2020 against Limerick, Tom Cunningham's was the feature interview in the *Irish Examiner* and remained hopeful of a win.

> 'We are all conscious in the county of how long it's been, but you have to put that stuff aside at some point. The players have to want to do it for themselves... and for their families. It doesn't matter whether it has been 60 years or six years... or 600 years. It's immaterial. It's just two years since Limerick won it and they're every bit as anxious to win it again as Waterford are. The players have to put everything else to one side. Everything else is immaterial except winning. The first part of the job is to get to the All-Ireland final. It's very hard to get there but Waterford have done that. Now they have to win, which is the second part. It's as simple as that. Everything else is totally immaterial.'

Larry Guinan was interviewed for *The Irish Times* and wished he was on the field again.

> 'Part of me would love to be lining out, but Limerick have big men in their full-back line and I'm not sure I'd be able for them at this stage. Limerick are a fine team, but we have ball players and strong men and fit men... I can't pick a star from the present team because to me they are all stars, but Liam Cahill has them flying and I think we are nicely set up and I think we will win.'

'59: AN EYEWITNESS ACCOUNT OF HURLING'S GOLDEN AGE

Sadly, the win hasn't materialised but with Larry, Óg, Michael and Freddie still available, journalists won't be short of an expert comment, particularly from Larry Guinan.

> 'God Almighty... I'd do anything to see a Waterford man climb the steps of the Hogan Stand and lift the MacCarthy Cup... before all of us from 1959 are gone. There's not many of us left... we're drifting away, but I pray to God, while we are alive, that Waterford can do it.'

MODERN GAME

While the players are universally positive about hurling today, there are a few areas of the game which raise discussions. Michael O'Connor is impressed with the detailed tactics in place today but feels that the best hurlers of his time would easily adapt to it.

> 'There was very little technique, tactics or teamwork in the selection. It was nothing like the current professionalism. I could see that some of the players on that team would be absolutely brilliant in the current style... I would say Mick Flan and Frankie Walsh who had speed and were wonderful hurlers. John Barron was a very intelligent corner-back and he used his head... I would put him down as being a very intelligent player who never made a major mistake. I was very small and fast... in a sprint, Frankie, Flan or Grimes wouldn't catch me.'

Joe Harney, amongst many others, regretted that the disappearance of overhead striking takes from the spectacle of the game.

> 'I don't like the new rules that are in place. They have done away with over-head hurling, and to a certain degree ground hurling. The new rules have not improved the game in my view.'

As far back as the late 80s Seamus Power wrote an article entitled 'Obsession with Possession' which traces this change in the sport.

> *'Obsession with possession is taking from the modern game. Movement of the ball should be the primary aim. The team that pulls fast on the ground and in the air will win a lot more than they lose.'*

'59: AN EYEWITNESS ACCOUNT OF HURLING'S GOLDEN AGE

The tactical basis is explained by Jimmy Barry-Murphy in Val Dorgan's book on Christy Ring:

> 'I always thought ground hurling was over-rated. There are times when it can be the wrong option. The players are clued-in to what the percentage game is... there is a lot of movement. It is a picking, running, passing game but, on occasions... ground hurling is used.'

Eddie Keher accepted that the change was inevitable.

> 'Two hurlers pulling against each other under a dropping ball might be very thrilling for the crowd if one made a good connection, but the ball could finish with the opposition.'

Considering much of the previous discussion about tough play and foul play, it is natural for players of the 50s to consider the game to be less brutal. That is welcomed by Johnny McGovern but the resultant increase in the number of frees is not.

> 'There wasn't many frees at that time. There are too many frees now. Some of the frees are unnecessary... there wouldn't have been any dirty play. They should let the play flow a bit... they should leave it flow... all the scores are being scored from frees. Nearly all the frees are being scored too. Every team seems to have a good free-taker. TJ Reid does it every day... he's consistent. It is the only thing that spoils the game now, the number of frees.'

The fact that a free can now be scored from the half-back line is changing the nature of the game and, like many other commentators, Jimmy O'Brien points to the equipment being use.

> 'It is still a great game, but I think they are spoiling it with the ball now. The hurls are too small. To change the ball... you'd have to change the hurls and all those lads who have come up with it would have to readjust.'

The last area of the modern game to cause discussion is the crowding around the ball and the number of 'rucks' which develop. Players are so fit, that they can cover far more ground and keep running for longer than their counterparts in '59. Essentially, this has the effect of making the pitch smaller. The days of Larry Guinan watching the play from corner-forward, standing next to the corner-back, like the rest of the spectators, is gone. His modern equivalent Dessie Hutchinson is more likely to sprint the 100 metres back to assist his half-back line. This is not a new discussion.

In an interview with *Scene Magazine* in 1967, Christy Ring proposed that *'There are too many players in hurling, and they should be reduced to a maximum of 12 or 13, instead of 15 because it would help to improve passing skills'*. It would certainly open up the pitch and allow for a return to more traditional skills. Back in 1959, it was even trialled in the Ulster Colleges competitions for several years and it came before congress in 1960. This motion failed and one of the reasons argued by Pat Fanning and others was the prospect of the GAA losing players to foreign games if there were not enough opportunities for boys to gain a place on a hurling or football team. Two fewer players required by a team could mean two more players who defect to soccer. This was a similar argument to the one put forward to support 'The Ban'.

REUNIONS

Waterford's win in 1959 coincided with the 75th anniversary of the GAA. This was reflected at the time in the pageantry surrounding the opening of the new Hogan Stand. The more significant anniversary was the centenary of the association in 1984. This was a time of celebration and reflection. Many club histories were written at the time and the glories of days gone by were celebrated at every opportunity. Any organisation with a GAA connection considered their history. At Clover Meats, they held a special reception for current and former employees who had won All-Ireland medals. While this was mostly a group from Kilkenny, including the then president of the GAA, Paddy Buggy, there were three Waterford players from the '59 team. John Barron and Martin Óg Morrissey had worked in Clover Meats in 1959 and Mick Flannelly who worked there later.

The All-Ireland hurling final in 1984 was played in Thurles as a recognition of the founding meeting of the association at Hayes' Hotel in the town. Cork beat Offaly in the senior match. At half-time in the minor final between Limerick and Kilkenny, the Waterford team of 1959 was brought onto the pitch and introduced to the crowd. John A. Murphy, writing in the *Waterford GAA Yearbook*, described it as *'a moment of sheer nostalgia'* and *'an occasion of pride for hurling followers throughout the length and breadth of the Decies. The reception accorded each player individually bordered on the rapturous. Clearly, many of the Centenary Year All-Ireland final spectators still remembered that golden year of 1959'*. He also gave an update on how involved some of the team continued to be in the GAA.

'59: AN EYEWITNESS ACCOUNT OF HURLING'S GOLDEN AGE

'Today Seamus Power and Tom Cunningham are Waterford's two representatives on the Munster Council and have been for many years past. Donal Whelan has served Waterford on the Central Council and indeed went higher still when emulating his legendary grandfather, Dan Fraher, by becoming a Trustee of the GAA. Mick Flannelly and Martin Óg Morrissey have served as county senior hurling selectors in very recent years and Ned Power has served admirable in a coaching capacity; and to this day Frankie Walsh is an ever-present as trainer of Mount Sion senior hurling teams. A quarter of a century on Tom Cheasty is still playing and indeed only a year ago inspired his club, Ballyduff, to victory in the county junior hurling final.'

As a past president, the centenary year was a busy one for Pat Fanning. In his interview for the GAA oral history project, he recalls 'I was very prominent in that. I think I wrote Paddy Buggy's address that year. He asked me to do it for the opening in Clare. I had a big year that year. It was a big year for all the Presidents'. A photograph was taken to commemorate the occasion of the first formal reunion of the '59 team and shows that most of the team was present. Pat Fanning paid tribute to them all in the *News & Star*.

'These were the years of glory and the men who served us then are remembered with pride. In any game, some men stand out above the others, but in the making of these years of glory, it was the team effort that counted. And in that effort, there was not a man on the panel, nor a man among the back-room group, who did not make a particular and important contribution to the saga. You all have your particular hero as I have mine. You will have your high moments as I have mine. But we are as one united in this proposition that the men of '59 and those with them who served between 1955 and 1963, were the makers, the shapers of an imperishable chapter in our hurling story. They have been honoured in this Centenary Year, and the jubilee of their own triumph over Kilkenny. The greatest tribute of all will be paid – only when other men will don the jersey, serve it with equal pride and carry it again to All Ireland glory. Then again will the county walk in the tradition of '59.'

At this point, all of the players were still alive. The first death amongst the panel caused shockwaves throughout the world of hurling. Raymond Smith reported extensively on Philly Grimes' funeral in *The Greatest Hurlers of our Time*.

'59: AN EYEWITNESS ACCOUNT OF HURLING'S GOLDEN AGE

'Fittingly the coffin was draped in the club colours he had worn with such distinction on the day that he was laid to rest in Ballygunner cemetery, former county colleagues and Mount Sion men of his own era forming the Guard of Honour. There were famous players present from many counties. It would be impossible to name them all but picked out at the graveside were Paddy Buggy, Ollie Walsh and Pat Henderson (Kilkenny), Willie Rackard and Ned Wheeler (Wexford), Dr Jim Young and Con Murphy (Cork), Kevin Heffernan (Dublin), Joe Salmon (Galway), Pat Stakelum, Micky Byrne, Theo English and Donie Nealon (Tipperary).

'It was on the day of his 60th birthday in May 1989 that he died in his native Waterford, having battled for over a year with admirable courage in the face of a terminal illness. Even before his passing in Waterford Regional Hospital (Ardkeen) news had spread through all the great hurling strongholds that there was to be no reprieve. Yet, when the announcement of his death came, I could not escape the sense of shock and sadness that inevitably follows when you learn that another of those who gave you such pleasure because of the way they could wield a caman, especially on a dry sod in summer days, had departed the scene. Of course, he was long since retired when death claimed him but that is incidental to the way those who saw him at the height of his power still extol his virtues as a hurler.

'As Pat Fanning wrote of him in the Waterford News & Star... *"and so when I am asked to capture in one brief moment the flair, the elan, the power, yes, and the sheer glory of Philly Grimes in action, thoughts come crowing in on a day in Thurles many years ago when he switched to centre back in a crisis situation. There followed a display which is unforgettable and ranks as one of the greatest individual efforts in hurling in my lifetime. Yes, that is the occasion I recall when I think of Philly Grimes and whenever I attempt to convey to young people something of the unique quality of the man".'*

Even today, players still express their shock that their fittest, most athletic teammate could be the first to go. Many of the players considered Philly the best they played with, and he will be remembered for generations to come. Five years later, Tom Cheasty, in Jack Mahon's *The Game of my Life*, chose Philly as the best player ever.

'I suppose Phil Grimes was best of all. It'd sway me a little that he is dead now... I was really cut up when he died, and he fought a hard fight against cancer before dying. We were all at Philly Grimes' funeral. Very sad.'

'59: AN EYEWITNESS ACCOUNT OF HURLING'S GOLDEN AGE

For Johnny McGovern, Philly's death was on a par with the shock of Christy Ring dying. The great Jimmy Doyle, winner of six All-Irelands, spoke in his autobiography about how he still paid his respects to the great Waterford players of the era.

> 'Grimes, Power, Cheasty, Frankie – they're all gone now, and I visit their graves when I'm in Waterford, but it was an honour to have played alongside them.'

There was no celebration of the 30th anniversary but when it came to the 40th anniversary in 1999, Frankie Walsh was instrumental in arranging a big event. Phil Fanning, writing in the Waterford GAA Yearbook reflected on the occasion.

> 'Frankie decided that the time was right to mark the 40th anniversary of Waterford's last All-Ireland success and took it upon himself to organise a reunion of all the surviving players, and anyone involved at the time, in the Granville Hotel. With Frankie there were no half measures and he duly obtained sponsorship and the support of a reluctant county board for the event. With Micheal O' Muircheartaigh as M.C. it proved a magnificent occasion for all the surviving players honoured alongside family representatives of those deceased.'

A glossy programme was produced to commemorate the reunion. It was nicely produced and included photos of 1959 team, matches and celebrations. The menu for the celebration dinner was included. In what was surely a typo, the choice of main courses was either 'Fillet of Beef Country Style' or 'Roast Fillet of Beef with Baby Vegetables and Irish Whiskey Sauce'.

For their 50th anniversary, Seamus O'Brien, in the *Waterford GAA Yearbook 2009* describes the reunion of that year.

> 'On the 4th October 2009, which was the anniversary of the great 1959 victory, the county board rightly decided to honour the players who brought honour and glory to the Deise county, and at our county senior hurling final, the thirteen surviving members of the panel with relatives of the eight deceased members (Ned Power, John Barron, Mick Lacey, Phil Grimes, Tom Cheasty, John Kiely, Donal Whelan, Joe Coady), were present as guests and were later that evening honoured at a function in the Granville Hotel.'

In recent years, with fewer of the team surviving, it was down to chance for one player to bump into another, as Michael O'Connor mentions.

'59: AN EYEWITNESS ACCOUNT OF HURLING'S GOLDEN AGE

'Dungarvan used to have a dinner every year and I went to that, and I found it nice. You'd meet Cunningham and all those fellas. I'd meet Austin Flynn and Tom Cunningham casually... going to mass or something. I'd go to Dungarvan to mass, and I'd meet Tom Cunningham. Other than that, we wouldn't meet a whole lot. We'd be always friends... that bond was there.'

Jackie Condon still enjoys the reunions but the attention from hurling fans is still relentless.

'The last event I was at was in Dungarvan last year. They were presenting medals for the younger teams... there was a huge crowd there. It is amazing the way people keep honing into you. They hadn't seen you with years. When the thing was over, I went out to the toilet and when I was coming back in... I was mobbed. They were wanting to take photographs, but they were all saying, "Do you remember me?" and "I was at that match"... and "I hurled against you down in such a place"... and all that kind of stuff, and you don't know who the fella is from Adam.'

Considering that event was 60 years after the All-Ireland win, this gives an indication of how strong the limelight was in the immediate aftermath. In many cases, it caused the players to avoid the subject as much as possible. In speaking to John Barron's son, John, it became obvious that his dad had spoken relatively little about his hurling experiences. A quiet, modest man, John was never keen to be involved in discussions of the GAA. Similarly, Charlie Ware and the other players were described as 'reserved types. He didn't want to be in the limelight. He just got on with the game'. Another conversation with players' families brought out similar reactions. Seamus Power, Philly Grimes, and others avoided discussions with the public, but this was particularly difficult for pub-owner, Philly.

> **Tom Power** – 'My father never really discussed matches. What I learned about 1959 came from Frankie... Peter's dad. All I knew about Philly was that he'd never discuss hurling with anyone that didn't play inter-county... so I thought I'd keep my mouth shut when I'd go over.'

> **Kay Grimes** – 'Dad spoke very little about it. When people came in from around the country into the pub, people that watched him play kind of assumed they had this relationship with him and that they knew him really well. He was very shy and odd. Sometimes he'd try to be creative when people would come in and catch him on the

hop and talk to him about hurling. If he thought he knew them or had met them before, he'd produce a book of social club tickets from the pub and he'd say "Here will you buy a ticket for the social club"... and get them to write their name down. Then he'd have the person's name and he'd engage with them.

'If he had no way of finding out their name, sometimes he'd leg it out of the pub. He'd say "I'll be back in a few minutes,"... and he'd be gone. He just wouldn't engage about stuff if he was ill at ease with the person or maybe if he didn't respect their authority or they didn't play inter-county. I certainly didn't play inter-county so maybe that's why he didn't speak about it much to me. Maybe he knew I didn't have his understanding. What I do know in the family is that when he was captain in ' 57 and they were beaten, it was the Wednesday until he spoke to anyone.

'In that article with Charlie Mulqueen, he was talking about how much it hurt him all those years later. I mean he was 55 years of age, but he was still gutted at having been beaten in ' 57. In ' 59... you'd imagine he would have been delighted to be chatting about it. Frankie certainly got enjoyment from it. He'd be chatting to people in the pub about it but Dad... not so much. Maybe it was the fact that I don't think the pub business suited him. There was always people coming and it was relentless.'

Peter Walsh – 'Take any of the players... be it Austin Gleeson or Ken McGrath or Tony Browne. Everyone thinks they own you, I guess. Everybody wants to be your best friend and talk about the matches... and Philly wasn't that way. I remember Philly coming to collect me up at the club to go down and work in the bar one evening after training... passing down Barrack Street and somebody shouting into the car at Philly, and Philly basically telling him to feck off ... "I gave 25 years to it... how much more do they want out of me?"... and that was just him being honest about it.'

Jackie Condon found the intense interest wearying.

'You had to disappear. Even going to work... I had to go in at unorthodox hours to avoid people. They'd stay talking to you all day and it was the one oul' story from everyone. I couldn't go to work at eight o'clock in the morning... I used to go in at ten and I wouldn't come home for my dinner. I'd work on until seven. Fellas took licence and they'd be asking me "What about the match on Sunday? Blah, blah, blah". The next fella... the same thing.

'I got sick of it... I got tired of all that. You'd go into a pub for a drink and a fella would say "Hey, you shouldn't be here. That's not training in the pub at this hour of the night". If I went to a ceili dance with the wife, we'd go in there and dance the night away, but the problem was I'd be sitting down and I'd have three or four fellas talking to me and I couldn't get up for a dance. The night would go... and the wife wouldn't get a dance and she'd be giving out.

'That was the downward side of it. Everyone thought they knew you. That wasn't a bad thing... they wanted to talk to you, and they felt entitled to talk to you. When I opened a shop, I realised that's what did it for me. People came from everywhere to the shop and the shop blossomed due to being in the hurling. I was there one Friday morning, and the place was black, and Philly Grimes came in and said "Jaysus Jackie, how the hell are you getting a crowd like that into the shop?" I said "I was such a good hurler, Philly!" Philly had the pub just down the road.

'People thought they owned you. It is bloody 61 years ago... it's a long, long time. You had to shy away from it... you have no life otherwise. I was avoiding the people at that stage even. It was difficult.'

Michael O'Connor also received a lot of interest and like Jackie and Philly, he was the owner of his business which led to an awkward, but manageable situation.

'I didn't find it that intrusive. I suppose I was a bit different... my difficulty would have been that I was a businessman, and I was employing all them fellas in the town. I was the managing director and owner... and they were workers. It became a little bit of drag with people asking about it all the time but then you think back... and we achieved a lot. It is nice that it is being remembered but we would love that they would win a couple of them at this stage.'

Their status as the last winners dragging on was strongly expressed by Austin Flynn in a very honest interview with Enda McEvoy.

'Ask Austin Flynn if Waterford's greatest ever team should have won more than just the one of the All-Ireland finals they contested, he replies that the real tragedy is that it took them 45 years after 1963 to return to Croke Park in the autumn, another nine years to make their next visit and that the MacCarthy Cup still hasn't traversed the Suir in the meantime. He remains the last full-back to win an All-Ireland medal with the Déise. He's not exactly one of a kind, mind. There's a bunch of them still hanging in

there from 1959: Mickey O'Connor, Joe Harney, Mick Flannelly, Martin Óg Morrissey, Larry Guinan, Freddie O'Brien. Not that he minds talking about the glory days, although he remains uncomfortable with what he terms the "exaggerated importance" assigned to himself and the rest of the old stagers from 1959. "We're too old to be heroes anymore." And yet, for obvious reasons, they continue to be. Eleven years ago, after Waterford beat Kilkenny in the National League final, he was on the pitch in Semple Stadium with grandsons Gus, Cormac, and Cathal. Along came a husband and wife of a certain vintage. "God be with 1959," the woman beamed. "We came back from our honeymoon in London for the replay." All well and good, but sometimes he imagines how things would have unfolded had he been from, say, Kilkenny. He might have won a couple of All-Irelands, then retired and faded into the background.'

The phrase 'We're too old to be heroes anymore' resonates strongly with the other players. They would all like to see another All-Ireland win, for the sake of the county but also to take some of the pressure off them. In another interview with the Irish Examiner, this time with Steve Neville in 2017, Austin Flynn expressed a similar sentiment.

'Of that team there's great comradeship still there between the fellas who are still on the move. It would be great if Waterford won it again. It would put us fellas back where we should be - back in the armchair reminiscing.'

Humphrey Kelleher, who played with Austin, could see the impact on the quieter personalities of the team.

'I think that was the reason that Austin went out fishing all the time. He wanted to be on his own... he went down to the boat. A lot of people don't realise that these guys have lives as well. John Kiely wouldn't be gregarious or outspoken... he'd go with his head down and kept to himself. You have to respect those guys personalities and make-up. Frankie and Larry might wave to the crowd, but John wouldn't. That Waterford team was made up of all different people... their personalities, their education, their intelligence... and all of those things.'

Just because a player was strong enough to play top-class hurling didn't mean they enjoyed the limelight, as Kathleen Cheasty remembers of Tom.

'59: AN EYEWITNESS ACCOUNT OF HURLING'S GOLDEN AGE

'Tom enjoyed going to the reunions and catching up with all the lads but he wouldn't read anything about himself. He'd never read the News and Star or the Munster Express where he might be mentioned. He'd read The Irish Times or the Tribune. He didn't want to see what they were writing about him. He was shy, really... but not on the field.'

When this topic was put to Frankie Walsh's son, Peter, and Philly Grimes' daughter, Kay, they revealed that similar frustrations and disappointments had been expressed by their fathers as the years passed.

Peter Walsh – 'He was known as the captain, and he got more invitations than anyone else and dragged out for interviews by the newspapers all the time. It got to one stage where he would say "Why don't you try the other lads? You must be sick of listening to me". He would give the same party line all the time. He'd say nothing to leave the side down no matter what was the scenario with Waterford. I'm sure newspapers were sick of talking to him as well because he wasn't giving them any juicy bits. I'm sure Pat would have had Frankie at 22 or 23 years of age tutored a bit on the day of the match in what to say. I'm sure Pat had him well tutored which was only right. He was a young man. You need a guiding hand.'

Kay Grimes – 'Talking to Frankie over the years, as things moved on from 2008, I think it became a burden. He wanted to be able to hand on that legacy because he was tired of being hauled out all the time. He so looked forward to having a bit of success that he would be able to hand it on to somebody else... I think it was a great disappointment to him that that never happened. If you were sceptical, you would say he enjoyed being rolled out and he enjoyed the notoriety... and part of him did, but I do think towards the end he was quite conflicted about it. He was so desperate for them to win, and he was absolutely devastated any time they lost.'

When researching the book, I was told that several players were unlikely to talk to me about hurling. They had avoided discussion to such an extent that family members, friends and teammates warned me that I wouldn't get very far. As mentioned in the foreword, Tony Wall of Tipperary, at first sceptical, really enjoyed our discussion; Jimmy O'Brien of Wexford commented 'You have a very good idea of it. You are after hearing a lot about it. I don't talk about the hurling, but I find it easy talking to you now' and Jackie Condon was not just talkative, but entertaining and insightful.

'I ran all nine of the Dublin marathons until I was 54... and I gave it up. I enjoyed them all. It got me away from the hurling thing altogether. In that way, I was able to avoid meeting the hurling fellas. I wouldn't go into a pub where there would be there would be hurling on... I wouldn't go down to Philly Grimes pub for example... I'd keep clear of that. It was always an issue wherever you went... people recognised you. I suppose it is not a bad thing. I never went anywhere without my wife once we got married. When some fella would come over and start talking about hurling, she would put her eyes up in the air... asking when is this going to stop? She'd be out of the loop... she wouldn't be able to join in the conversation. That's the problem with it. People still ask me about the matches. I say I don't know anything about anyone anymore but that doesn't matter, they still come back asking your opinion on it.'

LEGACY

The Waterford team of 1959 and more generally from 1957 to '63 are lauded as one of the greatest ever teams. This story of the '59 team has been told, as much as possible, in the words of the players but their legacy is probably best left to others to assess. In any history of hurling, they are mentioned positively. In Raymond Smith's Book of Hurling, he captures the feeling for this great side.

> 'In the summer of 1959 we learned what speed, backed up by science and skill, can do on a hurling field. Waterford were in that era a real hurling power in the land, and one of the most exciting teams to watch when they really got going.'

Nicholas Furlong in The Greatest Hurling Decade describes the impact they had.

> 'They had gathered their plans and their men with diligence and stealth. When their full force burst on to the hurling scene, Ireland was rocked, and all previous concepts of field strategy were shaken.'

Those best qualified to make this assessment are the players who played against them at the time. Their achievements are celebrated by Donie Nealon of Tipperary.

> 'In my honest opinion they were one of the top teams to win an All-Ireland... with the manner and the class of their hurling. They gave super displays... they really proved their worth. I thought they were a fabulous team. It's not easy to go into a replay and win a replay... when you haven't won for years. That was great credit to them to be

able to go in and play even better in a replay. They were a top... top team. I really admired the type of hurling they played.'

The final assessment can be left to one of the greatest hurlers ever, Eddie Keher of Kilkenny.

'My view is that the makeup of the Waterford team was ideal for the modern game, with a strong backbone of Flynn, Morrissey, Cheasty and John Kiely. They had two long-striking, stylish centrefielders in Philly Grimes and Seamus Power... and speedy and accurate wing and corner-forwards in Walsh, Flannelly and Guinan. The wing and corner-backs were stick men and preferred to play the ball rather than play the role of stopper... which they were expected to do under the old rules. Tom Cheasty would be equally at home in any era. He loved the physical contact that was very much part of the old game... but his speed and love of scoring would have stood him in good stead had he been born a decade later. I had huge admiration for that team and the way they played. I have often said that they were ahead of their time... I loved the type of game they played. Their skill level... their innovation. I just regret that they didn't win more All-Irelands... but not against Kilkenny! They were a great team.'

Hopefully this book will help cement the Waterford team of '59 in GAA history. May they be remembered forever.

25TH ANNIVERSARY GROUP

Back (L-R): Freddie O'Brien, John Barron, Ned Power, Jackie Condon, Martin Óg Morrissey, Joe Harney, Austin Flynn, Philly Grimes, Michael O'Connor, Joe Coady. Front (L-R): Paudie Casey, Tom Cheasty, Larry Guinan, Mick Flannelly, Frankie Walsh, Michael Fingleton (Irish Nationwide), Paddy Buggy, Tom Cunningham, John Kiely, Seamus Power, Mick Lacey, Charlie Ware, Donal Whelan.

◆

25th anniversary celebration: Recognition of the Jubilee Team at the 1984 All-Ireland final

◆

40th anniversary reunion programme

40th anniversary reunion (including other players from the era)

50th Anniversary Group including family members in place of deceased players.

◆

60th Anniversary Group (L-R) Jackie Condon, Freddie O'Brien, Martin Óg Morrissey, Tom Cunningham, Larry Guinan, Michael O'Connor (Mick Flannelly and Austin Flynn were unable to attend).

◆

ACKNOWLEDGEMENTS

CONTRIBUTORS

The players and their families, with all my respect and gratitude.

Eoin Fanning who carries on Pat Fanning's legacy through his lifelong involvement with Mount Sion. Eoin maintains his grandfather's archives and was particularly supportive in encouraging me to write this book. Thanks, Eoin, for all your help!

Ian Hannigan who colourised the cover photo. More of Ian's work can be found at Timeless Colours on social media. Thanks Ian!

OTHER AUTHORS

Many of the players had passed away by the time I started writing this book. While I regret the opportunities I missed to speak in detail to John Barron, Pat Fanning, Charlie Ware and others, Waterford hurling supporters are lucky that authors such as Brendan Fullam, Dermot Kavanagh, Diarmuid O'Flynn, John Scally, David Smith, Raymond Smith, and all those listed in the bibliography who got there before me. Where players are quoted directly in their books, I copied the quotation for use here, without using their analysis or commentary. While I was lucky enough to have surviving players' comments on a particular topic, it adds huge depth to the discussion to include the comments of Mick Flannelly, Austin Flynn, Tom Cheasty, Ned Power and others, as captured in these interviews. My aim was to use the players' words in all cases and only use my own when really necessary. I'm indebted to these authors for capturing the large swathes of the history of 1959 that I missed.

The same approach was taken with feature articles written by talented journalists like

Enda McEvoy, Michael Moynihan, P.M. O'Sullivan, Adrian Flanagan, Matt Keane, and Liam Kelly.

For further reading on the history of Waterford Hurling, I can particularly recommend:
- *The Colours Blue and White* by Tom Keith covering the 1938 and 1948 teams.
- *Unconquerable Keane*, David Smith's biography of John Keane covering the early history of Waterford hurling, particularly Mount Sion.
- *Erin's Own, A Centenary History* for the coverage of that same period.
- Conor Power's biography of his father *Ned: My Father, a Hurling Revolutionary, The Life and Times of Ned Power.*
- *Kings for a Day*, Martin Óg Morrissey's autobiography with Dermot Keyes.
- *The Ecstasy and the Agony*, Damien Tiernan's story of Waterford's recent hurling teams.
- *A Story of Hurling in Waterford* by Dickie Roche.
- *Waterford Game of my Life* by Tomas McCarthy.
- The journalism of Pat Fanning and Phil Fanning in the *Waterford News & Star*.

PHOTO CREDITS

Many of the photographs used to illustrate the text are items of memorabilia from the author's private collection. In most cases these were professionally photographed by Davi Matheson of DGM Photography (www.dgmphotographic.com).

The cover photo is used with the permission of Sportsfile.

Other photos are from the private collections of:
- Brian Kelly
- Eoin Fanning
- John Barron
- Freddie O'Brien
- Kathleen Cheasty
- Kay Grimes
- Joe Condon
- Mary Ware
- Larry Guinan

HERO BOOKS

This book was written with the full support of the Hero Books team. Particular thanks to Liam and Jess for making this long-term ambition a reality. Heroes indeed!

'59: AN EYEWITNESS ACCOUNT OF HURLING'S GOLDEN AGE

While every effort has been made to be factually correct, errors are inevitable and are entirely my responsibility. Thanks to the technology used by Hero Books, you can have your say and help to correct any mistakes. The book is available for sale on Amazon websites and is printed to order. If I am notified of an error, I can update it, and all future copies ordered on Amazon will be printed with the corrected information. If you spot any errors, please email briankellywaterford@gmail.com and I will make the required adjustments. If you have any positive comments, memories, photos, or '59 memorabilia to share, I would also be very pleased to hear from you.

COLLECTORS

Jim Whelan for access to his extensive book and programme collection. Thanks to Jim and Rita for their friendship and support. PJ Maxwell, John Nagle, Neville O'Donoghue, James Lundon, and other GAA memorabilia collectors.

ARCHIVES

- The local history room at Waterford City Library.
- The Waterford County Museum in Dungarvan.
- The New York Public Library which hosts an archive of the *Irish Echo*, an Irish American weekly newspaper.
- Thomas N. Tryniski who runs www.fultonhistory.com which hosts an archive of old American newspapers, including *The Advocate*, an Irish American weekly newspaper.
- The *Irish News* Archive, which hosts archives of most Irish regional and national newspapers.
- The GAA Museum at Croke Park and their reading room, run by Adam Staunton.

FAMILY

Writing a book can be a selfish activity, taking time away from other responsibilities. Thanks a million to Laura, Hannah, Theo, John, Mam, Dad, and Neil.

APPENDIX 1

1959
COMPLETE RECORD

MATCH 1
WATERFORD 4-6 • WEXFORD 1-4
COMPETITION: Challenge
DATE: January 18
VENUE: Gaelic Field, Waterford
WATERFORD: Ned Power, Joe Coady, Joe Harney, John Barron, Jackie Condon, Martin Óg Morrissey, Mick Lacey, Seamus Power, Phil Grimes, John Flavin. Tom Cheasty, Frankie Walsh, Larry Guinan, Tom Cunningham, Donal Whelan. Subs: Bill Dunphy, Michael White, Mick Kelly, Paddy Troy
Scorers: Guinan 2-0, Walsh 0-4, Whelan 1-0, Grimes 1-0, Cheasty 0-1, Power 0-1
WEXFORD: M. Butler, T. Bergin, Nick O'Donnell, Joseph English, Jim English, T. Morrissey, P. Barron, Seamus Hearne, Sean Power, Oliver Gough, L. Keogh, J. Cullen, Dick Murphy, P. Ryan, Joe O'Reilly
Scorers: O'Reilly 1-0, Gough 0-1, Murphy 0-1, Cullen 0-1, Keogh 0-1.
REFEREE: J. Vaughan (Lismore)

MATCH 2
WATERFORD 1-8 • KILKENNY 3-6
COMPETITION: National League
DATE: February 8
VENUE: Gaelic Field, Waterford
ATTENDANCE: 10,000
WATERFORD: Ned Power, Joe Harney, Austin Flynn, John Barron, Jackie Condon, Martin Og Morrissey, Mick Lacey, Seamus Power, Phil Grimes, John Flavin, Tom Cheasty, Frankie Walsh, Larry Guinan, Donal Whelan, Michael White. Subs: Mick Flannelly (for White), Joe Coady (for Barron), Mick Kelly, Paddy Troy.
Scorers: Whelan 1-0, Grimes 0-2, Walsh 0-2,

Lacey 0-1, Power 0-1, Guinan 0-1, Flannelly 0-1.
KILKENNY: Liam Cleere, Tom Walsh, Jim Walsh, Mickey Walsh, Paddy Buggy, Tom Hogan, Johnny McGovern, Mick Brophy, Paddy Kelly, Denis Heaslip, Dick Carroll, Mick Fleming, Mick Kelly, Billy Dwyer, Tommy O'Connell. Subs: N. Fenlon (for Hogan)
Scorers: M. Kelly 1-3, Dwyer 1-1, P. Kelly 1-1, Heaslip 0-1,
REFEREE: S. O'Dwyer (Tipperary).

MATCH 3
WATERFORD 1-5 • CORK 10-11
COMPETITION: Cork City Juvenile Board Tournament
DATE: March 17
VENUE: Athletic Grounds, Cork
Waterford: Ned Power, Joe Harney, Bill Mulcahy, Austin Flynn, Jackie Condon, Martin Og Morrissey, Mick Kelly, Paddy Troy, Mick Lacey, John Flavin, Tom Cheasty, Frankie Walsh, Larry Guinan, Seamus Power, Donal Whelan. Subs: Phil Grimes (for Troy), Michael White (for Lacey), Pat Spratt (for Kelly).
Scorers: Troy 1-0, Walsh 0-2, Lacey 0-1, Cheasty 0-1, Power 0-1.
CORK: Mick Cashman, Jimmy Brohan, Gerald Mulcahy, D. Kelleher, D. Murphy, P. Duggan, Mick McCarthy, Terry Kelly, Noel Gallagher, Mick O'Regan, Paddy Barry, P. O'Leary, C. Cooney, Noel O'Connell, Christy Ring.
Scorers: Ring 4-3, O'Connell 4-1, Barry 0-4, O'Leary 1-0, Cooney 1-0, Duggan 0-1, Kelly 0-1, O'Regan 0-1.
REFEREE: Moss Walsh (Cork).

MATCH 4
WATERFORD 2-13 • ANTRIM 0-5
COMPETITION: National League
DATE: April 5
VENUE: Loughgiel, Antrim
Waterford: Ned Power, Joe Harney, Austin Flynn, John Barron, Jackie Condon, Mick O'Keeffe, Martin Og Morrissey, Seamus Power, Phil Grimes, Bill Dunphy, Mick Lacey, Paddy Troy, Larry Guinan, Tom Cheasty, Donal Whelan. Subs: Michael White, John Flavin, Dominic Enright (withdrew).
Scorers: Cheasty 1-1, Lacey 0-4, Whelan 1-0, Troy 0-2, Guinan 0-2, Grimes 0-2, Dunphy 0-2.
ANTRIM: E. Collins, V. Kerr, J. Giles, G. Walsh, R. McMullan, J. Wright, E. McMullan, Sean Gallagher, Noel McMullan, P. Mullaney, R. Elliott, J. Harkin, P. McMahon, P. Morgan, E. Stewart.
Scorers: Mullaney 0-3, Elliott 0-1, Gallagher 0-1.

MATCH 5
WATERFORD 6-9 • GALWAY 2-11
COMPETITION: Cork City Juvenile Board Tournament
DATE: April 19
VENUE: Athletic Grounds, Cork
WATERFORD: Ned Power, Joe Harney, Austin

Flynn, John Barron, Martin Og Morrissey, Phil Grimes, Jackie Condon, Seamus Power, Mick Lacey, Larry Guinan, Tom Cheasty, Frankie Walsh, Paddy Troy, Charlie Ware, Donal Whelan. Subs: Michael White (for Ware), John Flavin (for White), Bill Dunphy, Mick O'Keeffe, Joe Coady.

Scorers: Troy 2-1, Whelan 2-0, Cheasty 2-0, Walsh 0-3, Guinan 0-1, Lacey 0-1, Condon 0-1, Morrissey 0-1, Flavin 0-1.

GALWAY: F. Benson, E. Derrivan, P. Burke, M. Glynn, Jimmy Duggan, Mike Sweeney, J. Lyons, Joe Salmon, P.J. Lally, Tom Sweeney, P. J. Lawless, Jack Whyte, S. Devlin, Paddy Egan, M. Fox. Subs: Conway (for Burke), Burke (for Conway), Conway (for Sweeney).

Scorers: Whyte 1-2, Egan 1-1, Sweeney 0-3, Lally 0-2, Lawless 0-2, Fox 0-1

REFEREE: Moss Walsh (Cork)

MATCH 6
WATERFORD 0-7 • TIPPERARY 0-15

COMPETITION: National League, Final
DATE: May 3
VENUE: Nowlan Park, Kilkenny
ATTENDANCE: 21,870

WATERFORD: Ned Power, Joe Harney, Austin Flynn, John Barron, Martin Og Morrissey, Phil Grimes, Jackie Condon, Mick Lacey, Seamus Power, Larry Guinan, Tom Cheasty, Frankie Walsh, Paddy Troy, John Kiely, Donal Whelan. Subs: John Flavin (for Troy), Bill Dunphy (for Power), Charlie Ware, Mick O'Keeffe, Joe Coady, Michael White

Scorers: Walsh 0-4, Lacey 0-1, Cheasty 0-1, Whelan 0-1.

TIPPERARY: Terry Moloney, Mickey Byrne, Michael Maher, Kieran Carey, Jimmy Finn, Tony Wall, John Doyle, Theo English, Donie Nealon, Liam Devaney, J. McDonnell, Jimmy Doyle, T. Larkin, M. Maher, L. Connolly. Subs: P. Hennessey (for Larkin).

Scorers: Doyle 0-5, Nealon 0-4, Devaney 0-2, Connolly 0-2, McDonnell 0-1, English 0-1.

REFEREE: Stephen Gleeson (Limerick)

MATCH 7
WATERFORD 7-9 • KILKENNY 4-9

COMPETITION: Challenge
DATE: June 11
Venue: Gaelic Field, Waterford
ATTENDANCE: 6,000

WATERFORD: Ned Power, Joe Coady, Austin Flynn, John Barron, Paudie Casey, Freddie O'Brien, Jackie Condon, Phil Grimes, Mick Lacey, Martin Óg Morrissey, Tom Cheasty, Frankie Walsh, Donal Whelan, John Kiely, Charlie Ware. Subs: Mick Flannelly, Jim Phelan.

Scorers: Ware 3-2, Whelan 3-1, Cheasty 1-1, Morrissey 0-2, Walsh 0-2, Lacey 0-1.

KILKENNY: Ollie Walsh, J. Hogan, Mickey Walsh, E. Dwyer, Tom Walsh, J. Hennessy, John McGovern, Paddy Kelly, Paddy Buggy, Denis Heaslip, Sean Clohessy, Mick Fleming, Mick Kelly, S. O'Brien, Tommy O'Connell. Subs: Liam Cleere, W. Fitzgerald

Scorers: Clohessy 2-2, O'Connell 0-4, Kelly

1-0, Cleere 1-0, Fleming 0-2, Heaslip 0-1.
Referee: John Maddock (New Ross).

MATCH 8
WATERFORD 1-5 • WEXFORD 2-13
COMPETITION: Dr. Kinane Cup, SF
DATE: June 18
VENUE: Gaelic Field, Waterford
ATTENDANCE: 8,000
WATERFORD: Ned Power, Joe Harney, Austin Flynn, Joe Coady, Mick Flannelly, Freddie O'Brien, Jackie Condon, Mick Lacey, Phil Grimes, Paudie Casey, Donal Whelan, Frankie Walsh, Charlie Ware, John Kiely, Larry Guinan. Subs: Seamus Power, Tom Coffey, Joe Condon, M. Kiely
Scorers: Walsh 1-3, Casey 0-2
WEXFORD: Pat Nolan, Martin Lyng, Nick O'Donnell, Mick Bennett, Jim English, Billy Rackard, Sean Power, Seamus Hearne, M. Bergin, Oliver Gough, Padge Kehoe, Oliver McGrath, Jimmy O'Brien, P. Ryan, Tim Flood. Subs: J. Kennedy (for ?), Ned Wheeler (for Bergin), J. Fenlon (for Bennett)
Scorers: Gough 0-7, Flood 1-3, McGrath 1-1, Kehoe 0-1, Hearne 0-1.
REFEREE: Paddy Buggy (Kilkenny)

MATCH 9
WATERFORD 7-11 • GALWAY 0-8
COMPETITION: Munster Championship, QF
DATE: June 28
VENUE: Gaelic Grounds, Limerick
ATTENDANCE: 15,000
Waterford: Ned Power, Joe Harney, Austin Flynn, John Barron, Mick Lacey, Martin Og Morrissey, Jackie Condon, Seamus Power, Phil Grimes, Larry Guinan, Tom Cheasty, Frankie Walsh, Charlie Ware, John Kiely, Donal Whelan. Subs: Mick Flannelly (for Power), Paudie Casey, Freddie O'Brien, Joe Coady, Tom Coffey
Scorers: Walsh 1-7, Whelan 3-0, Power 2-0, Guinan 1-1, Cheasty 0-1, Ware 0-1, Kiely 0-1.
GALWAY: Ignatius Gavin, R. Stanley, P. Bourke, E. Derrivan, Jimmy Duggan, Jim Fives, Mike Sweeney, P.J. Lally, N. Murray, Tom Sweeney, Paddy Egan, Joe Salmon, P.J. Cormican, M. Fox, T. Conway, Paddy Fahy. Subs: Paddy Fahy (for Gavin), J. Conroy (for Egan), G. Cahill (for Lally).
Scorers: Sweeney 0-3, Egan 0-1, Fox 0-1, Murray 0-1, Conroy 0-1, Cahill 0-1.
REFEREE: Moss Walsh (Cork)

MATCH 10
WATERFORD 3-5 • KILKENNY 2-5
COMPETITION: Challenge
DATE: July 2
VENUE: Nowlan Park, Kilkenny
ATTENDANCE: 3,000
WATERFORD: Ned Power, Tom Coffey, Austin Flynn, John Barron, Mick Flannelly, Martin Og Morrissey, Mick Lacey, Seamus Power, Phil Grimes, Larry Guinan, Tom Cheasty, Frankie Walsh, Charlie Ware, Donal Whelan, Freddie O'Brien.

SCORERS: Walsh 1-0, Whelan 1-0, Grimes 1-0, O'Brien 0-2, Flannelly 0-1, Power 0-1, Ware 0-1.
KILKENNY: Ollie Walsh, Tom Walsh, Jim Walsh, J. Hennessey, Tim Kelly, Mickey Walsh, John McGovern, Paddy Kelly, Mick Brophy, Denis Heaslip, Dick Carroll, P. Moran, S. O'Brien, S. Leahy, Mickey Kelly. Subs: Martin Treacy (for McGovern), P. Johnson (for P. Kelly), Nick Teehan (for Leahy).
Scorers: O'Brien 1-0, Johnson 1-0, Carroll 0-2, Leahy 0-1, Heaslip 0-1, Teehan 0-1.
REFEREE: P. O'Brien (Eire Óg)

MATCH 11
WATERFORD 9-3 • TIPPERARY 3-4
COMPETITION: Munster Championship, SF
DATE: July 12
VENUE: Athletic Grounds, Cork
ATTENDANCE: 27,236
WATERFORD: Ned Power, Joe Harney, Austin Flynn, John Barron, Mick Lacey, Martin Óg Morrissey, Jackie Condon, Seamus Power, Phil Grimes, Larry Guinan, Tom Cheasty, Frankie Walsh, Charlie Ware, Donal Whelan, John Kiely. Subs: Mick Flannelly (for Morrissey), Martin Óg Morrissey (for Power), Seamus Power (for Ware), Freddie O'Brien, Paudie Casey, Joe Coady, Tom Cunningham, Tom Coffey.
Scorers: Guinan 3-0, Walsh 2-2, Power 1-1, Ware 1-0, Whelan 1-0, Kiely 1-0.
TIPPERARY: Terry Moloney, Micky Byrne, Michael Maher, Kieran Carey, Mick Burns, Tony Wall, John Doyle, Theo English, Donie Nealon, Jimmy Doyle, Liam Devaney, Gerry McCarthy, M. Maher, Jim McDonnell. B. Moloughney. Subs: R. Mounsey (for Moloney), Pat Stakelum (for McDonnell).
Scorers: Doyle 1-2, Nealon 1-2, Wall 1-0.
REFEREE: Gerry Fitzgerald (Limerick)

MATCH 12
WATERFORD 3-9 • CORK 2-9
COMPETITION: Munster Championship, Final
DATE: July 26
VENUE: Sports Field, Thurles
ATTENDANCE: 55,174
WATERFORD: Ned Power, Joe Harney, Austin Flynn, John Barron, Mick Lacey, Martin Óg Morrissey, Jackie Condon, Seamus Power, Phil Grimes, Larry Guinan, Tom Cheasty, Frankie Walsh, Charlie Ware, Donal Whelan, John Kiely. Subs: Tom Cunningham (for Condon), Mick Flannelly, Freddie O'Brien, Joe Coady, Paudie Casey, Tom Coffey, Micky O'Connor
Scorers: Kiely 2-2, Walsh 0-5, Power 1-0, Cheasty 0-2.
CORK: Sean O'Brien, Jimmy Brohan, John Lyons, Gerald Mulcahy, Paddy Fitzgerald, P. Duggan, Martin Thompson, Eamon Goulding, Willie Walsh, Noel Gallagher, Paddy Barry, C. Cooney, Terry Kelly, Mick Quane, Christy Ring. Subs: M. O'Regan (for Cooney), M. McCarthy (for Duggan).
Scorers: Ring 1-5, Barry 1-3, Quane 0-1.
REFEREE: Gerry Fitzgerald (Limerick)

MATCH 13
WATERFORD 1-17 • KILKENNY 5-5
COMPETITION: All Ireland, Final
DATE: September 6
VENUE: Croke Park, Dublin
ATTENDANCE: 73,707
Waterford: Ned Power, Joe Harney, Austin Flynn, John Barron, Mick Lacey, Martin Og Morrissey, Jackie Condon, Seamus Power, Phil Grimes, Larry Guinan, Tom Cheasty, Frankie Walsh, Charlie Ware, Donal Whelan, John Kiely. Subs: Tom Cunningham (for Ware), Mick Flannelly (for Condon), Freddie O'Brien, Paudie Casey, Micky O'Connor
Scorers: Walsh 0-6, Power 1-2, Cheasty 0-4, Kiely 0-2, Guinan 0-2, Grimes 0-1.
Kilkenny: Ollie Walsh, Tom Walsh, Jim Walsh, John Maher, Paddy Buggy, Mick Brophy, John McGovern, Paddy Kelly, Mickey Walsh, Denis Heaslip, Mick Fleming, Sean Clohessy, Dick Carroll, Billy Dwyer, Tommy O'Connell. Subs: Tim Kelly (for McGovern), John Sutton (for Fleming), Mickey Kelly (for Brophy), Mick Fleming (for Sutton).
Scorers: O'Connell 3-0, Carroll 1-2, Dwyer 1-1, Clohessy 0-1, Kelly 0-1.
REFEREE: Gerry Fitzgerald (Limerick)

MATCH 14
WATERFORD 3-12 • WEXFORD 2-10
COMPETITION: Challenge
DATE: September 20
VENUE: Gaelic Field, Waterford
WATERFORD: Ned Power, Micky O'Connor, Austin Flynn, John Barron, Phil Grimes, Martin Og Morrissey, Jackie Condon, Seamus Power, Mick Lacey, Tom Cunningham, Tom Cheasty, Frankie Walsh, Larry Guinan, John Kiely, Donal Whelan. Subs: Joe Harney (for O'Connor), Freddie O'Brien (for Grimes), Mick Flannelly (for Cheasty), Charlie Ware (for Whelan).
Scorers: Flannelly 2-0, Kiely 1-1, Walsh 0-3, Cunningham 0-2, Lacey 0-2, Cheasty 0-2, Guinan 0-1, Whelan 0-1.
WEXFORD: Pat Nolan, Jim English, Nick O'Donnell, Joe English, E. Colfer, Ned Wheeler, E. Fenlon, Sean Power, B. O'Leary, Oliver McGrath, Padge Kehoe, Oliver Gough, R. Murphy, J. Colfer, Jimmy O'Brien. Subs: J. Kennedy (for Murphy).
Scorers: Gough 1-3, Kehoe 1-1, McGrath 0-4, Colfer 0-1, Kennedy 0-1.
REFEREE: C. Crowley

MATCH 15
WATERFORD 3-12 • KILKENNY 1-10
COMPETITION: All Ireland, Final (Replay)
DATE: October 4
VENUE: Croke Park, Dublin
ATTENDANCE: 77,825
Waterford: Ned Power, Joe Harney, Austin Flynn, John Barron, Mick Lacey, Martin Og Morrissey, Jackie Condon, Seamus Power, Phil Grimes, Mick Flannelly, Tom Cheasty, Frankie Walsh, Larry Guinan, Tom Cunningham, John Kiely. Subs: Micky O'Connor (for Lacey), Donal Whelan (for Cunningham), Freddie O'Brien, Charlie Ware, Joe Coady.

Scorers: Cheasty 2-2, Walsh 0-8, Flannelly 1-1, Guinan 0-1.
KILKENNY: Ollie Walsh, Tom Walsh, Jim Walsh, John Maher, Paddy Buggy, Tim Kelly, John McGovern, Paddy Kelly, Mickey Walsh, Denis Heaslip, Mick Fleming, Sean Clohessy, Dick Carroll, Billy Dwyer, Tommy O'Connell. Subs: Eddie Keher (for McGovern)
Scorers: Dwyer 0-5, Heaslip 1-1, Keher 0-2, M. Walsh 0-1, Clohessy 0-1
REFEREE: Gerry Fitzgerald (Limerick)

MATCH 16
WATERFORD 6-10 • WEXFORD 2-7
COMPETITION: National League
DATE: October 11
VENUE: Gaelic Field, Waterford
ATTENDANCE: 2,000
WATERFORD: Ned Power, Joe Harney, Austin Flynn, Joe Coady, Mick Flannelly, Martin Óg Morrissey, S. O'Brien, Joe Condon, Seamus Power, Charlie Ware, Tom Cheasty, Frankie Walsh, Larry Guinan, Tom Cunningham, Donal Whelan. Subs: John Meaney (for Flannelly)
Scorers: Whelan 2-1, Walsh 0-7, Guinan 1-0, Power 1-0, Meaney 1-0, Cunningham 1-0, Cheasty 0-2.
WEXFORD: Pat Nolan, Jim English, Nick O'Donnell, Martin Lyng, M. Fenlon, Billy Rackard, Sean Power, Ned Wheeler, B. O'Leary, O. Gough, Padge Kehoe, M. Bergin, Oliver McGrath, J. Colfer, Tim Flood. Subs: T. Morrissey (for O'Donnell), Butler (for Nolan)
Scorers: Kehoe 1-3, McGrath 1-0, Gough 0-2, Colfer 0-1, Flood 0-1.
REFEREE: Moss Walsh (Cork)

MATCH 17
WATERFORD 4-6 • KILKENNY 4-6
DATE: October 25
COMPETITION: National League
VENUE: Nowlan Park, Kilkenny
ATTENDANCE: 28,000
WATERFORD: Ned Power, Joe Harney, Austin Flynn, Freddie O'Brien, Mick Flannelly, Martin Óg Morrissey, Jackie Condon, Seamus Power, Mick Lacey, Larry Guinan, Tom Cheasty, Frankie Walsh, Donal Whelan, Tom Cunningham, John Kiely. Subs: Charlie Ware, Mick O'Connor, Joe Coady, John Meany, Sean Foley, Percy Flynn, Joe Condon
Scorers: Whelan 2-0, Kiely 1-3, Cunningham 1-0, Power 0-2, Walsh 0-1.
KILKENNY: Ollie Walsh, Tom Walsh, Jim Walsh, John Maher, Paddy Buggy, Tim Kelly, Mickey Walsh, Sean Clohessy, Paddy Kelly, J. Murphy, Liam Cleere, Eddie Keher, Denis Heaslip, Billy Dwyer, Tommy O'Connell. Subs: John McGovern (for Cleere).
Scorers: Dwyer 2-0, Heaslip 1-1, O'Connell 1-0, Clohessy 0-3, Keher 0-2.
REFEREE: Seamus O'Dwyer (Tipperary)

MATCH 18
WATERFORD 1-9 • DUBLIN 3-10
COMPETITION: National League
DATE: November 8

VENUE: Croke Park, Dublin
ATTENDANCE: 10,000
WATERFORD: Ned Power, Joe Harney, Austin Flynn, Freddie O'Brien, Sean Foley, Martin Óg Morrissey, Jackie Condon, Seamus Power, Joe Condon, Mick Flannelly, Tom Cheasty, Frankie Walsh, Donal Whelan, Tom Cunningham, Larry Guinan. Subs: Paudie Casey (for Foley)
Scorers: Walsh 0-7, Guinan 1-0, Cheasty 0-1, Flannelly 0-1.
DUBLIN: Jimmy Gray, Des Ferguson, Brian Young, Paddy Croke, Christy Hayes, Mick Bohane, Achill Boothman, Larry Shannon, Fran Whelan, Kevin McLoughlin, Des Foley, Jim Byrne, Jack Finan, Tony Young, Billy Quinn.
Scorers: Shannon 1-5, McLoughlin 1-1, Byrne 1-1, Whelan 0-3,
REFEREE: L. Conroy (Laois)

APPENDIX 2

No.	Name	Surname	Club	Age	Height	Weight	Appearances	Scores
1	John	Barron	De La Salle	23	5'9"	11-7	13	0-0
2	Paudie	Casey	Ballygunner	24	5'11"		2 + 1	0-2
3	Tom	Cheasty	Ballyduff	25	5'8"	12-11	17	6-19
4	Joe	Coady	Erin's Own	24	5'11"	12-7	4 + 1	0-0
5	Tom	Coffey	Cappoquin				1	0-0
6	Jackie	Condon	Erin's Own	21	5'8"	11-5	16	0-1
7	Joe	Condon	Erin's Own	19	5'7"		2	0-0
8	Tom	Cunningham	Dungarvan	28	5'9"		6 + 2	2-2
9	Bill	Dunphy	Dunhill	25	5'9"	11-0	1 + 1	0-2
10	Dominic	Enright	Abbeyside				0*	0-0
11	Mick	Flannelly	Mount Sion	29	5'7"		6 + 5	3-4
12	John	Flavin	Mount Sion	19	5'7"	11-2	3 + 2	0-1
13	Austin	Flynn	Abbeyside	25	5'11"	12-10	17	0-0
14	Percy	Flynn	Mount Sion				0	0-0
15	Sean	Foley	Ballydurn				1 + 0	0-0
16	Phil	Grimes	Mount Sion	29	5'11"	12-10	14 + 1	2-5
17	Larry	Guinan	Mount Sion	21	5'9"	11-8	17	8-9
18	Joe	Harney	Ballydurn	23	5'9"	12-2	15 +1	0-0
19	Mick	Kelly	Dungarvan				1	0-0
20	John	Kiely	Dungarvan	33	5'7"	13-4	10	5-9
21	Mick	Lacey	Cappoquin	28	5'9"	12-0	16	0-11
22	John	Meaney	Erin's Own				0 + 1	1-0
23	Martin Og	Morrissey	Mount Sion	25	5'8"	13-2	17	0-3
24	Bill	Mulcahy	Mount Sion				1	0-0
25	Freddie	O'Brien	Mount Sion	21	5'10"		6 + 1	0-2
26	Micky	O'Connor	Cappoquin	29	5'9"		1 + 1	0-0
27	Mick	O'Keeffe	Ballygunner	23	5'11"	13-6	1	0-0
28	Jim	Phelan	Ballygunner				0**	0-0
29	Ned	Power	Dungarvan	29	5'11"	12-0	18	0-0
30	Seamus	Power	Mount Sion	29	5'8"	13-10	16 + 1	6-9
31	Pat	Spratt	Brickey Rangers				0 + 1	0-0
32	Pat	Troy	Ballygunner	23	5'7"	11-6	4	3-3
33	Frankie	Walsh	Mount Sion	22	5'7"	10-8	17	5-66
34	Charlie	Ware	Erin's Own	24	5'8"	11-6	9 + 1	4-4
35	Donal	Whelan	Abbeyside	28	6'0"	14-4	17 + 1	17-3
36	Michael	White	Dunhill	28	5'8"	11-6	1 + 2	0-0

*named in original squad for Antrim league match (April 5th) but withdrew
**named in original squad for Kilkenny challenge (June 11th) but withdrew

APPENDIX 3

1960
SELECTED MATCHES

MATCH 1
WATERFORD 5-9 • CORK 1-5

COMPETITION: London Tournament, Semi-final
DATE: March 27
VENUE: Gaelic Field, Waterford
WATERFORD: Percy Flynn, Freddie O'Brien, Austin Flynn, John Barron, Joe Condon, Martin Óg Morrissey, Jackie Condon, Seamus Power, Phil Grimes, Mick Flannelly, Tom Cheasty, Frankie Walsh, Larry Guinan, Tom Cunningham, Donal Whelan. Subs: Mick Lacey, Mick Gallagher, Tom Kennedy
Scorers: Whelan 3-1, Cunningham 2-0, Walsh 0-5, Power 0-2, Cheasty 0-1.
CORK: Mick Cashman, Mick Horgan, Denis O'Rioradan, Jim O'Brien, Pat Fitzgerald, Jerry O'Sullivan, Martin Thompson, Eamon Goulding, Pat Harte, Joe Twomey, Terry Kelly, Joe O'Flynn, Paddy Barry, John Young, Mick Quane. Subs: J. Quigley (for O'Flynn).
Scorers: Kelly 1-0, Harte 0-2, Barry 0-1, Quigley 0-1, Twomey 0-1.
REFEREE: John Maddock (Wexford).

MATCH 2
WATERFORD 2-8 • REST OF IRELAND 2-8

COMPETITION: Challenge
DATE: April 10
VENUE: Gaelic Field, Waterford
ATTENDANCE: 9,000
WATERFORD: Percy Flynn, Freddie O'Brien, Austin Flynn, John Barron, Joe Condon, Martin Óg Morrissey, Jackie Condon, Seamus Power, Phil Grimes, Mick Flannelly, Tom Cheasty, Larry Guinan, Tom Kennedy, Tom Cunningham, Donal Whelan. Subs: M. Murphy (for Kennedy)

Scorers: Guinan 1-2, Grimes 0-5, Whelan 1-0, Cheasty 0-1.
REST OF IRELAND: Ollie Walsh, Jimmy Brohan, Nick O'Donnell, John Doyle, Ned Wheeler, Mick Bohane, John McGovern, Joe Salmon, Larry Shannon, Tim Sweeney, Sean Clohessy, Jimmy Doyle, Paddy Barry, Billy Dwyer, Christy Ring. Subs: Jimmy Smyth (for Ring), Padge Kehoe (for Shannon)
Scorers: Doyle 0-8, Barry 1-0, Dwyer 1-0.
REFEREE: T. O'Sullivan (Limerick).

MATCH 3
WATERFORD 2-16 • KILKENNY 6-16
COMPETITION: London Tournament, Final
DATE: June 6
VENUE: Wembley Stadium, London
ATTENDANCE: 37,000
WATERFORD: Ned Power, Joe Harney, Austin Flynn, John Barron, Joe Condon, Martin Og Morrissey, Jackie Condon, Seamus Power, Phil Grimes, Mick Flannelly, Tom Cheasty, Frankie Walsh, Larry Guinan, Tom Cunningham, Donal Whelan. Subs: Freddie O'Brien, Bill Dunphy, Percy Flynn, Tom Kennedy, Mick Gallagher.
Scorers: Power 1-2, Guinan 1-1, Walsh 0-4, Cheasty 0-4, Grimes 0-2, Flannelly 0-2, Morrissey 0-1.
KILKENNY: Ollie Walsh, Tom Walsh, P. Dillon, John Maher, Mickey Walsh, Seamus Cleere, John McGovern, Mick Brophy, Paddy Kelly, Phil Walsh, Sean Clohessy, Eddie Keher, Denis Heaslip, Dick Carroll, Nick Teehan.
Scorers: Heaslip 3-4, P. Walsh 3-2, Keher 0-7, Brophy 0-1, Clohessy 0-1, Teehan 0-1.
REFEREE: F. Sheehan (Wexford).

MATCH 4
WATERFORD 3-4 • NEW YORK 7-7
COMPETITION: Challenge
DATE: June 12
VENUE: Gaelic Park, New York
Attendance: 5,000
WATERFORD: Ned Power, Joe Harney, Austin Flynn, John Barron, Freddie O'Brien, Martin Og Morrissey, Jackie Condon, Seamus Power, Phil Grimes, Mick Flannelly, Tom Cheasty, Frankie Walsh, Larry Guinan, Tom Cunningham, Donal Whelan. Subs: Charlie Ware, Micky O'Connor, Joe Coady, Paudie Casey.
Scorers: Walsh 1-2, Guinan 1-0, Flannelly 1-0, Power 0-2.
NEW YORK: Patrick Fleming, Kevin Long, Brendan Dillon, P.J. Bermingham, Johnny Murphy, Brendan Hennessey, Pat Philpot, Paddy McGuirk, Christy O'Connell, R. Prendergast, James Carney, Joe Carey, Michael Furlong, Sean O'Meara, Pat Kirby. Subs: Martin Murphy (for Prendergast), M. Lonergan (for O'Connell), L. O'Connell (for Lonergan), Paddy Hearne (for O'Meara).
Scorers: O'Meara 3-2, Carney 1-2, Murphy 1-1, Furlong 1-0, Kirby 1-0, Hennessey 0-1, Philpot 0-1.
REFEREE: Jimmy O'Grady (Limerick)

MATCH 5
WATERFORD 4-6 • NEW YORK 4-6

COMPETITION: Challenge
DATE: June 18
VENUE: Gaelic Park, New York
ATTENDANCE: 5,000
WATERFORD: Ned Power, Joe Harney, Austin Flynn, John Barron, Freddie O'Brien, Martin Og Morrissey, Joe Coady, Seamus Power, Phil Grimes, Mick Flannelly, Tom Cheasty, Larry Guinan, Charlie Ware, Tom Cunningham, Donal Whelan. Subs: Micky O'Connor, Paudie Casey, Frankie Walsh, Jackie Condon
Scorers: Grimes 1-4, Guinan 1-1, Ware 1-0, Cheasty 1-0, Flannelly 0-1.
NEW YORK: Patrick Fleming, Kevin Long, Jim Carey, P.J. Bermingham, Johnny Murphy, Brendan Hennessey, Pat Philpot, Paddy McGuirk, Christy O'Connell, Martin Murphy, James Carney, Joe Carey, Michael Furlong, Sean O'Meara, Pat Kirby. Subs: Vincent Sammon (for Fleming), P. Guilfoyle (for Jim Carey), Norman Allen (for O'Connell), Paddy Phelan (for Furlong), R. Prendergast (for Murphy).
Scorers: Furlong 2-0, O'Meara 1-1, Murphy 1-1, Carney 0-3, Philpot 0-1.
REFEREE: Jimmy O'Grady (Limerick)

APPENDIX 4

IN MEMORIAM
Passing of Heroes

Philly Grimes	8/5/89
Mick Lacey	9/12/97
John Kiely	18/6/04
Tom Cheasty	10/8/07
Ned Power	15/11/07
John Barron	28/4/08
Joe Coady	5/8/08
Donal Whelan	20/9/11
Frankie Walsh	28/12/12
Charlie Ware	24/11/13
Paudie Casey	20/10/14
Seamus Power	25/6/16
Joe Harney	17/4/20
Austin Flynn	26/4/21
Mick Flannelly	11/9/21
Tom Cunningham	28/4/22
Jackie Condon	10/7/23

The Hurler's Prayer

Grant me, O Lord, a hurler's skill,
With strength of arm and speed
Of limb,
A flashing eye for the flying ball,
And the courage to match
Whatever befall,
May my stroke be steady
And my aim be true,
My actions manly and misses few,
No matter which way the game
May go,
May I rest in friendship
With every foe,
When the final whistle for me
Has blown,
And I stand before God's
Judgement throne,
May the great referee when
He calls my name,
Say you hurled like a man;
You played the game.

— Seamus Redmond

REFERENCES

ORAL INTERVIEWS

- Larry Guinan
- Martin Óg Morrissey
- Jackie Condon
- Michael O'Connor
- Tom Cunningham
- Freddie O'Brien
- John Flavin
- Joe Condon
- Billy Kelly
- Humphrey Kelleher
- Jimmy O'Brien (Wexford)
- Jimmy Brohan (Cork)
- Donie Nealon (Tipperary)
- Tony Wall (Tipperary)
- Eddie Keher (Kilkenny)
- Johnny McGovern (Kilkenny)
- Jimmy Gray (Dublin)
- Peter Walsh (Frankie's son)
- Kay Grimes (Philly's daughter)
- Tom Power (Seamus' son)
- Mary Ware (Charlie's sister)
- John Barron (John's son)
- Kathleen Cheasty (Tom's wife)
- Phil Fanning (Pat's son)
- Michael Dowling (Charlie Ware's nephew)

NEWSPAPERS

- Sunday Press
- Irish Press
- Irish Independent
- Sunday Independent
- Sunday Review
- Waterford News & Star
- Munster Express
- Evening Herald
- Dungarvan Observer
- Cork Examiner
- Irish Examiner
- Irish Echo, New York
- The Advocate, New York
- Daily Mail, London
- Limerick Leader
- Nenagh Guardian
- The Nationalist
- Connacht Tribune
- Kilkenny People
- Sunday Review
- Most newspapers accessed via www.irishnewsarchive.com

JOURNALISTS

- Pat Fanning (Deiseach) — *Waterford News and Star*
- John D Hickey — *Irish Independent*
- Sean Quigley — *Irish Independent*
- Con F. Kenealy — *Irish Independent*
- Mitchel V. Cogley — *Irish Independent*
- Seán Óg O'Ceallacháin — *Evening Press*
- Joe Sherwood (In The Soup) — *Evening Press*
- Art McGann (Fear Ciuin) — *Sunday Press*
- Eamonn Mongey — *Sunday Press*
- Peader O'Brien — *Irish Press*
- Mick Dunne — *Irish Press*
- John Barrett — *Irish Press*
- Paddy Downey — *Sunday Review*
- Paul Russell — *Sunday Review*
- C.P.
- Gerry Ahane — *Irish Weekly Independent*
- Sean Coughlan (Green Flag) — *Irish Press*
- Padraig Puirseal — *Irish Press*
- 'Vigilant' — *Irish Press*
- Jim O'Sullivan — *Cork Examiner*
- Dick Cross — *Cork Examiner*
- Val Dorgan — *Cork Examiner*
- Phil O'Neill (Sliabh Ruadh)
- Paddy D Mehigan (Carbery)
- Declan Goode (Taobhline) — *Dungarvan Observer*

NEWSPAPER INTERVIEWS

- Tom Cunningham, *Irish Examiner*, 12/12/20, P.M. O'Sullivan
- Joe Harney, *The Hinterview*, 26/4/12, Matt Keane
- Larry Guinan, *Irish Times*, 11/12/20, Barry Roche
- Phil Fanning, *Waterford News and Star*, 26/6/20
- Austin Flynn, *Irish Examiner Interview*, 9/12/17, Enda McEvoy
- Philly Grimes, Master Craftsman, *Munster Express*
- 1959 Team, Caught in Time – *Sunday Times*
- Pat Fanning, *Waterford News and Star*, 1984, Pat Fanning

- Johnny McGovern and Seamus Cleere, *Kilkenny People*, 24/2/12, Barry Henriques
- Philly Grimes, *Sunday Independent*, 14/2/82, Liam Kelly
- Martin Óg Morrissey, *Waterford News & Star*, 5/9/08, Adrian Flanagan
- Ned Power, *Sunday Independent*, 14/2/82, Liam Kelly
- Mick Flannelly, *Irish Examiner*, 7/9/13, Michael Moynihan
- Mick Flannelly, *Irish Examiner*, 13/9/21, Michael Moynihan
- Philly Grimes, *Irish Press*, 16/12/70, Jimmy Meagan
- Austin Flynn, *Irish Examiner*, 30/8/17, Steve Neville

BOOKS

- Cody, Joe, *The Stripy Men, Kilkenny's Hurling Story to 2008*, MacÓda Publishing, 2009
- Cronin, Mike; Duncan, Mark; Rouse, Paul, *The GAA, County by County*, Collins Press, 2011
- Dalton, Noel, *A Déise Boy*, Self Published, 2009
- De Búrca, Marcus, *A History of the GAA*, Cumann Lúthchleas Gael, 1980
- Dorgan, Val, *Christy Ring*, Ward River Press, 1980
- Doyle, *The Greatest Hurling Story Ever Told*, John Harrington, Irish Sports Publishing, 2011
- Freeman, Norman, *Classic Hurling Matches 1956-75*, Gill and Macmillan, 1993
- Fullam, Brendan, *The Final Whistle*, Merlin Publishing, 2000
- Fullam, Brendan, *Captains of the Ash*, Wolfhound Press, 2004
- Fullam, Brendan, *Hurling Giants*, Wolfhound Press, 1995
- Fullam, Brendan, *Legends of the Ash*, Wolfhound Press, 1997
- Fullam, Brendan, *Decades of Stars*, Wolfhound Press, 2011
- Fullam, Brendan, *Giants of the Ash*, Wolfhound Press, 1991
- Fullam, Brendan, *The Throw-In, The GAA and the men who made it*, Wolfhound Press, 2004
- Furlong, Nicholas, *The Greatest Hurling Decade*, Merlin Publishing, 1993
- Gleeson, Stephen, *Tipperary Game of My Life*, Hero Books, 2020
- Griffin, Pat, *Gaelic Hearts, a History of London GAA, 1896-1996*, 2011
- Hanna, Fergus, *History of the GAA in New York*, Belfast Press, 2014
- Kavanagh, Dermot, *Ollie, The hurling life and times of Ollie Walsh*, Blackwater Press, 2006
- Kavanagh, Dermot, *The Story of Interprovincial Hurling*, 2016
- Keane, Colm, *Hurling's Top 20*, Mainstream Publishing, 2003
- Keher, Eddie, *Hurling Heroes – Fourteen Hurling Greats Profiled*, Blackwater Press, 2000
- Keith, Tom, *The Colours Blue & White, Waterford's Successes in Hurling and Football*, 1998
- Keith, Tom, *The Christian Brothers in Dungarvan 1807 – 1992*, Litho Press, 1996
- Kelleher, Humphrey, *GAA Family Silver, The people and stories behind 101 cups and trophies*, Sportsfile, 2013
- Kelly, Dowling, Kelly et.al, *Erin's Own, A Centenary History*, 2024

- Kennedy, Tom, *The Erin's Own Hurling Club Story*, 1999 (unpublished)
- Mac Lua, Breandan, *The Steadfast Rule*, Cuchulainn Press, 1967
- Mahon, Jack, *The Game of My Life*, Blackwater Press, 1993
- McCarthy, Tomas, *Waterford Game of My Life*, Hero Books, 2021
- McEvoy Enda, *The Godfather of Modern Hurling, The Father Tommy Maher Story*, Ballpoint Press, 2012
- Moore, Cormac, *The GAA v Douglas Hyde*, Collins Press, 2012
- Morrison, Tom, *For the Record, A history of the National Football and Hurling League Finals*, Collins Press, 2002
- Morrissey, Martin Óg with Dermot Keyes – *Kings for One Day*, Hero Book, 2022
- Morrissey, Mick, *Hurling and my hurling stars past and present*, Munster Express, 1977
- Mulhern Robert, *A Very Different County*, Self-Published, 2011
- O'Flynn, Diarmuid, *Hurling, The Warrior Game*, The Collins Press, 2017
- O'Flynn, Diarmuid, *The Boy Wonder of Hurling, The Story of Jimmy Doyle*, Sliabh Bán Productions, 2015
- O'Connell, Peter, *Clare Game of My Life*, Hero Books, 2021
- Ó hEithir, Breandán, *Over the Bar*, Poolbeg Press, 1984
- Power, Conor, *My Father, a Hurling Revolutionary, The Life and Times of Ned Power*, Three Good Boys, 2009
- Power, Patrick, *Off the Ball, Waterford's Re-Emergence as a Hurling Force*, Mahon Press, 1999
- Puirséal, Pádraig, *The GAA in its Time*, The Purcell Family, 1982
- Roche, Dickie, *A Story of Hurling in Waterford*, Intacta Print, 2005
- Ryan, Tony, *A History of the Dungarvan GAA Club from 1885 to 2017*, 2018
- Scally, John, *The GAA Immortals*, Black and White Publishing, 2017
- Scally, John, *The People's Game*, Black and White Publishing, 2020
- Smith, David, *Unconquerable Keane*, 2010
- Smith, Raymond, *The Hurling Immortals*, Bruc Spicer, Dublin, 1969
- Smith, Raymond, *Clash of the Ash*, Creative Press Ltd, 1972
- Smith, Raymond, *Book of Hurling*, Creative Press Ltd, 1974
- Smith, Raymond, *The Greatest Hurlers of Our Time*, Sporting Books, 1990
- Sweeney, Eamonn, *Munster Hurling Legends*, The O'Brien Press, 2002
- Tiernan, Damien, *The Ecstasy and the Agony*, Hachette Books, 2010
- Wall, Tony, *Hurling*, GAA Publication, 1966

YEARBOOKS
- 75th anniversary of the GAA - Capuchin annual
- The Carbery Annual 1959/60

- Cuchulainn Annual, 1959
- Sidelines, WRTC GAA Magazine, late 1980s
- Sidelines 2, WRTC GAA Magazine, 1990
- An Cúl, Vol. 4, No. 2, April 1973
- GAA Golden Jubilee Supplement, Irish Press, 1934
- Ballygunner Days of Glory, The Centenary Yearbook of Ballygunner GAA Club
- An Deiseach 100, Waterford Yearbook 1986
- Deiseach, Waterford GAA Yearbook, 1988
- Waterford GAA Yearbook, 2007
- Waterford GAA Yearbook, 2008
- Waterford GAA Yearbook, 2009
- Waterford GAA Yearbook, 2013
- Port Lairge 84, Waterford GAA Yearbook, 1984
- Dunhill GAA Centenary Book
- An Deiseach, Waterford GAA Yearbook 1972
- Munster Gaelic Games Annual Vol 1
- Munster Gaelic Games Annual Vol 2

MAGAZINES

- Sports Illustrated 8/11/1954; 20/6/1960
- Waterford Sport, Hurling Special - Tom Cheasty interview
- Gaelic Sport, May 1966, Vol. 9, No. 5, - Frankie Walsh interview
- Gaelic Weekly, April 6, 1960, by Gerry McCarthy

PROGRAMMES

- Waterford v Cork, 29/6/03 (unnamed author)
- Waterford v Tipp, 2/7/89 (Tom Morrison)
- Waterford v Clare, 11/8/02 (Seamus O'Brien)
- Waterford v Tipp, 30/5/02 (Paddy Dunphy)
- Waterford v Limerick, 1/6/03 (Noel Horgan)
- Waterford v Kilkenny, 24/2/02 (unnamed author)
- Waterford v Kilkenny, 20/2/05
- Waterford v Tipperary, 17/8/08 (Eamonn Seoige)
- Waterford v Kilkenny, 3/3/91 (Seamus MacGrainne)
- Waterford v Clare, 24/5/92 (Pat Fanning)

VIDEOS
- Junior Final, Antrim v London https://www.youtube.com/watch?v=y9XLVOKWfMI
- Gaelic Park
  https://www.rte.ie/archives/2014/0502/614794-the-home-of-the-gaa-in-new-york-1966/

OTHER
- Thomas Fewer, Amateur Film
- John Lyons, Amateur Film, New York
- Waterford Treasures Museum, Waterford's sporting history display
- Munster Council Minutes 1959 and 1960, Croke Park Reading Room
- Central Council Minutes 1959 and 1960, Croke Park Reading Room
- Waterford County Board minutes 1959 and 1960, Croke Park Reading Room
- Annual Congress Report, 1959 and 1960, Croke Park Meeting Room
- 50th Anniversary documentary, Kevin Casey, Radio Series for WLR FM
- Eoin Fanning – college project on Pat Fanning
- Letters between Pat Fanning, Padraig O'Caoimh, Paddy Kenneally and Tom McGuinness – Private collection of Eoin Fanning.
- Pat Fanning's private notebooks – Private collection of Eoin Fanning.
- Programme from Bohack Cup match, New York v Waterford, Jun 12th, 1960.
- Programme from New York GAA 26th Annual Banquet, Feb 6th, 1960.
- Pat Fanning Interview, GAA Oral History Project, 21/11/2008.
  https://www.gaa.ie/the-gaa/oral-history/pat-fanning/

Printed in Great Britain
by Amazon

399b3011-f5cf-4cec-ba70-e130eff6ba39R01